WELCOME TO

LOOKING BACK 90 YEARS

84* TRUE STORIES ABOUT FAMOUS AND NON-FAMOUS PEOPLE, IMPORTANT AND INTERESTING EVENTS, AND SPECIAL PLACES, FROM 1919 TO 2009

BY

L. MACON EPPS

This book is dedicated to my wife, Elizabeth, and my children, Christina and Rebecca, who shared many of the events, or at least heard me tell about them. L.M.E.

* With 165 sub stories

PREFACE:

The true stories in this book are just a small sample of the people, places and events I have known, seen and experienced. Actually, there are many, many other stories I would like to write down, but that takes time and energy, both of which are in short supply when you reach my age, which is 89 as I write this Preface.

Each story is short enough to be read at one sitting, and the table of contents can help you pick ones of most interest. Naturally, some are longer than others, and some may be of more interest to different readers. All should give some insights into the past 90 years, and some may even be of interest to historians.

Since most of the stories are from my memory, I may have embellished them a bit, but they are basically true. Besides, I doubt if there are any witnesses still alive who could even challenge them, much less prove that their memory is better than mine. Each story stands alone, so there may be overlap between stories. For example, some may contain the same people and events and similar, but not identical, writing that is included in other stories.

I would have left out some of the stories if I had been much younger, less they tarnish my reputation; but at my age I can stand a bit of tarnishing. Some of the stories are reactions to events, and not really stories, but more like essays. I also snuck in a few poems that looked back.

This book is organized by decades, starting with 1920-1930 and ending with 2000-2010. Some stories covered more than one decade, so they are listed under Multi-Decade and are after 2000-2010. Most of them are a collection of true experiences that flashed through my head so vividly that I was inspired to write then down. I have left out many stories about my career and family since they may be in a future book(s); likewise for some of my other activities. Because of the somewhat random selection of stories, it is not an autobiography. However, it might give some insight into the virtues and vices of each decade. All stories bear the copyright date of this book, but I have put the date when I first wrote the story down in ( ) when possible.

I have included the names of friends and family in many stories, except in some I only used first (or fake) names to avoid possible embarrassment. I have not included an index, but I have underlined names when first used in a story to make them easier to spot. So if you are friend or family and want to find a story that may include you, please browse through the book quickly, or read all of them.

I have never been rich or famous, and consider myself an ordinary guy from an ordinary background. However, like many of my "ordinary" friends, I have been blessed with a rich and wonderful life, sufficient money to live well, and a bit of fame in limited circles, even nationally, all for which I am thankful. In fact, I suspect that many of us have had fuller and richer lives than the rich and famous because we didn't have to undergo their problems.

I hope you will find stories that both interest you and bring back memories of similar people, places and events in your life. For younger readers, I hope you will get some lessons from my stories and remember my main message: "You don't have to be rich and famous to have a WONDERFUL LIFE!

L. Macon Epps   8-12-2009

P.S. Teachers and other people who want to reproduce up to five stories for non-commercial use may do so without my permission. Above that number, or if you want to use some or all commercially, please write to me for permission at 17236 Village 17, Camarillo, CA. 93012.

P.P.S. Some people like to find errors in a book, so I have left a few for your pleasure. Also, I am 89 and proof read it myself.

ABOUT THE AUTHOR

L. Macon Epps was born in Mt. Airy, NC, on January 16, 1920. He grew up and finished high school in Newton, NC, following which he obtained a Bachelor of Mechanical Engineering degree from N.C. State College in 1940. He worked as an aerospace engineer/manager for 37+ years at Grumman Aerospace Corporation, and earned a Master of Aeronautical Engineering degree from New York University in 1947 during after work hours. He has also attended special courses given by Cornell University, Columbia University, California Tech., University of N.H., plus other non-university Courses.

His Grumman experience included: Shop orientation; structural design; Structural-analysis Project Engineer; Chief of Weight and Balance; Assistant to the Chief Technical Engineer; Assistant Director of Research and Advanced Development; Chief Value Engineer; Assistant Program Manager for the Lunar Module; and Assistant Director of Advanced Civil Systems.

He retired in 1977, and was founding president of the I-Cubed Corporation, which specialized in: new innovations; temporary jobs for other retirees; and sales representation for other corporation. Following his second retirement in 1986, he and his wife moved to Dover, New Hampshire. In 2001 they moved to Camarillo, CA.

His part time activities during his working and retirement years included: Various community and church positions; do-it yourself home improvements; tennis (a lifetime commitment); golf; water and snow skiing; sailing; oil painting; and various musical activities (He played a baritone horn in five different bands and was President and board member of the Huntington Concert Association.) He and his wife have traveled extensively, visiting all continents except South America and Antarctica.

He attended several creative writing classes and it became one of his principal activities during his retirement years. In 2004, he co-authored a book "Universal Spiritual Thoughts," published by AuthorHouse the same year. He was the originator, editor and contributor of two limited-edition anthologies titled, "The Creative Community," and "Imagination and Reality," published during the nineties by the Dover, NH Rotary Club. He was also the originator and chairman of a Rotary project to paint a large mural on a building in downtown Dover.

His most recent books are: "Senior Short Stories," and "Old Granddad's Children's Stories," both of which are Print on Demand books published by createspace.com and also available from amazon.com. He has five more books partially completed, and hopes to get at least three more published.

In 1945, he married Elizabeth Jean Warren, a Vassar College graduate in Mathematics and they celebrated their 64th anniversary on 5-6-09. They have two daughters. Christina Warren Saul, and Rebecca Catterall, both of whom are happily married. Elizabeth and Macon have three grandchildren and one great.

He is in good health and hopes the genes that let his Mother and two of her siblings live to 95, 95, and 96 will let him keep writing for many more years.

TABLE OF CONTENTS:

2000-2010

Multi-decade

A BIG RACE

It was very crowded, but I waited patiently for my turn to enter the race. When my turn finally came, my instincts said: "win. Win, WIN!" The odds against me were in the millions, but, thankfully, I was ignorant of that fact.

The starting gun was explosive and I was quickly thrust into the race. I was somewhere in the middle of the pack, but since it was a marathon there would be time to forge ahead. Eventually, I reached the finish line and entered into the glorious winner's circle. My mission to win had been accomplished, but now I must act like a winner and start the long road to true championship.

For many months, I was warm and comfortable with my efforts and my new status as a one-time winner. I sensed that I was making tremendous progress. Considering my tiny beginning, my accomplishments were stupendous. Percentage wise, I never equaled them again. But, as I learned later, all my efforts were just a stepping-stone toward something much more exciting.

One day I was squeezed and pushed until my face grew cold. Then someone tugged at me and I was chilly all over. "What's going on here," I wondered. And then my bottom was spanked so hard that I let out a lusty yell! I guess yelling was the right thing to do, because it made me gasp for air, fill my lungs, and keep me from an untimely death. Unknown to me, my stepping stone was my entry into a new, more complicated race.

I was cleaned and clothed, and then delivered to my mother's waiting arms. They were warm and gentle, and her caresses were a new, but delightful, sensation. I could again hear the rhythmic beat that had comforted me during my months of seclusion and darkness. A bonding process had begun which lasted a lifetime

The picture is clear now. As a microscopic, swimming sperm I had reached the finish line of a tiny, stationary egg. I had prevailed over about 300 million other sperm cells and had started on an incredible journey called life. And what a wonderful journey it has been. Not only did I win the initial race against incredible odds, but I was blessed with many things: Caring parents, worthy siblings, dedicated teachers, inspiring preachers, loyal friends, and a wonderful family of my own. All of the above have helped me accomplish more than I ever dreamed possible. Two engineering degrees; a job that was varied and demanding that I liked, and which helped win several wars and let men land on the moon; a small, extremely interesting business of my own; and a long retirement. Along the way I found time for many worthwhile and enjoyable "extra-curricula" activities, including travel to exotic, interesting and beautiful places.

My life experiences have been so wonderful and varied that they inspired this book. Although it is quite lengthy, It covers only a tiny bit of what my memory cells hold, so maybe I will create new volumes if I don't run out of time and energy.

I consider myself part of the great orchestra of mankind. It performs overtures, symphonies, concertos, oratorios, operas, dance rhythms, etc; in fact, all the music of life. It even plays requiems, but so far it has not played mine. When my requiem IS played, I will think of my tiny, humble beginning and all the "races" I entered, many of which I lost, but which gave me valuable lessons in return.

I thank God that I didn't lose the first and really big one, because it was the beginning of my long, fruitful life, along with some six billion fellow voyagers!

Authors note: Although I don't remember this event, it helped me claim to look back 90 years, so my book title is not far from the truth.

A FEW PRE-SCHOOL MEMORIES

1. OBJECT LESSON

I must have been about two-years old when something happened that hurt and taught me a lesson. Our family of four was living in Tarboro, NC, and I was playing in the yard with my older sister, <u>Ruth</u>. It was late spring or early summer, because we were both barefooted. The grass felt good on our tender feet, and everything was fine until I spotted a nice brick on the edge of the yard.

'Ah', I thought. 'That pretty red thing is something I want'. I then walked over to it to pick it up. It was heavier than my young, inexperienced mind realized, so it slipped out of my hands. Determined to posses it, I tried again. This time I was successful and started carrying it toward the house.

After walking a few steps, I stumbled and the distraction caused me to lose my grasp. Suddenly, it fell from my hands toward the ground. That is, until it landed on one of my bare, sensitive feet. I then experienced the worst pain I could remember in my young life. Naturally, I yelled out in pain, and then started crying and sobbing. Ruth saw what had happened, and yelled for our Mother.

<u>Mom</u> came quickly and soothed me as she carried me into the house, where she wiped the small amount of blood and soaked my foot in a pan of cold water, Her hugs and comforting words, plus her quick action, eased my pain greatly.

The bleeding stopped and there was minimal swelling because of the cold water treatment. Several days later, my foot had returned to normal and Mom had gotten rid of the tempting red brick, where I know not. Nature's wonderful healing process had done its trick, but it was years later before I marveled at how our bodies heal themselves.

So what lessons did this little two-year old learn?

a. Don't pick up an object that is too heavy to carry with ease.

b. Never, never do the above when you are bare-footed.

c. Even if you have your shoes on, make sure you move your feet away from the path of a falling object.

Now my immature little mind didn't express the lessons in those words, but believe me they crept into my mind without saying them. My most important lesson, or perhaps it was just reinforcing one I already sensed, was: MOMS ARE WONDERFUL CREATURES THAT DESERVE OUR GRATITUDE, RESPECT, ADMIRATION, AND ETERNAL LOVE!

2. NAUGHTY BOYS:

When I was about four, we moved to Newton, NC, which is the small town I lived in until I earned my College degree. Our first house there was on South College Avenue, named after Catawba College, which later moved to a larger place.

Across the street was a young lad named <u>Bobby Cochran</u>, who was about a year older than I. Since we lived in a sparse neighbor, kid wise, we soon became fast friends. Sometimes we played at his place, and sometimes at mine.

I remember talking about what we would be when we grew up, mostly about how tall we would be. We both planned to be 7 or 8 feet tall; not in those terms, but relative to objects we spotted. Little did we know that we couldn't control our ultimate height, but must wait for our genes, and our diet and exercise to do the trick.

Now in those days, coal was the fuel most households used. It was delivered by a truck, and shoveled into a basement bin by the driver. Inevitably, some small pieces didn't make it into the basement, but lay peacefully on the ground, waiting to see what destiny had in store.

Bobby and I were their destiny, because we picked them up, put them in our pockets, and used them as throwing "stones" with trees as our targets.

One day, we decided that moving targets would be more fun. No, we didn't aim them at dogs or cats, but at the few cars that came along. We were smart enough to hide behind a bush and wait until the car had nearly passed before throwing them, hoping the driver not only wouldn't know what had happened, but, more importantly, wouldn't spot us.

We liked to hear the clang of coal chunks hitting metal, or perhaps the thud when it hit a tire. We also liked to see the car slow down while the driver wondered what happened. Even when someone stopped to look, the coal had shattered to smaller, undetectable bits, or if not shattered the driver thought they were droppings from a coal truck. Yes, we were naughty boys, and we not only knew we were naughty, but gloried in our naughtiness.

One day, a perceptive driver either spotted us, or figured the coal particles were the cause of the big bang. He stopped, got out of his car, and started coming toward our hiding place. 'What to do,' was in both our minds, so we simultaneously high-tailed it toward the back of my house to find another hiding place. I quickly opened the basement door and closed and locked it; we kept so quiet that we hardly breathed.

We even heard the man muttering to himself, wondering where we had disappeared. When he tried the basement door, I was thankful I had locked it. We both felt we had gotten away Scott free, but the man was smart and persistent. Unknown to us, he knocked on our door, told my mother what had happened, and left.

Mom soon surmised that we might be in the basement, so she came down and started cross-examining us:

" Why are you boys down here in the basement?"

" It's cooler", I said.

" How long have you been down here?

" Oh, a long time."

" The last time I looked you were playing in the front yard, so it couldn't have been very long. Have you been throwing coal at cars?

" No ma'am" we both lied.

" Then empty your pockets."

We looked sheepishly at each other, and did so. She picked up the pieces of coal that fell out and told us about the man who came to our door. We knew we were caught, so we confessed.

Mom looked sternly at both of us, saying," Bobby, you had better go home now and tell your mother everything. I will call her later to make sure you did. Macon Junior, you will go to your room until your father gets home!"

When Dad came home, I got his usual stern lecture before he took off his belt, lowered my pants, and whipped me until I cried with pain. He ended the session with; "You'd better not lie to you mother or me, or throw coal or anything else at cars ever again."

I meekly said, through my tears, "YES SIR!

As to lessons, here's what I learned, and I expect Bobby did too:

a. Naughtiness can be lots of fun.

b. If you're caught, there's hell to pay, so don't get caught.

c. Kids that throw "stones" should stick to targets that can't fight back!

3. GENDER DIFFERENCES:

I was about five years old when Mom and Dad bought a three-bedroom bungalow on west 6th street in Newton. The house on South College Avenue was a rental, and I think they bought a house of their own for three reasons:

a. They felt that Newton was a good place to settle down.

b. Mom was expecting a baby again.

c. It was closer to the schools, and since Dad was the Superintendent, Ruth was going to be in the third grade and I in the first grade, it made a lot of sense. We could all walk to school and come home for lunch, or dinner, as we called it then. Furthermore, we kids only had to cross one street, so danger from the sparse traffic was minimal. Besides, our parents had carefully taught us to look both ways and cross only when it was safe.

In May 1925, Ruth and I had a little sister, Mary Louise. She was something new to our lives, although we had seen babies in other families. But the main point of this memory occurred when Mom and dad took us shopping for new clothes. They wanted to outfit Ruth and me from head to toe with new garb, including hats. They added to the adventure by driving to Hickory, a much larger town about ten miles away.

Everything went well until it came to hats. Ruth was older and a girl, so she went first. After reviewing several candidates, she picked one that had flowers all around its brim. When it came my turn, I said, "I want one just like Ruth's!" Mom showed me several she had picked out for me, but I was adamant. "No, I don't like those. I want one like Ruth's because it has all those pretty flowers on it. If Ruth can have one, why can't I have one too?"

Dad came to Mom's rescue. He took me aside and gave me a lesson on our culture, although he didn't mention that term. (I figured it out later.) Anyway, he explained that girls and boys are different. (Which I already knew because of Ruth's dresses and my pants.)

He then explained that the difference included hats. (Which I didn't know.) He went on to point out the difference in his hat and Mom's hat. But the convincing bit was when he said, "If you go to school with flowers on your hat, the other kids will laugh at it and call you a "sissy".

We then went back to Mom and I picked out a little boy's hat, but deep inside I still wanted one with flowers. To make amends, they let me pick a little overcoat that was black outside, but with a bright red lining. WOW!

Lessons?

a. Gender differences affect how one dresses.

b. Girl's clothes are fancier and prettier than boy's clothes. (Maybe it's because they are prettier than boys)

c. Cultures change, as I later learned. Look at the colorful garb men now wear and the popularity of pants with women. In today's world, dresses are getting to be more and more rare.

d. Changes aren't always for the better. I still prefer women in pretty dresses and men in nice looking and less colorful garb!

FROZEN IN TIME

I am staring at an object; strangely enough, it is staring back at me. It is frozen in time, but I am still a live human for whom time is even now moving at its usual pace. The object is younger than I am, since it was created circa 1927, about seven years after I arrived on planet earth. It is important to me, and is hanging on a wall in my house so I can see it frequently.

The object is a framed photograph of my parents and their first three kids, of which I was the middle one. About three years later, twin boys joined our family, so their photos are in another frame, but also important.

We are sitting on the living room sofa in Newton, N.C., and I can still hear the photographer, Mr. Scott, giving directions before he flashed his powder to illuminate the scene.

I am sitting on the arm of the sofa next to my Dad. Mom is next to him and holding my baby sister, <u>Louise</u>, on her lap. Older sister, <u>Ruth</u>, is next to her. We are all dressed in our best clothes, and no one is smiling, so this must have been a serious occasion, or perhaps just part of the times. Today, the photographer would say "Cheese", or "Sex" to get everyone to smile, but not then.

I was wearing my first long-pants suit, complete with tie, and looked like I was ready to smile. I hate to say it, but I was a good-looking kid in those days, but time has taken its toll. Dad was an impressive man, about 6' 2", and very stern looking with his horn-rimmed glasses and slightly balding head. This was not his everyday pose, and we all knew he could laugh and smile with charm and grace.

Mom looked very pretty with her dark hair and trim figure, and she too looked ready to smile. In contrast to Dad, she had beautiful teeth, so her smiles were a joy to behold. Of course her laughter was higher pitched than Dad's, and more musical and scintillating.

Louise had a pleasant, somewhat quizzical look on her face, probably because it was her first sitting. She was a precious little girl, and at the age where everyone wanted to hug her. Ruth was wearing knee-length stockings and a pretty dress, but looked uncomfortable and a bit awkward.

Once Mr. Scott had finished and departed, we resumed our normal lives by changing our clothes to something less formal and going about our usual activities. I doubt if anyone thought about the future, and the role the photo would have in it. We saw through a "glass darkly" in those days, but the future that faced all of us then is now clear. That is one of the wonderful gifts of looking at an old object. It not only let's our minds go back to those early days, but lets us foresee the joys and pleasures, as well as pains and sadness, of the future, as this brief summary will show:

Dad left his position as Superintendent of Public Schools a few years later and bought a printing and office supply business, which he ran successfully until his death in 1954 at age 68. He was also a Justice of the Peace, and since I was an apprentice in his shop, I witnessed many cases he adjudicated, plus some marriages. He weathered the great depression, managed to get all five kids a college degree, and was a much loved community and church leader. He was also loved and respected by the "colored" folks, as evidenced by three of them standing with the other honorary pallbearers from the Men's Bible Class. (I was proud of my southern state's open attitude in 1954, long before the Civil Rights Movement)

Dad was an inspiration to all us kids and was a loving father most of the time; he became a disciplinarian only when necessary. (Which in my case was frequently.) He was the only one of eight kids to get a college degree, so he knew and promoted the value of education and the persistence needed to overcome adversity. His lessons and words of advice were invaluable, not only to my siblings and me, but also to many others.

Mom was also an inspiration, and a wonderful caretaker of the whole family. She taught me to read and write, so when I entered first grade at age 5, I had a head start. Mom kept an immaculate house, sometimes to my regret when I had to wax the floor and do other chores. Her cooking was superb-- always tasty and plentiful, and in keeping with current customs.

I can still remember the pleasure I got from her pumpkin pies, Japanese fruitcake, and other good things. She was an excellent hostess, bridge player, and flower gardener, and through her we had a stronger relationship with her siblings than we did with Dad's.

She was quite a bit younger than Dad, but managed to find an interesting life in her long widowhood. As time took its toll, she went to a Life Care Facility; first to assisted care, and eventually nursing care. She lived to age 95, but the last five years were not good because she was so weak. Unfortunately, I was overseas when she died, so was unable to attend her funeral services. However, that didn't stop me from weeping and reflecting on the great and loving influence she had on my life.

Ruth got a degree from Appalachian State Teachers College with a major in music, plus graduate work at Davidson College. She became a fine pianist and vocalist, and taught piano and led choirs and choruses for many years, both before her marriage and later on after raising her three talented children. She lost her husband when he was 85, but she still enjoys many friends and her grand and great grandkids She is in reasonable health and is now living in Brevard, N.C., which is called "The Tanglewood of the South" because of its fine summer musical festival.

After getting a degree from UNC, Greensboro, Louise had a short career as a government employee before her marriage. Her husband died at age 60, so she became a widow much too soon, She was also an excellent pianist, but eventually let her talent fade away. She raised four talented children and lived in Charlotte, N.C until her death in 1985, at age 80. Two of her daughters lived near by, as did some grandkids, and great ones were not too far away, so her widowhood was greatly helped.

My own future unfolded beyond my wildest dreams. I earned a B. Mech. Engineering degree from N.C. State College, got a job at Grumman Aircraft Engineering Corporation, and earned a M. Aero. Engineering degree from N.Y.U. at night and weekends. In addition to important positions on most of Grumman's military aircraft, which were vital to winning WWII and subsequent wars, I spent time on non-military projects. My most memorable position was my seven years on the Lunar Module, which safely landed the astronauts on the moon and returned them to the mother ship. When Neil Armstrong became the first human to step on the moon, I had risen to the position of Assistant Program Manager. I retired from Grumman in 1977 and formed a small corporation, from which I retired in 1986.

In 1945, I married Elizabeth (Betty) Warren, a lovely co-worker in the engineering department at Grumman. She had been senior class prom queen and valedictorian at Arlington High School in Poughkeepsie, N.Y., and earned a degree in Mathematics from Vassar College; fortunately, I married both beauty and brains. We have two wonderful married daughters, and two equally wonderful grandchildren and sons-in law. We celebrated our 60th wedding anniversary on May 6, 2005, so as the movie title says, "It's A Wonderful Life", and I consider myself extremely blessed. Believe me, the little boy in the picture didn't have the slightest inkling of how wonderful it would be!

Some say, "The past is gone forever." However, I believe that one look at a small object, such as a photograph hanging on a wall, can not only resurrect the past in your memory, but also let you peek into what was the future when it was taken. Of course we can recall past pleasure and sadness without photos and other objects, but they are very powerful catalysts for getting the mental process going.

That's probably why we humans collect and cherish so many!

MY BOYHOOD HOME TOWN

It was a prototype of small town America-- neat, clean and friendly, but with a few unpleasant secrets buried beneath its pleasing exterior. It was the county seat of Catawba County, was called "Newton" in honor of Sir Isaac or a distant relative. It was in the Piedmont Section of North Carolina, and there were two basic groups: White and "Colored", as we called them in those days. Among the whites, the social scales were about like this: First were the professionals-- the doctors, lawyers, and preachers. Next were the mill owners, who may have been richer than the former, but not as admired. Merchants and businessmen were in third place, along with school officials. Mill supervisors, teachers and white-collar workers were in fourth place, but many of the teachers were greatly admired and respected. Farmers were next in line, although most of them didn't live in the town limits. They did shop and send their kids to school in Newton. At the bottom of the white list were the mill workers. Colored folks lived in their own neighborhood, and had their own social scale. It was a peaceful town, and most of the people were nice to each other. The colored folks were treated well and respected, but the "Jim Crow" laws were upheld.

Newton had a large granite courthouse, complete with Grecian columns, a flat roof and a grassy lawn which had two mementos of the Civil War-- a cannon and a statue of a Confederate soldier. The soldier's pedestal bore this inscription: "No braver bled for brighter land, nor brighter land had a cause so grand." Even as a teenager, I thought the verse "fulsome!"

The courthouse occupied a whole block and was surrounded by the major stores. A few stores spilled out from the square, but most people shopped "on the square", where they got a "square deal". While the courthouse was the predominant landmark, the two hotels always caught my eye because of their size. Both were three stories high and twice the width of other buildings.

One, the St. Hubert Inn, had a three story tower capped by a small "crows nest". That made it SIX stories high—practically a skyscraper for our little town of five thousand. My friends and I spent many happy hours sneaking up to the crow's nest to get a birds-eye view of the square and the local citizens, especially the girls.

Like most small towns, the stores must have been built at different times because no two seemed the same. I suppose each owner had different resources and requirements, not to mention individual tastes. These factors also explain the variety of sizes, shapes and decorative treatment. The total effect was not bad, and even had a primitive harmony.

The two banks occupied diagonally opposite corners, as if to emphasize their competitive position. The three drug stores were on different corners, with one in the Virginia Shipp hotel. As was typical of the south in those days, each drug store had a marble-topped soda fountain and grill, so that people could take a refreshment break and even have a light lunch. Customers were served in booths or at small round tables with twisted, metal-rod chairs, popularly known as drug store chairs.

The drug stores were the social center of town and the chief meeting place for young people, especially during weekdays and school vacations. I suspect that many business deals were consummated there; I KNOW that dates with the opposite sex were made there because I was a participant!

Except for the courthouse, most of the stores were of brick construction—common bricks for the stores and fancy bricks for the banks. Large, plate glass windows on the ground floor of the stores displayed the merchandise of the day--clothes, furniture, hardware, groceries, etc. The second floors were for the professional offices--doctors, lawyers, surveyors, etc. The streets were asphalt and there were plenty of parking spaces because few families had two cars and many none.

Metered parking was far in the future, as were shopping malls and other modern developments.

As to the unpleasant secrets, they mostly revolved around past wild oats. A prominent doctor had a son out of marriage, as did a prominent attorney. In the latter case, two attorneys had dated the same young woman and had flipped a coin to see who would marry her when she became pregnant. Upon arrival, the son looked like the lawyer who didn't marry her, which proved to the local citizens that "gambling doesn't pay." Somehow they all lived in the same town in apparent harmony.

There was at least one unwed mother that I new, and of course we had our fair share of shotgun weddings and guys who did the right thing on their own. Theft was rare, and cars and even homes were usually left unlocked!

The homes ranged from spacious mansions to small, frame houses. There were no real slums, even in the mill worker's section, or the section where the "colored" folks lived. Schools were segregated by race, but that was accepted by all as a natural condition. Textiles and furniture making were the principal industries and the local gardens and outlying farms provided plenty of food, plus raw materials for the mills.

My memory of my hometown, and especially the courthouse square of yesteryear, is still strong and, I hope, accurate. During a recent trip back I was glad to see that most of the buildings were still intact, although the nature and ownership of the businesses had greatly changed. Even the courthouse had changed functions, but not its outer appearance. Judging by the activity, the courthouse square seemed to be holding its own with the malls.

When I ambled around the square, I had a strange feeling; I seldom saw anyone I knew, whereas during my boyhood I seldom saw any strangers. Many stores had different names, almost all had different owners and clerks, and I was no longer privy to any juicy town secrets. But the buildings were so familiar that I felt at home again. It was a bittersweet experience and made me somewhat philosophical. Animate objects, such as people, move away, become unrecognizable, or die. Inanimate objects, buildings for instance, keep their identity much, much longer and can conjure up many memories.

But here's the bottom line: I'm glad that I returned! I'm especially glad that I'm an ANIMATE OBJECT!

1930-1940

Dirt

Western North Carolina has some of the reddest dirt on earth. The shade of red depends on the moisture content—dark red when wet, light red when dry.

It is also the 'messiest' dirt on earth. Just a puff of wind in dry weather and your clothes are soiled—almost beyond cleaning. Many time my Mother scolded me for getting too much red dirt on my clothes and shoes, but it was next to impossible for an active kid like me to avoid it.

During the early thirties, three other pre-teen boys and I were exploring a new area on the outskirts of town. It was a hot summer afternoon, so we were delighted when we came upon a clearing with a newly built pond in its center. Mounds of red dirt surrounded the pond and gave it a nice ambiance, but that's not how I would have described it in those days. Anyway, we were hot and it was cool, so we quickly removed our shirts, Sneakers and short pants, then plunged into the pond in our birthday suits.

John Cantrell quickly noticed that the wet earth made great mud and that it could easily be smeared over his body he then proceeded to give himself red-mud bathing trunks—just in case anyone came along and saw him naked. It wasn't long before the rest of us followed suit. In fact, we had an informal competition to see who could be most creative.

David Schrum. made a bathing suit in the latest fashion—over the shoulder top with double-hole armpits. Bill Cline made a long old fashioned bathing suit with horizontal stripes. I made shoes and socks with my bathing trunks and then made a light colored vest with mud buttons up my chest, starting with the one nature gave me.

It was the easiest thing in the world to change costumes. All we had to do was jump back in the water, swish around a bit and voila—we were our natural color again. We laughed the most at John C. when he covered himself from head to toe with red mud, dangerously leaving his bathing suit area au natural. He looked like an Indian with trunks. This sport lasted for about an hour or so. Finally, we heard someone coming, so we flushed off the red mud, put our short pants on and dried ourselves with our shirts and the hot sun.

As we were putting on our sneakers a man appeared and said, "You boys weren't thinking of going swimmin', were you?" I pretended that I was just taking my sneakers off and said, "No sir, we were just planning to go wading."

"Well you better not. This is private property and swimmin's not allowed—not even wading."

We left politely, but when we were out of earshot we laughed heartily at our trickery. However, all the activity and excitement created a huge appetite in each of us. Fortunately, we spotted a big fig tree loaded with ripe figs on the way home. There was no sign saying "Keep Out," so we assumed that some kind-hearted soul had planted it to feed hungry kids, so we ate our fill.

We had quintuple fun that day—we explored new territory, cooled off with a swim, enjoyed a bit of creative-costuming tom-foolery, used a forbidden pond with impunity and filled out stomach with luscious figs. I'm hard pressed to say which one I enjoyed the most.

One thing is certain—each has a fond place in my memory.

DRACULA

"Dracula", by Bram Stoker, is easily the scariest book I have ever read. It far surpasses in horror the 1934 movie, although I will admit that Bella Lugosi, the movie Count Dracula, is the mental image I still retain of the fearsome vampire. Movie scenes of Transylvania, Dracula's castle and the old abbey in England also made an indelible image in my mind. So the movie sort of pre-conditioned me when I finally read the book,

I first read it in 1938, when I was 18 years old and still very impressionable. I was attending summer school at N.C, State College in

Raleigh and the campus was almost deserted. Since campus life was near a standstill. I decided to get "Dracula" from the D. H. Hill library late one Saturday afternoon.

As I left the library I met my friend <u>Tommy Haynes</u>, all dressed up for a date with one of Raleigh's belles.

"What are you reading?" he inquired. I showed him the book.

"Dracula!" he said in awe—"Aren't you afraid to read such a scary book?"

"Why should I be scared", I replied, "Its only fiction."

"Well, I don't know," he said. "Some of the other fellows that read it told me they couldn't sleep all night. And you are living in the wooded end of 7th dormitory without a roommate. Boy, I wouldn't want to do that!"

"I'll be O.K.--it's just a book." He shook his head sadly and walked away with a solemn, "So long--I gotta run—but remember, I warned ya!"

I went back to my room, read a chapter or so and then went to the cafeteria for supper. After supper I walked for an hour or so to watch the sunset. As darkness fell, I went back to my lonely room and continued reading. Tommy was right. It was a scary book, made doubly so by the deserted dormitory.

Earlier in the summer I had moved my double bunk bed over to the twin windows to overcome the July heat. Around 11:30 I climbed into my upper bunk to relax, relieve the tension of the frightening tale, and read a bit more until I felt sleepy.

Jonathan Harker had finally escaped from Dracula's castle and his evil clutches. I had reached the end of the Count's sea voyage to London, where he planned to feast on the blood of the teeming multitudes of that great city. The poor wretches on the ship had all fallen victim to the evil Count and the ship had finally reached port. All hands were either dead or missing and the captain had bound himself to the wheel with crucifixes. Even that didn't help because he was dead on arrival, with horrible glassy eyes and a look of incredible fear on his countenance.

The seaport authorities were completely mystified, since the only living thing to leave the ship was a large, vicious dog--Count Dracula in another form. I was totally engrossed in the story.

Suddenly, I heard a loud, vicious growl just outside my window. Although I was flat on my back, I must have jumped a foot and my heart started pounding fiercely. I felt sure that Dracula (in the dog's body) had come to suck my blood and turn me into a slave vampire as he had done to so many others.

My sudden fright was calmed by the hilarious laughter of Tommy, who had concocted the impish idea of frightening me on his return from his date.

"Tommy, you bastard!" I shouted, "How could you do that to me?"

"Well, I warned you, didn't I," and he walked off still chuckling.

Naturally, I was greatly relieved that the evil count hadn't appeared—only my friend (?) Tommy. Even so, I decided to move my bunk back to the corner and as far away from the window as possible. After such a shock, I had a very difficult time falling asleep. Every time I turned out the light I could feel Dracula's presence in the room. Finally, I decided to leave my desk lamp on all night and eventually fell asleep.

It was a memorable event. In fact, I can't remember ever having such a powerful reaction to a work of fiction as I did that night with "Dracula."

A sharp hand salute to Bram Stoker for creating such a masterpiece; a sharp foot salute to Tommy's rear for his devilish trick. However, I must admit, albeit grudgingly, that Tommy's concept and his timing were also masterpieces!

P.S. I finished "Dracula" during daylight hours.

FIGHTS I REMEMBER

I must have been a good kid, because I don't remember starting any physical fights. That doesn't mean that I never had any, but as far as I can remember, someone else started them. The first one that I remember happened in 1934, when I was about 14 years old. It was in the afternoon, and I was headed for the bus depot to pick up my papers. Yes, I was a paperboy, and had 20 customers who subscribed to the Hickory Daily Record, an afternoon paper. I had my empty "paper" satchel over my shoulder.

As I passed the schoolhouse, four boys approached me somewhat belligerently. They were mostly kids of mill workers, who were at the bottom of the white social scale. I suspect they might have been annoyed because I was one of the upper-middle class kids. You see, I was the son of the ex-superintendent of schools and owner of Epps Printing Company, and my dad was highly respected in our small town of 5000 people. Most of the boys were my age and about my size, but one, named "Herman", was younger and a good bit smaller. One of the bigger boys said, "Herman claims he can beat you up, and is willing to fight to prove it!"

"I have nothing against Herman, and don't want to fight him," I replied. "Besides, he's smaller than I am, so it wouldn't be a fair fight."

"Then you must be yellow, and a scaredy cat if you won't fight him." He then looked at the others and said, "All of you agree, don't you?"

The others, including Herman started chanted, "yellow scaredy cat, yellow scaredy cat, yellow scaredy cat…."

Reluctantly, I said, "Well, if you insist, I guess I'll wrestle him." I took off my bag, grabbed Herman, quickly threw him down and pinned him to the ground in spite of his wiggling to free himself. Just as I was about to get up, two of the other boys grabbed me, threw me to the ground, and then placed Herman on top. "Look," one of them said, "Herman is winning!"

I quickly threw him off and pinned him to the ground again, only to have the two boys throw me down and place Herman on top. When I extricated myself once more, I said, "I can beat Herman, but I can't beat all of you, so I'm leaving." I picked up my bag and quickly walked away. They were a bit surprised, but once they recovered their wits they started chasing and throwing dirt clods at me from a nearby field. I used my bag to protect myself from the clods, and ran fast to escape them. They chased me for about two blocks, and then gave up because we were approaching the downtown area. Several blocks later, I picked up and then delivered my papers with no further trouble.

About a week later, I was in my <u>Dad</u>'s printing shop doing some light work. As I looked out the open door, I saw Herman walking by. "Aha," I said to myself, "I'm gonna teach him a lesson."

I then walked out the door, and as soon as he saw me, he started running across an empty field. I could run faster, so when I caught up with him I threw him to the ground and said, "Don't ever do that to me again. Remember, you won't always have those bigger boys around to protect you, so if you do it again I'll catch you and beat the daylights out'a you. Do you promise?"

"I promise, I promise," Herman said meekly.

Herman kept his promise, and the bigger boys never bothered me again.

Some years later, when I was returning to High School after having lunch at home, I was approached by a mill boy my age and size. "I don't like your looks, Epps," he said. "I think I'll punch you in the nose!"

"I'm sorry you don't like my looks, but that's no reason to start a fight."

"It is for me," he said belligerently, and started hitting me. Of course I defended my self and started swinging at him. I landed several good ones, including one on his nose, which began bleeding. He grabbed his handkerchief to stop the bleeding and went into the building to wash it off. I also went into the building and to my next class, wondering the rest of the day if he would report his bloody nose to the Principal.

I don't know if he ever got to like my "looks", but I do know that he never reported me to the principal!

In 1936, when I was a freshman in college, we were required to take boxing lessons. I suppose it was to teach us the manly art of self-defense. Anyway, we wore large boxing gloves, and even with the soft gloves most of us were gentle with each other. Oh, we would land blows beyond each other's defense, but not enough to hurt.

One day, I was boxing with a powerful boy who didn't seem to know the unwritten rules of doing no harm. Before I could prepare myself, he came at me swinging rapidly and powerfully. It wasn't long before he was hurting me, so the coach stopped the fight, telling him we weren't there to knock each other out, just to learn the art of boxing. He seemed to understand, but before long he was trying to land some more hard blows. By then I was on my guard, blocked his blows, and landed a few hard ones on him. Soon, we were going after each other like two wild cats. Again, the coach stopped us, and said, "I guess you two shouldn't box each other. Next boxers!

Eventually, I became the Southern Conference lightweight boxing champion. If you don't believe it, just ask <u>Dan Belvin</u>, one of my college buddies. He would tell this tall tale to pretty girls we met, and I, of course, would say, "Aw, Dan, you shouldn't tell these girls such things!"

When I was around 13 and feeling my oats, I was talking with my older sister, <u>Ruth</u>, in our kitchen. <u>Dad</u> was sitting at the table eating something and not paying much attention to our conversation. I started bragging about how boys were much stronger than girls, and that I could easily beat her up. I even gave a few light punches on her upper arm. I persisted too long with the punches, and Ruth attacked me, hitting and scratching with great vim and vigor. All I could do was put my arms up to protect myself and back out of the room, until she stopped.

Dad arose when we started fighting, but didn't do anything to stop it because Ruth was not being harmed and I was getting what I deserved. Once it was over, Dad said: "What's the matter, son? I thought you said you were stronger and could beat her. What happened?

"I know how to fight boys, Dad, but I don't know how to fight a girl!

Both Ruth and Dad got much pleasure by re-telling this story many times, and for many years. I'll admit that their tales gave me a bit of discomfort, but I always took it good-naturedly. Ruth is now in her 90's, and still reminds me of that memorable day.

FORBIDDEN FRUIT-SOUTHERN STYLE

They lay naked in the moonlight, an irresistibly tempting sight. I was not yet sixteen, but <u>Fred Huffman</u> had said that this new experience would be exciting, fun and satisfying. I knew that we were about to sample forbidden fruit and that there were some risks, but it was customary for red-blooded Southern boys to do this sort of thing by age sixteen. So why should I be different? Or retarded? Or left out?

My heart was pumping furiously as I drew closer to the one I had selected. Perhaps it was the moonlight, perhaps it was the excitement of the first such encounter, but it seemed to me that I had never seen one that was so attractive or whose skin glistened so exquisitely. I bent over to gather this tempting morsel into my arms— but wait, I am getting a bit ahead of my story.

The place was Newton, North Carolina, a sleepy little town of about 5,000 gentle people and maybe a few roughnecks. Even the roughnecks were honest, because no one ever locked their bikes, their cars, or even their homes, except maybe at night.

The year was 1935 and the Great Depression was in full swing. By today's standards we were poor, but I never felt poor. I never went without enough food, or a comfortable bed (except on camping trips). I always had decent clothes and lots of friends. Besides, there were many families worse off than mine, so we considered ourselves middle class. My <u>Dad</u> owned a small job printing and office supply business and made about $3,000 per year. That was enough to support my mother and us five kids. My <u>mother</u> was a very pretty woman and a good cook and homemaker. Both of them were good parents and our home life was harmonious and loving. Yes, we kids had all we really needed. The only two commodities that were in short supply were money and excitement. We had our own ways for overcoming the shortages, as you will soon see.

The month was August, and the long, hot summer showed no signs of letting up. One evening, my cousin and best friend, <u>David Schrum</u>, suggested that we go to the movies. Don't ask me the name of the movie or who was in it. All I remember is that it cost ten cents and it made us feel a bit reckless and in need of some excitement. As we left the movie, we encountered several other friends. They were in the same post-movie mood as we were. It was only about 9 p.m. so we started discussing what to do with the rest of the evening.

A friend named Fred said he had an idea that would be exciting, fun and satisfying.

"What is it?" we asked eagerly.

"Well," he said, "if you'll hop into my Model T, I'll drive out past old St. Paul's church and we'll raid a watermelon patch. I spotted it t'other day. I'll tell you fellas all about it if you'll bring back a melon apiece. I'll hav'ta stay with the car so we can make a quick getaway."

It sounded like a good proposition, so we hopped in and headed for the watermelon patch. At this point I guess I should sort of apologize for my provocative opening. If you will forgive me for misleading you, I will forgive you for any naughty thoughts you had. You did have some, didn't you? I guess you have forgotten (or never knew) how pure and relatively innocent young Southern boys were in those days.

There were seven boys who piled into that old Model T; in order of seniority, they were:

<u>Gus Arndt</u>, a short, powerfully built boy who was seventeen plus years old. Gus had dark brown, straight hair and was nice looking, but not handsome. He was a fun guy to be with and wasn't shy with the girls, like the rest of us. For example, he often greeted them with a friendly pat on the bottom, which got him a few slaps, but as he said, "More fun than slaps." Gus played end on the football team and was a good tennis player, swimmer and all-round athlete. He wanted to be a CPA when he grew up. At that age, I barely knew what CPA stood for, let alone what they did. Gus told me they made lots of money and had steady work, so that satisfied me. His father had a nice home near ours and ran one of the local lumberyards.

John Guy a big 6'4", 210-pound giant, also a bit over seventeen. John had light brown, straight hair and a big round face. His eyes were relatively small and nearly closed when he laughed, which he did frequently. Other kids called him "moon face", usually from a distance because John didn't take kindly to that appellation. John was very shy around girls and hated to be called on to read or talk in school. He got so nervous when he had to read that it made me uneasy. I couldn't fathom why a guy who could lick any kid in school would get nervous on those occasions, but he did. John was a star tackle on the football team and forward on the basketball team. His ambition was to be an athletic coach. His father was dead, but he had older siblings who kept the family going.

Fred Huffman, a medium-sized boy around sixteen years old, with straight black hair and a rosy complexion that got really rosy when he got flustered or excited. At first glance he looked like a "roughneck", but he was an OK guy. He was a bit on the plump side and was quick-tempered when crossed. He played substitute tackle on the football team and wasn't a very good student. His ambition was to finish high school and get a job. His father was a barber.

Macon (that's me), a 5"11" boy who weighed 135 pound soaking wet, and was 15 2/3 years old. (The 2/3 year was important to me in those days.) I had light brown, curly hair that my straight-haired sisters envied. ("Why waste it on a boy?" they often said.) I played right guard on the football team and baritone horn in the band. Like Gus, I wasn't handsome, but my curly hair scored a few points with the girls. I was one of the youngest kids in my class and graduated the following year, as did John. I wanted to be an aeronautical engineer and perhaps a test pilot. My father was ex-superintendent of schools, but left it to buy the small business I mentioned earlier.

David Schrum (my cousin), a 5' 11" boy who was a bit skinnier and a month younger than I. (I frequently reminded him of my seniority, especially when we had an argument or a decision to make.) David was a studious kid with dark red, wavy hair and a smattering of freckles. He wore glasses, which in those days was a sure sign of a good scholar. He played clarinet in the band and was one of the best tree climbers in town (almost as good as I was). He was a good guy to pal around with, but his folks' strict upbringing tended to inhibit his spirit of adventure. He seldom instigated any adventures, but could be persuaded if I promised not to tell his folks. He wanted to be an M.D., an ambition he acquired at the early age of five. His father was manager of the Western Union office and one of the best gardeners I ever knew.

Jack and Joe Gabriel, twin brothers who were around 14 and the smallest of the group. Normally, they were too young for us to pal around with and I didn't know much about their ambitions or their families. I did know that they were regular guys who knew how to have fun, so I accepted them as co-adventurers that night. Both had short, straight blond hair; pleasant, slightly freckled faces and big grins.

As the seven of us drove along, Fred started telling us his plan. "I'll park in the woods across from the church. I'll turn around and head back toward Newton so we can make a quick getaway. You fellas can walk down the road to the east. There's a small grove of trees just beyond the road goin' north toward Hickory. You can enter the grove and use it as cover 'til ya size up the patch and watch out for the farmer. If the coast is clear, grab the melons, fade back into the woods and bring 'em back here. If there's any sign of trouble, I'll drive away and meet ya here later."

It sounded like a foolproof plan to the rest of us, so we readily agreed. After parking, six of us started walking along the road toward the grove of trees, which was several hundred yards away. To our right was the graveyard of the old church. The twins expressed fear when passing so near the ancient tombstones, some of which dated back to the early 1700's as I had previously observed during daylight hours. They stayed close to John, feeling somehow that his huge size would protect them.

We entered the grove without incident; not a single car came along this deserted country road at this hour. We then made our way quietly and cautiously to the far side and stood in the shadows whispering to each other. Sure enough, they lay there naked in the moonlight, a beautiful, tempting sight if ever my young eyes had seen one. A murmur of appreciation rippled through the group. Everybody was ready to go harvest this delicious forbidden fruit, except Gus. He called to us softly, "I think I see a man coming toward the patch from the house—we'd better not go in or we may get shot!"

We all stopped in our tracks and peered into the moonlit night. We saw no sign of a man. All we saw were a few shocks of dried corn stalks that we thought Gus had mistaken for a man. It was 5 to 1—and we concluded that Gus was so nervous that he was seeing things. He insisted that he was right and the thought of being shot frightened the twins visibly. I came up with a compromise solution:

"I'll go into the patch with John and David. You and the twins stay in the woods 'til we get back safely. Then you go in and get your own watermelons." My solution was agreeable to all concerned.

Now I suppose you are thinking that we were greedy to want to get six watermelons. Perhaps you are right, but consider it this way: No one wanted to take all the risk alone so all six should share it equally. Fred furnished the car and the plan, so he deserved to stay with our getaway car. Since we all had to go into the patch, we might as well bring back a melon apiece. If we were lucky, all six would be ripe and we could enjoy them for a week. If a few were too green to eat, we would still have several days of good eating. Besides, it was part of our agreement with Fred. O.K.?

John, David and I then slipped quietly toward the watermelons, keeping a weather eye out for the farmer. No one was in sight. All we could see were the shocks of corn stalks, and they didn't move. As I approached a good-sized melon it <u>was</u> attractive and its skin <u>did</u> glisten exquisitely in the moonlight. And it certainly was a tempting morsel. So maybe I'll take back my apology!

Anyway, I bent over to thump it to see if it was ripe. It sounded "hollow" so that meant it was a "good 'un". This is about where my introduction left off, so you can start getting excited again, but now it is a different scenario from the one you first envisioned. As I reached over to separate the melon from the vine and take it tenderly into my arms, my reverie was rudely disturbed by a loud shot from the vicinity of the corn stalks.

Now we each had private, unspoken plans as to what we would do if accosted, which we immediately implemented. Gus and the twins faded back into the grove, crossed the first road and hid among the tombstones. The fear of the gun obviously was greater than the twins' previous fear of the graveyard. Gus's keen eyesight was exonerated, but no one thought of it then.

John and I lit out as fast as possible for the intersecting road and a patch of woods, which seemed closer and deeper than the shallow grove that we had used as first cover. I remember planning to jump into the high weeds on the other side of the road, figuring that I could hide there safely. If anyone started approaching my hiding place I would creep into the woods. I didn't want to go crashing into the woods for fear of hurting myself.

John, who was several steps ahead of me, was so frightened that he went crashing into the woods—all 210 pounds of him. Maybe he felt he was too big to hide in the weeds. I also remember hearing the second shot and, even scarier, the tinkle of the shotgun pellets in the leaves near John's point of entry. I guess the farmer was no fool. He shot at the biggest target. The tinkling sound made me fall flat into the weeds per my plan.

David had the most audacious plan of all, but I didn't know about it until much later. I figured he had joined Gus and the twins.

Well, it looked like we had all gotten away, but my heart was pounding so loudly that I was sure the farmer would hear it if he got within 20 yards of my hiding place. John had gotten far enough into the woods to stop crashing and make his way gingerly to where Fred had parked the tin lizzie. A few minutes later, the farmer started his car and began sweeping the road for culprits, or so I thought at the time. I breathed a big sigh of relief as he passed me in my weedy hiding place, only 2 or 3 yards in from the road. For one crazy minute I entertained the thought of going back for my beautiful watermelon, but my nerves were too frayed to risk it. I lay there a few more minutes and then went back along the road toward the car. I was ready to hop back into the weeds, or the woods, at the first sign of a car.

In about 10 minutes, Gus, John and I had made our way to the car, which was still there along with Fred. It seems that Fred had heard the shots, but since he wasn't able to start the model T, he hid deep in the woods. The twins were nowhere to be seen. Gus said they were still hiding behind the tombstones and weren't going to come out until it was really safe. No one had seen David and we all started to get worried. I was plenty worried too, but I knew he was very resourceful and figured he was O.K.

Gus said we should fetch the twins and look for David, so John and I went over to the graveyard and called softly for our missing buddies. Presently, the twins sheepishly came forth, kinda like Lazarus from the tomb. We were all amazed that they had overcome their fear of the graveyard so easily and teased them a bit about it.

We looked some more for David, both on foot and in the car, but could find no sign of him. Fred decided that he had to get himself and the car back home, or else face a big ruckus with his old man. We were all in the same situation, so reluctantly we drove back to Newton, going past David's house to try once more to find him before we called it a night. About a block from his house we finally saw him, headed for home. Boy, were we relieved to see him! We could hardly wait to hear his story.

His story went something like this:

"I'm O.K., but I got caught. My plan was to lie flat in the melon patch. I thought the farmer would chase John and Macon, who were hightailing it for the woods. I figured I could wait 'til he ran for them and then grab my watermelon and go back to the grove. It might'a worked 'cept he kept comin' toward me with the shotgun pointed at the ground. I was afraid it might go off accidentally if he came too close, so when he kept comin' toward me I yelled, 'Don't shoot, don't shoot!' and stood up with my arms over my head. He took me back to his house, started his car, and drove me to the police station in Newton to have me arrested. On the way he got the license number of Fred's car and wanted the names of the rest of you."

"You didn't tell him, did ya?" several of us shouted in unison. Fred uttered a low moan as if his goose was already cooked.

"Yep," David replied, "but hold your horses 'n let me tell ya the rest. The farmer, <u>Mr. Bost</u>, said that if I didn't tell he'd put me in jail and have the police track the rest of ya down from the license number. But, if I told him and we all came back and apologized tonight he might let us all off with a warning. I think he'll do it, but I can't guarantee it."

We discussed the situation briefly among ourselves and quickly decided to trust the farmer. We let the twins go home since they were the youngest and were already out too late. The rest of us drove back to Mr. Bost's farm at about 10p.m. He was waiting for us on his screened porch and showed us the cot he kept out there so he would be able to guard his melon patch and still get some sleep. His cue for a potential intruder was the sound and headlights of a car that came up the hill from Newton and then stopped within 4 or 5 hundred yards of his patch; he used the corn shocks to get from his house to the patch undetected. We were learning a lot about the other side of the coin.

We told him our names, apologized and assured him we had learned our lesson. Much to our relief, he said he wouldn't prosecute us. One of us asked if we could buy a watermelon, explaining that we had gotten powerfully hungry and thirsty from all the excitement. He allowed as how we could, so we each chipped in a nickel and bought a big one for 25 cents. (He kept a few melons near his house.)

Mr. Bost was a nice man and seemed to understand that we were just hungry young boys seeking some adventure. He implied that he had done the same thing in his youth, but didn't quite admit it. He said that the first shot was a warning, but that the second one was for real since we ran away. John and I felt lucky. Not only did we escape a painful (but not fatal) injury, but also we didn't have to explain any wounds to our folks. By the way, Mr. Bost told us he had rock salt in the shotgun shells. It stings like blazes, but cause minimum injury.

After thanking him profusely, we then drove away with the watermelon. We decided to stop near the original "getaway" spot and eat it. Most of us carried a pocket knife, but John's was the biggest, so he cut the melon in big slices and we started enjoying this delicious fruit, which was no longer "forbidden" but perfectly legal.

As we were eating, a lone car came along our road and all the other fellows slunk back into the woods to hide. "How come you're hiding?" I asked.

"Don't ask foolish questions," one of them replied. "If we're spotted eatin' watermelon here, they'll think we stole it and we could get into trouble again."

"Nonsense," I said, "We bought this melon and the farmer is our witness, so I'm not gonna hide from some passing stranger. I think you fellas are 'yellow'!"

"Suppose it's somebody who recognizes one of us and tells our folks? I don't want to take that chance."

"Fat chance of that happening," I said, calculating the odds mentally. "I'm gonna stay right here." And I did!

My argument was unpersuasive, but they did rejoin me once the car passed. We ate our fill 'midst good- natured patter and drove back to town a little before 11 o'clock.

The next day, some of us met and discussed the night's adventure and promised to keep mum about it, lest it get back to our parents. Fred got chewed out by his father for staying out so late, and the rest of us had a bit of explaining why we got home from the movie so late. My excuse was that I had stayed for the "second show", and that seemed to work. I didn't tell my folks that the "second show" took place in a watermelon patch!

A few days later I got a visible and very pesky reminder that there is a price to pay when one breaks the law, almost like a higher court ruling. It seems that the "weeds" I hid in at the edge of the road contained a bountiful supply of POISON IVY!! The itchy rash lasted two weeks, and I concluded that the person who said, "Crime doesn't pay" was dead right!

But I still think that a field of ripe, southern watermelons, glistening in the moonlight is a lovely, tempting sight!

Postscript

It has been many decades since this true adventure happened. I lost track of Fred and the twins, but think they finished high school, got good jobs and raised families. Gus went on to college, joined the Navy and became a naval aviator during World War II. I once saw him with his dive-bomber near Newton during a mutual visit home. He died in the Pacific fighting the powerful Japanese fleet, a real hero.

John became a first rate football player and athlete, graduated from college and was a high school teacher and coach when I last saw him. He became a high school principal before he died from cancer in the late 80's.

David and I have remained life-long friends. He became an excellent pediatrician and has taken care of thousands of children and saved the lives of many of them. He has been very successful, has a lovely wife, four attractive grown daughters and several grandchildren. Most of his practice was in Texas. Late in life he went to Oral Roberts University, where he was chairman of the Pediatrics department during its years of growth and challenge. He is now retired.

I pursued an engineering career and earned two degrees in Aeronautical Engineering. I had a successful and very interesting career at Grumman Aerospace Corporation. During WW II I helped produce fighters and torpedo bombers for the U.S. Navy, so Gus and I complemented each other. My most rewarding professional work was on the Lunar Module, which was extraordinarily successful in landing the astronauts on the moon and returning them safely. After an early retirement from Grumman, I started a small technical service and invention company; fun and fascinating, but only partly successful. My family is my greatest joy. My wife, Elizabeth, and I have been together since may 1945, have two lovely married daughters, two granddaughters and a grandson.

If any of the other surviving members of our adventure should ever read this account, they may have slightly different memories. I think my account is basically accurate. Should they quarrel with mine, my advice is, "Write your own version!"

I'm sure we would all agree on this point: IT'S SAFER TO BUY A WATERMELON THAN TO SWIPE ONE!!!

MEMORIES OF HIGH SCHOOL

We old timers sometimes wish we could return to our early years armed with the knowledge of decades of experience. Impossible to do, you say! Not necessarily, I say, provided we use our memory and the all-important ingredient of imagination! To illustrate, I will now return to those highly formative years known as "high school."

PRIDE AND FEAR:

It is September 1932, and I am walking a little more than a block up Ashe Avenue to Newton High School, in western North Carolina. I have a strange mixture of pride and fear in my mind; pride that I am now a high-school student and fear that I may find it a bit overwhelming. The fear is short lived once I see most of my former seventh grade classmates; at least I won't be the only one to endure any ordeals facing us.

I feel more disdain than pity for those who weren't promoted to our questionable new position as freshmen; yes, some were real dummies, but most were just plain lazy. Within a few days, I conquer the new routine and settle down to learning new things-- and discovering novel ways to have fun.

FUN IN CLASS:

Discipline is very strict in these depression days, but we kids can "invent" ways to have fun. An older "inventor" probably taught someone in my class this trick, but most of us boys soon became past masters at it-- humming in class. Now this isn't ordinary humming, but the kind that drives a teacher daffy! Why? Because s/he can never find its source. The hummer always stops as the teacher approaches and another boy far away picks up the exact pitch and intensity.

To make matters worse, each hummer feigns study or rapt attention, and when the teacher accuses one of us, we always stop humming, shrug our shoulders, and point in the direction of the new source. Sometimes we have group humming, which really exasperates "teach". There is one slight problem, however; we have to hold our laughter in until we leave the classroom, or face disciplinary measures.

Today, using my reservoir of experience, I just got all the boys to laugh in class — in unison-- so no one would be singled out. I even got some of the girls, who never participate in the humming, to join in the laughter and further insulate us from punishment!

BIG TROUBLE:

It is now October and I am in trouble—Big Trouble! <u>Rome Jones</u>, a tow-headed upper classman has caught me and pulled me into a little-used outside stair well. He growls, "I'm gonna get revenge for the beatin's your dad gave me a couple'a years ago when he was Superintendent!"

Rome twists my arm behind my back so I won't try to escape, and starts telling me details about the beatings.

I blurt out, "Hey, I'm innocent; it wasn't my fault he beat'cha, so please don't take it out on me!"

He yells, "Too bad, kid, I'm gonna beat'cha anyway!"– and he starts to do it.

But before he does, I dig into my vast experience reservoir and say, "And just what do you thing my Dad will do to you once he learns about this–shake your hand? You'd better think this out carefully, or you may get the wrong end of this deal. Besides, I happen to know that you're gonna make millions in your furniture company, and they're even gonna name a road after you- the one leading to your country estate!"

"Suppose I tell a newspaper editor of the future how you beat up a kid half your size! What then???" I walk away calmly, leaving him puzzled and slowly pondering my thoughts.

NON-ADMIRABLE CUSTOMERS:

Most of my newspaper customers are decent folks that pay me their "fifteen cents" a week each Saturday. (Tips are unknown, so my weekly take is one dollar even if all pay on time) Unfortunately, some of them are cheapskates, or worse yet, deadbeats. Several told me that they want to pay every two weeks, and then only a measly quarter. That cuts my weekly take by two and a half cents for each skinflint, but they threaten to stop the paper altogether if I don't. They drive their position home by pointing out that I go by their house anyway, so it's no extra work for me. Reluctantly, I agree.

Then there's a man called "Moon," who is also on the quarter-every-two-weeks plan. Sometimes he claims he paid me "last" week, but I usually win that argument by showing him my records. Frequently, he is short of cash and promises religiously to pay me "next week".

He is a master of excuses, and eventually cons me into waiting yet another week, and another, and.... Finally, when his unpaid bill reaches $1.20– eight weeks delivery and 40 cents in wages for me– I say, "Sorry, I won't deliver any more papers until'ya payup ."

I keep my word and, much to my chagrin, he keeps his money! I would like to dip all of the cheapskates and deadbeats up to their necks into my experience reservoir until they are soaking with remorse for taking advantage of a good-natured, trusting young lad. I suppose their sins against me were too small to deserve God's wrath, but perhaps He will chide them, or even forgive me for things I did later!

A YOUNG KID'S FANCY:

Its spring, and everything is blooming. I start noticing which girls are pretty and wonder what it would be like to kiss the prettiest one. But that's sissy stuff, so I dismiss it from my mind. I wander back to the big swing set at the back of the school, swing a bit and then decide to climb the fifteen or so feet up one of the slanting metal poles. I am about half way up when a strange sensation hits my groin. It is very pleasant, and I soon figure out that it has something to do with sex.

That's a highly forbidden subject in these times, so I keep it to myself. However, it doesn't stop me from trying it again now and then when I am near the swings! I am puzzled by this new phenomenon, and never learn exactly what it is. Dipping into my experience reservoir, I figure I may as well confess this incident since no subject is verboten these days-- besides, some reader may enlighten me about this totally dry experience.

MORE ABOUT GIRLS:

I am now a sophomore, and rising rapidly in the academic world-- or so I think. Not only that, I have just been invited to a party, so I put on my best white duck pants, a clean shirt, slick down my curly hair and head toward <u>Frances Raymer</u>'s house, our young hostess. She has devised a mixer, consisting of pictures from a magazine, which are cut, in half. I find the girl holding my matching half, and, according to the rules, enjoy fifteen minutes of conversation. They call this game, "Progressive Conservation." I guess its because we boys "progress" from one girl to another; but then, it may mean that I should make progress through my conversation. One thing is certain: it tests my ability to talk with the opposite gender. Somehow, I muddle through with some of the "wall flowers" I drew in the early rounds.

Gosh, my luck just changed-- my half matches a girl I sort of admire. She is <u>Dorothy Long,</u> the daughter of a Doctor, but in spite of her high social position, she is easy to talk with and seems to like me. We wander to a secluded part of the yard, and I gather up all my shaky courage and say, "May I kiss you?"

I feel like a fool, but much to my surprise she says, "I guess so. " I hold her in my arms and kiss her tenderly on the lips-- or is it tentatively? Anyway, I find the experience pleasant and a bit exciting, so I try it again, this time with more vigor. She responds cooperatively and says, "Wow! " I decide that it was more than a "bit" exciting.

Unfortunately, our fifteen minutes are up and I do not draw her again. As I wander home from the party I realize that I am growing up, having just enjoyed my first real kiss. I think of the sensation formed when climbing the swing, and make comparisons. Both were very pleasant, but some how the kiss, although less erotic, seems more fulfilling and natural. I wonder what else Mother Nature has in store for me? Again I draw from my experience reservoir and find the answer, but I don't change my first kiss experience one whit! It is part of the great unfolding of nature's plan to give her creatures something to make life worth living, joyous and productive!

MOONLIGHT MISADVENTURE

It was one of those delightfully warm August nights, made even more delightful by a full moon and fleecy white clouds gracing the evening sky. I was in my late teens, but since the great depression was going full bore I had very little money in my pockets-- maybe ten or fifteen cents. I decided to walk to the center of my small North Carolina town to buy a nickel cone of ice cream, or perhaps a ten-cent milkshake. I also hoped I could find a bit of excitement.

A few blocks before I reached the business district, I was greeted by a familiar voice, Lura Abernathy. "Hi Macon! Where ya headin'?" She was sitting on her large front porch with some others.

"Oh, just down town for a bit," I responded.

"Why don't cha stop in here--Katie Jean Rowe and Evelyn Sigmon are here, along with Buddy Yount and Bill Shipp!

It seemed like a good offer so I promptly accepted. We chatted a bit, laughed a lot and then Lura said, "Wouldn't a cold watermelon taste good—do ya suppose we could find a fruit stand still open and buy one?"

Bill replied, "Yeah, there's one in North Newton that stays open late, but my tank's so low I'll need a gallon a gas to make sure we don't run dry!

We three boys pooled our resources and came up with about thirty-five cents—eighteen for the gas and the rest for a cold watermelon. The girls had no change at all, so their contribution was zilch! This was par for the course in the thirties, since girls rarely had to share expenses. We then proceeded to follow our inexpensive plan, and soon we were enjoying a fifteen-pound watermelon in Lura's carport, which was adjacent to her porch.

Now a fifteen-pound melon is barely adequate for three hungry teenagers, let alone six, but we were now dead broke and HAD to be satisfied. Or so we thought, until someone suggested we drive out to the country and swipe one. Everyone liked the idea except me, and even I agreed provided I could stay in the car. I explained that I had been shot at a few years earlier in a melon patch, and had vowed to avoid that frightening experience forever!

We set off in Bill's car and headed out the Startown road because Buddy knew of a patch near the road that we could raid. About three miles later, we passed the patch and could see those lovely watermelons glistening in the bright moonlight. Everyone's spirits soared and our taste buds started warming up for another delightful experience, heightened by the thought that now it would be "forbidden fruit."

We then discussed who would go into the patch, and everyone had an excuse except Buddy. Bill, of course, had to stay with his father's car and be the getaway driver. All the girls were in high heels and pretty dresses, and I had already made my excuse. Buddy protested loudly, saying that it was unfair, and that the least I could do was flip fingers to see which of us would do the swiping. He called "even," so I put out one finger, hoping he would do likewise. But fate was cruel to me that night, because he stuck out two! Damn my luck, I thought almost out loud.

Bill turned off his headlights, stopped the car, and let me out, promising he would come back in five or, ten minutes. I wandered into the field and started thumping the larger melons. The farmhouse was four or five hundred feet away, and there were a number of corn shocks between it and me, so I felt secure. I was just about to cut the stem of my chosen one with my pocketknife, when I heard a man's voice say, "Stay right where ya are and I won't fire this shot gun!"

My heart trembled, and I cursed my luck once again. I put my hands over ray head and the man came closer. "You know you're breakin[1] the law, don't cha? I think I'll take ya to the police station and have ya arrested. But first, tell me who was in the car."

"Do I have ta? I don't wanta be a tattle tale!"

"You're dam' right cha do, or else I'll throw the book at cha! Also tell me your name."

"I'm Macon Epps, from Newton."

"Are you the son of Mr. Epps who runs the printing shop?"

My feelings were now quite mixed; on the one hand I hoped my Dad's good reputation would get me off. On the other hand I was afraid he would find out and I'd catch hell! I admitted that I was his son, and told him I was a student at N. C. State to add a little "grease" to alleviate my precarious situation.

"And who're the others?"

"Bill Shipp and Buddy Yount," I reluctantly replied.

"Is Bill related to Dr. Shipp, and is Buddy related to Mrs. Charlotte Yount.

"Yes, they're their sons."

"Well," he said, "I didn't expect to find boys like you stealin' my watermelons!"

I decided to risk a bit of humor, so I replied, "Neither did we!"

He chuckled a bit and said, "I heard some girls' voices in the-car—who're they?"

I decided to test his Southern chivalry, so I said firmly, "I can't tell ya—there's no reason to get the girls in trouble, it's not gentlemanly! Fortunately, he passed my test, and I even felt he respected me for my stand. He than said, "Let's go up ta my house and see if we can work somthin' out that'll keep you boys outa jail."

We ambled up to the house and headed toward his rear porch. On the way he told me that the corn shocks were to hide his approach so he could surprise me before I could run away. I mentally kicked myself for not remembering that lesson from my first watermelon misadventure. Once we reached the porch, I proposed that we pay him sixty cents for his trouble and as sort of a fine. I explained my reluctance to go into the patch and how I had lost the finger contest. I didn't mention my earlier experience.

He seemed sympathetic, but said, "I'll hafta think it over— when can ya raise the money?"

"By Friday– that's pay day for me" (I worked for my father and made the princely sum of eleven dollars a week—ten I saved for college expenses and one I got to keep and spend recklessly!)

"O.K., I'll be in town then and I'll stop by your Dad' s shop and let cha know my decision."

"I'd prefer you didn't do that; Dad might get suspicious and wanta know what's goin' on. Mind ya, I'm not afraida him, it's just that I would just as soon he didn't know about this. Suppose I drive out here Friday evening and have the money in case ya agree?" He nodded in agreement, and I silently sighed with a mixture of relief and hope in my mind.

" How' re ya gonna get back to Newton?– I saw your friends headed that way whlle we were talkin'." The farmer seemed concerned.

Again my heart sank, but I said, "I guess I'll hafta walk—it's only three miles." I hoped my bravado would impress him.

He wished me luck, went into his house and I headed for the road home. The moon helped me see enough to get to the road, and since there was hardly any traffic at about nine o'clock on this Tuesday night I felt reasonably safe. Every once in a while the clouds would cover the moon, so I decided it would be safer to walk in the middle of the road and scurry to the side if I saw any headlights. I probably saw less than three cars until I reached the streetlights of Newton. About an hour after I left the farmer I approached Lura's porch.

There they were, laughing and giggling after I had suffered the humiliation and danger of being caught, not to mention the long walk home. When they spotted me, they ran quickly and excitedly toward me, talking all at once. Lura's voice predominated, and she said, "Where on earth have ya been?—we've been worried sick and were 'bout to call the police to go and find ya!"

"Where was I?" I retorted, "Where were YOU? I had to walk three miles in the dark!"

Bill then explained that they had driven by the drop off spot several times, but his tank was so low they decided to go back to Newton. "We hated to leave ya there, but what else could we do. You had disappeared to God knows where, and if I ran out of gas we woulda all been stranded and hafta walk back!"

I accepted his reasoning and then proceeded to tell my story in great detail. They were a very attentive audience and commented frequently. The boys were annoyed that I had revealed their names, but the girls considered me a hero and a true southern gentleman for keeping their identity secret. Eventually, the boys forgave me, especially when I said I thought the farmer would accept my offer of sixty cents— ten cents a head or twenty cents each if the boys paid all of it. We chatted a bit more and speculated on what we would do if the farmer got mean. I asked all of them to keep mum about the whole affair for at least a year, and they all nodded in agreement. We then returned to our respective homes to try and sleep off our moonlight misadventure.

The next day, while I was walking by a hardware store opposite the Court House, one of the clerks said, "There's a telephone call for you inside." (It was a small town and I was well known.)

I went to the 'phone wondering who it could be, and how did they know where I was? It was Evelyn's mother, who worked at the nearby Court House, which explained how she knew my whereabouts. She was dead serious when she said, "Macon, there's a farmer from Startown in here swearing out a warrant to arrest you; also Bill Shipp and Buddy Yount; I thought you should know." I was flabbergasted, and before I could collect my wits she hung up.

That evening we all gathered at Lura's to discuss the new development. Buddy was really worried and nervous, and had called me earlier as soon as he heard about it through the grapevine. Bill was a bit on edge, but the girls looked like the cat that ate the canary. Finally, Evelyn confessed that she 'had told her mother, and her mother had decided to have a little fun— and maybe add to our lesson. (I decided she'd hung up quickly to hide her incipient laughter)

Again, I had mixed feelings—relief that it was just a joke and I wouldn't have to go to jail— and mild anger that Evelyn had broken her vow to keep mum. The other girls softened the anger by saying that they, too, had told their mother, or in Lura's case, the aunt that was raising her deceased mother's children. One of them explained that girls usually confide in their mothers. (I wonder if that's true today? I hope so.)

When Friday came I had collected the sixty cents and took it to the farmer to see if we had a deal. He had mellowed about the whole affair and seemed to understand how young people sometimes do foolish things. He felt we had learned our "lesson" and even offered to let us go Scott-free, but I insisted I pay him.

"Well", he said, "If YOU insist, I'll insist that cha take a nice big watermelon for your trouble." We then proceeded to select one from his supply, I loaded it in my Dad's car and the farmer and I shook hands. I took it straight to Lura's, with the understanding that she would cool it and invite the "gang" for a watermelon feast.

That had to be one of the best tasting watermelons we ever ate!

Epilogue: This true story happened in 1938 and all of the others are now dead or out of my radar scope. Buddy joined the Canadian Air Corps before Pearl Harbor and was killed in action, a terrible waste of a promising young life, but in a noble cause. Katie Jean and Lura married and had families, but they both died at a relatively young-age. Evelyn became my steady girl friend for a while, but it never ripened so we both married another. I last saw her about twenty years ago in a Lady's Clothing Shop, where she worked. Bill became a travel agent and started his own business, which I believe was successful. I graduated from N. C. State in 1940, earning a degree in Mechanical Engineering. (Aeronautical Option) I got a job "up north" with the Grumman Aircraft Engineering Corporation and became a "dam'yankee" to my Southern friends.

Those still alive have long since forgiven my straying from the South, and I in turn have never forgotten my roots, of which this story is a small, but important, piece. Incidentally, my Dad got wind of my escapade and had a lot of fun telling it to others and joking with me. The cost of things—ice cream, gasoline and watermelons- may seem impossible today, but they were true during the great depression. It's all relative, as Einstein would say.

But that was all in the distant past; life now goes on, with its memories and new adventures, but I can't help wonder what my next "Moonlight Adventure/Misadventure will be?

MY FIRST JOB

I grew up in a small, Western North Carolina town called Newton. It had about 5000 residents, not including the chickens, pigs, cows, and pets that many people kept in sheds in their back yard, or in their house for the pets. My Dad kept chickens, and I remember seeing new-born peepies in my pre-teens. Of course he had me help him on many occasions, but that wasn't a job; it was a chore. Yes, it was work, but there was no pay.

Actually, I had several paying jobs, all of which were different enough to be classified as FIRST. Here they are, in chronological order:

One summer, when I was about ten years old, I walked the three long blocks to the business section of Newton. The stores were nicely laid out around the County Court House. I was sort of idling along, looking at stores and trying to find something to pass the time. Suddenly, a strange man called me: "Hey, Kid-- how'd you like to have a job."

"I guess so," I replied. "What sort of job is it?"

"Well, hop into my car and I'll show you. It's not hard work and I'll pay you for a few hours of your time." Now this was in 1930, and it was perfectly safe to accept rides from strangers. At least no one had ever warned me not to do so. (Contrast that with today). After I hopped in, we drove about a half-mile to the First Presbyterian Church.

It was then that I discovered that he was an organ tuner. After he made his preparations, he placed a bunch of letters on the keyboard, and told me to hold down the proper letter whenever he called it out. He then proceeded to crawl under the organ and started tuning. It was an easy job for me, because all I had to do was sit on the bench, push and hold down the proper key, while he tuned it. About two hours later he was finished, thanked me for doing a good job, and gave me 35 cents.

Now 35 cents was a princely sum in those days. It would buy 35 pieces of penny candy, 7 double-dip ice cream cones, and 3 great big milk shakes, with 5 cents to spare. I felt very lucky, declined his offer to drive me home, and walked there with the money jangling in my little pockets. Both Mom and Dad were proud of me, and coaxed me to put some of the loot in my piggy bank. The rest I spent as described above.

Later that same year, my next job was when I learned about the barter system. As I was walking past the house of an elderly gentlemen with a long gray beard, he stopped me and asked if I liked to climb trees. "Yes sir," I replied.

"Well, I have a big cherry tree in my back yard that's full of ripe cherries. If you'll climb up and pick them, I'll give you half of all you pick."

I said "Yes sir, I'll be glad to accept your offer," and we walked to his back yard. On the way he got a bucket with a rope around it, slung it over my neck, and then led me to the tree, which was about 25 feet tall. Warning me to be careful, I easily climbed the tree. Once up, I followed his directions to the ripest cherries, and pretty soon I had a bucket full. He was pleased, and told me to come back in a few days when more would be ripe. True to his word, he divided the cherries in half and put my half in a paper bag. I ate quite a few as I walked home, where I proudly showed them to my Mother.

The whole family had ripe cherries for several days after each picking, and Mom made several jars of a drink, called "Cherry Bounce", with the remainder. We let the drink set for a week or so, and I had plenty of a brand new and tasty drink. I decided the barter system was a damn good one, especially with a Mom that could fix such a delicious drink free.

Now both of those jobs were temporary ones. My first permanent one was when I became a newspaper delivery boy at about age 12. I took over the route of an older boy who had found a better job. It involved walking three long blocks to pick up my 20 papers, six long blocks to deliver them, and three more to get home. The paper man gave me a large canvass bag in which to carry the papers; more about that later.

The paper was the Hickory Daily record, and I delivered it every afternoon, except Saturday and Sunday. Friday was collection day, and each customer paid 15 cents for the five-day week, of which I got to keep a nickel. Wow! That was a whole dollar a week, which was a fortune for a kid like me. It wasn't as easy as organ-tuner assistant, or as rewarding, but what the heck-- it was steady work and steady income.

It also gave me some valuable lessons on human nature and its idiosyncrasies. For example:

One of my jobs was to solicit new customers, and that taught me a lot. Some people were very rude in turning me down, others were crude, and some were plain old nasty, bad-mouthing the paper. Several stingy people subscribed, provided I would give them two weeks for a quarter. That meant two weeks of work for me for a thin nickel. They convinced me by saying. "You go by this house anyway, so it's better than nothing!"

Then there was the guy who paid at first, but then never seemed to have money on collection day. He talked me into waiting another week, at which time he convinced me that he would pay the whole bill. I got the same spiel each following week. Being an innocent kid of 13, I kept delivering for a whole month before I put my foot down: "No money, no paper."

Even then I realized that times were hard and he was short of money, but imagine a grown man doing that to a young kid. Incidentally, I had to pay the paper people 10 cents a week, or a total of 40 cents from my earnings, and the SOB knew it!

Of course, some people were seldom home on collection day, or at least didn't answer their doorbells. That meant I had to try and collect numerous times the next week and still deliver the paper. I soon learned to drop them once they got two weeks in arrears. Others would claim that I missed their house a day or two, and then refused to pay for papers they hadn't received. It was their word against mine, and I always lost.

Some were very talkative, and kept me standing and holding my heavy canvass bag for ten or more minutes. I had been taught to be polite to gown ups, and didn't have the skills to break off the conversation. My worst experience was when I was resting on a customer's steps, and a five-year old boy peed on my head and back! Unfortunately, there was nothing I could do but grin and bear it because he was the Police Chief's son

Although I got some new customers, I lost about as many as I obtained, so my weekly pay was seldom over a dollar, in spite of my extra effort.

Now my experiences weren't all negative. Some of the customers were very kind, especially the women. Some would offer me a cold glass of water on hot days; some even gave me fresh lemonade. Some of both genders would give me the full fifteen cents gladly, and even thank me for being such a good delivery boy. Some of the talkers taught me some new things, or told funny stories, and all my customers gave me a better insight into the great variety among people.

Some of the women were real Southern beauties, and I was a bit thrilled to see them each Friday, as they were the ones that usually paid. One was an outstanding beauty, and I will end my story with my lessons from her.

But first, let me describe her. She was about 5 feet 5 inches tall compared to my 5 feet 6 inches, so we could look into each other's eyes easily. She had long black hair that curled up at the bottom, and it was fine and silky, with a nice shine, especially in the afternoon sun. Her eyes were soulful and dark brown, and I got a queasy feeling every time I looked into them. Her face was movie star perfect, and her flashing smile would win an Academy award, at least from me. Her skin was very light and smooth, and when I touched her hand as she gave me my weekly money, I wondered what it would feel like if I ever touched her arms, or back, or other more delicate parts. The rest of her was perfection itself-- shapely legs, an hour-glass figure, a beautiful firm bosom, and an equally firm bottom. Although the movies of that day only cost 10 cents, I never saw an actress on the silver screen as completely beautiful as she was!

I was about 14 when I got her as a new customer. Her husband was an Eastern Airline pilot, and away from home a good bit. When he was away, she dressed casually, and partially displayed some of her charms. I was at the age when I was attracted to girls, but was too young to do anything about it.

She seemed to be a bit lonesome since her husband was away quite a lot, and would talk with me about various things, both on collection day and in between. I soon discovered that just looking at her made my pants swell up a bit, so I always put my canvass bag in front of my fly, so she wouldn't notice. I was afraid of what she would think if she ever saw my bulge, which seemed to increase the longer we talked. Fortunately, she lived on the edge of town and was my last customer, so I had time to un-bulge on my way home. You might say it was my own "Battle of the Bulge!"

One hot collection day in August, I decided to unbutton my pants and give my bulge more room, and a little air. I was careful to place my canvass bag way over it, so it couldn't even be seen from the side. When she came to the door she was scantly clad from the heat, and my bulge became the largest ever. My story should stop here, because she never saw what was behind my canvass bag. But my imagination was always active, so here is what I imagined while growing up:

Ending #1: Storm clouds had been gathering as I approached her house, and just as she was handing me 15 cents, a lightning bolt hit about a block away and the rain came down in torrents. The lightning startled us both, so she pulled me into the house, saying, "You'd better stay here until the storm subsides. It's too dangerous to go out in a storm like that. Here, let me take that bag off so you can relax and rest a bit." She quickly pulled my canvass bag from around my neck and my bulge was fully exposed. She quickly handed my bag back, and I apologized profusely. "May I stay until the rain stops?"

"Of course you can stay," she replied. She then patted me gently, and went into the kitchen for some light refreshments. We chatted amiably and enjoyed the goodies until the storm dwindled enough for me to leave. As to what happened during the following weeks, I will leave that to your imagination.

Ending #2: Once she saw my bulge, she said I have the perfect solution for your problem. You can call me Anita and come to my bedroom. Once I did, I had the most pleasurable experience of my young life. I'm sure I needn't go into details. All I can say is that I entered as an inexperienced young boy and came out as an experienced young man!

Warning: If you don't like to read about explicit sex, stop here.

Ending #3.

Naturally, I was horrified when she removed my canvas bag, and quickly tried to hide my bulge with my hands and by turning away, but it was too late. I could see by her eyes and hear from her gasp that she saw it fully. I tried to apologize, but I had never been in such an embarrassing situation before, so I made a mess of it. I was about to run outside, storm or not, but she held me back and said, "Don't be afraid-- it's natural for young boys like you to have an erection. I fully understand, and am not offended by it. In fact, I think it is something you should be proud of!"

I tried desperately to put it back in my pants and make it un-bulge, but it was obstinate. She then said, "Leave it out-- I kinda like to look at it. By the way, have you ever made love to a girl or a woman?"

"No Mam," I replied meekly.

"Don't you think it's about time you did?"

"Gosh, I don't know, Mam."

"Well, I think it's about time, especially for a young fellow as well equipped as you. Tell you what-- let's take advantage of the storm and go into my bedroom. I'll give you your first lesson, and I promise I'll be gentle"

"I'm not sure it's the right thing to do, mam. It may be a big sin if I do."

"No, it's not a big sin. People do it all the time; it's part of the pleasure of life. It might be a bit naughty, but haven't you done some naughty things you've really enjoyed? And quit calling me "Mam." Call me Anita, because we're going to be close friends from now on. But don't call me Anita when other people are present, they may not understand.

Hesitatingly, I said, "Yes, Anita!"

Ending 4. Anita then said, "Come on, let's go to my bedroom. If you're still uncertain, think of how unusual the circumstances were that brought us together-- you had it out and hidden by the bag; the sudden storm and lightening made me invite you in; my accidental taking the bag off exposed it; and the fact that you are attracted to me and I to you. Don't you see, it was meant to happen!"

Her logic was so good that I followed her to the bedroom, where we both disrobed completely. When I saw all of her feminine charms, my bulge lifted up even higher, and she caressed it lovingly while putting a strange rubber sleeve on it and pulling me to the bed. She also took my awkward hands, and placed them on her soft, warm breasts, and latter down to her hair covered cavity. I almost swooned with pleasure, but I sensed that it would get better. She then lay down and spread her legs, and I climbed on top and aimed my bulge where my instincts told me. After a bit of fumbling around and a little help from her, I entered her moist, warm cavity and started a slow pumping motion.

"You're doing great," she said. Just keep it up and don't be in too big a hurry. Something this good should last as long as possible."

Although it was difficult to restrain the wonderful feeling I was having, some how I did. I figured the rubber sleeve was partly to blame for the feeling of being a bit subdued, but that didn't last very long. After my rhythmic pumping increased, she started to moan and make little sounds. Thinking I was hurting her, I stopped pumping.

"No, No," she whispered. "You're not hurting me—it's just the opposite. It feels so wonderful that I'm making sounds of pure pleasure." She then wrapped her legs tightly around me to make sure I got the message, which I did.

Thus encouraged, I continued until her moans increased and she started yelling with sounds of ecstasy. Somehow, I sensed that the climax was happening, so I increased the pumping until I had to stop while my own fluid fill the rubber sleeve. It was the most wonderful feeling I had ever experienced, and so much better than the occasional masturbations I had previously enjoyed.

We lay coupled together for a minute or so, and then I rolled over and lay beside her. Her arms were wrapped around me and her lips were kissing mine passionately. She then said something that made me feel great; "You're the best lover I have ever had, and we've got to do this again and again!"

Meantime, the rain kept pouring down, and we knew that no one could have heard us, or come to the house. Eventually, we got up, put our clothes back on and went back into the living room. She brought out some light refreshments, and kept kissing and hugging me, until my bulge returned. She squeezed it playfully, but we didn't go any further that day. My imagination has gone even further, but, so far, I haven't typed it.

Once the rain tapered down, I left her house and started walking home, using my canvas bag top to cover me from the dwindling rain. My parents asked what happened to me during the storm, and I told them, "Oh, one of my customers let me stay in the house until it subsided."

"That was nice of them. We were getting a bit worried about you."

They didn't ask any more questions, so I didn't volunteer any more information, but kept it deep inside until this very day, 73 years later.

Author's note: One thing is certain: My first permanent, low paying job had its ups and downs, but I sure learned some valuable lessons about human nature and how the world works. I also learned how an innocent encounter with a beautiful woman could stimulate the imagination. Anyway, I hope you enjoyed my imaginary endings, and were not offended if you ignored my warning.

NEW YORK ON $2.00/DAY

As a person born and raised in a small North Carolina town, New York City was my ultimate dream destination. Although I was 19 years old and soon to be a senior in college, my travels were limited to two neighboring states: Virginia and South Carolina.

The year was 1939, and my six weeks at R. O. T. C. summer camp in Anniston, Alabama made it feasible for me to visit the Big Apple. It not only gave me reserve Army officer training and a fascinating experience, but enough cash to realize two of my dreams. The opening of the World's Fair in N.Y. City was an irresistible magnet for me to realize the first of my dreams.

I had hitchhiked to camp with my Aeronautical Engineering classmate, Dan Belvin. Since he shared my dreams, we decided to hitchhike to the great city and the World's Fair once camp ended.

We arrived in the city early afternoon the second day, and stayed at the Sloan House Y. M. C. A. on Eighth Avenue and 32nd street. It not only fit our budget, (which was limited because of the times and second dream), but was near the subway to the fair.

We decided to explore the famous sights in mid-town Manhattan the rest of that day and get an early start to the fair the next morning. After paying a nickel for the subway and five bucks for a five-day pass to the fair, we entered the gate around 9 a.m.

Wow! We were impressed. There were so many interesting sights we ogled and gawked like country bumpkins, which in hindsight we were. The Trylon and Perisphere were high on our list to visit because they were so well publicized, and they exceeded our expectations. For the next five days we wandered from exhibit to exhibit, taking plenty of time to absorb as much as we could.

For food, we ate an apple or banana for breakfast (5 cents), had a hot dog or hamburger and a soft drink for lunch, (15 cents), and splurged about 25 cents for supper. It wasn't long before we discovered that the food exhibits gave away free samples, so we saved our lunch or supper money for some of the night shows. We also discovered that the R. C. A. exhibit played lovely classical music and had upholstered chairs and sofas. It became a favorite spot to rejuvenate our bodies and spirits.

Our daily expenses were 75 cents for room, $1 for fair admission, 10 cents for subway, and 45 cents for meals; a grand total of $2.30! Actually, that was the expensive part of our trip, which averaged less than $2.00 per day, or about twenty bucks for eleven days. (I thought that was cheap until I learned that my cousin David did it for $5.00)

Using our saved meal money, and being red-blooded young males, we attended the "Girly" shows after dark. Three remain embedded in my memory:

o The "Nudist Camp", where nearly bare young women played and cavorted in the chilly night air. Desire was dampened by our concern for their catching the flu.

o The one where an oriental monk was tested by a sexy young woman trying to seduce him via an erotic strip tease and exotic music. (He resisted temptation more than I would have.)

o A stage revue with a bevy of young, dancing beauties. Dan and I had scrambled for front row seats, and were so surprised when they selected us to join them on the stage we were too bashful to accept. (We kicked ourselves the rest of the trip for missing the opportunity.)

On our last day we finished exploring the city, including a ferryboat ride to Staten Island for 10 cents. (Round trip). The next morning we walked to the Holland tunnel and hitched a ride south. By prior invitation we stayed at another classmate's home (Herb Posten) in Atlantic Highlands, N. J., where we received a day and night of free room and board!

We stopped in Washington, D. C. to see its sights, and then returned to our respective homes. The rest of the summer I worked for my Dad in his printing shop for $15/week, $14 of which I was to save for college expenses. After graduating in 1940, I landed a job with Grumman Aircraft on L. I., about 25 miles from my dream city!

Earlier, I mentioned that visiting New York was one of two dreams the extra cash from camp made feasible. The second one was flying lessons that fall, courtesy of President Roosevelt's Civilian Pilots Training Program. It cost $50 to enroll, but I received about 40 hours of flight and my Private Pilot's license. Two dreams realized, lots of interstate travel and exploration, and a great experience in Reserve Officers camp, all in one year!

Do you blame me for remembering 1939 as a wonderful year?

REMEMBERING WILL

In the 1930's, the most popular man in America frequently introduced his comments with: "All I know is what I read in the newspapers!

"Yes, it was the beloved comedian/entertainer/actor, <u>Will Rogers</u>, star of stage, screen, rodeo and radio. If T.V. had been around in those days, undoubtedly he would have had even higher ratings and exposure.

I was a teen-ager during his glory years, but even then I realized that he knew much more than he "read in the newspapers". I suspected that he had acquired knowledge from many other sources. I knew that my meager knowledge came from my parents, teachers, preachers, siblings, relatives, friends, books, magazines and radio, as well as the occasional newspaper I read, so why should he be different? I finally concluded that what he was really saying, was that his insights into the affairs of the nation, and the world, came from the details he gleaned from the papers.

Once he made that famous introductory statement, he would then give his inimitable commentary on the foibles and follies of the high and mighty people in charge of things. He was the champion of the common people, and believe me the common people needed one like Will during those frightening "Great Depression" years.

I think it was clear to us, his audience and fans, that we were getting much more than the newspapers, or any other media, could offer. We were getting a large dose of common sense and wisdom, served up on a delicious plate of good-natured humor. So powerful were his comments that I heard several educated adults say; "We should elect Will president!" Not a bad idea, I thought, even though I was enamored of <u>President Franklin D. Roosevelt</u> and his gallant effort to curb the awful depression.

In appearance, Will looked like a "common man". He was of medium build and stature, trim in figure, had a full head of "iron" gray hair and an unforgettable face. His grin was completely disarming in its charm and sincerity, although he could look impish when he chose. He was not a handsome man and was nowhere near the "matinee" idols of his era in looks. He was just an extremely pleasant looking man— one that you could identify with like a favorite uncle, or perhaps a beloved father or grandfather. I never encountered anyone who didn't like him— male or female, young or old, white or black.

His voice and mannerisms were also endearing. His Oklahoma accent made both southerners and northerners feel comfortable, and he sounded like a rural boy who had learned a bit about city ways

His diction was good and easily understood because he used common expressions, rather than pedagogical ones. His sometimes halting manner and gentle gestures made you feel he was a diamond in the rough, or perhaps one that had been cut but not fully polished.

He never talked down to people and one got the impression that he was a regular guy with something worthwhile to say. In fact, he seemed quite modest and almost surprised that so many people wanted to listen to him. Best of all, I believe he seldom followed a prepared script. He just seems to pick a topic and then ad-lib his witty and wise remarks. I understand he even did that during his movies, improvising his part of the dialogue that was better than the writer's prepared script. Even the political "big wigs" that he took down a few notches didn't seem to mind; his humor was that gentle, even though he made his points as sharp as a pencil. Remember, these are memories, not well-researched facts.

As I contemplate today's world from my 78 year old perch, I cant help but speculate what Will would have to say about all the things that have gone right-- and wrong-- with America. I'll bet that he would be proud that we and the other democracies dethroned Fascism. Nazism, and Communism. And he would be pleased with the rights won by minorities and women, although he would have found some wise and funny things to say along the way to speed up the process.

He would be thrilled at the rapid progress of aviation (his second love) and other high technology. And surely he would have been tickled about the relative prosperity and longevity of the elderly; but what fun he would have had at the way politicians of all stripes still pussyfoot around the economic plight of Social Security, Medicare, Medicaid, and Welfare. (Called Relief in his day.) I suspect the problems would have been solved long ago if Will had lived longer.

He would have had a "field day" with the lawyers and our litigious society, adding to the huge collection of "lawyer" jokes that the legal profession must now endure— on the way to the bank.

As to the "wrongs", I think he would have been shocked and even depressed at the inaneness and depravity of many T. V. programs, such as <u>Jerry Springer</u>, <u>Howard Stern</u>, etc., and the unkind humor of Saturday Night Live and other comedy programs. From where I sat, I couldn't detect a mean bone in Will's body; sick humor just wasn't his style.

Of course he would have marveled at the technical ability of the movies, as do I, as they recreate dinosaurs, ancient scenes, and natural catastrophes. He would have been in awe when they create space vehicles, strange planets and monsters, and scenes of terrible, life-like violence, wondering out loud if they weren't doing much more harm than good.

As to the growing obscenity in sexual scenes, he may have been in a quandary, as are many others. As a normal male he may have been pleasantly titillated, but as a husband-and father he would have been disgusted. (A mixed bag at best.)

But for a person whose motto was, "I never met a man I didn't like," those who practiced genocide–monsters like <u>Hitler, Stalin</u> and <u>Pol Pot</u> would have horrified him. Will would have been unable to stop such cruelties. After all, it still eludes our ability, even in this age, when we can walk on the moon, cure deadly diseases, process information at breathtaking speed, and live in a "global village", all of which Will would have applauded. Now these are just speculations, but I believe they aren't far from the mark.

As my generation realizes, Will's early death in the airplane accident with <u>Wiley Post</u> in 1935 took him from us much too soon. How I wish he had lived to see the things we did "right", urging us along the way with his common sense and humor.

As to the "wrong" turns we made, I suspect he would have been powerless to reverse the trend because of the greed for power and wealth involved in promoting sex, violence, corruption and depravity. Collectively they might have "overloaded" his great tolerance for mankind's foolish ways, because many of them now border on pure lunacy. The purveyors of the most extreme foolishness and cruelty may have been men Will DIDN'T like, but I feel sure he would have hung in by promoting common sense and decency.

So I remember Will with great affection and admiration, and I'm sorry that he couldn't have seen the good we accomplished, but glad that he was spared the depraved and lunatic elements of today's world. Unlike him, I have met some people I DIDN'T like; but had I been fortunate enough to meet him in my youth it would have become one of my most memorable moments. His life was a wonderful contribution to the first third of this century, perhaps a unique one.

Now if we can just find his counterpart in the twenty-first century, perhaps s/he can inspire the rest of us to reverse the distressing and deadly trends and concentrate on the good in most people!

RUNAWAY KID

As a ten year old boy, I loved my <u>Mother</u> dearly, but sometimes felt she made me do things that my older sister, <u>Ruth</u>, should do-- like wax the floor, peel potatoes etc. One sunny morning in the spring of 1930, my Mom and I had a big disagreement. Of course she won, but I took it badly and felt she no longer loved me. Maybe I should run away, I thought, and shared it with my younger sister, <u>Louise</u>. She was only five, and was so shocked that she yelled to Mom and gave me away.

I fully expected Mom to stop me, but instead, she was angry enough to say, "Let him runaway, it's alright with me!" The fact that she was about to give birth to my twin brothers, <u>Charles</u> and <u>Joe</u>, may have been a factor in her position.

Although it was Friday, my school day wouldn't start until the afternoon. That was because the school building had burnt to the ground the previous fall, and my fifth grade class was sharing the Sunday School building of the First Methodist Church, in my hometown of Newton, N. C. At first I thought I would wait until school was out, but since Mom seemed to want me to leave, I decided to go immediately.

It was a spur of the moment decision, and I didn't take anything with me except the clothes I was wearing and the raw peanuts I frequently kept in my pockets. I figured that Atlanta, GA, would be a good destination. It was a large city where I felt I could make my fortune, starting as a shoeshine boy.

I had a childish dream of returning to Newton many years later so rich and famous that Mom would regret her words and my schoolmates and my lovable teacher, <u>Miss Hassie Wall</u>, would admire my success. I then walked into town past Court House square and down College Avenue until I came to Highway 16. I figured I could get a ride from a traveling car once I was on the out skirts of our small town, population about 5,000.

I was too ignorant to use my thumb and hitchhike; instead I waved my arms to flag down the first car, as I had seen my <u>Dad</u> do when he had car trouble. By golly it worked, and the man said, "Where ya goin', young fella, and why aren't cha in school?"

"I'm gonna visit my Grandpa in Lincolnton, and since the school building burnt down I only go in the morning." By then it was early afternoon and he seemed to accept my falsehoods.

When we reached East Maiden, he let me out at a gas station, explaining he had some business to do before he went to Lincolnton. "I'll pick ya up later. Promise me you'll wait here".

There was a hint of suspicion in his manner. I nodded yes, but since I was suspicious of him too, I didn't want to wait around. Cars were scarce at that time, so I hitched a ride from a farmer driving a horse-drawn wagon. He let me out at St. Mathew's Church, several miles and over an hour away.

Oddly enough, my maternal Grandfather, <u>Sidney Schrum</u>, still owned a farm behind the church. I had attended services at St. Mathew's a number of times, so it was familiar territory. I wondered if the farmer knew my Grandfather, who now lived in Lincolnton, or perhaps the farmer lived near, or even on Grandpa's farm since he went down the same road.

After the farmer let me out near the highway, clouds started to gather and a few drops of rain fell on me. I was about to head for shelter at the church, or the open tabernacle near it, when another car came along. I flagged it down, and much to my surprise, my future uncle drove it: <u>Edgar Mauney,</u> from Maiden, who was then courting my <u>Aunt Mary</u>.

I was afraid he would foil my run-away plan, which he guessed was my intention after a few questions. After I resisted a bit, he cleverly persuaded me to hop in, saying, "You'll get all wet if you stay out there. Besides we can get some food and talk things over at your Grandpa's house."

Once we arrived, Edgar explained the situation and left for other business. Grandpa was a widower, and his stern face frightened me until I detected some amusement on it. Aunt Mary (and <u>Aunt Vera</u> who was visiting) expressed great concern about my recklessness. They hugged and kissed me in gratitude for my safety, and then these kind souls gave me all the food my growing-boy appetite could consume. One of them called my father, who asked them to put me on the next bus to Newton.

After spending a pleasant afternoon with them, which included Grandpa roasting some peanuts for me to take on the bus, I boarded it and arrived safely in Newton around five- thirty.

<u>Dad </u>met me, and on the way home he gave me a serious lecture about

my foolishness. I was afraid of a whipping once we arrived home, but he promised to defer that until my next foolish behavior.

I knew he soon forgave me because he liked to tell others the runaway tale. Mom quickly forgave me, and even admitted she spoke hastily, thinking I wouldn't have the nerve to actually run away.

Mom's cooking and my own bed felt especially good that night!

Final Thoughts: Today, at age 85, I think of how much the world has changed since those early depression days. What would happen to a ten-year old, runaway kid in today's world, with crooks, child-molesters, and their ilk around? Would the adults react the same way, or would they react very differently? Will we ever get back to the honesty of those days, when no one locked their car full of groceries, or even their house, except maybe at night? Will doctors ever make house calls again for $3.00, even allowing for inflation?

Most of all, I wonder what would have happened if my future uncle hadn't come along. Was that divine intervention or pure chance? And who, what, and where would I be today if he had come along a few minutes later, after I went to the church for shelter? Maybe I wouldn't' even be here to write this little episode, and would have missed the many other wonderful things that have happened to me-- so far!

Hopefully, those who read this piece will remember events in their own lives where fate, or some other force, steered them toward a better future. My own life has been so full of them that there must have been a Guardian Angel looking out for me. I hope s/he is still on duty!

1940-50

CHICKENS

I always thought chickens were—well—"chicken". They seemed about as peace loving and non-violent as any animal I had seen. This impression had been formed during my boyhood when my Father raised chickens. As I grew older, he taught me how to catch one and hold it in my arms until it calmed down. He then taught me to hold it by its feet, stretch it out on the chopping block and cut off its head with an axe.

I was always amazed at how long it would flop around headless before it died. Of course, I stayed at arms length during the execution, so that blood wouldn't get on my clothes. Now if you think this was a barbaric method, let me assure you that it was common practice in the 1930"s. My <u>Father</u> usually did the distasteful chore, but I have even seen my <u>Mother</u> do it. I also discovered that "different folks had different strokes". Some of my neighbors used a hatchet or a big butcher knife; some would wring its neck; and some would put its head between two boards and pull on it until it died.

A live chicken was less expensive to buy than a ready-to-cook one, which explains why execution was such a common practice in the depression era South, even among people who didn't raise chickens. Once prosperity returned, my family started buying them "fully dressed". That meant the head, feet and feathers were already removed. The entrails were also removed, but the butcher left the liver, gizzard and heart inside for those who liked those parts. I often wondered why they called them "dressed", since to my youthful eyes they seemed undressed—right down to their pimply skin! English sure is a funny language!

When I graduated from college and got my first job in Bethpage, New York, I rented a room with a family named "<u>Sengstacken</u>" that raised chickens. One Saturday, when I was in the backyard, I saw my landlord in the chicken yard feeding the chickens. I walked over and said, "May I come in?"

"It's OK with me," he replied, "but the rooster may not like it."

Since my general impression of chickens was that they were gentle creatures, I unlatched the gate and started toward my landlord. That was a big mistake! A big rooster spotted me and came running at me clucking loudly. Much to my surprise and dismay, the damn thing was attacking me!

At first I thought I would stand my ground and maybe kick him if he got too close, but I decided that might look too cruel to my landlord, so I beat a hasty retreat and exited the gate just in time. My chagrin at being chased by a mere chicken, albeit a rather large one, was deepened by the loud laughter of my landlord. The old fox had warned me, but he knew damn well that his rooster would tolerate no strangers in his private kingdom.

He told that tale on me many times thereafter, all in good humor. I even laughed with him and tried to come up with a clever excuse—but to no avail.

I had played "chicken" with a rooster in his territory—and I lost!

CLIMBING, CAMPING AND THE SIX "F's"

I just came up with a title for this story and a brief mental outline. I am now sitting at my computer and activating my memory cells. I momentarily close my eyes and I can see and hear my three buddies, who shared our one-week adventure in the White Mountains of New Hampshire in July

1944. I can also see some of the wonderful sights we saw, taste the good food we cooked, feel the tiredness and satisfaction we enjoyed after a hard days climb or descent, and some special events we shared.

It makes me realize what a wonderful thing the human memory is, which borders on a true miracle. My memories of this story go back over 65 years, so if that's not a miracle, I don't know what is!

Before I unleash my memories, I will explain the Six "F's". They are Friendship; Fatigue; Food; Fitness; Foresight; and Fun. Our adventure strongly enhanced our <u>friendship</u> and made us understand and appreciate the <u>fatigue</u> we all encountered, which a good night's sleep quickly fixed. It also helped us appreciate the need for <u>food</u> and water, and the skills we learned in preparing the food under primitive conditions. Although our leader and another climber started out very <u>fit</u>, two of us became much more fit when the week was over. As to <u>foresight</u>, our leader displayed plenty, and the rest of us pitched in our own during several tense moments. As to <u>fun</u>, we had plenty during the week, but we probably had more fun in the years after by recalling out adventure, especially when we saw the slides one of us took throughout the week.

My memory now sees our motley crew, all of which were engineers at Grumman Aircraft and on "Fitness Leave", which was the term for vacations during WW-2.:

<u>Lynn Radcliffe</u>, who was our leader because he had previous experience in the mountains, had the idea for the trip, and did most of the planning. He was very smart and exceptionally fit because he had been a championship half-mile runner during his years at Syracuse University and could have made the Olympics if they hadn't been suspended during the war. He was six foot two, quite handsome and with an impish grin. Best of all, he was exceptionally thoughtful for those of us with less stamina. He was the only married man.

<u>Brandeis Wehle</u> was the other fit climber and an excellent swimmer. He had been on the Harvard Swimming Team with future <u>President John F. Kennedy</u>, which we of course learned about in later years. He was also related to Supreme Court <u>Justice Brandeis</u>, hence his name. (We called him Brand.) He was a nice looking guy, about five feet eleven, and exceptionally smart and knowledgeable. He was a slow talker because he gave careful thought before he spoke, but he had the loudest and most delightful laugh of the group.

<u>Charlie Whitson</u> was the runt of the group, being about five foot six. He was average looking and a good engineer, as his subsequent career proved. He and I had both studied Aero engineering at N.C. State College, but he was several years behind me. He was probably the least fit of the group, with me just a few notches above him. He was also our official camera man, and took many photos of our adventure and the wonderful scenes.

<u>Macon Epps</u>, (me), who was five feet eleven, skinny, and an avid tennis

player. I won't describe my looks, but I guess they were passable because the girls seemed to like me and I married a real beauty.

Now that my brain has recalled the cast of characters as they looked in 1943, my memory now shifts into high gear for the story:

We had all bought army surplus rucksacks, packed a quilt and safety pins for a sleeping bag, a few extra clothes, cooking and other equipment, and lots of food. Our packed rucksacks weighed around sixty pounds, so climbing steep mountain trails with those aboard was a formidable task, which we soon discovered.

We left Friday afternoon in Lynn's old car, which had four nearly bald tires and used so much oil that Lynn took a five-gallon supply. Fortunately, his old car was very reliable and got us there and back with very little trouble, except the frequent re-supply of oil. We spent the night at his mother-in laws mansion, somewhere up the Hudson, near Albany, N.Y. It was on a beautiful lake, so we went swimming and boating in the morning, leaving in the early afternoon. That turned out to be a mistake, because we didn't get to our first mountain trail until sunset. We decided to climb Mount Liberty anyway, using our flashlights once the sun disappeared. The first part of the trail was easy and scenic, because it was beside a fast flowing stream. Soon it grew steeper, and our fitness encountered its first test. We all did well, but as it approached midnight, Charlie and I decided we couldn't go any farther. It was a clear night, so he and I proposed to sleep on the trail. Lynn tried to keep us going, saying, "Liberty Spring Shelter, (our destination) is just a bit further and a much safer place to spend the night."

We declined his advice, so he and Brand decided to climb the rest of the way and then come back and tell us how close it was. When they returned, Lynn said, " it just a few hundred yards further, and Brand and I will carry your rucksacks." Charlie and I reluctantly accepted the offer and made it to the shelter we had planned to sleep in.

Once there, hunger pains overtook us, so we built a fire and started cooking the whole chickens we all had bought on the way. Unfortunately, the chickens had turned bad during the heat of the day, and not only had a "fowl" odor, but also a "foul" odor. We all decided to throw them away, except Charlie, who was stubborn and cooked his. The rest of us cooked something else that was not very tasty, but Charlie really enjoyed his chicken. We were afraid he would get sick, but the heat must have killed any germs and Charlie outsmarted the rest of us. We slept well in the shelter until dawn, cooked breakfast, and then got ready for the next long day.

Before we left, Lynn showed us the latrine, which was about 70 feet away. It was on a steep slope, so it had no door. That meant that you could enjoy a spectacular view while you were sitting there doing your business. We nicknamed it "Buena Vista Latrine". Brand and Lynn were constipated, so they probably enjoyed the view longer than Charlie and me; more about that later.

We then started toward our goal for the day, Mount Lafayette. We had to go up and down over two other mountain peaks (Haystack and Lincoln) before we got there, so it was a difficult climb. We were over 4000 feet high most of the time, and Charlie and I had a tough time, especially when Brand took the lead. He didn't seem to notice when we got tired and needed rest, like Lynn had, so we asked Lynn to be our full time leader. We stopped for lunch, using raw food so we didn't have to cook, and finally reached our 5260-foot destination around sunset. It was a beautiful sunset, and we all enjoyed the gorgeous view of all the other mountains glowing in the sunset's hues.

Lynn said the weather was so clear that we could spend the night on this mile high open peak, explaining that a shelter was about 1000 feet lower if we needed it. There was a rock wall around part of the peak, apparently an old foundation for a hut that never got built because of the war. We ate supper and then got our sleeping equipment ready. There was a grassy area that the other three decided to use, but it was not sheltered from the wind. I was afraid of the night coldness that high up, so I decided to put my bed near a wall that could protect me from the wind. I was the odd man that night, but we all had a great nights sleep after a bit of conversation and looking up at the star filled sky. It was spectacular, since there were no city lights to mess it up, and the high altitude made it even clearer. I don't know about the others, but I was overwhelmed by the visible wonders of the universe and the divine force that created it, and said a little prayer before going into a deep sleep.

We ate a quick breakfast of dry cereal and then Lynn overcame his constipation in such a big way that he insisted we come and look at it before we departed. We stayed up wind, and it was a huge pile. Some years later, Lynn climbed back to the peak and claimed that he had found his huge deposit and that it was still warm inside. We laughed, but didn't believe it was still warm. Brand didn't have any relief, and we all started worrying about him, especially Lynn. (Later on, we found it proper to dig a hole and bury our waste, including food scraps.)

Our descent was relatively easy, and we reached Mt. Garfield in good time. We ran into a heap of trouble after Garfield. It seemed that the1938 hurricane had knocked down so many trees that the trail was obliterated. Resourceful Lynn told us to stay put on the still existing trail while he wandered around to find the next extension. We then followed his voice until we caught up. By golly that worked, and we used it many times during that day. We also saw a few critters, such as raccoons and porcupines, but no dangerous animals.

Somewhere along the way, we came to a steep cliff, about 500 feet high. We were standing on its top, so one of us decided it would be a good place to urinate, saying it would be the longest pee of our life. We all relieved ourselves and felt good that we had set a record; not a world's record, but a personal one, and probably a huge record compared to most of the men we knew. We made our next destination, Gale Head Hut, after dark and it was the toughest part of our trip, according to Lynn. The Hut was a large, well-equipped one, but, unfortunately, it was locked and unmanned because of the war, so we had no place to sleep.

Lynn suggested that it was an emergency and we could therefore break in. Besides, we had been alone in the mountains thus far, so who would know? After a bit of trial and error, we found a way in that did minimum damage. It was well worth the effort, because there were bunk beds with mattresses and other nice accommodations. All of us had another good nights sleep, but Lynn was so worried about Brand's constipation that he considered going to he nearest village, Bethlehem, to get Brand an enema bag. However, Brand finally overcame his constipation, so Lynn was spared the trip. I think the rest of us were more relieved than Brand, but in a different way. Incidentally, he didn't brag about it as Lynn had done.

Our next destination was Zee-Cliff Shelter, and we climbed South Twin Mountain to get there. We did run into a severe rainstorm, but it was in the valley when we were on a peak, and on the peak when we were in the valley. We all commented on the unusual luck we had, and Lynn hinted it was because of his leadership and his knowledge of the mountains. You can imagine how we handled that, but we all had to admit that it was an unusual coincidence.

Our shelter that night was a small lean-to hut, but it was good enough to protect us from the rain that night. Since we were going down to civilization the next morning, Lynn suggested we put our remaining food in one big pot and eat our fill. Believe me when I say we did as he suggested, and it was so good we ate it with GUSTO! Another night of sound sleep and an early breakfast, and it was mostly downhill all the way to our next destination, Crawford Notch.

We had lunch on the way, and I think we bought food for next day and our supper someplace that would accept us. You see, we had agreed from the beginning not to shave, so we all had scraggly beards and hadn't taken a bath for several days. As you might imagine, with all that climbing in the July heat, we sure needed one.

Lynn found us a new kind of shelter for the night--the Crawford Notch Rail Station. It had a covered wooden porch on three sides and we chose the one by the tracks, since it seemed the most secluded. We made our beds on the wood floor and went to bed early because the next day was to be our most demanding. We chatted a bit, and one of us was worried about a train coming in the night, since our feet were about five feet from the tracks. Lynn said there would be no trains at night, but he was wrong. A freight train came by in the middle of the night and woke us all up. I pulled myself into the fetal position just in case the train tossed something down on the platform.

Earlier, while we were awake but had stopped talking, a young couple was getting well acquainted on the platform around the corner. Their courting got hot and heavy, and it wasn't long before we heard the girl start her little scream of ecstasy. I suggested we go shine our flashlights on them, but Lynn vetoed it. To this day, I wonder how they would have handled our sudden intrusion.

Next morning, after breakfast, we started our long trek toward our ultimate goal-- Mt. Washington, which is 6288 feet high and the highest peak in the northeast. Later on, I climbed the highest peak east of the Mississippi River, Mt. Mitchell. It is in my home state of North Carolina and is over 6700 feet, but that's another story. What made next days climb so demanding, in addition to Mt. Washington's height, were the other peaks we had to climb on the way. They were: Mt. Clinton (4312 feet); Mt. Pleasant (4781 feet and now Mt Eisenhower); Mt. Franklin (5004 feet); Mt Monroe (5385 feet).

We passed the Lakes of the Clouds on the way to Mt Washington and admired its beauty and had lunch there. Then on to the summit, where we enjoyed all its splendid views. We didn't stay long because we wanted to get back to Crawford Notch before eight pm. Lynn told us we could have a real feast if we got to the Crawford House (an up-scale resort hotel) before it closed for dinner.

We went down the Amanoosic Ravine trail to the Base Station, where we could follow the road to Crawford Notch. On the way, we found a small waterfall with a deep pond at its base. We were the only ones on the trail, so we took off all our clothes, and, one by one, dove into the icy water. I do not exaggerate when I say icy water, because it was so cold it took our breath away and we climbed out as soon as we could. Brand was the only exception, since he wanted to show his masculinity by splashing around a bit.

Once we got to the road, Lynn set a very rapid pace to make sure we arrived at dinner on time. We scolded him several times for the rapid pace, but he kept saying, "You'll thank me once we get that big dinner in us." A bit later, I made a bad error. I decided to run ahead of the group and then sit down and rest until they caught up. Lynn warned me of bad consequences, but I ignored him. Once we got to the dining room, they decided we were too unkempt to be seated with the other diners, but when we told them where we had climbed that day, they took mercy and told us to go around to the kitchen. We paid a reasonable fee and then sat at a table with some of the help, who were having their meal. They fed us like princes, and we had the most delicious and well-earned meal that I can remember.

Now our hunger was well satiated, but some time during the meal, Lynn's warning came true. My legs started growing tight and painful, and they had to help me walk out. Lynn told me to keep moving until the pain grew manageable, and we then went to our next night's lodging place. We had spotted it that morning and agree it would be a good place to stay, much better than the Rail Station, in spite of its romantic interlude. It was the Golf Clubhouse, which of course was closed at night. We found an unlocked window and put our beds on a nice carpeted area. We were all exhausted, even Lynn, so we had a wonderful night's sleep.

Several caddies who entered the building awakened us the next morning. "Look," one of them said, "there are four tramps in here!" We quickly got dressed and took our rucksacks out of the clubhouse before the management arrived. We weren't offended by the term "tramp", because we all had very unkempt beards and scraggly clothes. This was our second illegal break-in, and could have gotten us in trouble. However, since we did no harm, we felt we could talk our way out of it.

We bought breakfast somewhere in town and then Lynn left us to hitch back to his car in Franconia Notch. Drivers were friendly in those days, so he returned in a few hours. We put our gear in his car, hopped in and headed back to Long Island. I think it was late Sunday when we arrived, so we took showers and shaved our beards. However, I decided to keep my mustache as a souvenir. It was then that Lynn gave me an Italian name, "Marconio Eppsicio, that he frequently called me in the following years, and remembers to this day.

Next morning, things were normal at work, except I got teased a bit about my mustache. One of the managers, Paul ?, told me I looked like Rett Butler, of Gone with the Wind fame. Since Clark Gable played that role, I considered it a big complement. However, my girl friend, Betty Warren whom I later married, didn't like it, so off it came.

In the following weeks, we saw Charlie's colored slides and re-lived our week's adventures. In fact, we saw them many times in the following years, and thus kept them imbedded in our memories. Unfortunately, we never got copies of the slides. As I write this piece, I am 89, and Lynn will be that age in July. Charlie died about ten years ago, even though he was about three years younger than me. Brand, who was a year or two older than me, died about two years ago. That was a bit surprising, because he kept himself in good shape, as did Lynn. We stayed good friends for many years, and did many other things together, including return expeditions to other NH mountains. My wife and I also saw them socially many times, especially with Lynn and Brand.

I have climbed and skied on many mountains since, but this weeklong adventure is still at the top of my list because it had the six "F's".

DAY OF IMFAMY

Most Americans of my generation remember where they were when they learned about Japan's bombing of our naval base at Pearl Harbor, Hawaii. It is still vivid in my own memory, as the following recollections show.

It was Sunday, December 7th, 1941, which started out for me as a special day. I was working as a young engineer for Grumman Aircraft Engineering Corporation, in Bethpage, NY, and World War II was going full scale in Europe and Asia. Somehow, the USA had managed to stay out of the war, but we were supplying equipment to the British, including some of the fighter airplanes I had helped assemble earlier. Having finished my apprenticeship on the assembly line, I was now doing design work on newer models and felt good that I was doing my small part to quell Hitler and Tojo. They were the main villains who had disrupted world peace, and were still a major threat

Because of the war, Grumman was expanding its facilities, and the completion of Plant 2 was one of the reasons it was a special day for me. Grumman and the Navy were having a dedication ceremony that morning for the huge new production facility, and, as a baritone horn player in the Grumman Band. I was part of the ceremony. I was only 21 years old, but in another month I would be 22, so I felt I was coming of age.

After lunch, my roommate Charlie Whitson and I drove to a small, local airfield to go for a flight around Long Island. I had earned a private pilots license my senior year in college, thanks to President Roosevelt's "Civilian Pilots Training Program," and wanted to take my roommate up for his first flight. That was another reason it was a special day. It was very windy, so when we got to the airfield all flying had been cancelled. While driving back to our rooming house in my new Chevy Club Coupe, I turned on the radio and heard the awful news about Pearl Harbor. We were both shocked, and continued listening to the radio after we got back to our room.

I remember some American Admiral saying something like this: "The Japanese Navy Is no match for the American Navy, so we can defeat the Japanese within a few months."

Those were re-assuring words; but, as we soon learned, they were extremely optimistic. The bombing triggered our entry into World War II, and I still remember part of President Roosevelt's speech in which he used the term "Day of Infamy."

Now Grumman was a leading manufacturer of carrier-based fighter and torpedo bomber airplanes for the Navy, so our entry into the war resulted in large orders. It also meant lots of overtime for Grumman employees, which was a mixed blessing. The extra money was certainly welcomed since salaries were still pretty meager, and we all had great pride when our airplanes became such a vital part of our victory in the Pacific. At peak production, we turned out 600 airplanes a month in Plant 2, a new record for the industry.

However, our long workweek, frequently 56 or more hours, meant that my social life was greatly reduced and the extra hours I was spending on a Master's degree in Aeronautical Engineering became even more difficult.

But what the hell—I was in my early twenties, had no family of my own, and was full of youthful energy and ambition. Somehow, I managed to work those long hours, get my master's degree, and find a lovely young woman to be my bride.

Elizabeth and I were married on May 6th, 1945, and spent the first part of our honeymoon in NY City. On May 8th, we were there for the celebration of V.E. day-- Victory in Europe. In August of that year, the Japanese surrendered and the war was finally over. A "Day of Victory" replaced the "Day of Infamy".

Grumman was so pleased that it gave all employees a week off with pay. That meant a trip to the Adirondack Mountains and a second honeymoon for us. It was a very happy ending for a sad and tragic beginning.

Now fast forward to 1965. Elizabeth and I visited Hawaii for two weeks, and of course one of the sights we visited was Pearl Harbor. There was still much damage, and I can never forget my feelings when we saw the battleship Arizona still mostly submerged in the water, and with the crews' bodies still trapped within.

Much to our surprise, we saw lots of Japanese tourists, including some during our trip to Pearl harbor. We couldn't help wondering why they picked this time of year to visit.

You see, it was December 7th, the 24th anniversary of The Day of Infamy!

DECISIONS! DECISIONS!   DECISIONS!

Lawrence Marcus Edwards was a young mechanical engineer with whom I became well acquainted many years ago because of our mutual love of tennis. After a hotly contested game we would discuss the young ladies in our life and seek each other's sage advice. I found his situation so interesting that I decided to write this story.

Marc, as he was called, worked for a major East Coast manufacturing company, and by age 23 he had risen up the corporate ladder several notches and had a promising future. He was almost six feet tall, with wavy brown hair, broad shoulders and a narrow waistline. He wasn't handsome, but his decent looks, pleasing personality and up-scale profession made him attractive to the opposite gender, so he didn't lack for female companionship. In fact, he took advantage of the situation whenever his busy schedule permitted, usually on a Saturday night. Lots of overtime, tennis and his pursuit of a master's degree were to blame for his busy schedule.

His two favorite young ladies were both very good looking and talented. Lois was a concert harpist and was receiving acclaim in the musical world. She was about 5' 6", had medium length blonde hair and a svelte figure. She was fair skinned and had a flashing smile that would wow her audiences and make even older men ask for her autograph. (Probably to get a closer look!) Her schedule was quite full too, and she was on tour frequently. On one occasion she had played at the White House for

<u>President Roosevelt</u>, as her publicity fliers usually proclaimed. Marc was a classical music lover, an amateur musician, and highly appreciative of her professional musical talents, as well as her many other gifts.

His other favorite, <u>Jean,</u> was a Vassar graduate with a degree in mathematics. She was valedictorian and Prom Queen of her high school class and had obtained a position in the same engineering department as Marc. She was about 5' 4", had gorgeous, shoulder-length auburn hair, and a trim figure, but with a few more curves in the right places than Lois. Her smile wasn't as flashing as her unknown rival, but it was sweeter and more sincere. And when the setting sun hit her auburn hair it glowed like a beautiful halo. Marc appreciated that and many other facets of her personality-- her wit, her natural charm, her cooking, her sincerity-- the list was quite long. Marc told her more than once, "You aren't beautiful--you're better than that-- you're lovely!

Later on, a third young lady, named <u>Aileen</u>, entered Marc's life; but distance made it hard to see her except when he visited his out-of-state parents and older sister. While this occurred only once or twice a year, its duration was up to a week at a time. His sister usually fixed him up with dates with local beauties, but none quite caught his eye as much as Aileen.

They had hit it off well on their first date and she had invited him to her father's mansion for a swim in the pool the next day. She looked good in a bathing suit and seemed quite athletic, a quality neither of the other two displayed. She was a university graduate and specialized in voice. She was 5'6", had shoulder-length, honey-blonde hair, a fair complexion and a trim, athletic figure. Of the three young women, she was the only one from a really wealthy family, but that didn't concern Marc. He planned to make it on his own--his pride demanded it!

For a while Marc's situation seemed ideal: three beautiful, talented, and personable young women to chose from, depending on circumstances. He would date Lois whenever she wasn't on tour, Aileen whenever he visited his sister, and Jean the rest of the time. Sometimes he would go out with other local girls, but usually as fill-ins when Lois or Jean weren't available. Yes, he had an ideal situation all right; but, as usual, there were, a few complications.

Lois lived about twenty, heavy-traffic miles away from Marc's house, which he shared with two other bachelors. It was difficult to see her on weeknights and her schedule took her away many weekends. Jean lived less than a mile away in a three-apartment complex with seven other girls, but was semi-engaged to a young Naval officer named Don. I say semi-engaged since he hadn't given her a ring because of the hazardous duty he was facing. And of course Aileen was too damn far away for heavy courting.

When Marc reached age twenty-four, he knew in his heart that he would have to make a decision soon and pursue one of the three seriously. Bachelorhood had its advantages, but something told him it was time to settle down. He was tired of attending other weddings, at two of which he was best man. Now he wanted his own best man, but more importantly, he wanted his own bride!

One Saturday night he drove the twenty miles to date Lois. She was kind enough to go out with him even though she had a bad cold. That not only meant no smooching, but an early "goodnight." As he drove back to his own town it was only about ten o'clock, so he decided to stop in and see Jean. Marc knew she didn't date any other men, and him only reluctantly because of Don. She was glad to see him, and they spent the rest of that night together—that is, until bedtime when Marc was asked to leave.

As he drove home he couldn't help but think about the two women he had just seen, and worse yet compare their qualities. Jean was sweeter, kinder, and more affectionate, even though in a reserved way, than Lois. Marc decided at that moment that she would make a better life-long mate and decided to taper off with Lois. He didn't want to make a quick retreat because Jean was still tied to Don, and conquest of her was very uncertain. Of course it was uncertain with the other two, but he kept thinking of expressions such as: "Nothing ventured, nothing gained!" "Faint heart never won fair lady," and "Perseverance can win seemingly impossible battles." He made up the last one to fit the occasion.

It was then that location and Mother Nature played important roles. Don was far away and Marc was near by, and as most people know, "Absence makes the heart grow fonder--for the one who isn't absent!" They were both human and nature caused their dates to grow more and more affectionate. Marc was pleased because it seemed that he was making good progress, but the time wasn't quite ripe for the big question!

One night, Jean dropped a bombshell, saying: "We can't go on like this--I think we had better stop seeing each other. I am getting too fond of you to continue— it's just not fair to either you or Don."

Although she had warned Marc earlier about this possibility, he was shocked at the brusque announcement. He thought a minute, and then responded with, "Yeah, I guess you're right. But let's not be too precipitous and stop all at once— lets sort of-- taper off!"

Jean pondered a moment before replying, "I think that will be O.K.-- but promise me you'll start dating other girls!"

"Alright, I will. In fact I just got a letter from a girl named Aileen from my home state saying that she was going to study for a year at the Julliard School of Music In New York City, starting next week. I can go into the Big Apple and see her!"

Jean nodded in approval, but later on she confessed that deep inside a twinge of jealousy had arisen. She was perplexed at this feeling, but dismissed it from her agile mind.

Marc then began his "taper-off" plan with Jean by dating Lois a few more times; but for some unknown reason he never made the trip into the city to see Aileen. Instead he concocted another plan. It was to take "no" for maybe, and "maybe" for yes. In short, he decided Jean was worth fighting for, even though his rival was thousands of miles away.

He than mounted a campaign that would have made a general proud. Here's how things ended up: Lois kept on playing the harp and eventually married an aviator who was killed a few years later. Aileen had a short singing career and married a local boy who grew wealthy through her father's business and his own skills. Marc's campaign was successful, and he and Jean tied the knot before any of the other "fair ladies" did.

Marc was proud of his four decisions. First to taper of with Lois in favor *of* Jean; second to convince Jean they should taper off when she gave him his walking papers; third, to use Aileen as a ploy to stroke Jean's jealous streak; and finally to pursue the one he wanted most with tenacity and determination.

Recently, I was able to attend Marc and Jean's fifty-second wedding anniversary and both are looking forward to many more. I'm happy to report that they seemed very happy with the tough decisions they made in their youth.

I ought'a know, because I was Marc in this story!

DIFFICULT CHILD

He came into the world in the usual way, and, as an innocent baby, no one could even guess that he would become a difficult child. Why he became difficult is still unknown. Did his father punish him too much? Was his mother too lenient or too harsh? Did his siblings taunt him until he cried? How about his classmates and playmates—did they tease him, ignore him, beat up on him, or do other unkind things? Then there were his teachers, who during his generation were not only strict, but used corporeal punishment. Were they to blame? I haven't even mentioned relatives, neighbors, strangers, diseases, birth defects, etc., so you can see how hard it is to learn <u>why</u> a child becomes difficult.

In the case of this child, I must admit that I don't even know <u>how</u> he was difficult. All I know is that what he became as an adult makes me think he was a difficult child. He even wrote a book about his early hardships, and used it as a steppingstone to his accomplishments. Some say that difficulties are a great incentive for accomplishments, provided they don't drag you into the gutter first. As for this difficult kid, I wish his difficulties had dragged him into the gutter as a young man and kept him there! I suspect that some of you may think I am being too harsh, but bear with me.

Now let me be a bit personal. When I was a kid, I caused my parents some worries, but they were normal for the era. However, I resented that they had given me names like Luther and Macon. They didn't seem to fit with the usual names of my friends, like <u>Bobby; Joey; Billy; Gus; Dave; Harry</u>; etc. Oh, there were a few other oddball names like mine, such as <u>Herschel, Virgil, and Clifford</u>, but they were little comfort to me because they became friends too late. Even my last name seemed a bit out of the main stream. Now I outgrew my frustrations, but the kid I am talking about didn't even like his last name, so he changed both his first and last name.

When he started accomplishing his ambitions, many applauded them. After all, he was trying to correct past injustices, and who is against that, except those who committed them in the first place? But then this difficult child became a very difficult man, as the world began to notice. To make matters worse, he was also clever, sometimes brilliant, and when those qualities are applied to evil actions, the rest of us are in trouble—deep trouble.

Then to compound the world's troubles, there was another "difficult child" on the other side of the planet that started down another evil road. Together, these two difficult children caused about 52 million deaths, plus untold pain and hardships. Yes, the difficult child of my piece is Adolf Hitler, and the other "difficult child is Tojo, the Japanese dictator that invaded China, bombed Pearl Harbor, and got the US into WWII. What I have said about the first difficult child probably applies to him also.

Now most religions call all humans, "Children of God", so I guess they both fit into that category. But they were surely "Difficult Children of God," and I wonder how God handles such "children" when he passes judgment on their lives?

Now I hope you will agree with and forgive my earlier statement: "I wish Hitler's difficulties had dragged him into the gutter as a young man and kept him there!" Ditto for Tojo, and all tyrants, past and present!

FLYING LESSONS
FUN, FOOLISHNESS AND FRUSTRATION

I'm holding a little green book in my hand that means a lot to me. It only has 44 pages and is not very big. (About 6 inches long and 3 wide.) On the cover it says, "CIVIL AERONAUTICS AUTHORITY, WASHINGTON; STUDENT PILOT LOG BOOK; L. M. EPPS. Inside are details of my lessons and solo flights up to the time I was awarded my Private Pilot License, so most everything I write is accurate, even the dates. It also has some of the flights that I made when I had passengers aboard after my license.

Let's start on the first page. It is November 27, 1939, and I am a senior in college and part of President Roosevelt's Civilian Pilots Training Program. I am training at the Raleigh, NC Municipal Airport, which is about 3 miles from the campus of N.C. State College. Since I have no car, I must take a city bus part of the way or walk all the way. Walking takes about the same time as a bus plus walking, so I frequently walk. Sometimes I am lucky and get a ride with another flying student, or hitchhike a ride. My airplane is a side-by-side seating Aeronca Chief, and my instructor is William Dameron, a very nice man. He grades me on the various maneuvers we do, and his log comment the first day is "At ease in air." During the following flights his comments are very pleasing. For example, "applies verbal instructions easily;" "Relaxed. Very receptive;" "Shows good progress;" "Retains instructions."

Then he says goodbye, because he got a co-pilot job with Eastern Airlines. My next instructor is <u>L. W. Clark</u>. He's a more demanding man as I soon find out. His attitude makes me a bit nervous, so after my first lesson with him, his log comment is, "Forgotten previous instructions." Some of his following comments are: "improving--tense;" "More relaxed, very willing student;" "Apt student;" "Poor judgment for cutting engine in glide;" "Flies into ground;" His scores on the various maneuvers are lower than Mr. Dameron, and he yells at me when I make a mistake, so I know I have a very demanding instructor. I wonder if that is good or bad, and finally settle with good, because I should become a better pilot with a hard taskmaster.

After 8 hours and 20 minutes of instruction, on February 5, 1940 I do my first solo. I have just turned 20, so I am pleased not to have him in the cockpit scolding me or making harsh comments when I make errors, no matter how small. I am thrilled at how quickly I take off and climb without his weight. I am elated as I quickly climb to my designated altitude, and surprised when I overtake a flight of large birds. It's fun to watch them look back at me and then scamper to get out of my way. I'm careful to keep a safe distance, because I realize that if my propeller hits one, it could be deadly for the bird and very serious for me.

I fly around and do a few maneuvers, then come in for a landing. We have to use designated runways and I am frustrated when the wind shifts and there's a strong crosswind, instead of the usual headwind. Just before I touch down, my right wing lifts way up and my left wing almost hits the ground. For a split second I'm not sure what to do, but instinctively, I do the right thing; I lower the wing to normal and come in for a decent landing. That's one of the rewarding moments in my flying days, because if I had done the wrong thing I would have crashed during my first solo!

There are some even scarier moments, but fortunately Mr. Clark is with me to make sure we both survive. One day, shortly after takeoff, he cuts the power, and says, "What are you going to do?" I know it's unsafe to return to the runway, so I pick out what looks like a field to make an emergency landing. As I get closer, I can see that it's an orchard with trees bare of leaves. He yells: "Do you see your mistake?"

"I sure do," I reply!

"OK, what are you going to do now?

I immediately turn on the power and climb higher. He then points to a real safe place for an emergency landing and says, "There's where you should have gone. Remember it, and always spot a safe place for an emergency landing anytime you use a new runway or a new airport. Also do it when you fly cross country, because you never know when the power will fail."

A month or so later, he does the same thing, except we are far from the airport and I have time to pick a nice field. I look at the trees to see which way the wind is blowing, and then head for the field into the wind. Unfortunately, I started my descent too soon because the wind is quite strong, and before we reach the field, several tall trees are in the way. This time, he gives it power and we climb back to the original spot.

"Remember the sideslip I taught you? You should use it during this type of emergency to make sure you get to the field safely."

This time I come in high, start my sideslip once I know I will clear the trees, and come so close to the ground that I'm prepared to land. Just before I do, he turns the power back on. He explains, "The farmer might not appreciate our landing in his new wheat field."

Another day, while we were at altitude, he says, "I'll take over." He immediately pulls the nose way up and rolls to the left, a position I have never been in. "OK—you take over!"

Somehow I push the nose down, made a turn to the right and recovered nicely. "Good job," he says quietly. I'm pleased.

When we get to tailspins, I'm a bit nervous, but manage to follow his instructions without getting into trouble. It's a fun maneuver, and I feel that I'm becoming a real pilot when I do them several times alone and recover in time. Incidentally, tailspins can be deadly if they occur accidentally near the ground, so we always practiced them with plenty of altitude. One day, as I enter the airport grounds, I see a crashed airplane. I am told three people died, and Mr. Clark then tells me how to avoid such an accident. A good lesson learned!

Now the most memorable and fun event happens when I take my solo cross-country fight to two other airports, with each leg about 50 miles. Except for a compass, light airplanes have zero navigation equipment in these days, so I have to find my way with a regular map and by following landmarks and a few signs that are visible from the air. I reach my destinations without trouble and land so I can get the airport manager to sign that I got there.

My instructions are to keep a safe altitude after take off and never go low unless I have an emergency. On my way back to Raleigh, the naughty boy in me arises, and I decide to fly close to the ground over the farm country, because the closer to the ground you are, the greater the apparent speed and the thrill. This I do, and several farmers wave me off and probably curse me for getting so close to them. However, I'm having too much fun, and my only concern is that they will spot my aircraft number and report my foolishness. I get within 10 feet of the ground at full speed, and even have fun pulling up just in time to avoid some approaching trees. I'm feeling my "oats" and having a great time.

I arrive safely in Raleigh and keep my low-level flight a secret, except to a few of my buddies, and not one farmer reported me. On May 8, 1940, my Private Pilot Certificate is awarded and I'm delighted. I'm now legally able to take passengers with me, so I take a few of my classmates up for scenic rides. My roommate, Roscoe Frank, is the only one to get airsick, so I open a side window so he can throw up without messing the cabin.

Most of my flights with passengers are safe and routine, but three are unusual. 1. I am visiting my parents in Newton, N.C., and <u>Watson Gabriel</u>, an old friend, is taking flying lessons himself, so I invite him to go with me in the rear seat. The local facility is a grass field with no runways, and my take off is good. As we climb due east to altitude, I spot some low, scattered clouds approaching us. I have never flown in clouds, and since they are scattered I feel I can find my way out safely. Watson is concerned as we enter, saying, "Do you know how to fly in clouds?"

"No, but I'm gonna learn now."

He seems really worried, so I say: "I can fly straight and level by watching my artificial horizon and listening to the engine. If it slows down, we're climbing—if it speeds up, we're diving. I'll use the compass to find my way back toward the airport."

All goes well and we both enjoy the new experience. After fooling around in the cloud, I make some turns and we start exiting it without descending. Watson says, "Do you know where we are? I'm lost!"

My compass says we are going west, and as I look down I see the flying field about a mile or so dead ahead. I show it to him, and he is amazed. I head for it and land safely. After we exit the airplane, he asks, "How did you navigate through the cloud and back to the field so easily?

"Oh, it's partly my sense of direction and partly watching the compass."

Today, I would add another reason, perhaps the major one: It was damn good luck!"

2. <u>Bernie Harriman</u>, a fellow engineer and friend asks me to fly him over his house in Hempstead, and offers to pay. I say, "I can't charge any money, but we can split the cost of the airplane." This we do, and soon we are on our way. I get to the general vicinity, and Bernie spots his house. "Can you go lower and circle it a few times. My wife will come out and wave to us."

I go down to about 600 feet and start circling. Both of us look down and see her waving, and are pleased. Just as I leave and start regaining altitude, I am shocked and scared. A bunch of F-40 fighter planes have left nearby Mitchell Air Force Base and whiz by me at great speed, and much too close for comfort. I wonder if they saw me, or if they just wanted to teach me a lesson. If it is the latter, it sure worked. Now, anytime I fly on Long Island, I keep my eyes open for all types of aircraft.

3. On this flight, I am taking my landlord's young daughter, <u>Adele Sengstacken,</u> on her first flight. I did it earlier with her younger brother, <u>Gene</u>. It is a windy day, but I figure that will make takeoff and landing easier and quicker, so off we go. We circle her house and other well-known spots, but now I watch carefully for other airplanes.

All goes well until I land, and even that goes well until I start to taxi back to the hanger. When I try to turn my little airplane, the wind is so strong that I can't head it back to the hanger. I try it several times, both left and right, but no luck. It's an embarrassing situation with a young girl that trusts my airmanship, so I decide to innovate. I throttle down the engine to idle, climb out, go back to the tail and lift it and move the stubborn airplane.

Hooray, it works, so I climb back in and taxi to the hanger. One of the attendants says, "We saw your trouble and were about to come and help, but your maneuver did he trick. Thanks!" I pretend it is something I have done before as I say, "You're welcome!

During the following years, I take up more friends, my two brothers, one sister and at least one girl friend. As I look at their names in my logbook, I can see their faces and even remember some of their comments during the flight as shown by the three special stories. At lest seven have now died and I have lost track of others, but the little green book triggers my mind to remember all of them. That's why it's such a treasure to me!

THE TOWER

THE CHALLENGE:

There it stood—tall and majestic—the latest addition to the "skyline" of my boyhood hometown. It rested on eight cross-braced legs, each about 140 feet long, and it reminded me of a humongous granddaddy longlegs spider. Its aluminum paint finish glistened in the early afternoon sun and contained large black letters, "City of Opportunity, Newton, N.C." From ground to top it was about 180 feet high and was clearly the tallest structure for miles around. The tank at the top held 500,000 gallons of water and was 45 feet in diameter by 38 feet high.

Before the tower was erected in 1948, the tallest landmark in town was the Eagle building, rising all of four stories above the city streets. During my boyhood, the old St. Hubert's Hotel was the dominant structure. It was three stories, plus a tower that rose another three stories.

As a teenager, some of my chums and I would sneak up to the top of the St. Hubert and sit in the open "crow's nest" to watch the "passing parade." It wasn't a very big parade because Newton only had about 5,000 citizens. However, it was my hometown, and I knew all the leading citizens and many of the others. So it was fun to look down at people I normally looked up to, whistle or yell when a pretty girl walked by, and philosophize with my friends about our unfolding lives.

Sometime during my college years, the hotel was torn down and a new Post Office erected in its place. Oh well, I thought it was just a big wooden firetrap. Still, I missed the high view and the hours I spent philosophizing and yelling and whistling. The latter was special fun because the girls couldn't figure where the sound came from.

When I first spotted the new tower I was about thirty. I had returned for a visit with my parents and other kin with my "Yankee" wife, Betty, and my half-Yankee, half-Southern baby daughter, Tina. I had brought along my 8mm movie camera and when I observed the 2-1/2 foot platform surrounding the lower rim of the tank and the ladder going up one of the legs, a sudden inspiration hit me. Why not climb to the platform and get a bird's eye view of Newton! Here's my recollection of the event:

RED TAPE CHASE:

Betty's home with Tina and my Mother, so I have the rest of the afternoon available for my project. *I* park my car near the base of the tower and enter the adjoining water treatment plant. Aubrey Moose, an uncle of my cousin David Schrum, is on duty and we easily recognize each other. I tell Aubrey my plan and ask permission to climb the tower.

Aubrey says, "I can't authorize it, but why don't you go see "Frosty" Lackey, the Superintendent of Public Works?"

"Where can I find him?" I ask.

"I think he's out on the Startown road putting in a new culvert. He should be easy to spot."

I thank Aubrey and drive about two miles out of town. Sure enough, there's Frosty and his crew. He's called "Frosty" because he has very light blonde hair. In fact, it's a family trait and his younger brother "Cotton" and their pretty sister, "Hazel", were real "blondies."

Frosty recognizes me and is sympathetic when I explain my project. "Sorry, I can't grant it," he says. "You'll have to see the mayor, Ed Haupt."

I thank him and drive into town to Ed's drug store. Ed is at his usual spot in the pharmacy department. We exchange pleasantries and I tell him about my project and ask permission to execute it.

"It's ok with me," he says, "but you'll have to get the town clerk, Loy Sigmon, to give you a release form to fill out. We need that to protect the city in case you fall."

Of course, I have no intention of falling, but I understand his desire to protect the city. About this time I am getting tired of the red tape chase, and tempted to just go climb the damn thing. However, my better instincts prevail, so I walk over to Loy's office. He seems happy to see me and we chat for a while. I inquire about his children, Katherine Reid and Loy, Jr. Katherine Reid was one of the prettiest girls in Newton. I had a silent crush on her in high school, but alas, she was several years older than I. Just as well, I think, because I found someone even lovelier when I met Betty.

When I ask for the release form, he says, "I don't have any—besides, that's not my responsibility; you'll have to go see Wade Leffler, the town attorney." Disappointed, but determined to follow the trail to the end, I walk the two blocks to Wade's office. On the way, I marvel that such a small town could produce so much red tape.

Hooray! Wade is in his office and greets me warmly. When I explain my project, he says, "No problem, I'll draw up a release right away." He writes on a piece of paper and gives it to his secretary. We chat amicably while she types it. I then sign it and the two of them witness it and stick it in an envelope addressed to Mayor Haupt. Believe it or not, he then asks me to hand carry it to the mayor! With this great display of confidence in my integrity, I comply immediately.

THE CLIMB:

I then walk down to the tower and tell Aubrey what transpired. He accepts my word and chuckles at all the red tape I encountered. "Be very careful, there's no guard cage around the ladder," he warns. "You'd better look down a few times during the climb to get used to the height—some people get dizzy and nearly fall. Don't want that to happen to you."

"Don't worry, I'll be careful," I say, "And thanks for the advice."

I then proceed to the base of the ladder. Access to it is difficult as the ladder leg rests on a 5-foot high concrete footing and the ladder itself is about 6 feet above the footing. I slip the camera strap around my left wrist and pull and haul myself up both.

Standing on the bottom rung, my eyes are over 16 feet off the ground—time to look down and check my "dizzy quotient. No problem. I take a deep breath and start a steady, measured climb. Finally, I am on my way!

As I climb, I have no fear, just lots of respect. Actually, I like height. I was an excellent tree climber as a boy and often dream of flying. I even obtained a private pilots license in college. My respect for the danger in this venture is heightened (no pun intended) by my new responsibilities of husband and father. I am also still fond of my own skin, so I have many reasons to be careful. I check my dizzy quotient three or four times on the way up—A-O. K.

The ladder is angled slightly away from vertical to conform to the slope of the supporting leg. However, as it approaches the tank platform, it rises vertically to meet the outside of the platform guardrail. No problem, I think, but I make a mental note of the anomaly for the return trip.

I soon reach the platform rail, climb over it carefully and stand safely on the metal platform. Success at last!

As I scan the horizon, I am nearly ecstatic—what a view. I think it's even better than I imagined!

I turn left and slowly circle toward the north to see what I can recognize...there's the high school, the grammar school—hey, there's my parent's house. I wonder if anyone's on the side porch—damn, the trees block my view. There's the Gaither house, the big red brick Garvin house, Sam Rowe's house. I look farther north beyond the grammar school—there's the Newton Glove Company, the North Newton business section... I look way north—gosh, that must be the City of Conover. I remember that it is so small they send their kids to Newton High.

I then circle toward the east...there's the County Court House (gee, it looks much smaller from this height); there's the Confederate Monument and the Daniel Boone trail marker; there's Ed Haupt's drug store; Wade Leffler's office.... I see many other familiar landmarks near the courthouse square and then gaze farther away.

There's the cemetery; the American Legion Hall; the municipal swimming pool. My memory goes back to a nude, late night, unauthorized swim when I was a teenager. There's the "Colored section;" ("African-American" in today's lingo); the Cotton Seed Processing Plant; Yount's Lumberyard; several hosiery mills....

I circle toward the south...there's my <u>Dad</u>'s printing and office supply business; the Post Office; the Chevy place; there's <u>Bobby Cochran's</u> house; the <u>Patterson</u> house; the ball park; Again memories flood my mind and I think of my football teammates during my last two years of high school, one of which we were Western N.C. Champions. The memories grow painful as I recall the trauma of my last game and the torn ligament that kept me out for the rest of the season. Beyond the ballpark I see the Startown Road and I imagine I see Frosty Lackey sweating out the culvert installation.

Circling toward the west I am immediately struck by the distant Blue Ridge Mountains glowing in the afternoon sun. Hey, there's nearby Baker's Mountain—gosh, it looks closer and bigger than ever from this height; there's Goshen Hill—those mill houses look pretty good from this angle. I look directly below at the treatment plant roof and the pools of water being treated. I even imagine doing a graceful swan dive down into those pools. Finally, I look directly down the ladder that will soon take me down. I'll confess that I'm a little dizzy at this point and a little nervous at the ordeal of climbing down. (Why is climbing up so much easier than climbing down?)

What a panoramic view of my old stomping ground. If there weren't so many trees, I probably could see everything! Maybe I should climb in late fall or early spring....

I then proceed to retrace my steps and film the whole thing, panning slowly so I will be able to recognize as much as possible. (How I wish the zoom lens had been available in those days.) I soon finish filming and decide to stay up here and enjoy the view as long as possible. After what I've been through to get here, I'm sure in no hurry to go back down.

After about an hour of viewing and re-living old memories, I begin thinking of going down. The sun is getting lower in the west and long shadows are already falling on the ground. Time to leave, I decide, so I strap my camera to my left wrist and walk over to the ladder.

THE DESCENT—AN EVEN GREATER CHALLENGE:

As I look down, the vertical part of the ladder looks steeper than it did coining up. In fact, it seems to be more than vertical—and in the wrong direction! I throw one leg over the rail and again look down at the dizzy height. A wave of excitement flows through me that soon intensifies to near panic when I spot four or five yellow jackets on the top few rungs, basking in the late afternoon sun. What a shock! What on earth are they doing way up here, just when I want to go down? If they sting me, it could be very dangerous at this height. They could make me loose my grip if I start swatting at them, and the venom could make me dizzy and cause me to fall. Needless to say, I am very disturbed at their presence. I remove my leg from the rail to contemplate my predicament.

Suddenly, a bright idea hits me—I'll take off a shoe and kill them, or at least shoo them away. (No pun intended). I kneel down on the platform, reach through the guardrails and try to swat them.

Damn, I missed! Hey, they're flying away--but wait--they're landing about 10 feet lower down. That's not fair, now they're out of my reach. I'm thankful I didn't drop my shoe during the swatting. A 150-foot drop wouldn't be good for my shoe and descending would be even more difficult.

I put my shoe back on and contemplate my situation. Here I am, 150 feet off the ground looking down a very steep ladder; the dinner hour is fast approaching and Betty and my folks are probably wondering where I am. What's worse, those damn yellow jackets are waiting to ambush me as soon as I start descending. Another fine mess I just got myself into. Why was I so damn persistent in getting the release?

For a brief minute, my imagination runs wild—is this the way I'm going to die? Has my time come? Did God send those yellow jackets to make me fall to my death? I can visualize the headline in the local paper—"Ex-Newton Man Falls To Death-Stung by Yellow Jackets While Descending Water Tower." It's funny how facing a dangerous situation alone stimulates your imagination and raises fear. Wait a minute, I think. You are a graduate engineer, a man of science. This is just an inconvenient coincidence. The yellow jackets are up this high just to catch the sun's rays, not to sting you. You can handle this situation if you keep your wits.

My first thought is: Wait 'til the sun sets further—maybe the yellow jackets will fly away. No good—Betty and my parents will be worried if I don't get home soon and the yellow jackets may stay there all night. Besides, I'd better go down while there's plenty of daylight.

Ah, I have it—I'll go down slowly and perhaps my presence will make the yellow jackets fly away and let me descend in peace. If they sting me, I'll steel myself to avoid swatting them and get down as soon as possible—before the venom makes me dizzy.

I feel better now that I have a plan, so I take another deep breath, look down to overcome any residual fear and swing my body over the railing on to the ladder. That first move into empty space is the hardest.

So far, so good. I slowly descend, making sure at least one hand and one foot are always in contact with the rungs. As I approach the area where the yellow jackets had landed, I move very slowly, half hold my breath and look straight ahead. Suddenly, I hear a buzzing sound, so I steel myself for the worst. My worry is unfounded; the yellow jackets simply move their position to get out of my way and now fly back to the higher rungs.

Hooray! No swats, no stings—my plan is working. Now if there aren't any other perils down below, I should make it easily. I look down to enjoy the height and make sure an accidental glance doesn't bother me. I repeat it several times.

In a few minutes I am near the bottom, so I prepare to dismount. When my feet touch terra firma, I breathe a big sigh of relief and say a little prayer. The ordeal is safely over!

THE AFTERMATH:

I then drive home to my waiting family only to be greeted with "Where have you been all afternoon—why didn't you at least call?" I mumble a lame excuse, but during dinner I tell them about my adventure and get mixed reactions. Dad gets a big kick out of it. He always did like to hear about my escapades. Mom seems relieved that I made it down safely, but scolds me for taking such a risk. Betty is like Mom, except more so, pointing out that I now have a family to consider and that I was irresponsible to even consider such a dangerous adventure. She's right of course, but secretly I'm glad I did it.

The movie shots? They were O.K., not nearly as good as the real thing, but they never are. They do let me relive the adventure whenever I look at them.

Today, in my seventies, I realize that I accomplished three positive things through the adventure:

– I demonstrated my perseverance in getting permission to make the climb.
- I used my mature judgment and kept my cool to overcome the yellow jacket threat.
– For a short while, I recaptured my boyhood spirit of fun and adventure.

Come to think of it, aren't they some of the important ingredients of life—perseverance, mature judgment and a youthful spirit of adventure?

AN UNEXPECTED ADVENTURE

In 1940, I earned a private pilots license, courtesy of Roosevelt's Civilian Pilots Training Program. Oh, it cost me 50 bucks, which was a lot of money in those days. On the other hand, I received about forty hours of lessons and solo flying, which would have cost about $320 if I paid for it myself.

Once I got my first job as an engineer at Grumman Aircraft, it wasn't long before I joined the flying club there. I especially liked the club because it was affordable and they had several different types of airplanes, so I got some interesting variety. Things were going well until WW2 hit America, at which time the club became inactive, probably because of fuel shortage or maybe because of security reasons.

When the war was over in 1945, I renewed my membership and contacted the club instructor for my check flight. I figured I might have to have a few lessons to make up for my long vacation from flying, so after the 30-minute check flight the instructor told me to contact him the next time I wanted to fly.

This I did, and once he looked at his logbook, I was surprised when he said, " You did pretty well last time, so you can take it up by yourself today. By the way, it's low on fuel so fly it over to the small field near Jericho Turnpike and they will fill it up. We have an account with them, so they will charge it to the club."

He made sure I knew where the field was, and off I went. It was only 5 or 6 miles away, so I spotted it quickly. I looked at the windsock, which all flying fields have, so I could land going into the wind. It was a very small grass field with no runways, so I knew that would make landing difficult. To make things worse, I spotted a problem that worried me a bit. It was a big trash dump at the end where I was about to make my approach, and there was smoke coming from it. I figured I had better come in high over the dump before I put the engine in idle, and then sideslip to minimize my landing distance.

This I did, but I soon discovered that the field was too short, so I gave it the gun and didn't even touch the ground. I climbed the standard 400 feet to go around again, wondering what to do next. I looked at my fuel indicator, and saw that I was getting near empty. I knew that there was a little reserve when it indicated empty, but I didn't know how much. Now I had three things to worry about. The short field, the smoking trash dump, and damn near no fuel!

I figured that maybe I should make a power approach and come in low over the dump. That way I would have power over the dump and cut the engine when it was safe. This I did, and I even touched down, but it was obvious that I would run out of runway. Again, I gave it the gun and circled the field, but this time I said to hell with the 400-foot requirement. I didn't want to run out of fuel and crash into the dump, so I knew it was land now or crash somewhere. I figured the bushes at the end of the field would be better than the dump, so I said a little prayer and came in very low over the dump with partial engine power to save fuel. Once I cleared the dump, I touched down as soon as I could and then used an old trick that I had previously learned. I slowly started turning left, so that there would be more field to slow the airplane down and hopefully stop it before it hit the bushes.

Much to my relief, it worked, and I taxied toward the hangar to get much needed fuel. It was then that I saw the field attendant waving at me. Once I stopped and cut the engine, he looked very excited. "Didn't you see me waving to you? We never land the way you did; the field is too short and that dump is too dangerous. We always land on a diagonal."

"But I followed the windsock, which is what I usually do on fields without runways."

"We don't do that here," he replied a bit less agitated. "A little cross wind is less dangerous than crashing into the bushes. So remember that next time you come here for gas."

I said, "OK," and once he filled the tank he said, "Do you know you were almost empty?"

"I sure did," I replied. "That's why I was so eager to land."

"Well you did the right thing when you slowly turned left. Otherwise you would have hit those bushes and damaged the plane, and maybe yourself."

I thanked him, started the engine and taxied to the end of one of the diagonals and took off. I went straight back to the company airfield with its long runways, and didn't do the practicing and sightseeing I had planned.

I figured I had enough adventure for that day. No, change that. I had enough adventure for a whole month!

1950-60

FASCINATING FOREIGNER

It's funny how small talk can lead to a great experience. That's what happened in May, 1954 when I happened to be seated next to John Van Lunkhausen, chief technical engineer for Bell Aircraft Company. I had been elected National Vice President of the Society of Aeronautical Weight Engineers and thus was assigned a seat at the dais during our annual conference, which was held in Buffalo, N.Y.—home of Bell Aircraft.

During my conversation with John, whom I had just met, I asked him if Bell was doing any work on rockets—a subject that had intrigued me since my youth. To my surprise, he said they were. In fact, he said, "We have hired Dr. Walter Dornberger, the German scientist, engineer and two-star general who managed the Rocket Development Center at Peenemunde." I was impressed.

I sensed that John was interested in rockets, so eventually I mustered the courage to ask: "Would it be possible to get Dr. Dornberger to speak to the Long Island chapter of our Society?" To my delight, he assured me it was and suggested I write him to confirm a date and other arrangements. It wasn't long after I returned to Long Island, N.Y. that I followed through and made the arrangements.

The following October, I drove to LaGuardia airport to meet Dr. Dornberger. I had invited him to stay in my home in Huntington and since he arrived shortly after lunch, I drove him there to relax a bit before going to the meeting that evening.

He was a garrulous man and spoke good English, with a slight German accent. He was mid-sized, stocky and had close-cropped gray hair and a full mustache. On the way home, I asked many questions and he seemed eager to answer them. I remember that he told me something of their work on inertial guidance systems. I was unaware of such work in the U.S.A., but I reminisced silently about the day another engineer and I had jointly conceived a primitive system using the same principles. Strangely enough, our concept arose when we were wondering how a rocket ship would navigate through empty space. (Regular celestial navigation depends on the earth's curvature.)

He also told me about being on the receiving end of allied bombing. It seems his and many other houses caught on fire and his reaction surprised me. Instead of saving as much of the contents as possible, he saved his favorite easy chair, took it to the curb and sat down in comfort to watch all his worldly goods become destroyed. He explained that the raids were so frequent that anything he saved that day would be destroyed another day, so he concluded he might as well enjoy the fire!

When we arrived home, my wife, <u>Betty</u> and two young <u>daughters</u> were there to greet us. We gave him our bedroom and, after unpacking, he joined us in the living room for cocktails. The kids were around 6 and 4 years old, so he took a fancy to them, talked to them like a kindly grandfather and even bounced them on his knee.

Suddenly, the significance of the event hit me. Here was a man who, a few years earlier, was a mortal enemy. And not just any enemy, but the one who was in charge of developing the most awesome and dangerous weapon that came out of WWII—except for the A-bomb. I shuddered to think what would have happened if the Germans had developed the Atomic Bomb and mated it with one of Dr. Dornberger's rockets—especially the V-2!

When the subject came around to <u>Adolph Hitler</u>, he told us things we never knew. He of course, knew the Fuehrer and met with him many times. Although they aren't exact quotes, here is the gist of what he told me:

"Hitler was a genius and, contrary to popular belief, a very good listener. It was his idea to mechanize the German Army. When one of his Generals told him it wasn't possible because his calculations showed that they couldn't depend on imported oil during a full-scale war, Hitler said, 'I didn't make you a General to tell me what I can't do; I made you one to tell me how to do what I want to do!' Then he added, 'We can solve that problem by making synthetic fuel out of potatoes and other organic material.'"

As to the good listener part, Dornberger said, "Hitler would meet with a dozen or so of his top generals and aides to make major decisions. He would outline the problem/opportunity and go around the table to get each person's opinion. He listened without interruption while each one said his piece. Then, he would give a brief summary of each person's position and reasoning, after which he would ask, 'Have I fairly stated your position?' 'Ya, mein Fuehrer,' they would respond."

"Hitler would then think a few minutes and say, 'Here's what we will do,' and describe his decision. If anyone objected to the decision he would coldly ask, 'Did I misunderstand your position?' Unless the objector came up with new ideas, Hitler would squelch him and insist that his decision be implemented." Dornberger said, "This method worked very well throughout the war until things got really bad and Hitler started loosing touch with reality."

We also learned that Werner von Braun, who was then gaining a reputation in rocketry in the USA, was Dornberger's Chief Engineer at Peenemunde. It seems that von Braun and some of his men liked to discuss space exploration over a few beers after work. Unfortunately, some S.S. men overheard them and promptly arrested them for not going full bore on the war effort. Dornberger came to their rescue by telling the S.S. how important and demanding their work was and that the space talk was simply a means of relaxation. Fortunately for Germany, but not for the allies, Dornberger prevailed and von Braun and his men kept developing those deadly weapons.

At the dinner meeting, I had the privilege of introducing Dr. Dornberger to about 150 people—about four or five times our usual attendance. His talk was entitled "Rockets, Satellites and Space Ships" and was very well received. After the talk, we adjourned to the bar and were joined by some other Germans who had emigrated to some of the local aircraft companies after the war. It was fascinating to hear them reminisce about Germany and the war, and I was thankful they spoke mostly English because my German was very limited, and still is.

Dornberger said, "Hitler once told me that he made only two mistakes during the war. One was when he invaded the Soviet Union and the second was in not backing my rocket programs soon enough and more strongly.

When Hitler asked what he could do for Dornberger, he said, "If you would confer Doctoral degrees on Von Braun and some of his top lieutenants, we would all be grateful." Hitler did just that in a subsequent ceremony. Incidentally, Dornberger had no need for doctoral degrees—he had already earned two, a doctor of science and a doctor of engineering.

Dornberger was regular army and not a member of the Nazi party. The allies tried to prosecute him at Nuremberg, but Dornberger was too smart for them. He insisted that he had done the same as allied scientists and engineers. He compared his rocket development with <u>General Groves</u> work on the A-bomb and with the men in charge of the Russian tanks and the B-29s.

When the allied lawyers reminded him that he was the one on trial, not the allied weapon developers, he said, "Very well, I will get three chairs during my trial and assign them to your developers. Whatever you ask me, I will ask the three absentee people for their answer and will use it as my own." The lawyers saw the power of his approach and never put him on the stand.

Several other German immigrants joined our table, and we talked far into the night. I felt lucky to be part of such fascinating conversation. He spoke highly of the work of the American Rocket Pioneer<u>, Dr. Robert Goddard</u>. Today, Goddard is generally conceded to be the "father" of modern rocketry. He acknowledged that Goddard's work had been extremely helpful during their developments, and was surprised that the American military had ignored the great potential that Goddard had uncovered. Needless to say, I was a very good listener that night. Eventually, we drove to my home and went to sleep. Next morning, we had breakfast and I drove him to the airport, conveyed my sincere thanks and said good-bye.

I arrived at work in mid-morning and was immediately besieged by fellow engineers about the meeting. All of them were very complimentary and said it was one of the best talks they had ever heard. One engineer, <u>Paul Anbro</u>, said, "It was a very good meeting and I enjoyed it a lot—but you don't believe we'll ever see the things he predicted come true, do you?"

"Of course, I do," I replied.

"Nah," he persisted. "Maybe in the distant future, but not in our lifetime."

"Would you like to bet on it?"

"Sure."

"OK," I said. "Since we will have to wait for years, let's make it a big one—say $50?"

"OK"

"Let's see," I said slowly. "A lifetime is about 70 years and we will be that age in 1990. So here's the bet: If an artificial satellite orbits earth before 1990, I win; if not, you win."

Much to my surprise, he agreed. I had used 1990 to take him literally and was prepared to back down to 1980 or maybe 1970, but he didn't negotiate, so I kept silent. We then put it down on paper, signed it and made a copy so we would each have one.

I filed my copy in a safe place and waited patiently. It wasn't long before

NASA announced that it was going to launch an artificial satellite within the next four years. I cut out the clipping and sent it to Paul with this note: "Five cents a day x 5 working days/week x 50 working weeks/year x 4 years = $50.00 Better start saving!"

He never answered the note, but when I next saw him he had a sheepish grin and admitted he was a bit hasty in making the bet.

In October 1957, the Russians surprised both of us—they launched Sputnik. The rest of the world was not only surprised, but shocked that the Russians were beating the Americans in the space race.

When I entered my office the next morning, I saw a check on my desk. Yep, it was from Paul and was for $50.00, so I looked at the Russian achievement with mixed feelings. I thought about it a while and then called him on the telephone. The conversation went something like this:

"Paul, this is Macon. Thanks for the check. It was nice of you to be so prompt."

"That's OK."

"I've been wondering what to do with it. At first I thought I would return it to you, but that was too easy. Then I figured you wouldn't learn a lesson if I did that. Next, I thought I would give it to some charity, but that seemed too easy and unimaginative. I'm still trying to decide what to do!"

"I know what I'd do," he said. "I'd take Jane (his wife) out to dinner and a Broadway show."

"Good idea," I responded. "I'll call her today and make a date."

He laughed nervously and after a bit more chatter we hung up. Later on I called Jane and made the invitation. At first she thought I should keep the money, but when she saw I wanted to spend it that way she reluctantly agreed. As an afterthought I said, "We can take Paul and Betty (my wife) if you like." She promptly agreed.

Several weeks later we had them over for cocktails, then I drove the four of us into the Big Apple. We had an exotic dinner at a mid-eastern restaurant and then went to the theatre. I wanted a play to fit the occasion so I selected "A Visit to a Small Planet"!

The evening cost a bit more than $50, probably about $60, but it was worth every penny. You see, my small talk with John Van Lunkhausen led to two great experiences!

Postscript: In 1963, nine years later, I started working on the Lunar Module (LM) contract, which Grumman Aerospace had won the previous year. I held various managerial positions for the following seven years. When Neil Armstrong stepped from the LM to the moon's surface and said, "One small step for man, one giant leap for mankind," I had risen to the position of Assistant Program Manager. Little did I dream during my brief time with Dr. Dornberger, that I would be an important member of the team that first accomplished "A visit to a small 'planet'"—the Moon!

MEMORIES OF MY FATHER

It has been over 55 years since I saw my <u>Father</u>, yet his memory still lingers in my mind. One of the strongest memories drifts back to the time he had a heart attack at age 68. Somehow, I feel compelled to start this remembrance during those trying days.

I was busy at work one morning in April 1954 when I got an urgent call from my sister, <u>Ruth</u>. "Dad's in the hospital in critical condition, so I think you should fly down as soon as possible. He and <u>Mom</u> were visiting us when it happened."

I agreed, and my assistant, <u>John Michael</u>, and my boss, <u>Grant Hedrick</u>, were very helpful in making flight arrangements and getting a company driver to take me to the airport. When I told my wife, <u>Betty</u>, the worrisome news, she was saddened, but immediately offered to pack a suitcase and bring it to work. Early that afternoon, I was on my way, and as I boarded the airliner I was grateful that all concerned had been so helpful, and so efficient. I had plenty of time aboard to worry about Dad, and how my Mother would handle the situation.

Ruth's husband, <u>Duncan Hunter</u> met me at the Asheville, NC airport and we went directly to the hospital in their small town of Brevard around 6 pm. Sometime later, my brother, <u>Charles</u>, flew in from Houston, TX, and he and I started an all night vigil at Dad's bedside. There was a cot near Dad's room that a nurse said we could use, so Charles and I took turns catching some fitful rest.

Dad was able to talk to us from time to time inside his oxygen tent, and was very appreciative that we had come so far to see him. I think he knew the end was near, because he philosophized about all the good things in his life and gave us some advice about our own lives.

Charles and I stayed all through the night. About 9 a.m., Duncan offered to take over, and Ruth drove us to their house so we could get some real sleep. Fatigue overcame my worries, and I slept fitfully until early afternoon. Ruth then drove Charles and me back to the hospital so we could relieve Duncan. As we approached the building, Duncan was walking toward us gesturing with his arms that it was all over—Dad had died!

Our hopes that he would recover were shattered, so we hugged each other and shed tears together. Charles, who was the strongest male in the family, was so overcome that he had to walk away and sob in private. Mom was still at Ruth and Duncan's home, so she was grief stricken by the news, but I think she had steeled herself for the worst. Next day, we drove her home to Newton, about 90 miles east of Brevard. Mom and Dad's visit with Ruth and Duncan had ended tragically.

When we drove into the driveway <u>Reverend Burgess</u>, a black minister, met us. He and two young black boys were working on the lawn. After he expressed his sorrow to my mother, we took her into the house and she laid down to rest. Charles and I went back to see the Reverend and he said, "Mr. Epps was a real friend to me and our church. He was a lay preacher there several times, and as a Building and Loan board member, he was the one that saw that we got a loan when we needed it. He was a fine man, so when I heard he had died, I asked <u>Mr. Mullinax</u>, head of the Building and Loan, what can I do to help. I told him I would do "nigger" work to help the family. He suggested that the overgrown lawn needed mowing, so here we are."

Charles and I thanked him for his kind words and deed, and we talked about Dad, his love of people, and other subjects. Reverend Burgess then surprised us by saying, "I sure would like to be one of the pall bearers."

"We'll have to discuss it with my Mother," I responded. " I'll let you know as soon as possible." I had a bit of trepidation about it, because Mom didn't seem to be quite as caring about race relations as Dad.

When I broached the subject to her, I was pleasantly surprised when she said, "I have already selected the men to carry the casket. However, the Men's Bible Class are going to be honorary pall bearers, so Reverend Burgess can join them. I would also like you to ask <u>Guy Sherrill</u> and <u>Otha Mullen</u>. As you know, they were janitors when your father was Superintendent of Schools, and he thought highly of them."

Since it was the South of 1954 and <u>Martin Luther King, Jr</u>. was far in the future, I was immensely proud of Mom. When I went outside to tell him, he was very pleased and offered to contact Guy and Otha for us. We shook hands and parted.

We had the wake at Mom's house, with Dad laying in state in the living room. Lots of Mom and Dad's friends visited, as did many of my former High School classmates. Many of them brought food, which lasted several days. It was so good that I was afraid I would gain weight, a commodity I didn't need in those days since I was "pleasing plump."

I was there when Mom's black cleaning woman came to the back door, as was the custom. She and Mom hugged each other, and Mom lost her composure and broke into tears. Her friend comforted her with words and pats on the back. Mom seemed more moved by her visit than she did with any of the others, except possibly her own sisters.

The day of the funeral was bright and sunny, and the service was very comforting to the family. The First Methodist Church Choir sang some of Dad's favorite hymns. One hymn, "Fairest Lord Jesus," brings tears to me to this day when I hear it because it was his favorite. The congregation was large and respectful, indicating that Dad had made his mark in our small town.

As the oldest son, I escorted Mom out of the church behind the pallbearers and the casket. The Men's Bible Class stood on either side of the broad sidewalk, and I looked for the three black men. When I spotted them, tall and erect and standing shoulder to shoulder with the white men, I was proud of my former church and hometown. I wondered how many Northern towns, including my then hometown of Huntington, NY, had seen similar affection and mixing of the races in times of travail.

After the graveside ceremony, I stayed with Mom for the rest of the weekend. It gave me plenty of time to contemplate how much Dad had meant to me. I remembered how he had seldom beaten me in anger. Oh he beat me, usually with his belt, and I deserved it; but he always preceded it with a stern lecture, expressing disappointment that I had done wrong. Sometimes he said, "Son, this will hurt me as much as it does you!"

My usual reply was, "Well, why don't you not do it and spare both of us. " Somehow my appeal fell on deaf ears, because he always beat me until I cried. Maybe I'm old-fashioned, but it didn't diminish my love for him; in fact, eventually, it increased my respect.

Dad taught me many things such as: how to care for the chickens we kept out back, even though we lived in town; how to catch and kill them, so Mom could pluck, dress and cook them; how to fold and press my pants so they wouldn't wrinkle so much (that was before permanent press arrived); how to bait a line and catch fish, and avoid being stung by the catfish; how to fire a shotgun, set the safety, keep the muzzle pointed toward the ground and not at people, and how to lead a running rabbit before firing; how to grow all sorts of fruits and vegetables in our backyard garden.; how to paint the fence and part of the house; how to split logs and kindling, and build the morning fire before he arose (that was one I didn't like); how to use good grammar, and pronounce and spell difficult words; how to play checkers, his favorite sedentary sport; how to wash the car, and, even more important, how to drive it. The list of practical things he taught me as a kid seems endless, and I'm sure I have omitted some important ones.

As I grew older, he let me work in his printing shop, which he bought once he left schoolwork. There I learned how to be a "Printer's Devil." I could set type by hand, run presses, cut paper, bind forms, and do many of the tasks his regular printer, H.H. Houser, could do, though not as quickly or well. I could also sell office supplies and make entries in his books.

Clearly, he was preparing me to take over someday, or at least know a useful trade. Incidentally, He paid me 10 cents an hour at first, but, when I went to college and worked full time, he upped it to $11 per 40 hour week, with the understanding that $10 was to be saved for college. That left me the princely sum of $1 to squander on dates and other pleasures!

Dad was the only one of eight siblings to go to college, so he and Mom created an atmosphere in which my two sisters, two brothers, and I knew that after high school came college. This was during the Great Depression, and most of my classmates went to work after high school. Some even dropped out earlier, so it wasn't and easy task for my parents. It meant scrimping and saving, but they were determined that all five of us would get a college degree, and by golly we did. Ruth and I even got master's degrees, which greatly pleased our parents.

Dad and Mom instilled good old-fashioned virtues in us kids. I remember Dad telling me the story about how my Grandfather was saved from drowning by his father's only slave, <u>Big Jim</u>. Dad said, "Son, never look down your nose at colored people, because if it hadn't been for Big Jim, I wouldn't be here-- and neither would you!"

He would also point out their neat, clean houses, and say, "They have the same needs and desires as we do, and are proud of their homes. They deserve to be treated with respect and dignity." His life was an example of practicing what he believed, as Reverend Burgess and others would testify to later.

Dad was very fond of my wife and two young daughters. He had away of endearing himself to our daughters, and soon came to be known as "funny old paw". It was a name he gave himself, which indicates that he wasn't too concerned with personal dignity if there was fun to be gained. For example, Dad had big feet and wore size 11 or 12 shoes. His friends often kidded him, but instead of complaining, he had a photo taken of him sitting on the sidewalk with his big feet looking gigantic because the camera angle distorted them.

Mom had raised five children, had several other grandchildren and didn't make a big fuss over ours. To this day my daughters remember her as being somewhat aloof and cool, which is a shame, because she could be warm and affectionate. She always shed tears and got choked up when we left to return back to Huntington.

In addition to the usual obituaries, both local newspapers ran editorials about Dad which Ruth and Duncan sent me. I filed them away, and although they are now yellow with age, I still take a peek at them now and then. What made them special was that they spotted many of the wonderful qualities my Dad had. It sort of proved that my love and admiration for him was not because of my special position, but that he had the knack of sharing with others and inspiring people to be better. Like other humans, I suppose he had some faults, but in my eyes they were rare. Imagine how much better the world would be if <u>everyone's</u> kids and the community had the same love and respect! © 2009 L. Macon Epps All rights reserved

A TENSE MOMENT

It was the mid 1950's and we were near the end of the proposal effort for Grumman's Design 97. The Proposal Manager, <u>Mike Pelehack</u>, and I had been debating the weight estimate for this jet twin-engine, carrier-based fighter airplane. As Chief of Weights, it was my responsibility to supervise mass property estimates for all proposals and follow-through with production values.

According to Mike, the weights we had estimated were hurting the aircraft's performance estimates, so he was trying to convince me to lower them. Mike had obtained some estimates from another source and we discussed the merits of the two estimates. His were highly optimistic, so I defended our estimates tenaciously.

Mike then decided to go to <u>Dick Hutton</u>, the Chief Preliminary Design Engineer, to arbitrate our stalemate. Mike went over all his arguments with Dick and I successfully rebutted each one. My main weapons were the new estimation methods we had recently developed. They used a preliminary structural analysis of all major components—wing, fuselage, empennage, landing gear, etc. They were more realistic for a specific design than the previously used statistical methods, especially when significant design changes were made. Design 97 had significant, changes from our previous designs, so I drove this point home.

Fortunately, I had kept Dick aware of our progress while developing these new methods so he appreciated their significance. I seemed to be winning Dick to my position, especially when I pointed out that our estimates were not only more realistic, but slightly optimistic—i.e., it would take careful design to reach them.

Mike, always a very resourceful person, came up with an argument I hadn't anticipated. It went something like this:

"O.K. Dick, I won't contest the accuracy of Macon's estimates any more. Instead, I think we should simply reduce them evenly through out the proposal by four- or- five percent. That way no single component will look ridiculous and we can improve our performance estimates. Let's face reality--the other bidders will underestimate their weights a few percent so we should do it just to stay competitive!"

Dick had the reputation of thinking through a problem and not jumping to conclusions, so I wasn't surprised when he lowered his head and started pondering Mike's new approach. I realized that Mike's approach had some merit, considering the tough competition we faced. Even so, I was somewhat stunned, so I decided to wait for Dick's decisions before putting forth any counter arguments.

It was a tense moment for both of us as we waited in silence for Dick's judgment. Mentally, I went over my counter-arguments in case Dick ruled in Mike's favor. I even arranged them in the order I would present them. They went something like this:

" Dick, the Bureau of Aeronautics weight people will not be fooled and will revise the new estimates upward. They will send them to the Bureau's performance people and we will lose doubly—performance and the new credibility I have established with my Bureau counterparts."

"One of my conditions when I accepted the Chief of Weights positions from <u>Grant</u> <u>Hedrick</u> (the Chief Technical Engineer) was that I would not fudge weight estimates. One of my predecessors had done this and had weakened his credibility with the Bureau. Therefore, we will have to review the decision with Grant."

"If both you and Grant insist I reduce the estimates I will step down as Chief and go back to the structural analysis department."

"If that isn't acceptable, I will resign from Grumman."

Now the last two may seem drastic, but I felt so strongly about the issue that I was willing to go that far if forced. I was pretty sure Grant would back my position and/or that it would take several days to resolve any drastic measures.

Much to my relief, Dick said, "I don't see how we can do that Mike. Macon and his people have put too much effort into the new methods and the proposal estimates to tinker with them now. I think you should find another way to solve your performance problems."

My already high opinion of Dick rose several notches. Later, I was especially gratified when Keith Dental, Assistant Chief of the Bureau's Weight and Balance section, showed me his comments on our weight proposal. He was very complimentary about our new estimating methods and the integrity we used in applying them. He backed our estimates without exception, which he assured me was a rare occurrence.

In my opinion, such events, multiplied by similar ones throughout the company, were major reasons why Grumman was so successful. By keeping and improving the Bureau's confidence in us, we were able to win the many contracts that fueled our growth.

My memory is a bit hazy as to whom, if anyone, won the Design 97 competition. I do remember that top management suggested we submit a proposal about the same time to redesign the F9F-6, called Design 98. It earned us a contract to produce the F11F series.

But that's another story!

1960-70

HIGH-LEVEL MEETING

I was busy working in my Value Improvement office in 1962 when I got a telephone call from my boss, VP Jim Zusi. The conversation went like this:

"Hi Macon, it's Jim. I just returned from the Business Development meeting and <u>Admiral Bolger</u>* said that you were trying to make an appointment with <u>Mr. Milne,</u> the Assistant Secretary of the Navy. Is that true?" * Our marketing representative to the Bureau of Naval Weapons.

"No it's not true, Jim. I don't even know his name, and I certainly wouldn't try to meet with someone at that high level."

"I thought so. I guess the Admiral has some bad information. Could you call your counterpart at the Bureau of Naval Weapons and see what's going on?"

"Yes, Jim. I call him right away."

I then called <u>Bill Feightenger</u>, the top guy in the Bureau's Value Improvement Program. Our conversation went like this after I explained the mystery:

Bill chuckled a bit, and then said, "I can solve the mystery, but it's a long story. Several days ago I was reviewing our program with <u>Captain Baxter</u>. He was so impressed with the money being saved that he suggested we talk with <u>Admiral Stroop</u>; as you know, he's the head of the Bureau, so I was impressed and a bit nervous."

"When we got to the Admiral's office, I had only gotten part way through my presentation when he said, "<u>Vice Admiral Hayworth</u> should hear this—lets go to his office. Once we got there, it wasn't long before he suggested we go to Mr. Milne's office, and it was there that I made my full presentation."

"When I finished, Mr. Milne wanted to know what Grumman was doing, so I told him that Grumman had the best program of all the Navy's Aircraft Companies. He then wanted to know who was in charge, so I gave him your name. When Admiral Bolger visited on other business, Mr. Milne told him he would like to meet with you, not vice versa. I was surprised that my meeting with the Captain went to such a high level, but it really emphasizes the importance of our work."

We chatted a bit longer, and after we finished I called Jim. When I explained the situation, we both chuckled. Admiral Bolger got the message backward—I wasn't trying to meet with the Assistant Secretary; he wanted to meet with me!

Sometime later, <u>Clint Towl</u>, President of Grumman, got a letter from Mr. Milne asking for a meeting in Washington. Clint then sent the letter to Senior VP <u>George Titterton</u>, who called a meeting with <u>Bill Robertson</u>, head of Purchasing, <u>Lew Scheuer</u>, a key electronic engineer, and me. I had a day to prepare, so I was not only able to answer all of George's questions, but provide the data to support them. George seemed very pleased, and I felt good because he was a tough executive. The other key people answered his questions, but they didn't have as much back up data.

Several weeks later, we flew on our corporate airplane to Washington for this high level meeting. It was held in Mr. Milne's office, and I was impressed with the size of his office and the huge desk. The previously mentioned Navy and Grumman people, plus a few more Navy people, were present. Now all the value Improvement Proposals went through my office, so I was the most knowledgeable person for Grumman. However, George did most of the talking for our group, and we had prepared him so well that he seldom called on the others or me.

After much discussion, including compliments from the Navy for our excellent program, one of my key proposals was singled out. It involved using forgings instead of machined parts on the A-6 attack airplane. At that time we got orders on an annual basis, and our limited production for that year meant that forgings would cost too much because of the one-time high cost of dies. Mr. Milne eventually authorized $2,000,000 for forging dies, provided the break-even point was 100 airplanes or less. Of course most of the money went to forging companies, but it meant the Navy saved at least $2 million for every 100 airplanes after the first 100, and the Navy's goal at the time was 400 airplanes. I think everyone was pleased with the meeting's result.

After the meeting, George said it was the highest-level meeting he had ever attended. I was not only surprised by that remark, but pleased because it was way above my level and my proposal had been the big payoff. Once I got back to work, I called for a review of all machine parts to compare each part's cost to the forged part's costs plus the cost of its die. Howie Krier, our forging and machine parts expert, was surprised at how many parts broke-even way below 100 airplanes. We saved about $10 million total on that proposal. There was even a hidden bonus, because forged parts are stronger than their equivalent machined part.

During the three years that I led the program our total savings were $80 million, and that was in 1963 dollars! Actually, we saved even more, because Bill Feightenger said our cost estimates were the most conservative in the industry.

Some months later, George Titterton called me into his office. Was he pleased with all the money our program was saving? Yes, but he was displeased because it was reducing our profits. Every time Grumman signed a new annual contract, we had to reduce the cost per the previous savings, and our profit was about 7.5 % of the cost, so the more we saved, the less our profit. Off course the savings put us in an even better competitive position with other companies, but George felt we shouldn't be penalized for saving the Navy so much money.

He then told me to visit the Bureau one day a week until I could convince the right people that we should be allowed to share the savings enough to keep the same profit we would have without the savings. This I did, starting by convincing Bill Feightenger and then going up the ranks until I got to the proper authority. I planned to have them as support when I reached the decision maker.

I was making good progress when I learned that Grumman had won the Lunar Module contract. I had heard that we were bidding on it and knew what was at stake. Although I was happy with my Value Improvement position, I decided that I HAD to be part of such a potentially history making program. I approached <u>Bill Rathke</u>, the LM Chief Engineer, and he gave me the position of Senior Resident Representative to North American Aviation, Space and Information Division (S&ID), in Downey CA.

S&ID was the principal contractor and had won the Command and Service Module Contract about a year earlier. There would be critical interface problems and many technical similarities between their two craft and our LM, so it was a challenging position. My <u>wife</u> and <u>kids</u> were in agreement to move, so I turned over my Value Improvement position to my assistant, <u>Tom Flynn</u>, and we headed for California.

It was the start of my seven years on the LM; two years at S&ID; one year as Test and Operations Manager at NASA, Houston; one year as Staff Assistant to <u>VP Joe Gavin</u>, who was the LM Program Director, and the balance as Assistant Program Manager to Bill Rathke, who had become Program Manager. I really enjoyed my work and joining the LM team was the best decision of my 30-year career with Grumman.

Following my LM experience, I became Assistant Director of Advanced Civil Systems, with <u>Al Munier</u> as Director. Previously Al was Director of Advanced Space Systems and was one of the major forces that won the LM contract. He was also the most creative engineer I had the pleasure of working with, and my years with him was not only rewarding, but fun.

But that's another story!

IMPOSSIBLE ACCIDENT

When they finally found the object that caused the accident, it would fit in the palm of your hand-- with plenty of room to spare. It wasn't the first time a Navy jet fighter had been disabled by a single shell, but I believe it was the first, and possibly the only time, that the shell was FIRED FROM the aircraft that it shot down!

Sounds impossible, doesn't it? But it actually happened--and to some one I knew personally who was flying a Navy jet fighter manufactured by my employer, the Grumman Aerospace Corporation.

When test pilot <u>Tom Attridge</u> took our jet fighter up for armament trials, he was careful to use the ocean area off the eastern end of Long Island that is clearly marked for that purpose. Fortunately, as you will soon see, he was at a high altitude for the firing. After the last burst of cannon fire he nosed his craft down in a moderate dive. Once he had descended several thousand feet, he heard strange noises in his single jet engine and it started running so poorly that he decided to shut it down.

Now shutting down your one and only engine is something a pilot doesn't do lightly, but Tom figured he could glide back to the home field, thanks to his high altitude and speed. He also figured that it would be safer than a potential engine fire or explosion. Good test pilots are known for their cool thinking in emergencies and Tom was a good, careful test pilot.

In fact, there is and adage that says, "There are hot pilots and old pilots, but there are very few hot, old pilots!" Tom's cool, analytical thinking on this and other occasions let him become an old pilot-- one who was able to retire from his risky job and assume a leading ground role on the Lunar Module Program some years later.

When Tom landed safely and made his report, the mechanics started disassembling the engine; they found that some of the air compressor blades had been shattered and bent by a 37mm shell. For a while everyone was perplexed as to its source. Could another jet have been firing at the same time? Could someone have fired from the earth's surface? These and other possibilities were quickly investigated and found to be most unlikely. So what was left to explain the cause of the accident?

For a while it had everyone perplexed. Then Hank Kelly from the Research Department had the audacity to suggest that it may have been fired by Tom and that he became like Superman--faster than a speeding bullet! On the surface that looked impossible; after all, the 37 mm shell had a muzzle velocity easily twice the top speed of the aircraft, and since it started with the jet's speed its actual exit velocity was three or more times the aircraft's speed.

To test their theory, the research people made dynamic time-history calculations and plots of the situation, using various dive angles and dive speeds. Here's what they found, expressed in laymen's terms:

Once the shell left the cannon, it immediately started slowing down due to air resistance. Unlike the aircraft, it had no jet engine to sustain its speed, and of course gravity exerted its inevitable tug to make it lose altitude.

When Tom started his moderate dive his speed actually increased, and a few miles later he was unlucky enough to overtake the shell, which at that time was traveling slower than he was due to the accumulated effect of the air resistance.

Hank and other research people were able to show that Tom had inadvertently dived at the only angle and speed that would cause the aircraft and the shell to collide. A half-degree shallower or steeper and he would have missed the shell entirely. A few feet to the right or left and the shell would have missed the engine intake duct and glanced harmlessly off the aircraft structure.

Talk about Murphy's Law, that day it was working OVERTIME and Tom was the unlucky victim. Tom and the rest of those involved soon appreciated the power of trajectories, the analytical tools to predict them and the persistence of Murphy's Law!

Some years later, when Tom and I worked closely on the Apollo Program, we both appreciated the importance of trajectories. We never would have landed on the moon had it not been for the excellent work of the trajectory, control and guidance engineers. They designed the systems that made the rocket engines head the spacecraft in the right direction.

This was no small feat because the rocket engines burn a relatively short time and then the spacecraft acts almost like a bullet for a 240,000 mile, five day, curved trajectory trip to the moon. I say almost, because it had some rocket power for mid-course correction and the systems had to account for both the moon and earth's gravity, both of which changed continually during the flight. But essentially, these tasks were well understood and readily within the technological skills of that era.

There was one important difference that Tom and I both understood. No astronaut could duplicate his shooting-himself-down experience in space, even if the spacecraft carried cannons. Why? Because there is no air resistance to slow the shell down!

That's one of the awesome aspects of space travel-- Once a rocket ship reaches escape velocity, approx 25,000 mph, it will go on FOREVER— unless a heavenly body stops it.

It's humbling to realize that Isaac Newton understood the principles involved hundreds of years ago.

INDELIBLE IMPRESSION

Walking on a crowded city street is not my favorite pastime, but I must admit it can be both interesting and provocative. It gives a brief look at the human race in all its fascinating diversity and commonality. It has been said that no two faces are the same, even though most of them have two eyes, two eyebrows, two ears, a nose, two lips, lots of teeth, and are surrounded by a plethora of hair--not to mention the wrinkles and other skin qualities that help create individuality. Perhaps it is a good thing, because many of the faces I see on a crowded street don't strike me as being too worthy of replication!

But once in a hundred faces, I usually see one that really catches my eye. Once in a thousand, I might see one that will linger in my memory for days.

Once in a million, I am privileged to encounter one that makes an indelible impression! Such was the case one sunny day in the 1950's on Eighth Avenue, in the great city of New York.

Suddenly, out of the great sea of faces, I saw that one in a million'. Was it a beautiful and famous woman? No! Was it a brilliant genius whose qualities couldn't be hidden? No! It was simply an old man with one of the most pleasant and memorable faces I have ever seen while walking any street, anywhere! He had a full head of snow white hair; large dark brown eyes topped by bushy, white eyebrows; a pleasing nose with large nostrils; dark skin', and an utterly charming smile, which he shared with me as we passed. He also spoke to me, in a deep, resonant voice, saying something like, "Hello--how are you today?"

Needless to say, I was somewhat surprised that a complete stranger would be so friendly, especially in the Big Apple, which is more famous for its busyness than its friendliness. I rose to the occasion, gave him my best smile and responded appropriately.

As I continued walking, my mind was in a turmoil. Who was this man, and why did he make such an impression on me? Talk about charisma, he had it in great abundance and seemed almost to glow, or be surrounded by some sort of a magnetic field. I glanced back to see what reaction he had on other pedestrians, and detected that at least some of them were impressed.

As I continued walking, I tried to analyze my feelings: Yes, his features were pleasant and his demeanor friendly, but that wasn't the answer. His spoken words were both warm and sincere, but that didn't explain matters either. Perhaps I was in a good mood--even a receptive one--but that also fell short. I stopped my analysis by deciding that he had some indefinable quality that made me feel I was SEEING HIS SOUL!

The other faces I encountered, I am sad to say, became sort of a blur. Even the displays in the shop windows, including the wonderful food ones, didn't grab my attention, as was their usually custom. I seemed completely mesmerized by that fascinating face, and even wondered, temporarily, if I had caught a fleeting glimpse of God!

Later on, I solved the mystery. The man I had seen and spoken to was Rex Ingram. He had played the lead role in the movie, <u>Green Pastures</u>, so my feeling that I had glimpsed God wasn't far from the mark!

As I recall this event from the distant past, I have two devout hopes. One is that my friendly response and smiling face had a fraction of the impact on him that his did on me. The other one is that the divine entity, which he portrayed in the movie, will someday let us meet again-- and smile on both of us!

A MONKEY'S UNCLE

Believe it or not, I was once a monkey's uncle. If that strains your credulity, would you believe that I was an uncle for THREE different monkeys? Before you put on your "Doubting-Thomas" hat, let me explain why I make these claims.

My younger daughter, <u>Becky</u>, loved monkeys and when she was in her pre-teens she asked if we could buy one as a pet. Her older sister, <u>Tina</u>, also loved them and strongly supported the idea. The little primates had always intrigued my deceased father and I had inherited his fascination for them, so I was a pushover. The only person who opposed the idea was my wife, <u>Betty</u>, but with three persuasive voices in favor, her opposition soon melted. She did have a proviso; the girls would have to do most of the care taking!

We decided we would have to drive into New York City from our Long Island home to get a pet that exotic. One day as we drove toward the city I began reminiscing about my previous monkey encounters.

My earliest memory was the organ-grinder man of my childhood. How I loved his tuneful music and his agile, costumed monkey. And I was impressed when the monkey passed his tin cup to collect coins from the well-pleased crowd that gathered around. I even put in a few pennies and giggled when he doffed his tiny hat to say "thanks".

My first personal encounter was with a pet monkey that a local merchant kept chained behind his store. I was about ten years old and bought a nickel bag of roasted peanuts so I could feed a few to the cute little fellow. As I started to hand him a peanut, the greedy little imp grabbed the whole bag from my other hand and spilled all its contents in his territory. Worst yet, when I tried to recover some for myself, he made a threatening noise and bared his sharp teeth. Needless to say, I gave up my efforts at retrieval and left the scene a very chagrined kid. Why? Because I had been outsmarted by a greedy, unappreciative little monkey who was one-tenth my size!

My thoughts then drifted to the time I had returned from college and told my <u>Dad</u> how <u>Darwin's</u> "Theory of Evolution" indicated that Man had descended from monkeys. Dad scoffed and said, " Well, maybe you descended from a monkey, but I didn't !"

Then there was the time Dad and I had gone to the New York World's Fair. When we got to the monkey "island", Dad seemed to lose interest in the other attractions and wanted to spend hours watching their antics. He was a keen observer of human nature and discerned many common traits shared by the monkeys and his fellow humans. However, his skepticism about Charles Darwin, who probably would have said that a monkey was more my uncle than I his, makes me believe that Dad would have accepted my terminology had he lived longer.

I also remember a framed cover from the Saturday Evening Post depicting a chimp and an orangutan playing checkers, a game Dad loved. Dad displayed it in his office, and his name was written below the chimp and the name "<u>Russell Whitner,</u> one of his checker buddies, below the orangutan. By golly, there was a remarkable similarity between these two close friends and their primate counter parts. His buddy had balding red hair and a round face, which fit the orangutan to a "T". On the other hand, Dad's dark hair, widow's peak, and elongated face made him clearly related to the chimp. Dad especially liked that picture because the smiling chimp had maneuvered himself into a winning position and the frowning orangutan was perplexed!

My last memory involved my bride and a visit to my home state of North Carolina. We had stopped for some refreshment at a country store, and lo and behold there was a monkey chained to a tree, with his owner near by. Of course I bought some peanuts to feed him, being careful to keep the bag way out of his reach. Much to our surprise, when Betty tried to give him a peanut he got excited and tried to attack her. The owner explained that the monkey was not a "him", but a "her", and that she liked men but detested women. To prove it, he invited me to step into the monkey's territory and pet her, which I did with impunity and pleasure. My poor bride couldn't get within ten feet without the monkey becoming mean. I'm afraid I rubbed it in by saying, " Hey, that monkey sure is a good judge of character!"

When we got to the pet store to buy our very own monkey, we chose a full-grown, female Capuchin, just like the organ grinders used to exploit. The store clerk taught me how to get the monkey in and out of her cage and we paid our fifty dollars. When we drove home there was a happy father, two delighted kids and a willing wife worrying about the caged monkey in the back of our station wagon!

For several days all went well as we got acquainted with "Marilyn Monmonk," as we had dubbed her. One day Marilyn was reluctant to re-enter her cage, and although I had taken the precaution to wear heavy gloves, she bit me hard on the thumb. She had previously nibbled my ears and neck a bit, but didn't draw blood. This time the blood came out freely, as I discovered once I got her back in the cage and took off the gloves to assess the damage. In fact, it was so great that I had to go to my doctor for shots and a big "soak" bandage. Next day at work I was constantly barraged with questions about my sore thumb; much to my consternation, no one would believe my story about being bitten by a monkey! Sometimes the truth is hard to swallow.

After a brief family pow-wow, we agreed to return Marilyn and swap her for a gentler breed. The clerk was very understanding and suggested a woolly monkey, because they never bite . The woolly was very young and cost a hundred bucks, so we had to shell out another fifty; but as things turned out she was worth it and then some. We named her "Cindy" because she was so dark, including her cute little face. Cindy proved to be a very loving and delightful pet, and the family had many happy hours with her. The girls were good caretakers and became little mothers to her, so perhaps I was more like a foster father than an uncle, but why quibble over terms?

However, when Cindy left a mess on the floor Betty was usually stuck with the clean-up detail, either because she knew how to clean the carpet or the rest of us were too "busy" to do the loathsome task.

One of Cindy's most endearing traits surfaced whenever I came home from work. If she was out of her cage, which she usually was at that time of day, she would emit a loud chirp and come running to me with outstretched arms, just as my girls had done when they were smaller. I would then pick her up and she would put her little arms around my neck, bury her little head in my shoulder, shake her head rapidly, and emit a delightful sound that I can only describe as rapid cooing. Having done that, Cindy would get down and I would collect my daily hugs and kisses from my darling daughters and my dear wife. Talk about feeling loved, I was the "King of the Mountain!"

Cindy loved to play outdoors as long as the weather cooperated, and occasionally she would climb a small tree and refuse to climb down. But when she saw me, she would come down and give me my hello hug. As I said earlier, monkeys are good judges of character!

The girls had full control after school and they spent many fun-filled hours with Cindy. Sometimes Betty and I would take Cindy into our bedroom and let her roam freely, but with the door shut. She loved to climb the drapes and swing around a bit. In fact, she damaged the drapes, and when Betty went to buy replacement ones she startled several clerks by asking for monkey-proof ones!

Cindy was also very smart. She soon learned that she could turn off the light by flicking the switch above the night table. It was her favorite trick, and Betty and I never failed to laugh as we turned it back on—over and over. Cindy was also smart enough to undo her cage latch, and one day when Betty returned home she found Cindy with a white face and the kitchen a mess. Cindy had investigated all of Betty's counter-top canisters, including one full of flour, and had spread the contents hither and yon, including on her little face and body. I never saw the mess because Betty had it cleaned up before I got home from work. Fortunately, Betty took it as an amusing incident and not as an unforgivable one, and we all had many laughs whenever she re-told it. A simple little lock prevented future escapades!

One day, Betty and the girls took Cindy to a zoo. Since we had acquired Cindy when she was very young she had very little experience with other animals. This became very evident when they approached the monkey cage. The monkeys stopped their activity and crowded close to the bars to see the monkey that had somehow gained its freedom. Poor little Cindy was scared to death of the strange creatures gaping at her, and clung to Betty like a frightened child. Betty swears to this day that Cindy believed that she was our child and not a monkey! In fact, Cindy was so frightened that she made a big mess on Betty's dress. It didn't faze her because we had long since learned that it was Cindy's most effective defensive maneuver.

One of the side effects of owning Cindy was that we got a reputation of being a somewhat eccentric family, or at least an extra-ordinary one. Our fame spread, and one day a kindred soul came to see Betty with her Gibbon Ape. I wasn't home at the time, but I can tell you that Betty was impressed with the ape's intelligence and training. It roamed the house freely and picked up all sorts of knickknacks, examined them carefully and put them back in place with zero damage. It even used our toilet properly and FLUSHED IT!

We were all protective of Cindy, and as it turned out we were too protective. We had placed her cage near a kitchen radiator to keep her warm and away from drafts. Unfortunately, this led to cage paralysis and Cindy could no longer walk, jump and run, but had to pull herself along with her arms. A few months later she died in Becky's arms and the whole family went into private mourning. We buried Cindy in our backyard and the girls put a little cross and flowers over the grave. In time, we overcame our grief.

A year or so later, another family with a monkey called us up with a proposition we couldn't refuse. They also had a woolly monkey, and we had swapped a few stories earlier. They invited us over for a drink and then outlined their offer. Business was going to take the whole family to South America for several years and they couldn't take their monkey. Worst yet, a relative who had promised to keep her had just backed out and their departure date was imminent. Their only recourse was to find a new owner or take her to a small zoo on Long Island, so would we please become the new owners? Of course we said yes, especially when they told us their monkey's name—"Mindy". Our friends' relief was exceeded only by our girls' joy.

Mindy proved to be an excellent replacement for our beloved Cindy, and we had many happy hours with her. Our relationship terminated when I got a two-year field assignment in California and we decided that we shouldn't take her with us.

We weren't able to find her a home, so we took her to the zoo after all. But we were glad that we had delayed that second choice for a year or two. When we returned from California the girls had discovered boys and a new monkey was not in our future.

But ahhh, what fond memories still linger in all our minds!

1970-80

CONNORS VS PANETTA

Recently, I was browsing through an old issue of <u>Tennis Magazine</u> and wondered why I had saved it. Then I came upon <u>Jimmy Connor's</u> article about the lessons he had learned way back in 1976 during a match with <u>Adriana Panetta</u>. My wife and I had seen that match, and the article brought to memory an usual experience. I would like to share it with Jimmy and his many fans in the form of a letter to Jimmy.

OK Jimmy, your '1976 come from behind" victory over Adriana Panetta at the U.S. Open taught you a valuable lesson. Thanks for sharing it with us hackers. But did you ever consider the other side of the coin—the lessons <u>we</u> learned by watching that match? Well, here's a first hand account of one fan's view and some surprising lessons he learned:

My wife <u>Betty</u> and I took our seats in the stadium in eager anticipation of a great match—and we weren't disappointed. You were my favorite player because of your great skill, your colorful personality and your fighting heart. I overlooked your occasional lapses of sportsmanship, but Betty didn't. She wouldn't even applaud your best shots, let alone cheer them. So we were an odd couple all through that match because I not only applauded loudly, but sometimes yelled my approval and support when the point was over.

Around the third game of the first set, a very attractive young woman about half my age, took the seat beside me. Her escort was in the seat next to her. I gave them a friendly hello and concentrated on the game. It didn't take long for us to see that there were two odd couples at the match—she was a supporter and her escort wasn't! She commented on it during a change over: "I see you are one of Jimmy's fans."

"Yes, I am," I replied, "He's my favorite."

"Mine too, he's the greatest!"

"You'll get no argument from me."

During the rest of the match we formed a local two-person cheering section.

During changeovers we maintained a lively conversation on why we liked you so much. At one point I said, "My wife doesn't like him—she can't stand it when he acts like a spoiled brat."

"Neither can he," she pointed to her escort.

"How do you feel about that?" I asked.

"Oh, I take the small amount of bad with the huge amount of good," she replied. "I guess his mother or his manager spoiled him a bit."

"I agree. Also, think of the pressure of finding yourself wealthy and world famous at his tender age. Then imagine the stress of constantly trying to stay at the top of the heap. Why if Jimmy has one bad day and his opponent has one great day, he could be knocked out of any tournament."

She agreed completely. Her escort and my wife either didn't hear our conversation or ignored it.

As the match progressed to the fifth set, it began to look like my "bad day, great day" scenario was going to come true. As I remember it, Panetta led by 5 to 3 in the 5th, and was about to serve for the match. My attractive new friend and I both got really worried.

"Come on Jimmy," we yelled, "you can beat him!" Your other friends were echoing similar sentiments.

I don't know whether we helped or not. Perhaps you dipped into that tremendous championship reserve you have. Perhaps that "I hate to lose" feeling took over. All I know is that I saw you slap your buns and get a look of sheer determination on your face.

Panatta's first serve would have been an ace to anyone but a determined Jimmy Connors. It pulled you way out of the court, but somehow you not only got to it, but hit a backhand winner down the line and outside the net post. Love 15! You shook your fist in the air in your inimitable style and Panetta looked shocked. The stadium went wild with cheers. My attractive friend and I jumped to our feet, as did many others. The stands quieted down to a whisper, as Panetta got ready for his next serve. It was not as strong, but still good and the two of you rallied until you found an opening and hit another winner. Love 30! Panetta looked really worried, you looked super charged and the fans went wild. Everyone sensed that the turning point had arrived and that you would win.

You know the rest score wise, but you failed to comment on the effect you had on the crowd, or our effect on you. I have never seen such a strong reaction from fans, nor heard such a contrast in decibels—from a hush just below a whisper when one of you started to serve; to excited 'ohs and ahs[1] when one of you made a good shot or spectacular save; to thunderous applause and cheers when you hit a winner !

Oh, there were a few glum fans, like Betty and the young woman's escort, but mostly the whole stadium was in your corner; and you and Panetta knew it. Your come back was spectacular and complete. From 5-3 down in the fifth set (with Panetta serving) to a 7-5 victory. Every point was bitterly contested by Panetta, but what could the poor guy do against your brilliant shots, your awesome determination and the lopsided fan support. I had a flicker of compassion for him, but it was quickly subdued each time you came closer to victory.

Finally it was over—game, set, match, and you won! Along with thousands of other fans, I leapt to my feet to cheer. My attractive friend not only jumped up, but she did a surprising thing—she threw her arms around me, hugged me hard and kissed me on the lips! It was so sudden and spontaneous that neither her escort nor my wife had time to protest. My reaction was surprise and slight embarrassment, but certainly not protest.

I never saw her again, but I am happy to report that my wife gained a healthy image of her aging husband's ability to appeal to young women. So as a fan, I did learn some different lessons:

o A real champion can raise the level of his game way above his opponent's—and Jimmy, in my book you are one of the all time great champions.

o Having the fans in your corner must help—even if it didn't affect you, it visibly affected Panetta.

o Sitting by an attractive fan that roots the way you do can have some surprising and pleasant results.

So Jimmy, thanks for the many great matches you have given the world, especially the one I just described. You and Panetta did all the work, you won another victory, and I had all the fun!

MY STROKE - LUCK OR BLESSING?

On August 20, 1977, I had a Cerebral Vascular Accident - commonly called a stroke. Many people have experienced strokes and have written books and articles describing them, so it is with some hesitation that I write about my own experiences. However, I have been encouraged to do so by Dr. David Schrum, in view of an unusual occurrence during the first 18 hours following my attack.

My problem occurred during a family reunion in the mountains of Western North Carolina. About two-dozen relatives had gathered at the home of my sister and brother-in-law, and we had just finished a delicious picnic dinner on the lawn. I was sitting near my sister, Ruth, and two aunts, Irene and Mary. We were part of a large circle of multiple conversations taking place after dinner. I first became aware that something was amiss when my right arm suddenly went limp and motionless. As I massaged it with my left hand, I was aware that my sister was moving her lips, but no sound reached my ears. I sat perplexed for perhaps 20 or 30 seconds, sorting out my symptoms in my mind, after which I said, somewhat urgently, "Ruth, something's wrong with me; something's wrong!"

Once she decided I was serious (I have a reputation for kidding around with my family) she called my wife, <u>Betty</u>, who came to me from another group, bringing my cousin, Dr. David Schrum, and his son-in-law, <u>Gary</u> Riggs. Gary is also an M.D., currently an intern in Psychiatry, so I guess this was certainly a <u>lucky</u> aspect of my stroke - having two doctors in attendance immediately!

By the time they reached me my right arm was no longer limp and seemed fairly normal, although I massaged it a bit more to reassure myself. David and Gary and several of the men lifted me from my chair and took me to a lawn chaise where I was able to lie down. David gave me a pill, (which I later discovered was Valium) and he told me to lie still while he gave me some reassuring words.

There was no feeling of pain or panic in me, although I realized something serious was happening. I remember I was aware that a hush had come over the assembled relatives and that I felt slightly annoyed that I was interrupting the festivities, and that something was happening to me so early in my vacation. I lay quietly for 10 or 15 minutes when I heard a vehicle arrive in the road and two attendants and David transferred me to a stretcher, and then placed me in an ambulance.

David and one attendant rode with me, and David started explaining what he thought had happened. His explanation ran something like this: "You have probably had a vascular spasm which temporarily blocked the blood flow to part of your brain. You seem to be doing O.K. but it is best to get you to the hospital for an examination and any treatment you may need. I suspect this came on you because of a number of factors - your long drive to North Carolina (about 800 miles in 2 days); the strain caused by your early retirement plans; your concern for your mother during the drive this morning (approximately 90 miles from the Piedmont to the mountains); the excitement of seeing so many relatives; and even the altitude change, which could slightly decrease the oxygen supply to the brain."

As I reflected on this later, I mentally added a few more factors - the lack of sleep the previous night (we had stayed at a motel with a lighted tennis court and had played until after 12 and then Betty and I got up about 7 A.M. to practice for 45 minutes or so; my strained relations with one of my brothers over an eleven year debt he had only partly repaid; and over-indulgence at the picnic.

The over-indulgence was of particular concern, since my wife and I had embarked four months earlier on a new diet plan with our doctor's approval. The diet followed the recommendation of <u>Nathan Pritikin</u> and others in their book "Live Longer Now", and was designed to check, or possibly reverse, arteriosclerosis in one's cardiovascular system. The irony of becoming a stroke victim four months after I had taken steps to decrease the risk of heart attack and stroke weighed heavily on my mind during the first few days of my stroke and I was especially concerned that my over-indulgence in desserts (I had sampled three or four of the big assortment available at the picnic) may have somehow or other "shocked my system."

Upon our arrival at the hospital, I was taken to the emergency room and met by Dr. James Keeley, who examined me and asked a number of questions. Normally I could have answered them but was unable to because the stroke had affected my speech. Fortunately, my wife and David knew enough about my general health to answer most of his questions, and I responded with signs and garbled words to questions about my present symptoms.

I was then taken to a room, given some aspirin (which I later learned was an anticoagulant) and subsequently put on a "starvation" diet of fruit juice, bouillon, and Jell-O. An EKG was also taken, along with some blood and urine samples for analysis.

Later in the afternoon, Betty and David were allowed to visit me, and at this time the unusual aspects of my stroke occurred. Before leaving on vacation, I had gotten perhaps half way through a book a friend, Vinny Rau, had recommended to me called "They Speak in Other Tongues" by John Sherrill. My attitude toward the book was, to say the least, skeptical, as I had been trained in Mechanical and Aeronautical Engineering, having acquired a Bachelor's degree in the former and a Masters in the latter. My 37 years as an engineer and manager with the Grumman Aerospace Corporation, including 7 years in responsible positions on the Lunar Module Program, had conditioned me to look for a physical explanation for any unusual occurrences. On the other hand, the success we had in landing the astronauts on the moon with our LM had conditioned me to believe that some "impossible" looking tasks were really possible.

In any event, it suddenly occurred to me while lying in the hospital bed that I could speak in "tongues", and I announced in garbled English that I could do so. I then proceeded to pour out a pattern of speech completely foreign to me but with a flow, rhythm and eloquence that I had never been able to do before. My wife later told me it sounded like Danny Kaye's impression of a foreign language. Mine had a singsong quality, which reminded her of a South Sea Island dialect, and, unlike Danny's impressions, mine had no words that even sounded like English. David's comment when he perceived that I thought I was speaking in "tongues" was, "Go ahead - you seem to be enjoying it and it won't hurt you."

As I poured out more and more of the strange language (or gibberish) I had a feeling that I can only describe as somewhere between euphoria and rapture. I was now speaking loudly enough to make my wife close the door to avoid disturbing other patients, and the feeling was so intense I later broke into a song in tongues, composing words and music as *I* went along.

I doubt that there was much artistic merit in them, but David's early comment that "I seemed to be enjoying it" was on the mark!

After my visitors had left for the day, I spent a restful night in the hospital. The rounds of the nurses who checked my condition interrupted my sleep once or twice, but I easily fell back asleep.

The next morning my wife visited me again and was present when Dr. Keeley came in. She had observed that my speech was much improved and Dr. Keeley was surprised and pleased at the rapid progress I had made. In fact, he said that my recovery was so rapid that he was inclined to think I had a vascular spasm, and that he wouldn't classify it even as a mini-stroke. Since this coincided with David's earlier diagnosis, I thought very little about it except that my luck was holding up. Incidentally, although I tried to speak in tongues, I was unable to, having neither the desire nor capability to do so.

I was kept in the hospital for another day, put on a regular diet, and kept under observation to make sure everything was O.K. On August 22, my wife's birthday, I was discharged around noon and went directly to my sister's home. I had been told by Dr. Keeley to rest there for a few days, continue to take 2 aspirin a day, and to let my wife do the driving back to Long Island, where I should go to a neurologist for tests the small North Carolina hospital was not equipped to make.

I followed the doctor's orders carefully and got a real good rest at my sister's for 3 days. Betty then drove leisurely back to Long Island, taking 3 days for what would ordinarily have been a 1-½ *or* 2 day journey.

After returning home, I called <u>Dr. Gerald Schroeder</u>, a leading neurologist in the community and an occasional tennis partner. He gave me further instructions and set up an appointment for an office examination, followed by an Rx for Papaverine, (a blood vessel dilator), and a series of tests - EEC, head X-ray, and a CAT scan. I later learned that CAT stood for "Computerized axial tomograph" and was a recent high technology tool that permits doctors to assemble X-ray mosaics of a complete cross-section of any part of the body.

The CAT scan was particularly interesting to me as I was able to review the pictures with the Radiologist, <u>Dr. Liebeskind</u>, on the cathode ray screen. He started at the base of my brain and projected the cross-section patterns approximately every 3/4 of an inch until he reached the top of my brain. At first he saw nothing and commented that everything looked fine. Then, at about the fourth or fifth projection he said, "Uh-oh, I think we have found something here." It was an anomaly, which I estimated to be 2" long, and about 3/4" wide at its maximum. As I recall, traces could be seen in subsequent cross-sections, so it must have been about 3/4" or so thick.

He commented that it was a clear indication of a stroke and appeared to be typical of one about two weeks old. It was a lighter shade than the gray shading of the brain tissue that I saw projected, but not as light as the skull bone which showed up as almost white. I asked him what caused it and he said, "You have been eating the wrong foods most of your life." I then told him about my new "Live Longer Now" diet, explaining that it was supposed to reduce the bacterial plaque that clogs the arteries and leads to stroke, heart attack, etc. His comment then was, "You should have started it much earlier, because the conditions that cause stroke accumulate over many years."

After Dr. Schroeder had reviewed the various test results he told me that I had definitely suffered a mild stroke caused by lack of oxygen to that part of the brain. He attributed it to a restricted blood flow, caused by a temporary thrombosis (clot) or the arteriosclerosis people get as they grow older. In answer to my questions on the new diet, he tended to agree with Dr. Liebeskind that I should have started it earlier. However, he was doubtful that it or my over-indulgence at the picnic contributed to the stroke. In fact, he felt that my weight loss and better eating habits may have lessened the severity of my stroke and could be useful in preventing another one. He advised me to hold my weight at around 170 pounds (it was 192 when I started the diet in April). He also said that there was no evidence that diet could reverse atherosclerosis or arteriosclerosis, but that it could help control further build-up.

I was given a post-stroke check up by my regular doctor, Delaney Glenn on October 15, 1977 and found to be in good shape except for a poor pulse indication in my left carotid artery, which he wanted to discuss with Dr. Schroeder. During this visit and a previous telephone conversation (after he had received the reports from Dr. Keeley and Dr. Schroeder) he relieved my concern over the diet as a causative factor by saying that the literature and his own experience tend to show that it was more likely to have lessened the severity than to have caused it in the first place.

After my discharge from the hospital, I was restricted from any physical exertion except slow walks and was not allowed to return to work for about four weeks. During this period I read several books on stroke and finished "They Speak In Other Tongues." Several points made by John Sherrill in the latter, that had particular significance to me, were:

-- The person speaking in tongues and others around him do not understand it and consider it gibberish.

-- St. Paul made reference to this fact and also to the fact that people sing in tongues.

-- Occasionally, someone can understand the "language" of the tongues and recognize it as his/her native language or one s/he studied. Others claim to be able to interpret the "Holy Spirit" present when someone speaks in tongues.

-- Frequently, a healing process accompanies, or follows, speaking in tongues.

-- There is a new movement in the world called the "Charismatic Movement", and there are a growing number of "miraculous" healings.

As I pieced out the evidence I began to wonder if maybe - just maybe - the Holy Spirit had visited me. My rationale was as follows:

-- During the afternoon of my stroke I spoke and sang in a strange language.

-- The experience created a feeling somewhere between euphoria and rapture,

--I regained my ability to speak in English the next morning, but was unable to speak in "tongues" as I had 12 hours earlier.

--The doctor was surprised at my quick recovery.

-- I wondered if some sort of healing <u>had</u> taken place that was unusual. Also, what did it mean in my life - a warning to watch my health; or perhaps that more was expected and even planned for me? Had my stroke been a "blessing?"

But then the pragmatic engineer in me took over and I conceived the following possible explanation:

-- I spoke English just after the stroke;

--My subconscious mind recalled the book "They Speak in Other Tongues"

-- I had experienced frustration because I was unable to speak in Englsh and shifted into a by-pass mode, eliminating the frustration in favor of a "stream of consciousness" of whatever came to my mind,

-- The by-pass mode triggered a psychosomatic healing process, or alternatively the stroke area had barely touched my speech center and a good night's rest was all I needed.

This line of reasoning led me to a feeling that maybe I was just lucky and that I should accept the mildness of the stroke as a warning to be more careful of my health in the future.

So now I was faced with a dilemma. My pragmatic nature told me to accept the last explanation; undoubtedly I would find that medical science some day or maybe even now, would be able to offer a rational explanation for the events. On the other hand, my spiritual nature and my past association with Methodist and Presbyterian churches made me reluctant to put aside the possibility that a spiritual blessing had been given to me. Should I acknowledge it somehow or other? Should I try to discover what it meant to my future life? Was it a sign that God had plans for me to do something meaningful after my early retirement in November 1977? These and many other questions ran through my mind, and I kept sorting out the various possibilities in an attempt to find an answer.

One night this answer came to me. Why not adopt a modification of the American code of justice, which says a person is innocent until proven guilty beyond a reasonable doubt. In this case, I decided to assume that the Holy Spirit had intervened directly and blessed me. Furthermore, I decided to leave it to medical science to prove beyond a reasonable doubt that my speaking in tongues and the rapid healing were occurrences that could be explained rationally.

This conflict between "Luck" and "Blessing, is the reason I decided to write about my experience. However, I am rooting for my quick recovery to be classified as a BLESSING from the HOLY SPIRIT!

1980-90

BROOM ART

Grandparents usually teach new things to their grandchildren/ but recently the process was reversed. My five-year-old granddaughter, <u>Hannah</u>, taught me a new art form, which I call "Broom Art".

Here's how it happened:

We were living in Dover, NH, and our Grandkids and their <u>Parents</u> were visiting us from California. One summer afternoon after it rained, I took Hannah and her two year old brother, <u>Grady</u>, to a nearby paved tennis court to get it ready for the next morning's game. There were a dozen or so puddles of water scattered over the surface, and I was using my straw broom to thin them out to dry. By tackling the deepest ones first, I hoped to slow the children's tendency to splash in the puddles with their shoes on.

Naturally, Hannah wanted to help. It wasn't long before she noticed that the broom made large wet brush strokes and --voila--Broom Art was invented.

First, she drew a big heart about six feet by six feet. Next, she found an oblong puddle, and, by using it as a body, she added six broom strokes and proudly announced: "Look, Granddad, here's a big spider!"

By this time my grandson said, "Grady, too, Grady too--RIGHT NOW!"

I persuaded Hannah to let her little brother try to make his own broom art. With every stroke he said, "Look at that, look at that!" Obviously, he took great pride in his artistic ability.

With a little imagination, Hannah and I could see an object when he finished.

" Oh, Grady," she exclaimed, " that looks like an airplane."

On another one, I said, " Look, Grady, that looks like a doggie's face— see, here's his eye, here's his mouth, and here's his ear!" Grady was pleased, and rewarded us with his big, contagious smile.

They continued for another fifteen minutes or so, taking turns at my request. They even let me make a whale, but that was all. Soon all the puddles were gone, and I felt a bit like Tom Sawyer must have felt when he got the other kids to whitewash his fence.

When the warm July sun started to evaporate the spider's legs and other thin broom strokes, we were all a bit sad; but we had enjoyed our fun and went back to the house contented.

Each of us was happy with our individual accomplishments: o Hannah, because she had invented a new art form, o Grady, because he quickly became a happy, abstract master, o Granddad, because his persistence in wooing their 'Nana" forty-five years ago made it all possible.

As we walked back to the house, two questions clouded my mind: Will the creative juices continue to flow in these two precious children, until they make worthwhile contributions to mankind?

Or, will the juices evaporate into thin air, as did the spider's legs, under the hot sun of rote learning and adult discipline?

Knowing their parents, I think I have the answer in their case. I pose the questions so that ALL parents, teachers, and grandparents will recognize the wonderful opportunity (and responsibility) they have in developing creativity in our children..

Folks, oil those little pumps—keep the creative juices flowing!

IMPRESSIONISTIC INCIDENT

Works of art can be controversial. That is hardly earth-shattering news, but the way in which controversy arises can be a complete surprise. At least it was for me during a recent visit to the Currier Museum in Manchester, N.H.
I was with a tour group of senior citizens and was enjoying the fine collection of this first rate regional museum. As usual, I had wandered away from the group and the lecturer. I seem to have a different inner clock at such events. Sometimes I linger longer than the others and must catch up, but usually I spot something ahead and leave them to see it.

At any rate, I had finished one room a bit ahead of the group and had drifted into the next room, a large colorful painting caught my eye and I walked over to inspect it more closely. It was by the American artist, _Childe Hassam_. What a funny name, I thought; I bet I could use it in a pun. But the painting wasn't funny--it was impressive.

The painting featured a woman standing in front of a sunlit window near a fish bowl. The fish were shimmering iridescently in the water. My eyes focused on the beautiful pastel colors used through out the painting--the woman's dress, the fish, the drapes, and the flowers. I concluded that it was a provocative piece of impressionistic art.

As I left the painting I noticed a plump, pleasant-looking young person looking at the Hassam from a distance of about 25 feet. I thought it was a young man, but it could have been a young woman in slacks. What really caught my attention was the intensity of the viewing and the big smile. It was pleasant to see someone so caught up in a work of art--or at least that was my first impression.

As I wandered around the room looking at other works, I noticed that the young person hadn't moved. Furthermore, the smile seemed to grow bigger and bigger, I became intrigued by such a strong reaction to a work of art, so I approached the person with a friendly "Do you like that painting?"

The response was a bit surprising, but not menacing. "Do you like it?" s/he asked,

"Yes I do."

"What do you like about it?" s/he persisted,

"Oh, a lot of things—the colors, the texture, the composition, the subject matter... " My words were spoken slowly and thoughtfully, "Why do you like the composition?" s/he demanded in a shrill voice.

About this time I became aware that I wasn't getting any answers and that the voice was unisex—that is, it was high for a man but low for a woman. The voice compounded my initial confusion as to whether I was talking with a feminine man or a masculine woman. To make matters worse, s/he had hair that looked short for a woman but long for a man. Even the breast gave no clue due to its plumpness. The lack of sex identity was subliminal. The thing that penetrated my conscious mind was that s/he was ASKING ALL THE QUESTIONS, and rather rudely at that.

So I said," I believe I asked you a question first-- would you mind answering it?" Again my voice was pleasant and friendly, so I was really surprised to hear a very belligerent, "Who are YOU?" It was almost a snarl— definitely unfriendly,

I was so taken aback that all I could think to say was, "I'm sorry if I disturbed you--have a good day!" I then walked away and immediately regretted it. You handled that poorly, I chided myself.

Why didn't you take a bit more time and come up with a better reply? (It seems to be a human weakness to think of the right thing to say AFTER the opportunity has passed—and boy, am I human.) I wondered about the young person's impression of the incident and me.

The rest of the afternoon my viewing was clouded by the insistent demand of my mind to think of a better response to the question: "Who are YOU? Here are some of the responses I could have made if only I had stalled for time or been quicker witted:

o (Flippant) Don't you recognize me?--I'm your guardian angel! I have protected you all your life, but I guess you don't need me anymore. I think I'll let you handle things alone from now on, GOOD LUCK!

o (Sarcastic) Why I'm the damn fool that thought I could be friendly with you. Sorry for my big mistake!

o (Devious) Oh, I'm sorry, I should have introduced myself, I'm Childe Hassan Jr., the artist's son, I just thought it would be fun to get your reaction to my father's art.

o (Saintly) I'm a child of God trying to communicate with another child of God, or at least you look like a child of God--are you?

o (Counterattacking) Why are you so belligerent? I'm just trying to have a friendly conversation and you act as if I were trying to rob you of something valuable. Are your opinions THAT valuable?

o (Sinister) You act as if I'm the Devil. Take care how you answer, because the Devil is easily provoked!

o (Inquisitive) Are you always so unfriendly and rude, or are you having a bad day?

o (Humorous) Who do I HAVE TO BE to get a friendly and intelligent reply from you?

o (Literal) I'm Macon Epps from Dover, N.H. What's your name?

o (Naive), you look like a nice person— I'm a bit confused as to why you are reacting so negatively to my friendly question. Could you help me overcome my confusion?

o (Assertive) I'm the guy who needs to have my friendly questions answered—RIGHT NOW!

o (Brief) I'm gone,

Given more time, I could probably think of a few more answers. Obviously, there are no right or wrong ones. No one knows what reaction each answer would have elicited from the young person, because the opportunity for dialogue has passed. S/he may have laughed or been amused by some answers and become friendly. Others may have provoked a strong or even violent reaction, I might have left with a bloody nose, or at least a more bruised ego.

Perhaps my first answer was the prudent one, First impulses often are, as anyone who plays Trivial Pursuit can testify. One thing I do know; Hassam's painting provoked a surprisingly unfavorable last impression of the young person. S/he responded to my friendly overtures in an unfriendly, ungracious and downright rude manner to a person old enough to be his/her grandfather. I suppose s/he had a bad impression of me. Probably thought I was a nosey old geezer for interrupting his/her reverie and misunderstood my friendly intentions completely. Maybe it was the generation gap we used to hear so much about.

I wonder if Childe Hassam ever envisioned this sort of incident, or such unfavorable "impressions", when he was working on that painting?

Perhaps my reply should have been:

"My name's Sam Smith—Lawdy me <u>Childe, HasSam</u> Smith's questions upset you?"

MUGGING TO A HUGGING

On Saturday, December 12, 1981, I had two unusual Big Apple experiences. The first was a three-day, human-potential workshop called "Actualizations". It was held at the Parsons School of Design near 7th Avenue and 41st street. The leaders explored personal problems and interpersonal relations in a way that directly helped participants to solve current problems. The Saturday night session was a warm, friendly party, with many interesting, interactive games.

As I left the party for a Fifth Avenue bus at one a.m., I was glowing with positive feelings and good will toward all mankind. Little did I suspect that the lessons of the workshop would be tested so soon, but they were.

Busses were rare at that hour, and so were taxis, so I contemplated walking downtown to my weekend abode on 9th street, where my <u>wife</u> was visiting our daughter's mother-in-law. Just before starting, two young men of a minority race walked by. One continued walking, but the 6'3" one said, "What's your problem?"

"I have no problem," I replied. "I just had a beautiful evening."

He then walked nearer and said, "You have a problem now-- give me all your money!"

For some unknown reason, I had no fear. Perhaps it was the impact of the workshop; perhaps it was residual past advice I had absorbed from my spiritual leaders, especially missionaries I had met when I was Chairman of the Mission Council. Several of them had told me that they had overcome dangerous encounters with individuals, and even mobs, by being friendly, showing no fear, and appealing to the dangerous person's good side. All I know is that I smiled at him, placed my hand gently on his shoulder, and said, "You don't want to do that!"

"Yes I do," he barked. "My buddy has a gun!" "Hey, come over here," he shouted to the shorter man who was about 40 feet away.

I decided that I had a little discussion time before I would hand over my money, so I said, "No, you don't want to do that. You're too nice a person to do that to someone my age. I'm a retired man and old enough to be your father."

As his friend with the gun ambled over, the tall one said, "I like the way you're handling this-- I respect you for it."

"I respect you too," I responded. "I believe you're a good person. You know, I hugged a young man like you at the meeting I just left."

The shorter man had now reached me, but there was no gun in sight. He reached under my overcoat to get my wallet, but the tall one chided him, "Don't do that. This man has my respect and we shouldn't take money from some one his age. I'll give you a couple of bucks if you need 'em."

He then proceeded to embrace me and I him. He then asked the shorter man to do likewise, but he offered me a puff of his "joint". Before I could decline, the tall one said, "No, no, don't give him that-- give him a hug!" This he proceeded to do and I returned it. We then chatted a bit and I asked if they had jobs. Neither one did, so I said, " I hope you can find work-- that might be the answer." They seemed to agree, and the tall one asked me how far I had to go.

When I told him that I might have to walk to 9th street because of the late hour, he expressed concern:

"I wish we could walk with you to protect you-- someone else may jump you-- but we've gotta get home." We parted with vigorous handshakes, and I started my lonesome walk downtown. Eight blocks later, at 33rd street, I finally got a cab and just had to tell the driver of my experience. He was amazed and told me how lucky I was. When I arrived safely at 1:45 a.m., my wife was sound asleep, so I decided not to tell my experience until the workshop ended the next afternoon.

Sleep was delayed, because these thoughts crept through my mind: 'Somewhere in the great city of New York, two young men who made a big, positive impact on my life have probably arrived home. They reaffirmed that most people are basically decent and intelligent. They also confirmed the workshop's teachings and the missionaries' lessons that we can solve tough situations if we are willing to communicate and take a few risks.'

I realize that the risks I took could have turned out badly. I could have lost all my money, been beaten up, even killed. So I'm thankful that their instincts were good and that we made contact as humans and not jungle beasts.

Before I fell asleep, my fervent wish was this: 'I hope I made a good impact on their lives and that they will seek and find work. Once they do, I hope they will make their mark in a world that needs all the help it can get!'

L. Macon Epps (Revised from the original on 2/18/04)

Note: This is a true experience, and the quotes are verbatim because I wrote them down the next day, while my memory was fresh. A slightly different version was published in the 12/24 /81 issue of Newsday, Long Island's leading newspaper, but they left out the "minority race" words. The aftermath of my experience was almost as interesting as the actual "mugging turned to hugging".

For example, when I told my story to the Actualization group the next day, I received the only standing ovation of my life. Later on, a NYPD officer told me he had been on the force for 20 years and had never heard of a mugging turning out that way. Then there was a strange co-incidence when a friend who lived in California accidentally read about it when his mother sent a clipping from Newsday, with my story intact on the back. He thought I was foolish to take such a chance.

When my wife told people at our church about it, I was able to share it with many other members, as I am doing now. I hope it will be helpful to anyone who encounters a dangerous situation! © 2009 L. Macon Epps

NO BUGS!

I finally found it—a semi-tropical resort with NO BUGS! Hard to believe isn't it? But I swear by my tourist nametag, flight bag and camera that it is absolutely true. There are no gnats to swat, no mosquitoes to slap, no flies to brush away, no ants to step on, no moths to flicker around lights, and no creepy, crawly bugs to squash! Here's a hint—there aren't even any las cucarachas to trap.

If you have ever been to a semi-tropical resort you know how attractive the folders make them--palm trees, gentle trade winds, tropical fruit piled high, spectacular shorelines, craggy mountains, splendid waterfalls, championship golf courses, lighted tennis courts, luxurious swimming pools, fantastic restaurants and congenial people. Now all of those things are generally true, but have you ever noticed that the folder-people look more like movie stars than tourists? Not a pound of fat, no gray hair or bald spots, no flabby thighs--just pure, unadulterated perfection!

But when you get to the usual resort, all eager and excited after a long flight and perhaps too many drinks, what do you find? You guessed it; the beautiful people of the brochures left last week and you are greeted by a lot of BUGS! And not the usual bugs named above, but some you never even suspected—huge ants that bite like the devil, big hairy-legged spiders, moths as big as bats and a wide assortment of indoor and outdoor creepy, crawly ones. (Great for entomologists, but bad for vacationers.)

To make matters worse (the brochures call it colorful) there are human bugs—street vendors that won't let you go until you buy a trinket, even though you just glanced at it for a millisecond; street urchins that bug you for money--and then call you °cheapskate" when you finally run out of coins; and waiters that take forever to serve you the wrong order–and forever and a day to bring your bill. (I keep planning to walk out after unreasonably long waits, but my wife and friends won't cooperate.)

So far, I have not found any of the third kind of bug at a tropical resort—that is, eavesdropping bugs. Once on a trip to the Soviet Union I suspected they were there but didn't spot any. But the Soviet Union is hardly a semi-tropical resort—interesting, yes, resort no.

The resort I found didn't even have very many of the most common resort bugs—the microscopic ones that get your system out of kilter and leave you weak and sometimes feverish. There was only one 24-hour period during my 14-day stay that I felt a little queasy, but it didn't keep me from tennis--I just played poorly.

The people were friendly and the sales clerks were very helpful and not pushy. Oh, they looked a bit disappointed when I didn't buy the sweater I tried on, but they were gracious and usually said *adios". (Hint) Even at the Arab market, (Hint, hint) the man we dealt with spoke perfect English, smiled and shook our hands when he learned we were Americans, and finally sold my wife a beautiful malachite necklace "below his cost".

As to street urchins, we saw none! No one approached us for a hand out and that was a pleasant surprise. Some of the waiters were much too slow to suit my taste, but they always got the order right and spoke enough English to communicate. We had dinner at a casino one night, and I was lucky enough to net about 1500 pesetas (about $14), Not bad for an evening of fun, especially for a 25-peseta slot machine gambler like me.

Of course there were plenty of gray-haired, bald, flabby, even fat people around the pools, but the tennis group was pretty trim and the visiting soccer team was very trim—but messy. Our apartamento was very comfortable but hardly a decorator's dream. The view of the pounding surf and the craggy cliffs from our bedroom, living room and balcony was superb and all the decor we needed. The soothing sound of the surf lulled us into a deep sleep every night and my wife and I were delighted to be right on the ocean.

The kitchen and open walkway to the elevators looked up at 12,000 foot, snow-covered mountains. Although clouds frequently obscured them, we saw enough of them to drool in anticipation over a forthcoming day trip to Mt. Teide. What a delight that was. On the way up and down the narrow, winding, unprotected, steep roads we admired the skill of our driver and silently prayed that he wouldn't lose it—or us! We passed banana plantations (level 1), citrus groves (level 2), peach, apricot and apple groves (level 3), pine and fir forests (level 4) and finally a snow-covered volcanic crater, capped by Mt. Teide, also snow-capped (level 5),

We thus saw five climate zones in a few hours. Later we went to the southern part of the crater, which was about 13 miles across, and found a most interesting, desert-1ike landscape with fantastic rock formations and spectacular cliffs. That region gave us a SIXTH climate and was the place where "The Planet of the Apes," and its sequels were filmed, so you may have seen it at the flicks.

If you haven't guessed where this fascinating place is, here's a final hint: We didn't see any small yellow birds that went tweet-tweet, but we did see and hear lots of dogs. In fact, it got its name from the Latin "Insula Canaria." (Islands of Dogs.) Yes, it was the Canary Islands, a Spanish possession about 70 miles west of Africa and geographically a part of it. Our island was Tenerife and our hotel, The Marltime, was near Puerto de la Cruz, a charming small city on the west coast. Our two-week stay was delightful, made even more so by the presence of three other couples—long-standing friends and charter members of our old Thursday night paddle tennis group. Some of us had moved away from our mutual, working-year hometown of Huntington, N.Y., so it was a mini-reunion. Our friends were <u>Sam</u> and <u>Connie Rogers</u>; <u>Brand</u> and <u>Ann Wehle</u>, and <u>Ray and Barbara Weeks</u>.

But why were there NO BUGS on this fascinating island when they seem to abound at other semi-tropical resorts? Well, according to our genial guide, Jose, the island of Tenerife is of volcanic origin and is very porous. Therefore, there are no rivers, no lakes and no streams to support an insect population. And it is not only porous, but too hilly to have stagnant ponds and pools as breeding grounds. So voila--NO BUGS!! However, no bugs mean very few birds— not even canaries. What would they eat?

As to the lack of the other types of bugs, all I can say is this: the main industry is tourism; it is a prosperous island; and the people are smart enough to discourage ANY type of bug that will damage a good thing.

When you are having fun, two weeks pass quickly. As I write these thoughts down we are winging our way back home to New York, Iowa and New Hampshire via Iberia Airlines and its connections. Being from the first primary state (N.H.) and since the political season is in full swing, I have just taken a poll of our small group. We can't agree on our choice for president,

but we are unanimous about our trip:
    TENERIFE, YOU'RE TERRIFICK!

SMOKE

Ah! I can take a short nap. My wife, <u>Betty</u>, and her cousin, <u>Joyce Gardiner</u>, have gone shopping. That usually takes at least two hours. Joyce's husband, <u>Dan</u>, has used the other car to do some errands and meet someone at the Chappaqua, N.Y. railroad station. That should be good for at least an hour—plenty of time for my nap.

<u>Sarge</u>, <u>Michael</u> and <u>Meg</u>, the Gardiner's kids, are watching T.V. in their den; Sarge is in his early teens so I figure he can supervise his younger half siblings. With luck, I can sack out in peace and recover from the rugged platform tennis we played before lunch. I take off my shoes and lie down on the guest bed. Sleep comes fast, as it usually does for those with a clear conscience. About thirty minutes into my nap I am rudely awakened.

Sarge knocks loudly on my door and in an excited voice cries, "Uncle Macon, come down stairs--the fireplace is smoking!" I jump up and run down the stairs in my stockings, with Sarge just ahead. When we get to the living room it's starting to fill up with heavy smoke. Sarge begins apologizing for making a fire without his father—apparently it's the first time he tried it alone.

"Did you open the damper?" I ask as we approach closer.

"Gosh, I guess I forgot—I don't even know where it is," he replies.

As luck would have it, the fire is doing pretty well without a draft. In fact, it's too hot to use my hand to open the damper, so I grab a poker. After a little probing up the chimney, I finally get it open.

"There," I say, "that'll stop any more smoke from coming in— now all we have to do is get rid of the smoke that's in here—We'd better open all the windows!"

Apparently the T.V. action isn't as exciting as the L.R. action because Michael and Meg join us—they even help open the windows. The smoke starts to dissipate, but progress is barely perceptible.

"Do you have any large cardboard panels we could use as fans?" I ask.

"Gee, I don't think so," Sarge replies. Then his face lights up. "We have a big attic fan—shall I turn it on?"

"Let's try it," I say,

Sarge goes up stairs to the switch and soon I hear a whirring sound and feel a nice draft, I check to see if the living room smoke is disappearing and am shocked at what I see. The fan draft is so strong that it pulls the smoke out of the chimney and back into the 1iving room!!!

"Shut it off," I yell," It's making things worse."

By the time he shuts it off the room has about twice as much smoke as before. I feel like an idiot, but how could I know it would happen, especially with all the windows and the porch door wide open?

"Close off the rest of the house and lets get out of the living room before we suffocate," My tone is almost a command. We beat a hasty retreat and wait for the smoke to clear.

When Dan arrives I tell him the story and apologize for the attic fan boo-boo. He is very considerate with me, but is quite annoyed with Sarge for lighting a fire with the damper closed,

"Don't worry, Dan," I say. *Sarge has learned a good lesson and will open the damper from now on—and so will Mike and Meg." Dan agrees and eases up on Sarge.

"Come to think of it, Dan, I learned two lessons myself."

"Like what?" he asks,

"Taking a nap can sometimes be more exciting than restful."

"Yes," he agrees, "and the other lesson?"

"Never, I mean NEVER, turn on an attic fan when there's a fire in the fireplace!"

He chuckles, as do the kids. By the time Betty and Joyce get back, most of the smoke is gone; but enough had lingered on to let me tell my story again.

That's what I just did—but this time it's for posterity!

1990-2000

HAND BELLS

A hand bell produces a simple, almost primitive form of music. It takes relatively little skill to play one because all you have to do is shake it at the proper time, for the right duration, and at the correct volume level.

There are no worrisome scales to learn, no complicated fingering to master, no difficult lip movements or breathing challenges to overcome, etc. All of these awesome talents that most musicians must develop fade into oblivion for hand bell performers. Of course some hand bell musicians play two or more bells, but they still have only two hands to worry about at a given time.

The major talent in a hand-bell ensemble resides in the director. S/he must coordinate the output of the group and produce pleasing music. The talents of scales, timing, note duration and volume, feeling, expression and other things are all involved, and a good director can bring out the best in the ensemble members.

In the fall of 1999, my wife and I each played a single bell in an ensemble at a beer hall in Germany. It was part of the audience-participation entertainment, and I was surprised at how well it went because we were randomly selected.

The director announced that we would play "Edelweiss", which is a well-known and lovely tune. He pointed at the appropriate person at the proper time and for the right duration, and by golly the results amazed me. He even coaxed fortissimo and pianissimo from us by subtle hand gestures.

It was a delightful experience for me to participate in making music, and was especially meaningful since it had been nearly six decades since I played a baritone horn in several bands.

My greatest hand bell delight came when I witnessed a hand-bell choir composed of retarded children. Their I.Q.'s were way below normal, but the skilled director had coached them well. All of the compositions they played were melodic and moving, and much appreciated by the audience. But the greatest delight was the big smiles on the children's faces during the heart-felt applause and shouts of support. It was one of those unforgettable experiences.

As I drove home, these thoughts came to me: There they were, seemingly representing one of nature's bad tricks on mankind, yet able to do something useful, beautiful and moving. I contemplated the almost universal tears in the eyes of the audience, and they welled up in my own again just by remembering. I was proud of the human race for taking these apparent misfits into their hearts, and especially for those dedicated few who had devoted their time, talent and treasure to their well-being.

Music is truly the universal language, because it touches the very souls of both the high and mighty and the least of our brothers and sisters-- the mentally challenged!

LETTER TO GOD

Dear God: 3/31/97

I have written many letters during my long life. They were to friends and relatives; to business and non-profit organizations; to political leaders, including the U.S. President; to editors of newspapers and magazines. However, I have never written one to you. Although I have expressed my thoughts to you as Creator, Sustainer and Redeemer many times in vocal and silent prayer, I have never done it with paper and ink. This letter, written in my 78th year, corrects my oversight; hopefully, it will become a semi-permanent record and give me a better insight into our long relationship, which I treasure. You have endowed your creatures with five senses, so permit me to explore my thoughts about our relationship in that context.

Like most mortals, I long to SEE your face, but I have never had that privilege. Oh, I have imagined it in my mind and even seen artists' renditions, but they have not fulfilled my longing. However, this thought occurs to me: I <u>have</u> seen your handiwork—the beauty and vitality of nature; the splendid creative powers of your children, mankind, be they for good or evil; the ability of all your other creatures to survive, even flourish, in environments which are usually benign, but can sometimes be harsh and demanding; the majesty of the sky, the mountains, and the eternal sea; the glorious display of color in autumn; the awesome detail in plants, animals, insects, and even your microscopic creatures; and the nightly glimpse of outer space, with all its mind-stretching wonders. Truly, the magnificence of your creation enlarges my vision of your face, and perhaps it is so huge that what I see <u>is your face!</u>

I have often wished that I could HEAR you speak to me audibly, even in reprimand. It would provide my scientific mind with evidence that you are really there and not just a product of my imagination. It would quell the "Doubting Thomas" part of my nature and let my faith flower into full fruit. But, I confess that, indirectly, I have HEARD your glorious voice. I heard it in the care and concern of my earthly parents; in the sweet voice of my loving wife; in the first coos and gurgles of our children and grandchildren; in the laughter and advice of our friends and relatives; in the new-awakening sounds of spring; in the loud crash of thunder; in the wailing and moaning of fierce winds; in the persuasive sermons of your ministers; in the written words of the Bible; and in the still, small voice of my conscience. So although I yearn for direct communication, I will consider all the above, and more, as your way of speaking to me.

Sometimes I wish I could FEEL your presence, like I feel when I hug my wife, children, and grandchildren, I wish that <u>You</u> would hug me, or at least make your presence positively known. Although I have never FELT your presence the way I do with my fellow humans, sometimes when I am lonely I feel the warmth of your breath near me; when I am gratified by a worthy accomplishment, I sense your Parental pride in me.

When I am ashamed that I succumbed to earthly temptation, I feel your pain and disappointment; when I am saddened by the death of a loved one, I imagine the comfort of your embrace, reminding me that soon they may be with you forever; when my faith wavers, as it sometimes does when bombarded by the vicissitudes and realities of life, your love, patience, and grace renew and strengthen it! And although I yearn to feel your presence directly, I realize that it may be too overpowering for my mortal frame so I will wait until your final judgment of my worth.

I have never SMELLED your fragrance as I have with other humans, but I have smelled the many fragrances of your creation: the lovely aroma of flowers; the appetizing odor of a gourmet meal; the delicious scent of fresh-picked fruit or a tasty dessert; and the clean, exhilarating smell of most things in nature. While there are odors that are unpleasant, or worse, they serve to warn us of danger and protect us from harm. I can only imagine the divine aroma of your being, but it must be something truly remarkable.

You know how we humans delight in the TASTE of good food and drink, and use it as the centerpiece of our social affairs. It is there that we have the chance to sample some of the multitude of tastes that you have created, and one has to be near death not to revel in them. I suppose we mortals need not taste you, for you are not food or drink. But like food and drink, we need you for our very survival. In fact, without the sustenance you have made possible, our species would be on the endangered list. Natural calamities such as drought, floods, tornadoes, etc. are frightening to us, but they do remind us how dependent we are on your graciousness. I am mindful that it was you who created the precious sense of taste, and give grateful thanks.

You have given Your creatures five senses which let us see, hear, feel, smell and taste so that we may enjoy all the good things of this world, and avoid most of the bad ones. As I put these thoughts on paper, I believe that you have given humans another sense that tops all the others — the sense that we belong to you and you belong to us! And, if we cultivate it properly, our spirits may enjoy you and your wonders forever! I say all these things with sincere humility, realizing that when you judge my worth you may find me wanting and will cast my spirit into outer darkness. When that awesome judgment day arrives, I hope that this simple letter will be Exhibit One of my witness and that your love and forgiveness will make me acceptable.

Your loving son,
Macon

MARBLES

"Here, Granddad," three year old <u>Grady</u> exclaimed as he handed me a small marble from his large assortment.

"Thank you," I replied, as I patted his small blonde head in silent praise for his willingness to share with me.

He returned to play with the rest of his marbles and I started admiring the smooth, shiny, glass sphere in my hand. I became entranced with the bright splashes of blue and white colors that swirled near the surface and finally disappeared into its crystal-clear interior. It wasn't long before I drifted into a quiet reverie.

Suddenly, sixty-three years vanished!   I was seven years old again and standing in the schoolyard with <u>Zeb Yount</u>. Zeb was a-year older than I, and the best marble shooter in the primary school, I had just received a large bag of marbles for my birthday and made the mistake of showing them to Zeb. He "generously" offered to teach me some of his skills.

At first I thought we would play just for fun, but crafty Zeb soon convinced me that I would "learn to play quicker if we played for keeps!" Eyeing my large bag, I figured it might be worthwhile to risk part of them. Zeb lent me a, "steelie", drew a ring in the dirt and let me go first. My shot missed the initial bunch of marbles that I had placed in the center. It was then Zeb's turn and he proceeded to knock all of the marbles out of the ring, one at a time. He was kind enough to explain his technique with each shot.

I restocked the ring and Zeb showed me how to hold the steelie, aim it toward the nearest marble and flick my thumb sharply to drive it on its way. Alas, my shot wasn't much better than before. Again, Zeb cleared the ring with his masterful shots and told me to restock the center. I balked a bit, but he told me I was catching on and shouldn't quit. About that time the bell rang to go to our class and I tried to use it as an excuse to stop; but Zeb knew he had a real sucker on his hook and convinced me to stay by saying, "This may be your only chance to really learn to shoot marbles!"

About five minutes later, a little girl approached and told us that our teacher wanted us to come to class immediately. Believe it or not, Zeb persuaded me to keep playing. We were both really into the game, I had started winning some of my own marbles and Zeb repeated and embellished his previous persuasive arguments. He clinched his con job by assuring me that our teacher would "just scold us a bit".

In spite of my few wins, I was no match for Zeb. In ten more minutes he had ALL my marbles and we went into class. Our teacher was furious that we had ignored her request and told us to report to <u>Mr. Snipes</u>, the Principal, right after lunch.

Needless to say, I didn't get much out of my lessons that morning. I was too busy mentally kicking myself, not only because the Principal might give me a beating, but because I had lost ALL my marbles! In later years when my friends used that quaint expression about me, they didn't know that it was literally true.

After lunch, we reported as directed. Zeb had previous experience and showed me the padding he had placed in his pants to soften the blows. He was surprised that I didn't know that trick, so he advised me to "yell real loud, and Mr. Snipes will ease up."

When Mr. Snipes hit my bottom with his belt, I yelled loudly and kept it up until he stopped—which was quite soon. Although he had closed his office door, he must have been embarrassed by a kid yelling so loudly and with so much agony. Hollywood, you missed a good child actor.

I concluded that a beating wasn't as bad as I had imagined; most things in life aren't, but I was still upset over losing my marbles! Incidentally, I never did get very good at shooting marbles, so I applied my talents elsewhere.

After I re-lived my marble-losing experience, the marble in my hand led me into reminiscing about the steelies Zeb and I had used. I recalled my discovery, several years after Zeb's costly lesson, that steelies were the balls in ball bearings and that I could actually get them FREE from garages and the local machine shop. I also discovered that they could be used in my sling shot for greater accuracy and more lethal power. Many years later, when I studied engineering, I not only learned to appreciate their role in reducing friction, but also learned, how to specify them in machine design.

After I left my reveries, I looked at Grady's marble again and wondered what else this shiny bit of glass could conjure up in my mind: a fortune teller's crystal ball that shrank and grew cloudy; a cloud-filled, miniature earth; more memories from my distant past....

Suddenly, I really went back in time—right to the beginning of the universe over SIXTEEN BILLION years ago. It dawned on me that the WHOLE COSMOS was once an incredibly dense chunk of matter about the size of the tiny marble in my hand! That's not my concept, but the view of modern science as propounded in the Big Bang and Expanding Universe theories.

So what I was holding in my hand was a replica, or if you prefer, a symbol of everything that is, ever was or ever will be. What an exciting thought!! Consider some of the sub-thoughts that this shiny symbol inspired:

o Smooth and cool when felt, it represents the feelings of ALL the creatures that ever existed or will exist.

o Intriguing to behold, it symbolizes EVERYTHING that the mind can see, or even imagine.

o Soundless, unless it strikes another object, it contains the incredible sound of the 'Big Bang' and all sounds since,

o Virtually odorless, all the odors of creation lie locked in its tiny interior.

o Existing in its present form for only a short time, it signifies the very beginning of time.

o Occupying a tiny bit of space, it epitomizes the infinite enormity of the cosmos,

o Seemingly powerless, it stimulated my mind to contemplate the magnificent, creative powers of God!

As I continued to contemplate the little marble in my hand, I was amazed that a little child's plaything had the ability to awaken distant memories and stimulate deep, imaginative thoughts about creation, the cosmos and God.

Grady, what did you unleash when you shared this tiny marble with me? If I save this essay until you and your sisters are in your mid teens, will it evoke memories and deep thoughts in your expanding minds?

Will it make you appreciate the power of sharing, the joy of an active imagination, and the awesome significance of the "insignificant"?

THE TORTURE CHAMBER

I thought that advanced civilizations had made them obsolete, or at least relegated them to museums. Of course, I was aware that some of the more primitive cultures still used them, but never in my wildest imaginings did I think I would encounter an operating torture chamber, much less one in the U.S.A.

It took me some time to realize that I had actually entered a real torture chamber, because it seemed so modern and harmless. Others who have encountered them may disagree with my opinion, so I will describe my experience and let you, dear reader, make up your own mind.

Recently I found myself in a room full of people. Some had excited looks on their faces, others looked worried, but most looked bored. In due course, I went with the people into a tunnel that led to another tunnel-shaped enclosure. But once I entered it sufficiently, I discovered that it was a dead end tunnel, more like a small cavern. A wave of claustrophobia swept over me, but I quickly subdued it. I suppose I took comfort in the large number of people going into the cavern with me.

I quickly found a space that looked relatively comfortable and waited. It hadn't dawned on me that torture was about to commence, because it was so gradual. For example, dripping water can go on for quite a while before it becomes torture, and the cavern's slowly rising temperature was similar. It wasn't long before I took off my coat and loosened my tie; even so, I was still too damned hot and very uncomfortable. To make matters worse, they sealed the entrance to the cavern and we were trapped like a bunch of rats in a small cage, with no reasonable means of escape. Furthermore, the temperature kept rising so much that I was almost ready to take off my shirt!

My complaint about the heat fell on deaf ears, but shortly after voicing it my own ears heard a loud roar, as if a pride of lions were lurking outside the cavern. The roar grew louder and louder and was frightening to hear. It soon subsided into a steady rumble that wouldn't go away. It sounded like a large waterfall, except there was no splashing water sound.

The roaring sound had one good feature—the cavern became cooler, so I was able to keep my shirt on. I was then tied down with a locking device that indicated I had better stay in my small, cramped space. I tried my best to get comfortable, but to no avail. I squirmed and wiggled a lot, and wished there were some place to lie down so that my demise would be peaceful. Foolish wish!—it was impossible to lie down.

The discomfort, plus being trapped in the cavern with so many others, heightened my latent claustrophobia and mental anguish. Just as they reached their peak, nature called. Fortunately, I was able to open the locking device and make my way to some cramped facilities, but a long waiting line delayed relief. After much fidgeting and shifting from one foot to the other, blessed relief was finally achieved.

Then back to my cramped place where I tried to relieve the torturous confinement, first by reading and then by a nap. But by then my feet had started to swell and my legs ache. What next, I thought, and it so stimulated my mind that sleep was limited to short nods that were completely unsatisfactory.

I knew that my confinement in the torture chamber was supposed to be limited to five or six hours, but reports by others indicated that the time element could be much greater. Worse yet, other reports indicated that mass death was possible by asphyxiation, cavern collapse or other frightening modalities. Supposedly, mass death had a low probability; but its very existence added mental torture to the physical torture. When I thought of the large sum of money required to enter the torture chamber, I started to doubt my sanity!

The one bright element of the experience was that I didn't get thirsty or hungry.

The torture chamber officials had provided food and drink, hoping I suppose that it would help us endure all the elements of torture. However, it was difficult to consume them in such cramped quarters and the food was nothing to brag about. Besides, the combination hastened further calls from nature, so the same long wait and cramped facilities had to be endured several more times.

Shortly after my fatigue and weariness let me fall into a deep sleep, I was rudely awakened by an official announcement that our confinement was nearly over. If all went well, and we survived the enhanced threat of mass death during the next fifteen minutes, we would all be released. I was greatly relieved at the prospect of release, sorely annoyed at being awakened after my long struggle to go to sleep, and mentally apprehensive that the threat of mass death was at its peak!

My patience and perseverance finally paid off, and I exited the torture chamber with no ill effects except for my swollen feet and residual mental anguish. I immediately buried all ill effects deep in my subconscious mind once I saw my <u>California daughter and grandchildren</u>.

Their smiling faces and warm embraces were a real tonic for my tortured spirit. Naturally, my daughter asked," How was your flight from Boston?" Much to my surprise, my wife responded, " It was great— no problems at all!"

At that point I became acutely aware *of* these truths:

1. People can have diametrically different views of the same experience.

2. A man's size is a distinct handicap in an airline seat, a woman's size a blessing.

3. Compared to other modes of travel, airlines have a big advantage—the torture is short-lived!

4. The probability of an airline having the guts to publish this article is extremely low!

5. A vivid imagination can be a curse, but, hopefully, its product is entertaining!

UNEXPECTED DELAY

My wife, <u>Elizabeth</u>, and I had reached the gangplank area in plenty of time to join the group in a fifteen-minute walk to a restaurant in Rudesheim, Germany. It was led by our fabulous tour director, Bart, and was one of the included features of our three-river cruise. We went from Vienna, Austria, to Amsterdam, Holland, aboard the M.S. RIVER RHAPSODY. The rivers were the Danube, the Main, and the Rhine, plus connecting canals and over 100 locks. The restaurant was said to be a fun place, so we were eager to go with the group. Besides, my thrifty nature told me never to miss an included treat.

To add to the festive atmosphere, the tour people were offering a local specialty—brandy-filled, chocolate candy. I put my piece directly in my mouth and could feel the warm, intoxicating flow of brandy as I chewed. Elizabeth was too much of a lady to eat it whole, so she bit it in half. That was a mistake, because the brandy spilled out on her hands. Again, she was too much of a lady to lick or wipe it off, and decided to go to the nearest rest room to wash her hands properly. By the time she returned, the group had left and was about 150 feet ahead of us because of our unexpected delay.

Unfortunately, her health problem kept her from walking fast enough for us to catch up, so I sometimes walked ahead to keep the group in sight. I didn't know the restaurant's location, and even its name was fading from my memory, so it was imperative that we keep track. We were doing fine until the group reached a sidewalk full of people and started blending with them. I thought I still had them spotted, and even ran ahead to confirm my belief. When I got there it was a different group; our group must have made a turn, or perhaps entered a restaurant unnoticed by me.

I walked back to Elizabeth and told her the bad news. "They probably turned down this gasse (alley), but I don't see them. Do you remember the name of the restaurant? I think it's the Rudesheim something, but I have forgotten." "No, she replied, I have forgotten it too. Rudesheim is the name of this city, not the restaurant."

If I had been smart, I would have gone down the gasse to try and spot the restaurant, but instead I said, "I have my boarding pass with the emergency telephone number for the ship, so I'll call them for directions. Wait here while I find a telephone."

I went into a restaurant to find one, but the waiter, who spoke "a liddle English", sent me to a pay 'phone in an obscure place. When I got there, the written instructions were in German, which I know only slightly. To make matters worse, I had left my reading glasses on the ship. I tried to solicit help from people on the street, but either they didn't speak English, or weren't able to help for various reasons. I even went into a store, explained my plight to an English-speaking clerk, and offered to pay for help, but to no avail;

When I returned to Elizabeth I said, "Telephoning isn't going to work. Why don't you find a comfortable place to wait while I return to the ship for help? I'll take a taxi back."

She saw the wisdom of that solution, and cautioned me to be careful. I then retraced my steps at a brisk walking pace. Adrian, the cruise director for the ship, was surprised to see me back so soon. I told him the story and he made a copy of a map with explicit instructions. Reception called for a taxi, but when they told me it would take 15 or more minutes to arrive, I cancelled it. "I can walk back quicker," I explained.

It took 8 or 10 minutes to walk back, and just as I spotted Elizabeth, I saw the familiar face of Bart, our tour guide. Our travel friends had missed us, and good old Bart had offered to search for us. It was a welcomed deed, but I had the situation under control thanks to a lot of walking and the ship's help. After explaining things to Bart, we went to the restaurant, "The Rudesheim Schloss". When we entered the area where our friends were saving us a seat, the entire group applauded, and some yelled. It was the sort of recognition we would have preferred to avoid, but we accepted it gracefully.

We thanked Bart and our friends for their help and concern, and I told our friends and a few others what had happened. I ended my story by saying, "The brandy-filled candy was dandy, but I wish it hadn't been so handy!"

Elizabeth and I were served our soup and our "bottle of wine for two", and soon caught up with the others. It turned out to be a fun-filled evening, with "gut essen und trinken", music, song, and audience participation. The latter started with some group liquor swigging. The restaurant people had fastened five shot glasses to a long board, got five volunteers, and then everyone shouted, "Ein, Zwei, Drei", at which time the volunteers chug-a-lugged. One of our friends, Comer Bates of Kansas City, was a volunteer, but missed his gulp and spilled some on his shirt. Fortunately, it didn't stain, so all was well.

Later on, Elizabeth and I volunteered to be part of a hand-bell group, and upon direction of the leader, we played a decent rendition of "Edelweiss." Everyone else either sang or hummed, so everybody participated.

Earlier on our trip, one of the guides told a story about Goethe, the famous German poet and author. When asked, "What are the most important things in life, he replied: "Wine, women and song."

"Suppose you had to omit one, which one would it be?"

"Song." the master replied.

"Suppose you had to choose between wine and women?

"In that case", he wisely said, "it would depend on the vintage!"

After an evening of fun, German style, we returned to the ship aboard a rubber-tired, three-coach, street trolley, a fun experience itself. A frustrating beginning had a great ending, as do many other worrisome things in life.

Whoever said, "Don't sweat the small stuff, and it's all small stuff", was right on target that evening.

WAHGEE

Do you know what a wahgee is? Have you ever seen one, or touched one or tasted one? No? Well you are not as experienced as my grandson because he not only has seen, touched and tasted a wahgee, but he invented the term!

My grandson is one year old and his name is Grady James Catterall, For the past two weeks, he and his four year old sister, Hannah Beth, have been staying with their 'Nana' and 'Granddad', Hannah and I communicate in English, but Grady has been doing his best to communicate with me in his own language. Thanks to his persistence, I think I am beginning to understand it.

At first, I thought wahgee was his name for our Don Quixote woodcarvings, because he said wahgee whenever he saw them. Of course he had to touch and taste them once he saw them. I got a bit confused when he started calling other objects 'wahgee', but suddenly it became clear.

Wahgee is a very complex term- it is a generic noun like the word 'object' or 'thing' is for us, but it is more. It is also a request, almost a command, that means 'I want it' or 'give me that right now!'[1]

How do I know? Because he points to a wahgee when he sees one and then, shifts to the request by the inflection in his voice—"wahgee; Wahgee; WAHGEE !"

Grady has some other interesting terms. One of his favorite ones is 'bight'[1]. Some of our friends think it should be spelled 'byte' and that it is a sign that he will be a computer genius, but I know better. He only uses the term when he sees an electric light. He can't say 'l' yet so he uses a 'b'. That's why I spell it bight.

Of course he may be a budding computer genius, but at this stage 'bight'[1] means 'light'. If it is any kind of sign it is that he may become an educator (spread light) like his mom and dad, or perhaps if I add an 'r' it means he is 'bright'[1],

Grady is very fond of 'bights'. Turn an overhead one on and he will start saying the word loudly. When I am sitting in my easy chair he will crawl over, point to the reading lamp and repeat the word 'bight' until I turn the lamp on. He then, looks at me and gives me a big smile, I turn it off and on several times just to see that look and that smile.

His favorite 'bight' is in the dining room, When we are there he insists that I lift him up and let him work the dimmer switch. His big smile tells me that he enjoys the feeling of power he gets by controlling the 'bight'.

Another favorite word is 'mama'. Now most people think that is his way of saying mother, but again I know better. He says it to me when he wants some food. He says it when he has had enough food and wants to get out of his "sassy seat," He says it again when I give him his bottle to go to sleep. Again, it is a generic word with many different uses. It's amazing how one so young knows about generic words, isn't it?

Grady is a good-looking kid-- light blonde hair; bright blue eyes; smooth pink skin; and a big eight tooth smile that will melt your heart in a millisecond. That's not just grandfather talk, because perfect strangers stop and tell me the same. His sister is very pretty, very cute and smart. Total strangers have also confirmed that.

Grady is very active and can crawl better than any kid I have ever seen. He can even shift into high gear by lifting his knees off the floor and crawling on hands and feet, I can't believe the speed he achieves and it keeps all of us very alert. In that gear, he can get into trouble in nothing flat! Grady has very sharp eyesight and seems to be especially attracted to little things—like wall outlets (plugged for his protection); cupboard door handles; drawer pulls; stereo equipment knobs; lamp cords; etc. He is strong and quick.

One day before I could react, he upset a big, heavy table lamp near the sofa. He didn't get hurt, just surprised, but the three-way bulb refused to work after the mighty crash.

He is starting to walk and has taken up to eleven steps before he loses his balance and sits down--kerplunk! Sometimes he falls forward and uses

his little hands to cushion his fall. Occasionally, he falls hard and frowns, wondering whether to cry or laugh. So far, his optimistic nature has made him opt for laughter,

Grady has already learned some of the universal sounds of mankind. Give him a bite of ripe banana or melon and he will say 'mmmmmm' to show he really likes it. Give him a big drink of milk from a cup and he may say 'ah-h-h', or perhaps 'mmmmm',

If he doesn't like something, he loses no time in letting us know by a big "WAH-H!" When I carry him in my arms in a crowd and someone stops to admire him, he smiles and coyly puts his little head on my shoulder as if to say 'aw shucks'. No one taught him that winsome maneuver; it just came naturally.

He wakes up early every morning and for the past two weeks he has never cried or fussed. He just sits in his playpen cooing, talking his special language and waiting for one of us adults to pick him up and change his diaper. He likes his bottle while being changed., so he has a lot to learn about aesthetics. Oh well, no one is perfect,

As I write this article his mom and dad are packing to return to California. I could go on and on with other words, sounds, actions, etc.--you know how grandparents are--but I will resist the temptation and help them get ready..

One thing is for sure-- someone in New Hampshire is going to miss that little boy, his cute sister and his mom and dad!

Recently, I heard another grandfather talking about his grand children. He concluded his remarks with the witty observation, "If I had known they would be so much fun, I think I would have had then first." Amen!

© 2009 L. Macon Epps All rights reserved (1986)

2000-2010

ANCIENT SWINGERS

BREAKING NEWS:

A recent discovery revealed that there are some fast ladies in Leisure Village, a retirement community where the average age is around 75. Your reporter, age 89, has been running around with them, but they are much faster than I am. Now this may shock some people, but we are all "swingers," and change partners frequently. To relieve the shock, let me explain: "We are all members of the Racquet Club, play tennis four times a week, and swing our rackets often!"

A TOAST:

Here's to the fast ladies in my life;
I run around with them, 'though none is my wife.
They are much faster than I am,
So frequently I say, "Thank you, mam!"

Now all of us are long-time "swingers,"
And sometimes we create big zingers.
We have more fun, when partners we change,
Which by consensus, we usually arrange.

Now none of us commit a big sin,
Because it's the racquet club were in!

©   L Macon Epps   10-22-08

CAMPAIGN QUESTIONS

After a year of campaign talk, it's time to give worn-out voters some relief. Here are some humorous questions for voters to consider: (hopefully with a chuckle)

Can Obama capture Osama; will Barrack put us back on track? Will the name "Hussein" drive some voters insane?

Will the USA walk better with McCain, or will he need a <u>cane</u> before he retires? Will John prove to be a con, or perhaps like Ron?

Can Hillary command our Military, or will she lead us to hilarity? Will women voters make a giant leap forward--- or backward?

How long will Huckabee wait and see? When will Mike take a hike?

When will Nader become a fader, and will he need a cane before McCain?

Will Edwards now head bed wards?

Why couldn't Romney buy more votes with all that money?

Will Dodd complain because God didn't give <u>him</u> the nod?

Is Dennis no longer a menace?

Will Rudy become very moody?

Will Ron Paul start a brawl?

I'll leave it to voters to answer these questions!

© 2009 L. Macon Epps All rights reserved (2008)

GLIMPSE OF PARADISE

It is morning, and I look southward out my bedroom window. Although it is late February, the thermometer reads 58 degrees and I marvel at the flowers on my patio, which are in full bloom and delight my eyes.

The dew on the wide expanse of grass sparkles in the bright sun like tiny diamonds, and I am entranced . Two golfers amble by and start chipping their little white balls toward the eleventh green. My reverie is temporarily interrupted.

I look at the houses 200 feet across the fairways, which are partly in sunlight and partly in shade. The patterns resemble a giant checkerboard.

My eyes rise up toward the mountains, which are 3 or 4 miles away. The upper part of the window blocks my view, so the mountains seem to touch the sky. I hear an airplane flying over them and bend down to see it. It shows that the sky is much higher than the mountains, which are only a few thousand feet above me. My mind's eye recalls photos of Mount Everest and I realize that even that giant can't quite touch the sky, so I am content with "my" mountains".

If I tried to climb them, I would be even more content because of their height and steepness. They undulate up and down like giant static waves, with cliffs and ravines spilling off them, and boulders standing erect like surfers. But surfers can never ride these waves, although hikers and climbers can accept their beckoning challenge.

Half way up the slope of one mountain men have paved a freeway, which makes a thin, diagonal slice into it. Cars and trucks speed up and down its steep grade, which bottoms in Pleasant Valley and its many strawberry farms. My mouth starts watering at the thought of them, and I grow impatient for the season to start.

Camarillo, my new hometown, blends with Pleasant Valley and is now bustling with its daily business. The multi-mountain view out my window is the fulfillment of a lifelong dream, which took almost 82 years to realize, and I am grateful that my bride of almost 57 years is here to share it with me. Similar views can be seen from our living and dining rooms, and even better ones from the patio.

Our previous home on Long Island had a small winter view of Huntington Bay, and our condo in Dover NH had a tiny view of the Bellamy river, but they were only appetizers, not the main course like our present view. Of course, like many others, I have enjoyed spectacular views from temporary places, like our timeshare with its full view of Lake Winnepesauke and the Ossippee mountains in NH. Then there were vacations where views of the Alps the Rocky Mountains, Alaskan Mountains, etc. not only thrilled me, but whetted my appetite for a permanent place with a mountain view.

Although our view seems fixed, it makes subtle changes everyday. When sunset and twilight arrive, the changes are no longer subtle because sunset's brilliant hues work their magic, and the fading light and deepening shadows of twilight cast an aura of mystery over it.

Head and tail lights from the fast moving traffic on the freeway, heightened by red blinking lights on mountain-ridge towers, remind me of a video game. I wonder if my grandson would appreciate my comparison to his favorite pastime.

Sometimes the scene is changed by strong winds, and the trees and bushes wave hello to us, their new neighbors. Rabbits also bounce across the scene, waving their little powder-puff rears at us.

Squirrels flick their frisky, bushy tails at any passerby, and birds fly past, peck at things in the grass, or sing joyfully in the nearby trees.

Occasionally, a humming bird whirrs by, flitting and hovering among the flowers to emphasize the scene. I remember the old joke that says "they hum, because they don't remember the words."

Clouds sometimes overshadow the mountains, and when they stoop to kiss the earth, they engulf our valley with mist. Even the fairway and houses beyond the golf course become partially enshrouded, as if a mystery novel was about to begin.

Sometimes clouds bring rain, rarely hail, but never the snow and ice storms that I enjoyed back east, especially in New Hampshire. Although we miss the great beauty of fresh-fallen snow and its attendant winter sports, it is a small sacrifice for the valley's delightful mild climate. I console myself for the lack of snow by thinking of the lower energy age brings, and the fact that there are higher, snow-covered mountains a few hours away. My only consolation for the friends we left back east lies in the airlines. They can whisk them out to us, or us back to them, in half a day, or less.

In spite of the delightful climate, insects are rarely seen so there are few annoyances. To the contrary, the active retirement community where we now live, called "Leisure Village", has dozens of worthwhile activities within walking distance. We can't possibly indulge in all of them, but we can pick and choose the ones we like best. Most of the people here are mature folks, with an average age of 75, so for once in our life we are above average! They are gentle, friendly people; are easy to meet; and almost always say "hello" when we walk by.

Our younger daughter Rebecca, her husband James, and our teen-aged grandkids live in Topanga, only an hour away/ Our older daughter lives in Denver CO, closer than when we lived in NH.

Sometimes I wonder how long this semi-paradise can last, especially at our age. But then a pleasant, almost divine thought enters: 'Don't fret the diminishing time, old boy; just enjoy every minute. It may be part of the acclimatization training for the real paradise.'

The thought comforts me, and makes me appreciate our fascinating view and delightful situation even more. I then contemplate the magnificent wonders that may await us in paradise, and my head spins.

But suppose there is no paradise? Suppose it is just a figment of man's vivid imagination and sincere longing? I quell those negative thoughts by reminding myself of my natural optimism, positive thinking, and basic instincts.

They tell me that God has great surprises in store for humans, and that our gorgeous view and delightful situation are our GLIMPSE OF PARADISE!

HISTORICAL PERSPECTIVES

Imagine this: It is 1860, and Southern State leaders have decided to secede from the United States. They have many reasons for doing so, including the fact that they are free people who joined the other original colonies to become independent of the tyrannical rule of the British. They feel that the Northern States will not block their decision to sever their ties with the union, much as a man and woman decide to sever their union via a divorce. Now divorce is not a pleasant task, but first it should be discussed logically to see if reconciliation is possible. If not possible, then it should be handled diplomatically, reasonably, according to existing laws, and without violence. Certainly a divorce should not cause the quarrelling couple to kill their own children. So the Southern States hoped the Northern States would agree that they were perfectly correct in using their rights to secede.

I do not know how much reason and diplomacy was used to resolve the Southern States decision to "divorce" the Northern ones, and go their separate way. All I know is that tempers flared, the North refused to withdraw from Ft. Sumter, which was off the coast of South Carolina, and the newly formed Confederate States tried to remove them by force, on the basis that it was their legitimate territory. Actually, the North invaded the South earlier in a small battle, so the South's Ft. Sumter attack was more legal than the North's.

President Lincoln was the chief executive and the leader of the remaining United States. I understand that he had two main goals at that time. One was to free the slaves, which many in the North felt was an evil practice and not worthy of a nation that put so much emphasis on individual freedom. The other goal was to preserve the union, thereby avoiding the inherent weakness of two smaller countries being overtaken by European powers. Another reason, some say, was to prevent future wars with the South as a separate country.

Southerner leaders saw things differently. Their economy was highly dependent on slave labor; they had paid for slaves on an existing and legal market; and they felt the slaves were not capable of freedom. Besides, the Holy Bible did not condemn slavery; it gave many examples of it, so it was not considered evil provided the slaves were treated decently. As to preserving the Union, the divorce analogy and their rights as free people, gave them good reasons for going their own way. As to two weaker countries being victims of European takeovers or having future wars with each other, the benefits they perceived via session, outweighed the risks.

Besides, should Europe invade either North or South, they could always become allies in a common cause. Furthermore, they simply wanted a "divorce", and had no intention of invading the North, so it was not an imminent threat to the Yankees. Bottom line: Why not try to persuade the

South to stay, or let it go in peace?

I understand that there was much argument in the North as to whether going to war to reach Lincoln's goals was worth it, but eventually, Lincoln and the Congress decided the cost in lives and treasure <u>was</u> worth it. One of the reasons for that decision was original estimates, which indicated that costs would be slight, and the war would soon be over. They didn't use the "slam-dunk" analogy, but it must have been similar.

What followed was a big mess. Lincoln's handling of the war as Commander in Chief was fraught with mistakes, as shown by the number of generals he had to replace before he picked a winning one. About 624,000 military men's lives were lost, with about two-thirds Union men. Almost as many American military men were killed during this war than all others combined, and as a percentage of the total population, it was far greater. Undoubtedly there were also civilian deaths, but I don't know the number. Worse yet, it was a case of Americans killing Americans. They were all the same people, even relatives, who had known and worked together for years, and basically were Christians with similar values and cultures. Terrible property destruction occurred, and devastating hardships were imposed on the people, not only for the four years of the war, but in the years following. The South bore the brunt of the destruction and hardships, which engendered bad feelings that lasted for many decades. Some bad feelings still haven't completely vanished.

What would have happened if the North let the South secede? No one knows for sure, but some think the slaves would have been freed within a few decades, so the huge cost in lives and treasure doesn't seem to be worth the few extra years of freedom the war provided.

As to what would have happened with two independent countries, there are many possibilities. One is that they would have rejoined after a few years of thinking things over carefully, especially after the South freed the slaves on its own. Even if they remained separated, it is probable that they would have become allies if a European power threatened them. Another possibility is that the USA would not be the super power it is today. Perhaps neither country would have entered WWI, and Germany would have won, thus avoiding Hitler's cruel power.

Perhaps there would have been no WWII, because Germany and its allies might have ruled Europe properly, or strongly enough, to avoid it. On the other hand, the future may have been even worse, although with the death and destruction of WWII, it's hard to imagine it being worse. (52 million total deaths, $2 trillion to US)

But the above is pure speculation as to what would have happened. So was speculation by the leaders of that time about an uncertain future worth Americans killing 624,000 military men and an unknown number of civilians, destroying huge amounts of property, and imposing hardships on citizens for generations? My logic says NO!

Lincoln was severely criticized during the war, but eventually won it and achieved his main goals. The slaves were freed and the Union was preserved! However, he was assassinated, so he wasn't able to enjoy the fruits of victory, or carry out his admirable reconciliation plans. But history has been kind to him. He is now considered one of our greatest Presidents, and his image is one of four on Mt. Rushmore. One can only speculate as to how many people during the course of the war envisioned him as being labeled "Great" by future generations. While I am not a scholar of history, I would like someone more knowledgeable than I am to tell me what's wrong with my analysis, and why Lincoln is held in such high esteem today?

Now let us turn to 2007, and consider the Afghanistan and Iraq wars. When Islamic extremists flew airplanes on 9/11/01 into the World Trade Center and the Pentagon, the American people finally woke up to the threat of a small group, called Al Quaeda, which didn't represent any particular nation. It did represent dangerous religious extremists, whose goal was to destroy us, and either convert the world to Islam or destroy it. According to their beliefs, winning would make them heroes to Islam; losing would make them martyrs and get them a big batch of virgins in Paradise. While there had been other Al Quaeda incidents in the past which had warned us of their intentions, including a failed attempt to destroy the World Trade Center, they were more or less shrugged off by the public.

But the devastating 9/11 attack on our <u>own soil</u> was different. It stirred the public greatly, and when President Bush decided to invade Afghanistan, whose government had sheltered Al Quaeda, it was widely supported. However, many Americans, plus France and other key UN members, were skeptical of his decision to invade Iraq, even though there were the following reasons to do so: 1. It had ambitions to control the mid-east and its vast oil reserves; 2. It had attacked Iran, and then Kuwait, as part of its ambitions; 3. It had to be forcibly removed from Kuwait by the United Nations under US leadership; 4. It had used a weapon of mass destruction (poison gas) on Iraqi Kurds; 5. It was still violating cease-fire agreements and shooting at our airplanes, which were enforcing those agreements; 6. It had kicked out all UN inspectors, contrary to the agreements; 7. Most Western-Nation intelligence agencies agreed that they had more poison gas, some biological weapons, and might be working on nuclear ones.

The UN Security Council turned down President Bush's appeal to implement its previous resolution warning Iraq of "serious consequences," and France, whom we saved during WWII, actually threatened to veto if the council agreed with Bush. Following the UN decision, Congress voted to invade Iraq. It wasn't unanimous, but it had a large majority.

Initially, the invasions of both Afghanistan and Iraq were very successful, and the "slam-dunk" description by officials seemed fulfilled. Large numbers of both people seemed to be grateful for their liberation, particularly the Iraqis, because Sadam Hussein was a terrible dictator. (He is reported to be responsible for over one million deaths, mostly his own citizens.) But then things started to go wrong-- President Bush and his military advisors started making bad decisions, or perhaps not making the right ones. And radicals, extremists and die-hards within Iraq and less so in Afghanistan, made things very difficult, even for our superb military and less superb DOD officials.

When American military deaths reached 3,000, criticism of Bush grew stronger and stronger. High-ranking retired generals and political leaders were, and still are, demanding a new course of action, including complete withdrawal. The voters showed their distaste for the war by electing a Democratic Congress in 2006, and several moves were then taken to correct the Iraq mess. However, some leaders still say that even though many mistakes have been made, withdrawal before we achieve Iraq stability could make things much worse.

No one can be certain who is right, but our system requires the Commander–in-Chief to make the final decision, as was true in Lincoln's day. Right or wrong, we must either abide by President Bush's decisions, or impeach him _and_ Vice-president Cheney, because the VP seems even more determined to stay than the President. If impeachment is successful, Speaker Pelosi would be the new President-- the first woman one in our history. Many citizens would appreciate the uniqueness of a woman President, but how many would be pleased with her decisions?

Although we are still fighting in Afghanistan and Iraq, it might be helpful to make a comparison of Lincoln and Bush as Presidents and Commanders-in- Chief. See chart below:

	Lincoln	Bush
Threat of physical harm to citizens without going to war	negligible	large
American military deaths: (approx.)	624,000	3,000+
Deaths as a percent of population:	1.8%	.00001%
Per Capita Cost (1990 dollars)	$3153	$3000*
Mistakes made during war	many	many
Criticism by citizens	substantial	substantial, plus international
Stubbornness (Perseverance) in seeking ultimate victory	very	very
Could war have been avoided	yes	maybe, but With great risks
Was war a conventional one? (From a military standpoint)	Yes	no way

* Assumes $900 billion eventual total Also, Iraq war takes less than 1% of GDP; Vietnam: 14%; Korea: 9%

Readers are invited to supply more accurate data and to change the judgment opinions in the rest, if they disagree. The numbers given above are from Internet sources that are considered fairly reliable. Readers are also invited to supply any flaws in my logic, and in the following conclusions I have reached:

1. President Lincoln is highly over-rated. Had he been a great leader, he would have avoided the war, or at least given up before so much harm was done. (for reasons, see previous points).

2. President Bush is not someone I admire very much, but when I compare his position with Lincoln's, I believe it is only fair and logical to withhold final judgment until the air clears more. After all, the Islamic extremists we now face are a different and much more deadly threat than the Confederacy was, which was minor provided the North had let it secede peacefully and try to woo it back later. The Islamic extremists are dedicated to destroying us, and no amount of reasoning or diplomacy is likely to work with their ilk. Our best hope is to use tough and fair diplomacy on Islamic nations who either support them or don't stop them, but that's a formidable task, even if Bush starts to pursue it more vigorously.

3. If history has been so kind to Lincoln, with all his tragic and costly mistakes, and his stubbornness while seeking to reach his goals, isn't there an even better chance that history will be kind to President Bush? I know that is hard for some people to swallow in the heat of the turmoil, but how will you feel if it comes true?

Please give this article some serious thinking with an open mind. And remember, my mind is open to a better analysis!

LONG AGO AND FAR AWAY

The title conjures up strange feelings that grow more meaningful as we age. Long ago grows more ancient; far away closer.

LONG AGO takes us back to our childhood and the wonderful world that was unfolding: stable, but changing; safe, but uncertain; kind, but with splashes of cruelty; beautiful, but with its share of ugliness. Memories of those early days can bring both pleasure and sadness. Pleasure when we recall the happy times we re-live in our minds; sadness when we think of the parents, relatives and friends who are no longer with us, and the realization that those days are gone forever.

Books, movies and plays can take us back to places and events we never experienced, such as the Middle Ages. Vicariously, we relive those frightening days, with their multiple horrors: famine, pestilence, wars, persecutions, etc. Somehow our ancestors survived long enough to produce offspring that kept the gene pool going. All who are alive today have dipped into that pool.

Then there are the glory days of Rome, Greece, Egypt, China, and other ancient civilizations. Glorious, yes, but built on massive human rights abuses by modern standards. Even so, we still marvel at what they could accomplish without modern technology, and we admire the great intelligence of their philosophers, artists, builders and organizers. We also learn that modern man, basically, hasn't changed much in the several millennia that have gone by.

A visit to a natural history museum takes us way back to the age of dinosaurs, which ruled the earth for millions of years before mankind appeared. We are fascinated by the size and power of those large creatures, and wonder what it would be like if man had been co-habitants. Movies do a wonderful job of answering that question. But the age of dinosaurs was so long ago that it stretches our imagination.

FAR AWAY takes us to remote regions of the world, which lose their remoteness with age and travel

Richmond, Virginia was remote in my early youth because I had never traveled beyond my native North Carolina. But around age twelve, Richmond left the far-away category.

New York City, a favorite far-away place of my youthful dreams, became a nearby neighbor when I got a job on Long Island at age twenty. Multiple visits to its museums, theaters, operas, ballets, concerts and sporting events made it a nearby pleasure land.

California, a whole continent away, became familiar with several business trips, a two-year field assignment, and eventually my third retirement home, which I have now enjoyed for over a year.

As I write these thoughts, I am sitting in the lounge of a riverboat cruising down the Rhone River headed for Avignon. Another far-away place now conquered by the wonders of jet flight and my earlier thrift.

Last night, I sat on the upper deck and watched the shadowy hills and mountains glide by, partially illuminated by a full moon. Now there's a far away place that I will never visit, I mused. Vicariously, I, like people through out the world, visited it when the astronauts landed the Lunar Module and walked or rode on its hostile and barren surface. A sense of pride flickered in my mind as I recalled the seven years I spent helping produce the Lunar Module as a Grumman Aerospace engineer and manager.

Earth now has no far-away places that travelers can not reach, although the arctic regions are still hostile and difficult. My flight over Greenland, with its vast snow and ice-covered wasteland, gave me a fleeting glimpse of the wonderful and strange beauty of the Polar Regions.

Mankind's new far-away place is now Mars, and it too will be visited given time, money, energy and human ingenuity. But there are still the stars and their planets, which are so far away that we may never visit them except via telescopes and other scientific marvels. However, if the extra-terrestrial investigators, or Star Trek fans are right, star visits may come sooner than we think.

The Hubble telescope and television have shown us some wonderful views of the outer reach of space. Astronomers tell us that some of the pictures may be 13 billion light years away. Since light travels at 186,000 miles per second, we can calculate their distance in miles by multiplying 13 billion years by the number of seconds in a year, and then multiplying that product by 186,000 miles per second. The number we get, 76,254,000,000,000,000,000,000 miles, stretches the human mind to the breaking point. Even more amazing, is the fact that what we see is what was happening billions of years ago.

Now that's really long ago and far away!

POLITICAL HUMOR?

The end is in sight! The 2008 presidential campaign will soon be over, and the world will get back to normal, whatever "normal" is. No more long speeches on TV. No more biased reporting. No more verbal bashing by one candidate of the other candidate. No more discussions with friends and family as to which candidate you are backing, and no more arguments as to why you are stupid enough to back candidate X. Yep, it will soon be decided, and your candidates will either smile in victory, or give a weak smile to show what good sports they are.

I, for one, will be glad that the great American Public has made its choice and we can then discuss, or argue, about many other things, such as: "Was the election full of fraud? Will the congress cooperate with the new president, or will there be all the bickering we have gotten used to? How about the new cabinet—will we like, or dislike its members? Will the economy be fixed? Will the energy problems be solved? How about global climate change? Will we get hotter or colder, and when will it be so bad that everyone will yell, "Fix it!" Will the new guy get us out of Iraq and Afghanistan, capture <u>Bin Ladin</u>, and restore peace to the world, or will even worse threats dampen or stop all the new programs he has planned?

Unfortunately, the election will not immediately solve all the current and unknown problems, but we can all hope that great progress will begin. So while we are all waiting for the election to be over and the new administration starts its humongous task, I thought we could use a bit of political humor to tide us over. Warning: some will be groaners, but hopefully some will bring a few chuckles, and maybe even a few hearty laughs. (Remember, I am an optimist and have a thick skin, so react naturally). Here goes:

Should <u>Barrack Obama</u> have used the nickname "Barry" and put an apostrophe after "O" to get more Irish votes? Doesn't Barry O'bama sound better than his real name?

My <u>wife</u> is for Barry, and uses a cane, which she calls "John." When I asked her why, she said, "Because it's my cane, and I don't want to use that name!

Joe Biden has sought the presidential candidate nomination several times. He finally got the VP nomination, so I guess he was "Biden" his time. Anyway, it's good his last name is "Biden" instead of "King"; otherwise we would say he was "Joe King!"

If you look at Sarah Palin's white face, you can see that its "Palin" color. However, when her fans cheer her, they "Say Rah" for Palin.

How about the candidates that didn't get nominated:

Some who didn't like Hillary Clinton called her, "Hilarious Rotten Clinton."

Mitt Romney lost because his "mitt" wasn't large enough to catch more voters.

Chris Dodd may have lost because his name sounded "odd" or to much like "God," especial with his first name being "Chris."

Mayor Guliani's name may have been too feminine for some male voters. Isn't Julie Ann a girl's name?

Jonathan Edwards may have lost because the public found he was inclined to go "bed wards."

Mike Huckabee was a "wannabe" but he didn't have the right key.

Did Dennis Kuchinich lose because the voters thought he might become "Dennis the Menace?" Or was it because his last name sounded too much like "sandwich?"

Now lets examine some of the current political leaders:

When Bush ran against Gore, a friend of mine said, I voted for Bush. Then he told me, "I figured I'd rather be "Bushed" than "Gored."

Some folks say that VP Cheney is a bit "insaney"

Will Henry Paulson's "bailout" help some or maul some"?

Some say that Ben Bernaki is a bit "whacky'.

Do some call Nancy Pelosi, "Fancy Nancy", or Speaker Pee-loosey

Is Harry Reed appropriately named? He's as thin as a reed, and almost as strong.

If Barney Frank ever ran for president, should he select a running mate named "Stein"? The ticket would then be "Frank and Stein"!

With the economic crisis hurting most everyone, I tell my sister, "Don't cry, sis"!

If our Writing Club leader, Kenney Nelson ran for president, he just might win. The wrestlers would say, "We can use a good "full nelson". Others would say, "Vote for him-- he's one of our kin".

If I ran for political office, my opponents would probably say, "Watch out for Macon—he may con you!

Those who want to pell me with fruit, please make sure it is still edible!

PRESIDENTIAL CAMPAIGN 2000

As thirteen-year residents of New Hampshire, my <u>wife</u> and I have enjoyed meeting as many Presidential Candidates as possible. We especially enjoy the small audience atmosphere, the availability of the candidates for questions, and the feeling that we are real participants in our great democracy. We even enjoy the personal handshakes and photo opportunities, as our photo albums can attest.

When we heard that Presidential Candidate <u>Bill Bradley</u> was having a "town meeting" in nearby Somersworth, we were eager to attend. Earlier this year we had met and talked with Senator <u>John McCain</u>, Texas Governor <u>George W. Bush</u>, and Vice-President <u>Gore</u>, so Bradley would be the last of the four leading candidates.

When we arrived at the Maplewood School there was a large crowd already there. Fortunately, I spotted several seats in the front row, so we decided to be bold and take them. Several friends saw us and came up to say hello. Sitting next to me were two young high school girls with whom I chatted, commending them for their interest in Presidential elections. Adjacent to my wife was a pretty young woman with a very cute baby in her arms. The rest of the audience was made up of a nice cross-section of New Hampshire citizens.

After a local supporter introduced Candidate Bradley, he launched into a friendly talk about his family, his careers, and his vision for America. He was relaxed, spoke well, interspersed his talk with humorous and interesting stories, and projected a vision that drew frequent applause. 'This man has possibilities,' I thought.

During the question and answer period, I listened attentively. I had a question of my own, so when the Senator recognized me I stood up and looked the tall Senator in the eyes to see his reaction. While it is not verbatim, here's our dialogue as I recall It:

"Senator Bradley, I'm Macon Epps from Dover and ...."

"Are you a native of New Hampshire?" (I was surprised at his interruption because I was still headed for my question, but it turned out to be a pleasant interruption.)

"No sir, I was born and grew up in North Carolina, but I think New Hampshire is a wonderful state."

He smiled and said, "Was it Western North Carolina?"

"Yes sir. You have a good ear for regional accents."

He then looked at the audience and said, "I could tell this man's origin because he speaks with the soft, pleasant sound of that region." He turned to me saying,

"Please continue."

"Sir, I've been around a long time and I've attended many meetings like this; but one thing I've noticed is that when a candidate wins and goes to Washington, too many of his promises are quickly forgotten. Now I realize that the world changes and new situations can arise that may cause you to alter course, but what I really want to know is this: What promises can you make tonight that you can keep through thick and thin?"

At this point, the audience applauded loudly, and when I sat down a man behind me patted my back and said, "That was a damn good question!" I waited eagerly for the Senator's answer.

He became serious as he said, "I promise to make health insurance available to more people; to reduce the number of children in poverty; to reform our campaign financing system so that the people's voice will be much stronger than that of special interests; to help families cope with a changing American society; to maintain steady economic growth and see that it benefits not only corporations, but individual families; to continue improving the environment; to work for more inter-racial unity; and to strengthen The United States' image throughout the world so that peace and democracy will flourish. Those are my major goals, and in working for them I promise to always act with integrity and in the best interests of our country."

There was loud applause from the audience, during which I said to Senator Bradley:

"The last two are the ones I wanted to hear most!"

After the meeting adjourned, a reporter from a local N. H. newspaper, Foster's Daily Democrat, interviewed my wife, Elizabeth. She not only told the reporter her assessment of Senator Bradley, but also added that it was her Republican husband who asked the question that got so much applause. In typical newspaper fashion, what got printed about me was this: .

"It was her registered Republican husband, Macon Epps, who asked Bradley which of his campaign promises would be expendable if he were elected president."

They were kind enough to include a photo of me with a caption that said I asked, "If he is going to keep his campaign promises." That was closer, but I felt that both texts were watered-down versions of my original comments and question.

The next day my picture, my question, and Senator Bradley's answer, were in the N. Y. Times and the Washington Post, so I got a few seconds of fame. (The Post was mailed to me from a friend in another state)

There were many other good questions from the audience that Candidate Bradley answered thoughtfully and with seeming sincerity. I wish that Foster's had included most of them, because they display the interest and intelligence of the voters, and are crucial to our system working better. The comments of a young woman who had been part of Americorps were especially appropriate. They not only showed how one person can make a positive difference, but reinforced Bill Bradley's admonition to all of us: "Get involved, quell the special interests, and make our democracy work for all the people."

As a thinking and concerned citizen, I find many things I like and dislike about all political parties. I wish we could choose the best ideas and policies from each party, and discard the self-serving and unworkable ones. I especially wish that our elected officials would work together to find the best solution to our many problems by adopting policies and programs that will make our nation stronger, more united, and prosperous for all our citizens. I also wish that the U.S.A. could be more effective in making the world a more prosperous and peaceful place by example and leadership.

For the 2000 elections, I believe that Senator McCain is more in tune with my political philosophy than Senator Bradley. Both espouse needed reforms, but McCain seeks less Federal Government and more and better state governments, per the tenth amendment. However, I find that both men have the three "I's" that I seek in a candidate: "Intelligence, Integrity, and the Interest of the people, so I hope both will get the nomination of their party. If they do, I will have to think long and hard before I vote, but I will do so with the feeling that our beloved country will be in good hands!

SATURDAY MORNING REVERIE

My plants need watering, so I turn my hose to soft sprinkle and slowly quench their thirst. First, my 8 flower boxes, next my 2 dwarf citrus trees in large pots, then four potted plants, plus some left over poinsettias.

It's a balmy, slightly overcast day, and the nearby mountains dominate my horizon. Recent rains have made them sparkling green, bringing new life to the formerly dry plants and grasses. I pause to admire the scene's majestic beauty.

As I contemplate this peaceful and pleasant picture, a humming bird suddenly appears. It seems to have been attracted by the hose water, because it hovers just beyond the main stream. I ponder: Is it inhaling the mist of the spray, thus quenching its thirst? Is it taking a quick shower to drive dust from its smooth, sleek feathers? Or is it just delighting in the tinkling, musical sound of the flowing water?

My questions aren't answered, so I just stare and marvel at this fascinating, tiny creature. I can barely hear its hum, so I turn off my hose to quell its competing sound. The tiny creature quickly flits away, but returns just as quickly once I resume the water's soft flow.

During the silent interval, I hear its humming sound easily, and notice this: Although it has variable pitch, I can't detect a tune like humans make while humming. Other birds create a tune while singing, but this little bird is just whirring its wings; hence no tune.

I notice how quickly it can move, and feel slightly vulnerable. Suppose it darts swiftly toward my exposed face and pokes its sharp, pointed bill into soft flesh, or worse yet my eyes. I remember that I am wearing glasses, so my precious eyes are protected. I wonder if my empty hand would be fast enough to ward it off, if it did attack.

I realize that it has no intention of harming me. Perhaps my huge size, and my power to control flowing water have made it feel vulnerable toward me. Then I remember that most animals act mostly in self-defense, or to satisfy bodily hunger. Both are traits that I wish my fellow humans would follow more closely.

I wonder if its tiny brain can think cognitively, or does it operate purely by instinct. Either way, I marvel at its ability to fly forward and backwards, up and down, sideways or at any angle, and hover in one place. Surely it is nature's helicopter, and it existed eons before man finally learned to copy it.

I recall the course I took at N.Y.U on "Helicopter Theory", under Dr. <u>Alexander Klemin</u>. It led to after-hours work for <u>Peter Papadakis</u>, President of the Gyrodyne Corporation of America. Gyrodyne was in its formative years at that time, so the stock I worked for paid off once it became successful.

After the humming bird flew away, I know not where, my wife opened a window to talk to me. She had not seen the bird, but guess what she said? "When you come in, bring the humming-bird feeder and I will fill it." Of course I said "O.K."

As is their custom, large trees have dropped pine needles and leaves on my patio. Spotting them, I turn my handy hose on full blast and squirt them and any accumulated dust away. My patio is now sparkling clean, so I turn the hose off and coil it up, like a long green snake, on its hanger. I pluck several tangerines from my tree, unhook the feeder, and go back inside.

It is now noon, and I sense my own hunger and thirst. Suddenly, I discover a stronger feeling, which is mental, not physical. It is the desire to preserve my "Saturday Morning Reverie" on paper, before it gets tangled in the regular routine of living.

As I complete this short piece, these thoughts come to mind:

1. How many small, but wonderful, experiences have I encountered in my 85 years on earth, and why didn't I write more down?

2. I'm sure that other people have similar, and even more meaningful, experiences. I hope they write them down; even if they don't, I hope they will fully appreciate them, and store them away until life's pains and sorrows surface. Remember, the meaningful experiences of life are a good antidote for tougher times!

SCENES FROM A JETLINER

As I look out my window on American Airlines flight 2445 from Dallas to Los Angeles, the many fascinating scenes intrigue me. Even though I have been flying since 1939, I remain amazed at the great variety that Mother Earth presents to those who take time to observe. Here are my observations as recorded in my little notebook:

Take-off is now mundane, yet there is still a thrill when I hear the engines roar and feel the increased pressure on my back from the acceleration. Soon the local buildings and even those in Dallas, some miles away, have faded from view. I see small cities, even smaller towns, and tiny villages, and wonder what life is like there. I suppose it is home sweet home for the inhabitants, and my memory takes me back to the small city in North Carolina, where I grew up. (Population 5000). Although I loved it dearly, college and my subsequent work as an aeronautical engineer took me far away from it. This scene sends me back in time to those good old days in Newton, N.C.

My reverie is interrupted when I spot some large circles on the ground. They are near farmhouses, so I realize they are the current way some people grow crops. The circles didn't exist in my youth, and I speculate that the farmers must have an advantage doing it that way. Perhaps more efficient tilling, planting, watering and harvesting will result. I notice that they have a road that is a radius, leading from the circumference to the center. The circles and the radius are pleasing; they remind me of my High School Geometry teacher, Leila Shore, and the importance of mathematics during my career.

When I see distant lakes and small ponds and streams just below, the flashing lights that strike my eye intrigue me. They are like brilliant strobe lamps in their intensity and short duration. They occur when the bright sun and the water are directly lined up with my eyes, and I catch them even when the water is too small to spot. I suppose that even the smallest mud-puddle wants to let me know it is there, driving home the point that size is not the only criteria for judging things.

Soon, all signs of civilization vanish, except for a few sparse, feeble-looking roads. Even the roads have no traffic, so I conclude that we have reached a vast desert, but it too has its own attractions. Sparse vegetation, variegated patches of soil, even a few little hillocks here and there. The flat, barren land starts rising, and I see a wild pattern of hillocks and gullies, and then some large flat mesas, outlined by sharp, curvy cliffs. They look like pieces of a gigantic jigsaw puzzle, which has yet to be assembled.

When the terrain grows higher and steeper, I see rugged mountains that seem to have vegetation, but it is too small to see from 34,000 feet. Time and erosion have carved wonderful patterns that become cliffs and canyons, ridges and gullies, and long, serpentine forms that are dry rivers and creeks.

Suddenly, a new feature forms, which puzzles me. The land below now has thousands of irregular spots, as if some pestilence struck rapidly and then departed. Unfortunately, I cannot solve the mystery from my comfortable seat, and the beverage being served distracts me.

As we continue on, some of the mountains are strangely "soft" looking, in spite of their twists and turns, and undulating forms. The softness doesn't look like vegetation, but simply that nature was very gentle when carving out this fascinating landscape. Incidentally, it has turned more colorful, with reddish hues blending with the mixed brown ones. The colors are not as vivid as the Painted Desert, which I have seen several times on previous flights.

So far, it has been a cloudless sky, but now a few small cumulous ones appear. They seem to be moving eastward at a good pace, or is it an illusion caused by our westward speed? I pick a landmark under a single cloud and trace the clouds progress. When it moves substantially away from the landmark, I conclude that there is a strong wind from the west. Fortunately, the clouds don't congregate, but remain widely scattered so the landscape remains mostly in view.

We have now traveled over an hour over the deserted land, and the terrain is still mostly devoid of human signs. I marvel at how much unused land exists in the good old U.S.A. I wonder if the scientists and engineers will ever be able to send some of the torrential rains that now plague the East Coast states westward, thus making the barren land a new "Eden".

I spot a long, straight road, which crosses a dry, flat desert and ends at the bottom of an isolated and rugged mountain. Who caused this road to be constructed, and why? Was it some nutty millionaire, or some politician exercising his wasteful "pork" privileges? Is there a logical answer? If so, it eludes me!

As I gaze at the distant horizon, it is too filled with polluted air and haze to form a distinct line. I recall my flying lessons of 1939-40, and how we used the horizon to check level flight, but now pilots most everywhere must use an artificial horizon instrument. Once again, "Necessity is the Mother of Invention."

During my piloting days, the ground seemed to move swiftly by, even though my craft's top speed was less than 100 mph. Now, we travel at around 600 mph, but our much greater altitude makes it appear that the earth is moving much slower than yesteryear. I am grateful that the flight from Dallas to L.A. now takes only 3 hours in spite of the optical illusion of slower ground speed.

We are now descending into the L.A. Basin, and I see a mass of clouds ahead. I look below and backward and admire the last visible, rugged mountains. Civilization, with all its marvels and problems, is just a few minutes away, so I leave my high-altitude observations with these thoughts:

During my exercise walks up and down the aisle, I noticed other passengers reading, talking, using computers, watching on-board TV, and sleeping. Even those at the window seats didn't seem to be focused on the wonderful scenes below, as I had done. What a waste, I thought, especially since only modern man and the angels have such a privilege. Hopefully, those who read this article will grab the opportunity on their next flight.

Or perhaps some enterprising person will make a video or DVD of all the wonderful scenes the airlines give us free, make a fortune, and satisfy some of the basic needs of thoughtful people!

SENTIMENTAL SOUNDS, SPLENDID SCENES

It is three a.m., and I'm wide-awake. I place a C.D. in my bedside player, put on my headphones, and listen to the "Musical Sea of Tranquility" with classical melodies from a celestial harp. There are: background sounds of a crashing surf; plaintiff cries from a soaring seagull; and delightful yells of children cavorting in moist sand. They send sentimental sounds to my head.

The sentimental sounds soon perform their marvelous magic by creating many splendid scenes in my darkened bedroom. My mind's eye sees the wondrous waves of the dark blue sea, swelling, peaking, crashing onto the shallow shore, and then slithering slowly back to the sea. It sees not just one, but many seagulls darting to and fro, then landing with fluttering wings to snatch some loose scraps of food from the beach-- squawking furiously when anything dares to intrude on their find.

It sees sleek yachts with multi-colored sails, and on the far horizon the stacks and hull of an ocean liner destined for distant places. The children and their sandcastles pop into view, and I revel in the delight of the children, and the pride of their parents as they contemplate their offspring's' creativity. Crabs scurry to the water, fish leap in random acts of joy, and a dog's eager catch of a flying Frisbee completes the scene.

High above this tranquil tapestry, I spot a jet plane's vapor trail-- a slender, elongated cloud that seems out of place with the ponderous, puffy clouds floating over the shore. It will vanish quickly, because mere mortals, not divine nature, make it. But the jet is one of the amazing accomplishments of the human race, so I look in awe.

I find myself looking out the window of the jet, marveling at the distant diorama below. It has become and impressionistic image which morphs into splendid scene after scene. In a flash, I am back on the beach sneaking glimpses at a few beauties in stunning swimwear.

The music now re-enters my consciousness, and I recall the concerts and operas that enriched my life-- way, way beyond belief. My mentality marvels at the genuine genius of the magnificent minds that condensed so much beauty into a thin, round disc. It marvels even more when I contemplate other technological advances-- I-Pods; MP3 players; computers....

My thoughts then flee way back to those super humans who composed these memorable melodies out of thin air, and to today's talented men and women who lovingly make the composers' scribblings come alive with their marvelous instruments and incredible interpretive skills.

My mind then drifts toward infinity as I contemplate all the humans and the zillions of hours it took to develop the music and the equipment I am now listening to in the comfort of my bed. Among the humans who deserve great credit are: scientists; engineers; inventors; entrepreneurs; miners; manufacturers; teachers; instrument makers; truck drivers... the list is endless.

I become grateful for my own mind's capacity to enjoy these memorable melodies, appreciate those who made it possible for me to hear them, and then create unforgettable images in a darkened room with my wide-opened eyes staring at a dimly lit ceiling.

My eyelids finally grow heavy and I fall asleep, only to hear new sentimental sounds and see more splendid scenes, both of which are beyond description. I awake to a beautiful new day-- refreshed, renewed, and ready to revel in the exciting, exhilarating enterprise called
LIFE!

TEARFUL TUNES

I suspect that everyone has some tunes that will bring tears to their eyes. Why? Because the words and music bring back memories that touch us to the core. Now words and music together can be very powerful, but they can also be powerful alone. There are words of poetry, literature and scripture that move us deeply, and music alone can move even more people because it is the universal language!

Sometimes the words, or music can be very simple and common; sometimes they are very complicated and high class; sometimes they are so personal that even close friends wonder why we are so moved. Here are some examples from my 88 years on earth:

At a recent violin concert, the last piece was the famous Hawaiian song, "Farewell to Thee." It always moved me because the music was emotional and the words meant that someone was saying goodbye, frequently after a pleasant visit. Usually, that doesn't bring any tears because there will be other times when we can "meet again." But as I looked at the audience of senior citizens and contemplated my own age, these thoughts went through my head: 'You have recently lost some new friends, and last year you lost some old and very dear friends. Because of time and distance, you weren't able to say "farewell to thee" to most of them. Even when you were able to do so, it was a sad occasion.'

Once I started thinking of all the friends and relatives I had lost, tears filled my eyes and I had to remove my glasses and wipe them away with my handkerchief.

Today, March 16, 2008, my <u>wife</u> and I attended church and heard the hand bell choir play the song, "Long, Long, Ago." Again tears welled up in my eyes as I recalled my boyhood and college years. Those happy, eventful, and formative years were certainly "Long, Long, Ago," and I was saddened that they are now just memories. Those days are <u>gone forever, never to be</u> <u>repeated!</u> If that isn't tearful, what is?

Classical music has the power to bring tears, even without any sentimental words. The third movement of <u>Mahler's</u> first symphony comes to mind. It starts with a slow tempo using the notes from the folk song, "Freré Jacque," or in English "Brother John." The notes are played in a minor key, so the combination means that many people don't realize their roots. Now "Freré Jacque" is neither a sad or happy song, just a pleasant one. But Mahler makes it a deeply introspective piece, which catches your attention. Then he adds some new and extremely beautiful tunes that are so moving that they bring tears.

I once read a story about <u>Franz Schubert</u>, a great composer that died at age 35 from Syphilis. According to the story, a friend asked Franz to compose a piece for a birthday party for a family member. Franz was an invited guest, so he willingly accepted. On the day of the party, the friend saw Franz and said he was looking forward to the composition. Franz was too embarrassed to admit that he had forgotten about it, so he rushed home to create it in the few hours before the party. When asked to play it at the party, he did so, but for the first time. The host and guest were deeply moved by its beauty, and so was Franz. There wasn't a dry eye in the room, especially Franz's eyes, when he finished his famous "Serenade!"

Sometimes the words of a song are more powerful than the music. Even words alone can move us to tears. Consider these passages of poetry, which always move me deeply:

"Full many a flower was born to bloom unseen
and waste its sweetness on the desert air.
Full many a gem of fairest ray serene,
the deep, unfathomed caves of ocean bear."
<u>Thomas Gray</u>, "Elegy written in a Country Grave Yard."

or

"Once upon a midnight, dreary,
while I pondered, weak and weary
over many a quaint and curious
volume of forgotten lore.

Softly, still, I heard a tapping,
as of someone gently rapping--
rapping at my chamber door.
This I heard, and nothing more.

Ah, how well do I remember;
it was in the bleak December
and each flickering, dying ember
wrought its ghost upon the floor

Vainly, I had sought to borrow,
from my books surcease of
sorrow; sorrow for the lost Lenore....
Whom I have lost--forevermore!
<u>Edgar Allen Poe</u>, "The Raven."

Also consider these words from <u>Shakespeare's</u> Romeo and Juliet, when

Romeo finds Juliet, supposedly dead in her tomb:

"Here I will remain—here with worms that are thy chambermaids; oh will I set up my everlasting rest; and shake the yoke of inauspicious stars from this world-wearied flesh."

"Eyes, look your last! Arms, take your last embrace! And lips, oh you the doors of death seal with a righteous kiss...."

"Here's to my love! (Drinks) Oh true apothecary! Thy drugs are quick— Thus with a kiss I die!"

If these words bring tears, imagine what would happen in a darkened theater when Romeo says them with great meaning and passion!

The Holy Bible, both the Old and New Testament, have so many words that move us deeply that I will not try to give examples.

Now the previous examples can bring tears of sadness. Fortunately there are music and words that can bring tears of joy. What parent or close friend hasn't had joyful tears once a beautiful young bride came slowly down the aisle to Wagner's "Here comes the bride."? Or had even more joyful tears when the bride and groom kissed, and left quickly to the bouncy tune of Mendelssohn's "Recessional."

Even the words of a minister during the wedding ceremony can bring tears of joy or sorrow, or both. I recall such an occasion when I was "Best Man" at my friends Dan and Jane Belvin's wedding. Dan was so moved by the words that tears flowed down his cheeks, and he sobbed audibly.

As "Best Man," I felt I should do something, but what? Give him my handkerchief? Pat his back? While I was making up my mind, Jane reached over and wiped away his tears with the handkerchief she held in her hand, and all was well. Now I couldn't classify Dan's tears as joy or sorrow, so I guess they were tears of emotion—sort of a combination of joy and sorrow.

I realize that I have just exposed a few examples of music and words that are "tearful," but given time I could fill a book. Instead, I will ask you— the reader or listener—to jot down some examples of your own and give me a copy. Perhaps we can make copies for family and friends. Any takers?

UNIVERSE

Students learning the English language might think that the topic of this essay is about a short form of poetry—one verse. Or, they might think it is some way to unite all poetry—united-verse. Actually, it is about a subject that stretches the human mind to its outer limits—and then some. Yes, it is about THE UNIVERSE, or as some call it today, THE COSMOS.

As a retired aerospace engineer who worked seven years on the Lunar

143

Module and its voyage to the moon with humans aboard, I have long had an interest in the Cosmos. I not only watched <u>Carl Sagan's</u> TV program about the Cosmos, but attended one of his lectures in Boston and spoke with him at the end. I find the work of modern astronomers and cosmologists both fascinating and admirable. These guys sure are smart, and they come up with theories that boggle the mind.

The first one that I remember was the "Expanding Universe." They found that distant galaxies were moving away from our galaxy because there was a red shift in incoming light. This was easy to understand, because most of us have noticed the change in pitch when a train that is blowing its whistle passes by. It is a higher pitch when approaching and a lower pitch when moving away. The train's speed shortens the sound waves (higher pitch) when approaching, and lengthens them (lower pitch) when receding.

Experiments on earth have shown that light that is moving away from the observer changes its wavelength, and, if the speed is huge it shifts to the red part of the light spectrum. Conversely, if it is approaching the observer, it shifts toward the blue part of the light spectrum. So far, so good regarding my limited intellect.

Next they came up with the BIG BANG THEORY. Their rational was based on retracing the path of the galaxies to their origin. Their conclusions was that the cosmos was once a tiny chunk of matter with incredible density, and that some time around 14 billion years ago it exploded with a huge force, sending huge amounts of matter away from its center at incredible speeds. Of course that is just a theory, since no one was there to observe the Big Bang, but their calculations made sense to the theorists, so who am I to dispute them. I still find it very hard to visualize that the whole universe was once the size of a child's marble, or smaller, and I suspect most other humans have the same problem.

Later on, I learned about Black Holes, which were huge accumulations of galaxies with so much gravity that light couldn't escape from them. Somehow, scientists were able to detect them and make calculations about their mass.

I often wondered how these scientists handled their mundane, everyday affairs. With such intimate knowledge of the enormity of the Universe, the infinity of time, and all the complexity of the Cosmos, are they upset when a waiter spills something on them? What happens if they get in a big argument with their wives or cohorts? And will they get upset if one of their investments loses a lot of dough? Alas, I never found an answer, but Carl Sagan seemed to be a very cool guy on his TV program and when I talked with him after his lecture. So I conclude that at least he remained cool when it came to everyday affairs.

Recently, I read some really provocative findings in my Scientific American magazine by the scientists who look at the big picture, as represented by the Universe. Here is a summary for those who are too enmeshed in everyday problems to look at their astounding findings:

In 1908, scientist thought our galaxy was the universe, and that everything beyond it was empty space. Today, in 2008, science has discovered 400 billion galaxies, and there could still be undiscovered ones. Since a galaxy contains billions of stars, similar to our sun, the cosmos is so huge it is hard to even visualize it. And when we consider the incredible amount of energy in our sun, the known energy supply in the cosmos blows the mind.

Recent observations indicate that the expanding universe is speeding up. This seems to be caused by some sort of "dark energy" in really outer space, which pulls galaxies toward it. Furthermore, it seems that this "empty" outer space has three times as much energy as the known universe. WOW!

Scientific observations and calculations indicate that the Milky Way (our galaxy), Andromeda, and some smaller nearby ones are not receding, but will come so close within five billion years that Andromeda will almost fill the night sky. Furthermore, our sun will become a red giant during the same time period, consigning earth to a very hot existence.

Within 100 billion years, the nearby galaxies will form a super galaxy, and all the receding galaxies will be un-observable by any creatures living in the super galaxy. This means that they will not be able to observe the origin of the universe through the Big Bang data.

In 100 trillion years, all the stars in the universe will burn out, leaving only dimly glowing black holes. Our super galaxy will become a black hole. Now the Scientific American article had a lot more information, including the formation of matter, but what I have reported in summary form is enough of a mind stretcher. Even with this glimpse of the big picture, I am still perplexed with the problems of today, let alone the ones five billion years from now when earth will lose its sun. But it does make me realize that even though we humans are a tiny part of the enormous cosmos, we may be the only creatures who can grasp and study such details of it.

Even among the billions of humans, most of us are relatively insignificant. Our insignificance becomes enormous compared to the cosmos, so what should we do? First, we can take pride that we are part of the race that has learned so much about the Cosmos. Next, we can do our part to make life more enjoyable and productive in the limited time we have on earth. We can also do our part to preserve our fragile planet during the next few billion years before it becomes extinct. Finally, we can turn to a faith of our choice that gives us hope that our spirits may be around for at least part of those future billions of years!

VISUAL PHENOMENA

What I am about to write is true, but there is no way I can prove it. When it was happening, I considered it a puzzling, but wonderful, experience. In fact, it had qualities that seemed spiritual, perhaps miraculous. If it has a scientific explanation, I haven't found it yet, and even if I do, it will remain a spiritual experience to me. I say that with confidence, because I have had other spiritual experiences that were easily explained by plain old common sense, let alone science.

Basically, here is what happened to me on Christmas night, 2002: Following Christmas day festivities with my Topanga, CA daughter's family, my wife and I, along with our Denver daughter and husband, returned to our Camarillo, CA home. I was joyous, but a bit weary, and closed my eyes after we sat down in our living room. It was then that it started-- a several day's sequence of wonderful visual images that occurred whenever both eyes were closed and I was fully awake.

What made them wonderful was their beauty; unforced creativity; brilliant and subdued colors; three-dimensional qualities; flowing motion; natural and artistic shapes and patterns; great detail; and ability to morph slowly into different objects or scenes. They didn't come with heavenly music or commentary, but I supplied that with my C.D. player and my descriptions. My wife, Denver daughter and husband supplied their amazed comments.

It is impractical to describe each of the huge number of visual images that I saw during the next few days, and there is no way I can convey their marvelous qualities. The latter would be like trying to describe a Monet, Bierstadt, or Turner painting, or perhaps a Disney cartoon feature with its motion and ability to morph. (Mike, my son-in law said it was too bad that I couldn't video tape it, as it might have a commercial market, possibly with Disney.)

Now I am not claiming that my images were the same high artistic level as those famous masters, or had the cleverness of the Disney people. My point is that descriptions can never do justice to the real thing. Even so, I will try to convey some rough ideas of a few of the images that I saw with 20-20 vision.

One of the early visions was a meadow with trees and bushes artistically arranged, much as Mother Nature does every day. The colors were varied, but subdued. There was no motion until it started to rain-- first slowly, and then torrentially. Puddles and little rivulets formed in the meadow, and I could see drops splashing in the water and off objects in the meadow.

After a while, the rain slowly turned into sleet and then snow, with flakes getting larger and larger. It was beautiful and fascinating, but it was similar to scenes I had seen with my eyes open. However, my eyes were now closed and the scene was a new one, at least to my conscious mind.

Granted that it may have been a scene from my sub-conscious mind, but why was I seeing it so clearly with my eyes closed and while I was awake and talking to my family?

A more puzzling and unusual scene was one in which there were thousands of thin black wires, artistically arranged on my new canvass. Their intersections made squares, rectangles, trapezoids and other geometrical shapes, and I marveled at their great number and detail. My marvel turned into amazement when the wires started changing into pleasing colors-- red, green, blue, orange, etc.-- and then started flowing in rippling and waving patterns. When I described this scene to my family, I assured them that I wasn't crazy, but was enjoying new, mysterious phenomena that brought me great pleasure.

My son-in law, <u>Mike</u>, said it sounded like I had been exposed accidentally to a psychedelic drug, adding, "If you find out what it was, let me know-- I want some!" My daughter, <u>Tina</u>, took a flash photo of me with my eyes shut and hands gesturing in a vain attempt to describe my "vision". My wife, <u>Elizabeth</u>, thought I was pulling one of my jokes, but soon realized I was dead serious. That, and their other testimony as eyewitnesses, is my only proof that I am telling the truth. But that is not real proof of what I experienced, only that I described something very unusual.

There were many other scenes that started with a vast network of thin wires, most of which eventually flowed or vibrated. Some had random and scattered patterns, but one formed a giant organization chart with all the spaces blank. I wondered if its significance was that there might still be a new role for me before I depart from this life. The vast network of wires reminded me that the human mind is composed of an even vaster network of interconnected cells, which is sometimes referred to as the mind's "wiring". Later on, I recalled that some scientist claimed that humans use only a small fraction of their mental capacity, so perhaps for the first time in my life I was using most of my brainpower.

This may be the right time to disclose some things about myself. That way, readers can decide whether I'm nuts or perfectly sane. It could also give some perceptive person a clue as to the cause of the phenomena.

1/16/03 marks my 83 birthday and I have led a mentally-active life. I earned two engineering degrees and had a long career in Aerospace as an engineer and middle manager for Grumman Aerospace Corporation. My first 22 years work was on military and commercial aircraft, followed by 7 years in several management positions on the Lunar Module. My last 9 years was in Advanced Civil Systems as Assistant Director, working on projects such as shipboard waste treatment systems and gigantic airship designs. Our department prepared all of the Civil System proposals and in a few cases followed through with detail design, manufacturing and testing My final project involved fusion energy, but that was so new, complex and demanding that I took the existing early retirement program at age 58 and started a small business in 1978.

I was the founder and first President of the "I-Cubed Corporation, which, as its name suggests, focused on Ideas, Innovations, and Inventions from various sources. After my second retirement in 1986, the corporation closed in another year or so.

During my early working years, and later at I-Cubed, I designed a number of original features and several products. While in management I made many design improvement suggestions. I personally conceived many inventions, but only got one patented. As can be seen from the above, my professional life was mentally active, creative, and stimulating.

My private life was similar, but lower keyed. In high school and college I played a baritone horn in various bands and formed a lifelong interest in music, especially classical. I dabbled with the piano and chord organ along the way and composed several pieces on paper and many in my head. Community activity included many years on the board of the Huntington, L. I. Concert Association, and President for two. Through out our life, my wife and I attended many performances of the N.Y. Philharmonic Orchestra, the Metropolitan Opera, and N.Y. theaters, as well as others elsewhere. These live performances were audible and visual inspirations.

Art was also an interest for years, and I tried my hand in it during my 30's. Several acceptable oil paintings and pencil sketches resulted, but my talents and interests lay elsewhere. That didn't stop me from appreciating the marvelous talent of others, and my wife and I have enjoyed many types of art during visits to museums and galleries all over the world. I even originated and chaired a massive art project for the Dover, NH Rotary Club that resulted in a 12 foot x 80-foot mural on the outer side of a store. Perhaps my close association with great art could explain the beauty of my mental Images.

Writing has also been a long-term interest which I was able to focus on during my retirement years, both in cooperation with others and personally. Two limited edition anthologies of short stories, poems and essays, featuring writers from Seacoast New Hampshire and Maine, were Dover, N. H., Rotary Club projects that I originated, chaired, edited, and contributed to.

I was founding chairperson of the New Hampshire Senior Writers' Action Group and editor for several years of its quarterly publication, "Senior Perspectives". The editorial committee selected a number of my writings for publication.

Individually, I have written numerous humorous pieces and jokes; short stories; essays; mini-dramas and movie scenarios; rhyming and non-rhyming poems; a "How to Book"; some aphorisms, which I call "Capsule Comments"; and true experiences, of which this is the latest. So far, they haven't made me rich and famous, and as a retiree it is not my goal, (However, more commercial publication would be pleasant.) Perhaps the busy mind that does so much writing helped me create the fascinating mental images.

My nighttime dreams are vivid, imaginative, and usually fun, and some of them are included in this book under "Old Man's Dreams." More importantly, I can usually remember them and some inspire my writings and inventions. My latest visual images are reminiscent of my dreams, but more beautiful, detailed and creative. Furthermore, they occur when I am wide-awake and talking to others, so perhaps my dream mechanism spilled over to my wide-awake mind. I have an optimistic nature, a pleasant disposition (most of the time) and this unusual experience not only did not frighten me, but I found it most enjoyable.

However, I am prudent enough to seek medical and spiritual advice to explore its meaning. My ophthalmologist has now examined my eyes and pronounced them fit for my age. He did say that some people see strange things at the start of macular degeneration, but that didn't apply to me.

I saw a neurologist, and he did a number of tests, including an MRI. Other than migraine headaches when I was middle aged, my only mental problems were a short-lived stroke when I was 57 (which the MRI detected) and the usual short-term memory loss of aging. The neurologist postulated that it might have been caused by a mini-stroke that was undetectable by the MRI, but admitted that there are many things about the mind that science is still puzzled by, but still exploring. He was unable to explain my visual phenomena from the test results, but said he was glad that I enjoyed it, instead of worrying about it as most other patients do when they encounter lesser phenomena.

As a main line Protestant Christian, I have been active in church affairs most of my life, which explains my spiritual outlook. I have gone into this much detail about myself hoping it will help those who read this article find a rational explanation for my experience, or perhaps see it as a spiritual encounter like I did.

For spiritual help, I called my minister, <u>Dr. Jim Decker-Mahin</u>, (who is legally blind, but has partial vision) to see if he had ever encountered such visions himself or known any others who had. He responded negatively, but agreed that it might be some sort of spiritual experience, adding, "It would be interesting to see if there is a scientific explanation." I mentioned that I had read about people during near-death experiences having strange and wonderful visions, and we both agreed that it hardly fit my case, except possibly peripherally. He recommended a book, "Life After Life," by <u>Moody</u>, which I read with great interest. He also said that I had handled these puzzling visions well by taking them as a wonderful and positive experience, rather than worrying about dire and negative concerns.

Now for some more examples:

Some of the scenes had buildings, plants and people. The buildings were usually masonry, and many were covered with artistic patterns of different colors. Some patterns resembled mold, but others were more like artists' designs. They were too varied, creative and numerous to have been made by my untalented artistic mind, unless it was working at maximum capacity, as I suggested earlier. An unusual feature of the buildings, or their components, was their ability to move in any direction. I wondered if movie scenes of earthquakes triggered that feature.

The plants, including trees, were normal, except that they looked like I was using 3-D glasses, which usually over emphasize the effect. Sometimes the plants moved slowly toward me and I could see great beauty and detail, but they never touched me. Sometimes the trees changed color, grew taller quickly, and even fell toward me in slow motion. Fortunately they never crashed into me, but I wondered what I would have done if they had.

The people were almost always middle-aged men and women. They wore old-fashioned clothes, including hats, probably from the 1890's. Their faces were usually somewhat blurred, but interesting and attractive. On several occasions a woman started walking toward me, but about half way she morphed into a man. Her dress slowly changed into a frock coat and pants, and her trim hat gradually became a broad- brimmed, western-style one. I took a positive interpretation of these changes, reasoning that some higher power was reminding me that men and women are basically the same and should have equal rights and responsibilities, but in accordance with their own special gifts.

Unlike some of my night and day dreams, especially in my youth, there were no sexual overtones in the images. There was no nudity, or even provocative clothes or positions. Freud's theories apparently will not be useful in interpreting those images, but perhaps some expert may think differently.

Many of the images involved bodies of water. There were flowing streams that accelerated and decelerated quickly. There were calm pools that were cloudy at first, but then grew so clear that the beauty of the sand, marine life and rock patterns of the bottom could be admired. Sometimes I was underwater completely, but could breathe normally and look horizontally and vertical at different sights. Sometimes I looked thru a glass window as if I was in a fish tank. Experts may say I was re-living my womb months.

Other images involved flocks of birds flying gracefully through the air; schools of fish swimming and leaping; hordes of insects partially clouding magnificent pastoral scenes; and mysterious strangers who lurked at the edges of my unusual canvass. Incidentally, some of the images filling my vision were close ups, some far away. The images slowly grew darker and then disappeared after 3 or 4 days. All of the above are just some of the many images that I saw, but they are enough to convey the puzzling and miraculous nature of my experience.

My cousin, David Schrum, a retired, but still very knowledgeable physician, thought there might be a possible connection with my earlier stroke. He reasoned that the re-wiring that takes place during a stroke's aftermath might have had some residual effects. He agreed with most of my minister's thoughts.

As I conclude this piece, I am still baffled by my unusual experience. Whatever their cause, the Neurologist I saw could no longer explore them directly, because he had no way to re-trigger them. He had encountered similar cases in the literature and during his practice involving the lower part of the brain, called the peduncle, but several MRI's and brain scans eliminated that explanation. Even the scars from my stroke, which he observed, were considered too small and too old to be of significance, so the mystery remains.

My only wish is that some reader will come up with a rational explanation. If it remains a mystery, I will be grateful that it was one of the most fascinating and puzzling experiences of my long life.

As to my future, I hope there will be other, equally marvelous experiences!

VULNERABILITY

It's a BIG word! It has thirteen letters and ranks right up there with other big words. Sure, some words are bigger, but on the other hand most words are much smaller.

It's an IMPORTANT word! It conveys a concept that affects all living things — people, animals, insects, plants…. Like it or not, life by its very nature is vulnerable to harm and eventually to death. It is more important than 'mortality', because it applies to every day of our life, not just the end of life. Of course different species may have differing DEGREES of vulnerability, but the bottom line is; WE ARE ALL VULNERABLE!

It is a FLEXIBLE word! it can connote individual vulnerability and its many subdivisions – physical, emotional, psychological, moral…. It can also connote national vulnerability and its many subdivisions– political, commercial, military…. It applies to individuals, groups, societies, nations, species–and the subdivisions are limited only by the imagination.

It is an UNAPPRECIATED word! As we go about our daily tasks, how often do we pause to consider the full extent of our vulnerability? (I wish more evil people did— maybe they would mend their ways,) Of course we all try to be careful, but how often do you wonder:

Will some drunk kill or maim me while I am driving safely?

Will someone cut me to the quick by a harsh judgment or unkind words?

Will a deadly disease select me for its next victim?

Will the I.R.S notify me of a serious tax problem?

Will some terrorist's path cross mine?

Will a poisonous substance invade my food, my water, or my air?

Will lightening, fire, flood, earthquake or some other natural calamity strike me?

The list is virtually endless! To make matters worse, it applies not only to you, but also to those you love—your mate, your children, your parents, your friends,,...

I realize that it may be unpleasant to contemplate our common vulnerability, but, unfortunately, ignoring it can't eliminate it. On the other hand, excessive contemplation could make us worry to the point of near paralysis. So are there any positive aspects to our vulnerability?

I think the answer is a resounding 'YES'! Consider these points:

Evil people are vulnerable. Hitler, Mussolini, Stalin and many other World War II criminals are now long dead. Their vulnerability finally overtook them—much to the relief of mankind,

Our vulnerability can deepen our appreciation of our blessings. It causes many of us to be more grateful when we experience:

The physical stimulation of sports, whether it be our favorite team's victory or the after glow of our own well-played efforts at golf, tennis – or tiddlewinks.

The intellectual stimulation of a good book, article, sermon or talk.

The emotional stimulation of a warm embrace. (Am I reaching you now?)

The wonder and joy of a healthy baby,

The pleasure of a good, wholesome meal that is shared with close friends or that 'special' person, (Made even more pleasurable when some one else does the cooking.)

The quiet satisfaction of a good days work—and an equally good paycheck,

The discovery of a new store or restaurant where friendly service and bargains abound,

The excitement of a successful investment that your friends considered "too risky".

The ecstasy of your first orgasm--and your 1000th!

The rapture of a genuine religious experience.

The sheer delight of doing whatever really turns you on!

We have many countermeasures for minimizing our vulnerability. For example:

Our bodies can heal themselves and will last over one hundred years if we take care of them and are lucky,

A good physician or other health professional can speed the healing and/or reduce the pain,

Insurance can relieve the financial burden of a serious problem. The support and prayers of friends and family can work miracles--or near miracles.

With six billion people in the world the odds are heavily in your favor. Only a small percent encounter real catastrophe or early death. If you can read this essay you are part of a select group with even better odds.

Confidence in yourself, or faith in a Supreme Being, can keep you going when things get really tough.

The above are just a sample of the many positive aspects of our vulnerability. Add your own to my list and you should have plenty to cope with the worries. Here are some specific suggestions for those who tend to accentuate the negative:

Recognize that vulnerability is a universal fact of all life. It is much more acceptable if you don't feel you are being singled out when your time comes to face disaster.

Realize that the wealthy and powerful are not exempt. To the contrary, they may be more vulnerable because thieves, scoundrels and assassins are drawn more to them than to you. In addition, they can afford more unhealthy pleasures. (My apologies if you are wealthy or powerful, but both situations can easily be corrected.)

Focus on the positive aspects: Evil people are highly vulnerable, your vulnerability can deepen your appreciation of your blessings and there are many countermeasures to minimize the bad aspects.

One final question needs to be answered—can we ever achieve INUVLNERABILITY ? The answer depends on one's faith.

For non-believers it appears to be impossible. What's worse, there is no hope– unless the 'nothingness' of the grave gives hope. Even if they find hope in the perpetuation of their genes thru their children, remember that they have the same vulnerability as their parents.

For believers, it appears to be possible! Best of all, hope abounds that there will be a joyous eternal life instead of the nothingness of the grave. The Bible gives many passages that give hope, so if you missed the movie you can easily get the book.
It is the most available one in the world!

MULTI-DECADE

AUTO FUN

How important have automobiles been in your life? If you are like me, you will say: "They've been very important, because they have brought much pleasure, a bit of pain and lots of fun." What sort of fun? Listen up and I'll tell you.

Do you remember cars before they had windows? Well, I do. I remember when they had isinglass curtains that had to be snapped on every winter, and even in warmer seasons when the weather got rainy or too windy. And having to sit in the back, as we kids did, it was usually windy because they could go 30 or 40 miles per hour once the road straightened out.

It wasn't long before they had glass windows that you could crank up and down; what a blessing that was. I could shut out the chilly wind, or open them wide when the weather was hot and muggy, then enjoy the cooling breeze. (A/C was many years away) And do you remember the great thrill when you owned your first car? I sure do, but before I tell you about that, let me tell you about some of my boyhood dreams of owning a car. I'm going to cheat a little, and have some grown-up fun with word play using the names of various cars to lighten this story. You may groan if you want to, but a silly giggle will please me more.

My first dream was of owning a model-T Ford. It was the first car that young men bought, usually a second- or third-hand one. Unfortunately, when they were in vogue, I couldn't afford one

Next I wanted a Chrysler, but I decided I was too old to cry for a Chrysler, so I went to the store and bought De soda. De soda made my teeth need work, so when I went to the dentist he tried to Ply my mouth open, so I tried to Dodge him.

I knew I would need a lot of dough to buy a car, even a very used one, so I tried to earn some by applying for a job as a caddy at the local golf course. Unfortunately they already had too many applicants, so I needed to find a course that had a Caddy Lack. A few weeks later, I went to a dog and pony act that was held on a deserted bridge. Some Italian gentleman called it a Ponte-act. As I entered my late teens, I was attracted to a used Oldsmobile, but figured I wasn't old enough to own such a mature sounding car.

As I matured, I was somewhat envious of people my age who had cars. I especially remember a girl named Sally, whose wealthy father gave her a brand new La Salle convertible. Our French Class called it La Sal's La Salle! I finally bought my first car when I was 21. The girls of that era were reluctant to give in to young men, and I was eager to have my first "lay", so naturally, I bought a Chevrolet!

Later on, a salesman named "Ed" tried to sell me an Edsel, but I wouldn't let Ed sell me an Edsel. When I discovered I couldn't even afford a brand new Ford, the Mercury in my thermometer rose. A Lincoln was way beyond my means; besides, I didn't want to run the risk of being assassinated! As to a Continental, who would buy a car named after a popular dance?

In my middle age, foreign cars intrigued me, so I bought a brand new Toyota. It was a good car, but I told the dealer that next time I was going to buy a real Ota, not a toy one. I didn't speak Japanese, so Nissan and Mitsubishi were out. I was interested in a Volvo, but they spelled it wrong. At first, a Mercedes-Benz looked good, but who wants a car that Benz? As to BMW, the first two letters sort of turned me off.

Currently, I own a Hyundai. Its warranty lasts for ten years, or 100,000 miles, so chances are that either my Honey or I will die before the warranty expires. If, perchance, the warranty expires before we do, I might buy a Saturn. It is the planet of old age, and during my working years I had jobs where I sat a lot. And since I plan to be cremated, my last resting place will be in an urn, so a Saturn seems like the right last car, or perhaps the last rite car!

If I've left a car out, please don't pout--
Don't even shout, or call me a lout--
Enter the game-- and tell me its name!
Then join the fun by making a pun! © 2009 L. Macon Epps   (4/1/07)

Cars I have owned: Chevrolet; Ford; Dodge; Chrysler; Plymouth Barracuda Convertible (My favorite); Renault (The worst); Volkswagen; Nissan; Subaru; Saturn; Toyota; Hyundai…

COINCIDENCES

There is something mysterious about the word as I use it here, because it describes events that actually happened, but are so unexpected and unlikely that they seem almost impossible. In fact, if a mathematician calculated the odds, I suspect most of the ones herein would be astronomical.

Coincidences happen to most everyone, but that only adds to the mystery. Some call it "fate," some "divine intervention", some "dumb luck".   Usually, they are positive incidents, but I suppose some are negative. The latter aren't told often, so it's hard to tell their relative number compared to the good ones. During my 87 years on earth, I have been involved in at least 25, which I am now putting on paper. This will provide a record of them in case anyone is compiling a book. If enough readers send me their own coincidences, maybe we can publish our own book of COINCIDENCES. Here are my 25 coincidences, all of which are remarkable, but some are in the "almost impossible" category.

1. When I was 12 years old, my folks sent me to a summer camp in the mountains of western North Carolina. It was my first time away from home by myself, so it left a strong impression on my youthful mind. I met other kids from my state, but a few were from South Carolina, and one was from Florida. The Florida kid was <u>Sidney Lanier</u>, and he was from Orlando, a city of which I had never heard at that time.

Later that summer, I met a very pretty girl from Florida named <u>Beebe</u> Shell. Guess where she was from? Orlando, of course, so now I knew two people from that city. Much to my amazement, when I told her about my friend from camp, she blithely said, "Oh, I know Sidney; he's a classmate in my school. Although I was only 12, somehow I knew that the odds were unbelievable.

2. When I was 15, my cousin, <u>David Schrum</u>, and I decided to hitchhike to Charlotte, North Carolina's largest city. Everything went well until after lunch, at which time we couldn't agree what to explore next. We were both hardheaded kids, and decided to go our separate ways.   I had walked perhaps half a block when I decided that I didn't want to explore and hitchhike alone, so I got a brilliant idea. I would follow him unseen and wait ten or more minutes before I surprised him. I reversed my tracks, and cautiously peeked around the corner of a building to spot him.

I was surprised-- no, shocked, when his face almost collided with mine; we both laughed heartily, and the only argument from then on was when I insisted we go his choice, and he insisted we go my choice. This was a low odds coincidence, because we both naturally came to the same conclusion about not getting separated. But the precise timing of our faces meeting still puzzles me.

3. At age 20, I had an engineering job at Grumman Aircraft Engineering Corporation on Long Island, NY. During my vacation back home in North Carolina the following summer, I met an attractive and talented young woman named <u>Emily Richardson</u>. She played the harp, and when she learned that I now lived on Long Island, she gave me information about a fellow harpist named <u>Lois Bannerman</u>. As a young bachelor, I called and made a date with Lois. I was so impressed with her beauty, charm, and talent that I called on her many times. That wasn't easy, since she lived in Hempstead, a city about 10 miles away from my small village of Bethpage, and she frequently gave concerts on weekends when I was off from my 52-hour workweek.

One weekend when she was away, I decided to go to New York City and continue my exploring of its many wonders. As I was walking on the crowded streets, whom did I spot? Lois, of course, and she spotted me. We talked for a bit, especially about the coincidence. I tried to get her to join me, but she had a work engagement and had to decline. It was a happy coincidence, but bad luck when she couldn't join me.

4. A few years later, I met a beautiful red-haired girl at work. Her name was <u>Betty Warren</u>, and she caught my eye immediately, and my heart not long after. Although I had a policy of not dating girls at work, I broke it after I met her. In less than a year, I proposed and we got married. We spent the first few days of our honeymoon in the city, and went to several Broadway shows. One day when we were approaching a box office for tickets, I almost bumped into a woman from my hometown, Newton, NC. Furthermore, she was the mother of <u>Dorothy Long,</u> a girl I had dated many times in High School, and a few times while we were both in college. Naturally, I introduced her to my new bride; she was gracious and wished us much happiness. It was a good coincidence, especially since her wishes for happiness came true and has lasted 62 years and counting!

5. When Grumman sent me away for six weeks to Cornell University for an Executive Development course, I met a number of bright and up-and-coming men. One day I was talking with a man named <u>Bill Baines</u>, who worked for a New Jersey Research and Development company. His face looked familiar to me, and mine looked familiar to him, so we started probing as to where we had met before. He was about six years older than I, and nothing seemed to work until he said, "Where did you go to college?"

When I told him N.C. State, he asked, "What years were you there?"

"I entered in 1936 and graduated in 1940."

"Did you take chemistry your freshman year?"

"Yes," I replied.

"Well, I was a Chemistry instructor there in 1936, and we must have seen each other in the building, or perhaps in a lab."

It was one of those explanations that can never be proved, but it satisfied both of us. We then marveled at how amazing the human memory can be. Even though mine has now slowed down a bit, I am still amazed at how much I can recall, sometimes in vivid detail!

6. This one involves my wife, but at least I played a part. As Chairman of the Mission Council at my church, I had arranged for a man from India, John Alexander, to come and talk to the Sunday school kids. He made a lasting impression on Betty, our kids and me, and we communicated for a number of years after he returned to India. A few years after his visit, Betty was a delegate from our church to a national Presbyterian convention in the mid-west. As she took her seat in the large assembly hall, she sat next to a woman from India. Although she knew it was impossible odds because there were about 800 million people in India at that time, she told the woman that we had a dear friend from India and gave his name.

You guessed it; she actually knew and admired John. Once Betty recovered from the shock, she figured the odds weren't 800 million to one, since they were both part of the relative small Christian community in India. We never figured the actual odds, but I'll bet they were still in the millions.

7. Through out our married life, Betty and I have loved to go to concerts, operas and the theater. While still living on Long Island, we frequently went to the half-priced ticket booth on Times Square. There were usually long lines there, so we passed the time by talking to those near us about shows they had seen, or ones we had seen. One day, we had an interesting chat with a couple from Ohio. Once we got our tickets to different plays and were departing, we both expressed our pleasure in meeting each other. The other man said, "Yes, it was fun, but unfortunately we'll never see each other again," We all agreed and left.

The next day, Betty and I decided to go to one of the city's fine museums. As we left one hall for another one, we bumped into the Ohio couple. We had a good laugh as we recalled his comments about "never seeing each other again." We agreed that the odds of it happening were almost impossible, but somehow we beat those odds. After a bit more talk we again departed. This time his prediction came true.

8. During our 46 years on Long Island, we had some good friends who owned a 38-foot yawl. We were fortunate enough to be invited by Lynn and Jean Radcliffe, to go on long cruises with them, some of which lasted two weeks. Several of the longer ones involved sailing from L.I. to Maine. After a few days of sailing we would anchor in a harbor to get supplies and find a place where we could take a shower. I needn't tell you that after a few days in the hot sun and doing the various tasks involved in sailing how much we needed them.

On one of the cruises, we stopped at Nantucket Island for supplies and showers. The Radcliffes had been there before and anchored near a fancy Yacht Club, and the only way to get to the street was through the clubhouse. Our ladies were a bit reluctant for us to be seen in our sailing attire and carrying bags for supplies, but Lynn convinced them by saying, "You won't know anyone here, and they won't know you, so why worry?"

Thus convinced, we made our way through the clubhouse, where well-dressed people were enjoying cocktails and light refreshments. We were about to exit, when I saw a good friend from L.I., Pierre Dupont. Naturally, we stopped, said hello and introduced the Radcliffe's. We chatted for a few minutes and then left. The ladies were a bit concerned that Peter, as we called him, had seen them in their condition, but agreed that the unusual coincidence was well worth the slight embarrassment.

Incidentally, Pierre was not related to the Pierre Dupont family of chemical industry fame, saying, with a laugh, "There are several billion dollars difference between their family and mine."

9. When I was 79, I took a hike up New Hampshire's Mt. Major with my Rotary Club. I was by far the oldest hiker, and the members were a bit concerned about me. Even so, I made it to the top somewhere in the middle of the pack. We had our bag lunches on the summit, and it was such a beautiful day I took some photos. Lake Winnipesaukee was easily seen, so I took several shots of its sparkling blue waters and surrounding mountains. After they were developed, I decided to send extra copies to my good friend, Lynn Radcliffe. Lynn was not only a sailing buddy, as shown by the previous story, but we had climbed a number of NH and other mountains in previous years, during which he had taught me to oil paint. We were also both avid music lovers and had many good evenings together at our homes listening and going to concerts. His folks had once owned a cottage on Lake Winnipesaukee, so I felt he would enjoy the photos.

One day, Lynn called me and said he could almost see his folk's old cottage from my photos, and asked if I would be willing to climb Mt. Major with him. I said yes, and the following fall we made arrangements for him and his wife, Jean, to visit us for several days. That way we could be sure of decent weather for our climb and enjoy each other's company. Our wives decided not to climb with us.

It was a beautiful November day when we started up. As usual, Lynn set a pace that I could keep up with although he was in much better shape than I, and more expert on mountains. There were hardly any other hikers that late in the season, but we met two coming down about half way up, We stopped to say hello, and one of the men said:

"I thought I would be the oldest guy on the mountain today, but you two may have me beat. I'm 60; would you mind telling me your ages?"

We both said, " We're 80."

He was impressed, and so was his son. We chatted a bit, and I asked his son what his work was.

"I'm a Naval officer", he responded.

"What branch are you in," one of us asked.

"I'm a Aircraft Carrier pilot."

"What type of airplane do you fly," we asked.

"A Grumman F14."

We told him that we had both worked as Grumman engineers for many years, and were impressed that he flew our F14, adding that carrier pilots are the best in the world and we admired his skill and dedication.

He and his father asked some questions about our previous work. When we told them that we both had not only worked on most of Grumman's aircraft, but also had important roles on the Lunar Module, they were impressed. The conversation ended with us praising him for the important work he was doing for the country, and he praising us for our previous contribution. If the father hadn't been curious about our ages, this coincidence would never have happened.

Somehow, the climb to the top seemed easier after this wonderful meeting. P.S. Lynn spotted his old family house from the peak; later on we drove by it and got a close up view.

10. I'm not sure this is a coincidence, but it was such an unusual experience that I'm going to tell it anyway. It happened when I was returning to Long Island from a business trip to Los Angeles on an airliner, whose first stop was Dallas, TX. I was sitting alone on the un-crowded flight, when I overheard an elderly woman in the seat in front of me tell the stewardess, "I just know I'm going to die. This is my first flight and I'm scared to death. Does this little window have a shade so I don't have to look out?"

The stewardess was very consoling, both with her soothing words and her help in moving the shade down. After she left, I said, "Pardon me, Mam, but would you like company on this flight?"

"Oh, would you mind?" she quickly responded. "I'm scared to death about flying-- it's so dangerous!"

Once I moved up to her seat, I made a bit of small talk. After I told her that I was an aeronautical engineer, I proceeded to convince her that flying was actually safer than her auto trip to L.A. (One of her sons had driven her from Dallas to L.A. to visit another son, but the one who drove her lived near L.A. and convinced his mother to fly home.) My words seemed to assuage her fears, and I even convinced her to lift the shade and enjoy the view. By this time we had risen to over ten thousand feet, so when she looked out the window she asked, "What are those little things moving around down there?"

"Those are automobiles and trucks," I replied.

"Then what are those bigger things?"

"Those are houses and buildings. We are so high up that everything down there looks small."

My answers not only satisfied her, but she started marveling about the wonders she could see from this height. She even said, "This must be the way the world looks to God!"

When I asked her what her L.A son did, she said, "Oh, he's in the movies."

I thought he could be a production worker, or maybe a musician or one of the many regular people needed to make a movie. When I asked her what he did, she replied nonchalantly, "He's an actor."

Again, I thought he might be a bit actor, but just in case, I asked, "What's his name-- maybe I've heard of him?"

I was pleasantly surprised when she said, "Dana Andrews."

Of course I told her that I was well aware of her son's work and admired him, which seemed to please her.

We continued talking all the way to Dallas, and she told me her deceased husband had been a Christian Minister and that she was disappointed that none of her sons had followed their father's calling. When I asked what they did, it turned out that they were successful in their chosen fields, had married and were supplying her with grandchildren. I was brave enough to tell her that she should count her blessings, because many other mothers had problem kids. She readily agreed.

When we landed at Dallas, I offered to escort her to transportation. However, another child was meeting her so she thanked me and declined. Thus ended her first airline trip--but a very interesting flight leg of many for me.

11. In 1986, after my second retirement, we moved to the wonderful state of New Hampshire. We left many good friends on Long Island, but took trips there about once a year to see those who hadn't moved to Florida or some other place. One year we decided to take a cruise down the Alaska coast, flying first to Anchorage, which we explored for three days.

On the last day in Anchorage, we were headed for lunch when I said, "Look; there's a man that looks like Arnold Jacobson."

Betty immediately said, "It is Arnold, and there's his wife Lillian." They had been good friends and neighbors on Long Island, but had moved to Florida. They were surprised when they saw us, and we all commented on the impossible odds and good fortune of our unexpected meeting. Arnold upped the odds when he said "We were going the opposite way a few minutes ago, but decided to go back to our hotel. Otherwise we would never have seen each other."

We all agreed, and made a date to have cocktails with them and their friends at their hotel, with dinner afterwards. It was a joyful reunion that would never have happened except for the wonderful coincidence!

12. During the Civil Rights Movement, led by Martin Luther King, Jr., Elizabeth and I were strong supporters. I had grown up in North Carolina during the depression and the colored folks, as we called them in those days, were discriminated against, but according to the customs of the times and never violently. Furthermore, there were many good friends between the races and there was lots of mutual respect. My father had been especially strong in that regard, and often told me that they were humans,

just like us, and had the same needs and wishes that we did. He even told me that his father had been saved from drowning by the family's only slave, emphasizing that if the slave hadn't saved Grandpa Epps, he wouldn't be here, and neither would I!

Dad was highly respected and loved by the black community, partly because he had spoken up for them when he was a director of the Building and Loan Business, but also because he had always treated them fairly when carrying out his duties as Justice of the Peace. When he died in 1954, at age 68, there were three black men standing with the Methodist Church Men's Organization as honorary pall- bearers. I was proud that I had made the arrangements, with my mother's full approval and the church's blessing.

Elizabeth and I had been privileged to hear Dr. King live at a rally in L. A. in the 1960's, when we lived in California for two years. We were saddened when he was killed, and still supported his cause. When his successor, Reverend Abernathy came to our hometown, Huntington, NY, we attended the dinner meeting in his honor. I went to the meeting place directly from work, planning to meet Elizabeth in the waiting area outside the huge dining room. I was sitting on a sofa, when a black man sat on a chair near me. He nodded hello, and I stuck out my hand to greet him, saying, "Hello, my name is Epps."

He was surprised at my name, because he said, "Are you kidding me?"

Now Epps is not a common name, as a glance at any telephone directory will confirm, so I assured him I wasn't kidding. When he told me his reason for the question, it was my turn to be surprised: "That's my name too. I'm John Epps, from Brooklyn."

I told him my full name and that I was a local guy. We then had a long discussion. Originally, he was from South Carolina, so our roots were from the same general area. When I told him that my grandfather's name was John Epps, he was even more surprised.

When Elizabeth showed up, I introduced them to each other and told her how we were both surprised by the same name coincidence. Elizabeth and I then went into dinner, but unfortunately not to the same table since his party still hadn't arrived.

Later on, I wondered if maybe, just maybe, he was related to the slave who had saved Grandpa John Epps and taken the name Epps once he was freed. That would have made it a really remarkable coincidence, but since I never pursued it further, I was satisfied with the coincidence of: meeting another Epps, of a different race, at a Civil Rights meeting, which we both happened to be attending and waiting in adjacent seats!

13. When I was in my early teens, my buddies and I liked to hike in the nearby countryside just to see if we could find some interesting sights, such as large gullies, steep hills with cliffs, or maybe a cave. We frequently left the unpaved country roads and crossed a field as a short cut to an interesting possibility. On one such occasion, we encountered a farmer

working in his field. He was friendly, and stopped us to talk a bit. After he found out what we were doing, which he approved, he asked our names. When I told him mine, he said, " By any chance are you related to John Epps, of Lincoln County?" (The one adjacent to our county, called "Catawba," after an Indian tribe)

"Yes sir," I replied. "He was my Grandfather."

"Well, you come from good stock." He then stated, with noticeable emotion: "He was the finest man I ever knew!"

I thanked him, and we soon departed. I don't recall any special sights we found during that hike, but I remember to this day those praising words. They became especially meaningful to me when, as an adult, I found that Grandpa Epps had died exactly five years before I was born. He died on Jan 16, 1915, and I often wonder what it would have meant to me as a child if I had known this man, who was called: "The finest man I ever knew!"

14. When Lee and Ruth Truman invited Elizabeth and me to a potluck luncheon, we promptly accepted. It was in honor of our good friends, Tut and Jean Hart who had moved away from our new hometown a year or so before. We had met both the Truman's and Harts at adult discussion groups at our Methodist Church in Camarillo, and felt privileged to be included with friends who had know them for many more years than had we.

During the luncheon, we met the Truman's daughter, who was visiting them for the weekend. Once we learned she was from Los Altos, CA, a good-sized city, I decided to try a long shot. "My college roommate, Jay Brandon, lives in the same city. By any chance do you know him or his wife, Jeannie?"

Much to my surprise, she said, "Yes I do. I worked closely with Jay on his WWII memorial project, which he and another man originated and brought to fruition."

"Yes," I said, "Jay has told me about the project. It is a large sculpture of a U.S. soldier holding a child in his arms, right? What was your role in the project?'

"I was the sculptor who won the competition. They liked my model and chose it over a large number of entries. I have a photo of it with me-- would you like to see it?"

"You bet," I quickly replied.

We were impressed with the sculpture, and so were other people at the table. We complimented the Truman's and their talented daughter, as did others who saw the impressive photo. We then discussed the unexpected coincidence, marveling at the confluence of events that made it happen. What are the odds that she would be visiting her parents the same weekend we had our one and only lunch with them? How many college people keep in close contact with their classmates 65 years later, even if both are lucky to be alive? And suppose I hadn't made the common-city connection and asked my question? There are probably a few other variables in this coincidence, but its probability of happening must be extremely low!

15. During the 1970's, Elizabeth and I went to Austria. We spent one week for sightseeing and one week for skiing in the mountains, near Kitzbuel. We both joined ski classes, but since we were on different levels of skill, they weren't the same classes. We usually rode up the large tramcar together, and separated at a higher altitude. To get to the slope with our instructors, we took different two-person chair lifts. One day I was on my lift with a young man not from our class, so I said, "Do you speak English?"

"Only," he replied.

"Are you American, like me?"

"Yes, I'm from Orlando, Florida."

(No, it wasn't Sidney Lanier from the first story, but a complete stranger.)

"I was in Orlando a few years ago," I said.

"Were you in Florida on business or pleasure?"

"Mostly business. I was at Cape Kennedy on business, and took a side trip to Orlando to see Disney World."

He then asked, "Were you involved in the Space Program?

"Yes I was. I work for Grumman Aerospace Corporation, and I spent seven years on the Lunar Module Program."

His next comment was a big surprise. "I have a cousin who is married to a man who worked on the same program. Her name is Winnie Rathke, and her husband is Bill Rathke. By any chance do you know either of them?"

"Do I know them? Bill was the Program Manager and my immediate boss on the Lunar Module. I've known Bill for about 30 years and worked on other programs with him. I've also known Winnie since she was an engineering aid at Grumman during WWII. In fact, we live in the same town near each other, and my wife and I see them socially. As I recall, Winnie's maiden name was Wilson. Is that your name too?"

"Yep! I'm Ken Wilson."

I introduce myself and we chatted a bit more until the lift reached the top, where we had to depart. I never saw him again, but you can bet that I told the Rathke's about this remarkable coincidence.

16. When I was about 23 years old, I was the principal engineer at Grumman Aircraft Corporation on an advanced development project for some new, high-strength, aluminum alloys produced by the Aluminum Company of America (Alcoa) and Reynolds Metals. The Navy's Bureau of Aeronautics sponsored the project, and it involved extensive structural and manufacturing testing of the new alloys so engineers would have the basic data to use in designing and manufacturing new aircraft. To prove our investigation was sound, we also re-designed and tested an existing wing from our latest model, The F7F.

I was pleased by four outcomes from my work. Praise from my boss,

<u>Pete Erlandsen</u>; Support from Grumman's Vice-president of Engineering, <u>Bill</u> <u>Schwendler</u>, who let me use it for my master's degree in Aeronautical Engineering from NYU; The Navy's Bureau of Aeronautics for using the results in a bulletin, which they gave to other contractors and for internal use; and finally, by very high praise from <u>Lt. Commander Emerson Conlon</u>, who was the Navy's key man on the project. I only met Lt. Cdr. Conlon in person once, and after the project was completed I lost track of him completely.

Sometime in the 1960's, around 20 years later, our path crossed again. It turned out that he had left the Navy and relocated to my hometown of Huntington, NY. Even more surprising, he joined the same Presbyterian Church to which I belonged. Furthermore, in the course of time, we were Ruling Elders together and spent many hours at Session meetings doing the church's work! Does this coincidence qualify for the saying, "God moves in mysterious ways?"

17. James was an assistant professor of education at UCLA and Rebecca was Director of the Lower School at an up-scale, private school in Brentwood, California. Both had been divorced recently and were coping with their new life style. Rebecca had a favorite place near her apartment, where she liked to unwind after work and have a snack or just a cup of coffee. One day she saw a nice looking young man sitting across the restaurant's outdoor patio. He saw Rebecca, she saw him, and their eyes made contact for a few seconds. When Rebecca left, the young man waited a moment, and then followed. Once she got in her car, he even followed her to her apartment. No, he wasn't one of those bad guys, but he was impressed enough to think it might be a good way to make contact with her another time. Another chance meeting at the restaurant would have pretty low odds, he figured.

Some weeks later, a woman friend invited Rebecca to a party. The young woman said, "I've invited a young man that I want you to meet. I think you'll really like him."

When Rebecca arrived at the party, the young man had not appeared, but a few minutes later he walked in and their hostess introduced them. Again their eyes met, and they instantly recognized each other. Yes, the young man was James, who had swapped glimpses with Rebecca at the restaurant and followed her home!

It was an unusual coincidence, but it was also one with a happy ending. They started dating and in due time they got married, bought a house, and had two kids-- a girl named <u>Hannah</u> and a boy named <u>Grady</u>. Now you may ask, "Why do you know so much about this coincidence? My answer is simple--<u>Rebecca</u> is our second daughter, and the marriage with <u>Dr. James Catterall</u> is still going strong. In fact, both Hannah and Grady are now students at U. C. Santa Cruz!

18. After my retirement from Grumman Aerospace Corporation in 1977, I started a small business called the I-Cubed Corporation. We dealt with new

ideas, innovations and inventions, hence the name I-Cubed. One of the things we did was help other inventors write business plans and raise venture capital for their idea. One of the inventors for whom I wrote a business plan, was named <u>Jeff Stein</u>. Now Jeff had a clever improvement on daisy wheel typewriters, which was then the leading way to type documents. (Word processors and personal computers were still a few years away) I had raised about $50,000 toward his goal of around 200K, and was still hoping to get more. One late afternoon, when I was playing tennis at my club, I was called into the clubhouse for an urgent telephone call. It was from one of my vice-presidents, <u>Norman McKinnon</u>, who told me a business club in Locust Valley, of which he was a member, desperately needed a speaker for their meeting the next day. It seems the scheduled speaker was sick and had to cancel. Somewhat reluctantly, I agreed, even though it was short notice. That evening, I prepared my talk, and gave it the next day without any problems. During the talk I told the audience about some of the new venture capital ideas we were working on, including Jeff Steins idea. After the meeting, Norman and I were approached by a man named Epstein, who happened to be a partner of Solomon Brothers, a leading Wall Street financial firm. <u>Mr. Epstein</u> was interested in the daisy-wheel typewriter, and asked if I could bring Mr. Stein to their Manhattan office to discuss funding the project with him and two other partners. Of course I said yes, and called Jeff the next day to set up a meeting.

Now I felt it was a nice co-incidence that I had obtained a potential client at a meeting in which I was the substitute speaker, but the real co-incidence lay in the fact that the potential client's last name was a combination of my last name and Jeff Stein's. I took it as a good omen that Epps and Stein were meeting with Epstein and two other partners.

We had been invited for lunch, which was served in the executive dining room. It was first rate, with gourmet cuisine and fine wine during it, and cigars passed out at the end. We then went to a conference room where Jeff and I told them details of our project. After a brief discussion among themselves, the three partners said they would like to finance our project, provided they could be the sole financiers. I had told them about the other subscribers, and said I would see if I could get them to release us, since they still hadn't put up any cash at that time.

On the train back to Long Island, I was quite optimistic, but Jeff wasn't, saying, "I've been disappointed too many times in the past, and won't feel good until they sign a contract and give us a check."

The next day, I got a telcon from Mr. Epstein, saying they had changed their mind and that I should proceed with my current subscribers. I was very disappointed, but glad I didn't have to talk with the current subscribers. Unfortunately, I wasn't able to get the extra subscribers needed to go ahead with the project, and it wasn't long before word processors and personal computers made daisy-wheel typewriters obsolete.

It was one of life's little defeats, even though the unusual nature of the co-incidence made it so promising!

19. In 1963, I had a field assignment in California on the Apollo Program. I was Senior Representative at North American's Space & Information Division for Grumman Aerospace, designers and builders of the Lunar Module. North American was the Prime Contractor for the Apollo Program, while Grumman was an associate contractor.

During our two-year stay, we met a couple from the Methodist Church we attended. We had invited Barbara and John Mitchell to our home for dinner, and after dinner we had a lively conversation about unusual people we had known. Barbara had just finished telling her story, which we all enjoyed. I then started telling about my friend Lynn Radcliffe without mentioned his name. I told about his many accomplishments and his perseverance to become an expert in whatever he decided to do. Among his accomplishments were sailing, cross-country running, piano and baritone horn playing, oil painting, mountain climbing, classical music expertise, etc. When I finished Barbara said, "That sounds like Reverend Radcliffe, our minister in Ohio."

"That's his father," I replied.

" Well, he must be a lot like his father, because Rev Radcliffe has the same skill and perseverance that let him masters whatever he chooses to master."

We were all impressed that my description of someone whose name I hadn't mentioned, caused her to think it was his father I was describing. What made it even more remarkable was the fact that we had recently moved to California, thousands of miles from Long Island, had met a couple from Ohio, and still came up with the unbelievable connection!

20. Sometime in the late 70's or early 80's, my wife and I took a European tour. I mentioned our plans to my dentist. Believe it or not, he was going to Europe about the same time. As we compared our itinerary, we found that we would be in Paris on the same day, so naturally we made arrangements to have dinner that night with him and his wife. During dinner, he said that his partner, Dr Harold Raymond and his wife Faye, would be in Rome about the same time as us, so he gave us their Hotel address and telephone number.

Once we arrived in Rome, we called his hotel, hoping to make meeting arrangements, but they were out sightseeing, so we left a message. We had dinner near his hotel, and decided to go to his hotel to see if he had returned. A quick check at the desk showed that he was still out, and was checking out the next morning. "Damn, we missed him," I said to my wife, Elizabeth. As we were leaving the hotel, we saw a taxi arrive, and who do you suppose emerged from it? Yes, it was Harold and Faye, and were they surprised to see us. We then filled them in with the details, and they invited us into the hotel bar for a farewell drink. We were all not only amazed at the unbelievable timing of the coincidence, but glad for its happy ending!

21. While still living in New Hampshire, <u>Elizabeth</u> and I liked to go to as many of the Presidential Primary meetings as possible. In 2000, we attended a meeting at which <u>Vice-President Al Gore</u> was speaking. After his speech, we went to talk with him. I was especially interested in his work regarding eliminating government waste and improving service, since I had a similar job at Grumman in the early '60's.

Standing near by was a man who had asked questions earlier about extra-terrestrial intelligence. Once I spotted him, I introduced myself and told him that my nephew, <u>Dr Steven Greer</u> was doing a lot of research on the same subject. I was pleasantly surprised when he told me that he knew Steve, was working closely with him, and that Steve had told him about my work on the Lunar Module. He was a Professor at UNH, and was even planning to get in touch with me since Steve had given him our address.

We had a long discussion that night, and I invited him to give a talk to my Rotary Club. Several weeks later he did so, and his talk was a big hit, even though some of the members were skeptics. However, one of the lady members wasn't, because she had an encounter with an extra-terrestrial being. She described it to both of us, and the Professor made notes to add to his database. So thanks, VP Al Gore; you not only made it possible to meet an associate of my nephew, but let me hear a first hand experience about ET contact. Two great coincidences!

22. <u>Elizabeth</u> and I moved to California again in 2001, settling down for good (we hope) in a retirement community called "Leisure Village." Early in 2006, we took advantage of one of the Village's local tours to the Jet Propulsion Lab. Also on the tour was a lovely lady, <u>Betty Stallman</u>, with whom I play a lot of doubles tennis and Elizabeth and I see at various club meetings. During the tour, Betty said, "Let's have lunch together-- there's a local Doctor I know that I want you to meet. He knows a lot about Extra-terrestrials.

During our lunchtime discussions, I found that <u>Dr. Roger Leir</u>, a Podiatric surgeon, was the author of two books on the subject-- "The Aliens and the Scalpel," and "UFO Crash in Brazil." Furthermore he knew my nephew, <u>Dr Steven Greer</u> and they had worked together in the ET field. Both Betty and I subsequently bought his books, and as Program Chairman of our Racquet Club, I was able to get Dr. Leir to give a talk to the members. Again, there were a few skeptics, but, unlike the Rotary meeting, there was no one who had a first hand encounter with ET's. Although this was not an "impossible" coincidence, as were some of the other ones, it was still a very pleasing and productive one.

23. In September 1989, my wife and I took a seven-week visit to New Zealand and Australia. Auckland, New Zealand was our first stop, and some how we had booked a hotel a mile or more from the downtown district. The next morning, we decided to go downtown to sightsee, and were told we could get a bus across the street. As we were waiting, a young woman in a car stopped and asked if we were going downtown. "Yes, I replied, we are

waiting for the bus."

"It will be a long wait, so since I am driving there I would be happy to take you."

Naturally, we accepted her kind offer and had a good discussion during the drive. She was even kind enough go eight or ten blocks out of her way to take us to the section she figured we should see. We thanked her, and had a fine day exploring Auckland. The next day, we hooked up with our tour bus and toured the North and South Island of this lovely country. We found the New Zealanders very warm and gracious people, and since they spoke English, we had no trouble communicating. We smiled a bit (privately) at their unusual accent, but they probably did the same with ours.

Sometime around 2004, while we were living in Camarillo, CA, We had to take a visiting friend to the local railroad station. After we had said goodbye and she boarded the train, we returned to our car. As we approached it, a middle aged woman asked if we could tell her how to get to the Outlet Stores, which is one of the big attractions of our new city.

I told her, "Straight up this road," pointing to Ventura Blvd. "But it is about two miles to get there. Tell you what, I'd be glad to drive you there, but you may have to walk or take a taxi to get back to the station."

"Are you sure it's not out of your way? I don't want to inconvenience you."

Although it was 90 degrees from our return home, we both reassured her it was OK, and she climbed into the car. As we were driving there, we asked where she was from. Imagine our surprise and delight when she said, "I'm from Auckland New Zealand."

We then told her about the kind Aucklander who gave us a lift, and told her how happy we were to repay the kindness we had been shown by her countryman. We were all pleased at the outcome, dropped her of at the Outlet, and never saw her again. At least up until now; but who knows what the future holds?

24. Many years ago, I used to go mountain climbing with my good friend, Lynn Radcliffe. He had a 1954 Porsche automobile that he was very fond of, because it was a very fine and sporty car. Usually we used it on our trips to the New Hampshire or Vermont mountains, and I recall those rides with fond memories. Not only because of the conversations with Lynn, but because we listened to great classical music on the way and shared our enthusiasm for it. During those trips I never dreamed that the Porsche would be the reason I met a new friend when I moved to California in 2001, about fifty years after my last ride in the Porsche.

It happened this way: A retired California man, named Steve Conger, decided to buy an old Porsche and fix it up. He was clever at doing this sort of work, and one day he found an old registration card in the glove compartment. The card belonged to my friend Lynn, and Steve was curious. Eventually, he made contact with Lynn, the original owner.

Because of their mutual interest in the Porsche, they communicated by mail and telephone for some time.

While addressing Christmas cards, Lynn noticed that Steve lived in my new hometown, so he sent me a note explaining his relationship and suggested I contact Steve. I noticed from Steve's address that he was in the same part of town as we were, so I called him and made arrangement to come have a drink with us. Lynn had told him about us so he accepted and brought the old Porsche, which he was still fixing. He even gave me a ride in it.

Since then, we have met on several occasions and have had fun talking about the Porsche and our mutual friend Lynn. I have told Steve many interesting things about Lynn, and his wife Jean, and our long friendship. Steve, in turn, has told me interesting things about his life. Our most recent meeting was when Steve took me on a long trip in Lynn's old Porsche, following very scenic, back roads that he uses with his biking bodies. Yes, Steve is an avid biker, and for a 66-year-old man he does very well. In fact, this trip was in celebration of his biking 1401 miles last month, a new record for him.

We not only had a delightful and very scenic ride, but Steve treated me to a very nice lunch at a very good restaurant in Ojai. I told him that Lynn would have liked the restaurant almost as much as I did, because it played classic music on a CD all during lunch, and had a lovely garden near our table. (Lynn is not only a classic music lover, but also a very fine pianist who has mastered many very challenging classical compositions.)

What makes this coincidence unusual is the role the ancient Porsche had in bringing Steve in contact with Lynn; Lynn's noticing the proximity of Steve and me; and the fact that Steve and I have become good friends. Now Lynn and I are much older than the Porsche, but for such an old car it did a splendid job in bringing Steve into our circle of friends

25. In 2002, we went on a river cruise in France with my cousin, David Schrum, and his charming wife, Betty. One day, my wife Elizabeth and I were invited to the captain's table, since we had toured with the same company many times. No, I didn't have a new wife; once we moved to New Hampshire Betty decided to go by her real name. I sometimes still call her Betty, which confuses our new friends who properly call her Elizabeth.

It was the first time we had been invited to dine with a Captain, and sitting with us at the table was a couple that we soon learned lived in Charlotte, NC. When I told them that I grew up in Newton, NC, the woman said, "So did I, and my husband grew up on a farm near Newton."

They were younger than we were, so I said, "My younger sister, Louise, may have been near your age. Did you ever know her in high school?"

"Yes, I was a classmate of Louise Epps, and I suppose she is your sister."

I of course agreed, and we marveled at the connection. When I told them that Louise was now living in Charlotte, the connection deepened.

Later on, I found out that her husband had been Executive Vice President of the Belk Department store chain. "Hey," I said. "My <u>Uncle John</u> was the part owner of <u>Belk-Schrum</u> in Lincolnton. Did you know him?"

"Yes I did. I knew him quite well. He was a good guy and a fine businessman."

Gosh, I thought. This is getting about as unusual as it gets, but I was wrong. His wife told me that he was the last man to shoot down a Japanese airplane in WWII, which made him unique.

Naturally, I asked, "What kind of airplane were you flying?"

"A Grumman Hellcat," he replied.

"I worked as an engineer for Grumman for 37 years and I helped design the Hellcat, as well as many of Grumman's other airplanes!"

He graciously replied, "It was a damn fine airplane, and it saved my hide on several occasions. So thanks."

"Thank you for your part in winning the war against the Japanese."

So there we were on a riverboat in the middle of France, an unlikely place to meet folks who: 1. Were from my hometown. 2. Knew my sister. 3. Were now living in the same city as my sister. 4. The husband knew and did business with my Uncle John, from Lincolnton, and 5. Flew with distinction an airplane that I helped design. Add to those, the fact that it was my first, and thus far only time to dine with the Captain, and you have an almost unbelievable coincidence.

As I finish jotting down memories of coincidences that happened to my wife and me, I hasten to add that they are the ones freshest in my mind. Given time, I will probably recall some other ones, but I doubt if any can top these, especially number 25! What do you think?

DIVINE PINCHES

I confess! When it comes to religious experiences, I have never had an earth-shaking one. No tongues of fire have crossed my vision. No blinding light has shown me "The Way", like it did for St. Paul. Clouds have never parted to show me God's magnificent face and there has been no rush of wind or speaking in many tongues, as occurred for the disciples on Pentecost. *

However, I have seen some fascinating, God-like "faces" in cloud formations and a mild stroke made me lose my normal speaking ability and compensate by talking in a gibberish sounding "tongue" that gave me a feeling of rapture. I have also heard some inspiring sermons that moved me to the core. But none of these experiences was "earth shaking", so I suppose I'll have to face it-- God has not given me a clear, unmistakable signal that I've been chosen to be one of

"His" earthly vessels.

Instead, I have received a lot of gentle, sometimes sharp, pinches to remind me that there is a powerful, creative force in the universe that mankind calls "God", "Jehovah", "Allah", "the Great Spirit", etc. Until lately, this force was usually described as masculine in nature, so I will use the name and personal pronouns that I have used most of my life; but in honor of the current, gender-neutral trend I will put quotation marks around the latter. In any event, the "pinches" that I received made it clear that I needed to learn more about God and the plans "He" has for "His" creatures, of which I am one. I have tried to do so by reading, listening and writing down some of my thoughts.

Some of the "pinches" were pleasing-- rugged, snow-covered mountains glistening in the morning sun; a hillside of rhododendron in full bloom; a gorgeous sunset; autumn in New England; the angelic smile of a baby; a ripe watermelon; a splendid meal; a loving family; a crystal-clear, star-filled night; ....

Some were unpleasant-- an upset stomach; a sick child; a violent thunderstorm that was too close for comfort; an angry friend; an unfair boss; a scolding teacher; a devastating hail storm on my garden; ....

Some were downright painful-- a broken arm; the death of a dear one; an auto crash; a dangerous operation; job-threatening layoffs; several failed ventures; ....

My "pinches" were slower, and probably surer for my doubting mind, than a sudden, earth-shaking conversion experience. Collectively, they have built a strong faith that is not easily eroded by the vicissitudes of life. And they are so numerous that it is difficult to forget ALL of them, so they compensate for my failing memory.

If you are like me, thank God for "His" little "pinches". "He" is being gentle with you!

* I did speak in tongues once when I had a stroke. See 70's decade.

DREAMS OF GOD

To some people, God is a very real presence that influences their daily lives directly. To others, He* is a fuzzy image that they turn to in time of need or during religious services. Still others consider him just a product of the human imagination—a useful crutch for those who can't quite cope with reality. There are countless positions between these three basic ones.

Unless you endorse the first position, you will probably agree that our conscious minds find many puzzles whenever we contemplate God: Why is He so silent and mysterious? Why does He let evil and injustice flourish? Why did He design the world with so much natural violence—predatory animals, poisonous snakes, devastating insects, destructive hurricanes, fierce volcanoes, frightening earthquakes and the like?

Even when science unravels some of the mysteries of the universe, we still wonder at its inconceivable vastness. How can it go on forever—yet how can it have an end? Shouldn't there be something beyond the end, even if it is just empty space?

We wonder why our solar system has only one planet that, as far as we know, can support life. We marvel at the great variety and abundance of living things on earth. We believe we are at the top of the pyramid among earth's life forms and feel very lucky—perhaps even special creatures.

We speculate that, with trillions of known stars, probability theory suggests there must be billions of planets like earth. We ponder whether they are populated by intelligent beings or if they are just waiting for us to populate them once we conquer inter-stellar space.

We are puzzled by the eternity of time. When did it start and will it ever stop? Sure, it stops for individual mortals, but from an objective viewpoint, how can it have a beginning or an end?

We question how the cosmos got there. Is it really still expanding and did it start from an incredibly dense chunk of matter about the size of a child's marble just before the "Big Bang," as science now says? Or was it like the account in Genesis in which God was the prime mover and super intelligence? Are they mutually exclusive explanations of earth events, or can they dwell in intellectual harmony?

There seems to be one inevitable conclusion: Active, conscious minds can raise many more questions than Science and Religion can answer!

The subconscious mind is different. The normal constraints of the real world no longer apply, and thoughts, images, ideas and visions flow freely. In fact, "impossible" events and capabilities are routine for the amazing subconscious mind. For example, in my own dreams I have experienced: flight without wings; breathing under water; safe falls from great heights; 300 foot broad jumps; 1000 foot trees; inter-stellar space travel; safe passage through the sun—you name it and the subconscious mind can do it. If it is a dream, the subconscious can conjure up images, colors, sounds and other sensations that make everything not only seem possible but perfectly natural!

So it seems to me that it would be interesting and possibly useful to tap the subconscious mind. By examining some of the dreams involving God we may gain a new and better insight of God, or at least human concepts of him.

* The writer is aware of the modern trend to avoid assigning gender to God. However, referring to God as "He" or "Him" makes for easier reading and hopefully will not offend anyone as long as we all understand that God may be masculine, feminine, or neuter, or perhaps all three at once.

Here are eight dreams of God from young and old people, male and female. Each dream is told in the dreamer's own words** and is grouped by gender and then arranged within the group by the approximate year in which they occurred. The geographical location is also given. This tact was followed so that it would be easier to ascertain whether or not gender, age, time period or location affects our dreams of God. Since dreams are personal and to many people private, I have omitted any identifying references.

[**] Minor editing was done, but the essence of each dream was retained.

Male Dreams;

1. Age: 18; Year: 1939; Location: Mid-South; The Dream:
Judgment day had arrived and those that were consigned to hell were told to start marching into a cave that led directly there. Unfortunately, I was in the group destined for the subterranean journey.

Like all the others, I was a bit shocked that my good deeds hadn't outweighed my bad ones. Unlike others, I didn't protest. In fact, I started my slow descent toward hell with a vocal admission that I undoubtedly deserved my fate. I also voiced the hope that God would see fit to release me once I had paid for my sins. I was going willingly but still harbored a faint hope in my heart. Much to my surprise, God's voice (I never saw him) said that we had been given a final test. Since I was the only one to accept His judgment without protest, He said I could ascend back to the surface and join the heaven-bound group. I woke up before I was able to get to heaven, but it was still a memorable dream.

2. Age: 19; Year: 1968; location: Vietnam (home state: Texas) Prologue;
I was assigned to the 67th Evacuation Hospital outside of Qui Nhon, South Vietnam. The night I am going to tell you about happened when I had been in Vietnam for about six months. It was the night Jesus came to me and said that I wasn't going to die.

I was raised in the '50's and early '60's and probably had the typical American Protestant education. I was raised a Methodist and was active in the Methodist Youth Fellowship. I uncritically and unquestioningly accepted the church's teachings. I was an intelligent boy and a good student, so I not only accepted the church's teachings, but learned them so well that many times I considered becoming a minister.

It was my fortune that the natural rebelliousness of my teenage years coincided with society's rebelliousness during the late '60s. It was a time when I questioned all of my values. I moved away from the Methodist church and began attending a Unitarian fellowship. But the move didn't satisfy me, it seemed like I moved away from a structured religion that I thought was perhaps wrong to an unstructured philosophy which was so full of shades of grey that it was too timid to call any act or thought wrong or right.

Eventually the erosion of my faith made me give up thoughts of becoming a minister. I spent a year in college as an English major, then dropped out, joined the army and went to Vietnam.

In Vietnam I was assigned to a first aid dispensary on a caserne that was also home to a Military Intelligence unit and an ammunition depot. We were located in a valley where it was a common occurrence to have the enemy lob mortar shells on us. They would fire a few rounds and retreat back into their caves and we would respond with artillery fire and helicopter gun ships and tens of thousands of dollars worth of pyrotechnics. I don't think anyone ever got hurt by the mortar attacks and we always enjoyed the US response—the rocket's red glare, etc.

However, our anxiety level was raised one night when sappers infiltrated the compound and destroyed several vehicles in the motor pool. The next night sappers blew up part of the ammunition depot. To the six of us in the dispensary these events seemed a serious escalation. For two nights in a row the enemy had quit waging a long distance war with laughingly inaccurate mortars and had actually been within a couple of hundred yards of where we slept.

The day after the two attacks was filled with rumor: the hills were filled with VC that were going to overrun us that night; the sappers had stolen poison gas from the ammo dump and would use it against us; Military Intelligence knew how bad the situation was and had bugged out. And there was just enough activity to give credence to the rumors: our aircraft spent the entire day blanketing the hillsides with mini-gun fire; a directive came down from headquarters saying that we should all review how to put on our gas masks; and no one was in the offices or barracks of the Military Intelligence unit.

By nightfall it seemed like everyone was resigned to the notion that we were going to die. And we all handled it differently. Some drank and got a little loud; others smoked grass and listened to music. I wrote a letter to my wife.

After midnight I went to my hootch and tried to go to sleep. I lay in bed thinking what a pisser it was that I would never see my wife again and never see my daughter grow up. I thought of how on my report cards my teachers would always write about how much potential I had, and now that potential was going to be snuffed out by someone who didn't know who he was killing. I thought of how, despite our protests to the contrary, we must really love war or we would have stopped it centuries ago. I thought about praying, but a last minute conversion seemed too cynical.

THE DREAM:
At some point I drifted off to sleep and had this dream: I was sleeping in my bunk when suddenly my room filled with light and I woke up. Jesus was in my room speaking to me. I didn't actually see anyone, the room filled with a diffused light, more of a glow than a bright light and I knew that Jesus was there. And even though I didn't see a physical form, my attention was directed to the foot of the bed as though he were standing there.

And when I say that he spoke to me, I didn't actually hear a voice—but I could feel the words and felt they were coming from the foot of my bed. Jesus told me that he knew I was worried and I shouldn't be. He told me that I would not die in Vietnam. He also told me that he knew I was struggling with my religious doctrine and that I should quit worrying about that also—he told me that my ideas about religion, philosophy, and morality were correct. Then the light gradually dimmed and I knew that he was gone.

Epilogue:
I woke up and went outside to smoke a cigarette. I was totally at peace. I had a feeling of serenity that I doubt I'll ever experience again.

The war stayed far away from us that night. No gas attacks, no human waves overwhelming the perimeter. In fact the war was quiet for a couple of weeks, then returned to the ineffective mortar attacks. And for several weeks I was certain that Jesus had come in the night to comfort me. I didn't tell anyone about the visit, but I kept the peaceful feeling.

Then I started thinking about what happened and realized that I had to have tricked myself into imagining the visit. Certainly the biggest incongruity was having Jesus tell me that my philosophy was correct when I knew that it was incomplete and contradictory.

I really think that I was so morose at the thought of dying that night that my mind created the visit to put me at ease. Certainly the two subjects on my mind that night were dying and my loss of religion.

3. Age: ? ; year: 1986; Location: Mid South; The Dream:
I have had only one dream of God. I intentionally hurt someone that had wronged me. I felt profoundly guilty about this. I later saw God in a dream. God was very angry with me and would not look at me. He was looking down with his eyes closed, saying nothing. How did I know this was God? Although there was not verbal communication between us, I sensed that he was God. He was very old. His face was aged in a way that seemed to show the accumulated wisdom of many, many lifetimes. This was the only dream of God that I ever had.

4. Age: 70; year: 1990; Location: Northeast; The Dream:
It was Doomsday! If it wasn't, it was as close as I ever want to be to it. As I looked over the landscape from a hill, I saw awesome clouds above and at least 30 tornadoes coming my way. Behind were mountains, so I headed for them hoping to escape the twisters.

When I reached the mountains, the earth started shaking and the mountains started swelling as if huge volcanoes were about to erupt. I saw one spot which looked relatively stable and headed for it.

I had gotten about halfway to it when the mob came—the thousands and thousands of people running for the refuge I had spotted. It was obvious that they would outrun and outnumber me, so I decided to quit running and await my fate.

Suddenly, the fear left me. "What are you running for," I said out loud. "If your time has come, God will find you no matter where you hide or seek refuge. If it hasn't, he will spare you on this or any other spot."

"God," I said, "I'm ready for whatever you have in store for me. I'll put all my trust in you. Save me for a few more years on earth if that is your will, or take me home with you now—your choice is my choice!"

I woke up with a strange feeling of peace.

5. Age: 72; Year: 1992; Location: Northeast; The Dream:

I dreamt that I was an American Indian youth about to undergo my tribe's rites of manhood. The chief and braves traditionally tested our endurance to pain—beatings, knife cuts, even hot embers from the campfire. I was among the first of the youths to be tested, but instead of submitting willingly, I said. "Why do you want to inflict pain on your own flesh and blood? Pain may test us but it degrades you, because only cruel men hurt their sons. I have heard of a better way that Jesus of Nazareth used on himself. Many people say that He is truly the son of the Great Spirit, and although He died nearly 2000 years ago, he still lives in the hearts and minds of his followers."

About this time Jesus Himself appeared, walked slowly through our midst, through the flames of the campfire and disappeared into the enveloping darkness.

"Behold," I said. "He has shown Himself to us and given credence to my words."

The chief said, "There is truth and wisdom in your words and the man who appeared to us does confirm them. What did he do to test his manhood?"

"He went into the wilderness for forty days and nights," I replied. "There he fasted, meditated deeply and prayed earnestly to the Great Spirit whom he called "Father."

The chief then spoke in a solemn voice, saying:

"Then from this day forth, let this tribe do likewise. You young men shall now go alone into the forest and follow the example of this Jesus."

I gathered up my blanket, my weapons and went into the darkness. I found a large overhanging rock for partial shelter and re-entered the dream world! When I awoke I was perplexed by the dream, because my ancestors came from Germany! However, unconfirmed reports say that one of my great grandfathers married an Indian maiden, and it made me wonder if some of her genes triggered the dream.

Female Dreams:
1. Age: Early Twenties; Year: 1984; Location: Northeast
Prologue:

I was raised with no real church affiliation until my father's death when I was 15. My mother took us to a Fundamentalist Church where God seemed to be all wrath and brimstone to me, and I was afraid. Later, I became a Seminary student, working toward an M.A. in religion, but I felt that nothing I did would please God.

The Dream;
One night, I dreamt I was walking along the shore and I saw a dark man in white pants and a colorful shirt, which was unbuttoned. He was throwing stones into the sea, feeding seagulls, and laughing. It made me feel happy just to hear his laugh! We talked and it was as though he already knew who I was and everything about me. He had a thick Jamaican Patoi, a place I've never been but associate with calm seas and tranquil people. "Don't you know who I am?" He asked. I knew then, somehow, that He was God. "Why did you come to me in this form?" I asked. (I am white, have nothing against black people, but it was not what I had expected God to look and sound like.) "Because, my child" he said, in a soft voice, "You were afraid of me in the form you expected me to appear."

2. Age: 77 Year: 1961; Location: Oklahoma

Prologue;
I was visiting my parents. They lived in a one-bedroom apartment so I was sleeping in the living room on the sofa. I had gone to sleep about ten o'clock the evening of my dream. There was no clock in the living room, but I estimate that my dream occurred about 2 o'clock in the morning.

The Dream;
I dreamed that I saw a figure in a long white robe standing in the middle of my parents' living room. A bright light surrounded this figure which had long brown hair and was looking straight ahead,, rather than facing the sofa on which I was sleeping, which would have been to his left side. The dream was so vivid that I woke up and saw this vision while awake, but just momentarily. My intuition gave me to believe I had just seen God. I have never forgotten that dream.

3. Age: 28 ; Year: 1994 ; Location:

The Dream;
I was walking down a long and wide path of marble, with pillars of marble on both sides of me. Near the bottom of the pillars was a long pool of sparkling water. Some people were coming and going down this long hallway. I stopped at the waters edge and was thinking of playing in it.
Then the Lord spoke to me by thought and said, "You can play here as long as you like." There was no hurry to be anywhere and I felt no

pressures of any kind. No condemnation for wasting time, plus I knew I was delighting the Lord by just enjoying myself. Then I looked down the hall because I heard the sound of dishes clinking. At the end of the hall was a huge dome of glass-like material, cut in intricate shapes with beveled edges. Underneath the dome were big round tables and people were eating on fine dishes and being served by waiters. Now the Lord was going to mix earthly people in this to show me something. As I walked toward the restaurant entrance, I remember thinking, "They probably won't let me in because my clothes aren't good enough," but I wanted in to see this place; so I decided to go ahead and see if they would seat me.

The host looked me up and down, and seeing I wasn't dressed well said, "And who is at the head of your table?"

That statement really irritated me so I said "I'll tell you who is at the head of my table! Jesus is at the head of my table!" The host said "Uh huh, right!" He then took my arm and started to escort me out, but then checked to see whose gem stone keys were hanging on the wall (The important people left them there as they entered.) Their names were attached so they were identifiable to the host. When he saw the key with Jesus' name on it, he thought the Spanish word for Jesus and figured I was at a table with a Mexican named "Hey Suess" (The sound out word for Jesus in Spanish).

So he said, "Oh! Right this way!" Then he took me to a booth where Jesus was sitting with others. One small section had a few booths. Isn't it just like Jesus to sit at a booth? Why? Because the work he had for us wasn't quite done and this was a business meeting. Obviously, it wasn't time to reap rewards, at least for a few of us. Jesus was on the very inside of the booth. The first thing I wanted to do was kiss His feet! But because He acknowledged it in thought, and because it was kind of awkward at this time it was unanimously agreed to skip it. (Because thought is even acknowledged as the action!)

The waiter was worldly and when he heard Jesus order "Communion," he heard "Or Derves,"(sounding out again, you know, appetizers!). But we knew Communion was bread and wine. The waiter went to get them and Jesus asked, "Where shall we evangelize today?" And I said, "Let's go to the slums." A child in the booth behind me said, "Yes, let's go to the slums! That's where my father used to beat me." The father was at the head of the table and he had three children on each side. The father said "Yes, son, that's where I used to beat you." He then looked at Jesus and Jesus with all His love, gave him the most loving and forgiving look, and the rest of us all knew we had all been there and we were no better than that father, so we all understood. The best part, we felt no condemnation!

Then the dream changes to another scene because once again Jesus wants to show me something. I was on a slow moving train and it was packed with happy excited people, because it was going to Heaven! There were so many people on it that some were on the roof, some were hanging out the windows! We happened to be going through a New York

Substation. The people watching us all appeared to be in a daze. They were moving in slow motion and zombie like fashion. Jesus was on a platform parallel to the train. The platform was red and it had a ramp for people to get on.

As it moved slowly past the people, Jesus would ask, "Are you a sinner?" Just then a stockbroker (we just knew his occupation) was thinking, (we heard his thoughts too!) "I wonder why those people are so happy? He started to feel our joy, but when Jesus asked him "Are you a sinner?" the little smile he was starting to have left and he shook himself and said, "Don't be ridiculous!" and continued on his zombie way.

Well, a housewife heard this from far away. The Holy Spirit was bringing her to life. This was the only way she could have heard it—in her spirit!. She yelled "Yes! Yes! I'm a sinner!" and she came running for the train and as she went up the red platform, it was revealed the red on the platform was the shed blood of Jesus! The only way we get to go to Heaven!!! A few others did the same. We were on our way to Heaven! Kind of a last call before Rapture. The others just zombied off!

That was the end of the dream. So I hold it dear to me knowing we only have a short time to grab someone to take with us, and seriously think of who needs help, and even make a list! Pray for them. Get up each day and say, "What can I do today, Lord? Write someone? Visit someone? Help me to speak up now before the train is out of their reach! Amen!

So there you have eight dreams of God. Dreams from both males and females; dreams that occurred at different times of life and in different places; dreams that involved God directly and indirectly, and as Father and Son.

I suppose that a good psychiatrist could offer a rational explanation of each dream, but that's not the point. I also suspect that a learned theologian or deeply religious person could view some or all of the dreams as non-scriptural, false, or sacrilegious. Again, that's not the point. The point is: what do you, the reader, see in these dreams?

o Did some of them contain moral truths that could be useful in your life?

o Did the dreamer get valuable new insights that are applicable to you?

o Is it possible that God uses the dream mechanism to contact humans?

o Does age, sex, location or time period affect the content of the dream?

o Were the dreams a mystical experience or just a piece of undigested food?

o Will we ever get satisfactory answers to our many questions about God during our time on earth?

o Do you care? Should you care?

EMBARRASSING MOMENTS

GIRLS' BEDTIME HAIR:

When I was out of college and a dashing young bachelor, I dated my life-long mate, <u>Elizabeth (Betty) Warren</u>. At that time Betty lived in the garage apartments of a large estate, with seven other girls. The estate was called "Point Siesta," but we bachelors called it "Passion Point!"

One night, as I was about to leave, some of Betty's housemates invited us to have a cup of hot chocolate with them. They were all in their bathrobes, and had their hair done up for the night, which meant it was raised up and tied with different contraptions. Of course they apologized for their bathrobes and hair, but it was all prim and proper, so I told them not to worry. Then I made a big mistake. I started making comments about their bedtime hair. One of the girls was not a regular, but a guest, so when I got to her I said, "Gee, your hair looks real nice, even though its bedtime." I was sincere in my comments, because even though it was raised above her ears, it still looked nice.

Someone then whispered, "That's not her bedtime hair, it's the way she usually wears it."

I felt like a damn fool, and I would have been very embarrassed by my mistake, except I mitigated it by these words: "I hope you'll forgive me. You see, I'm still ignorant about girls' bed-time hair!"

TRACK TEAM TRYOUT:

Along about my junior year in college, I decided to try out for the track team. I had always had embarrassingly skinny legs, and hoped I could put larger calves on them. One of my dorm mates, <u>Jack Nelly</u>, was a member of the track team, so I approached him about it.

"We are having try-outs this Friday," he said. "I'm going running this afternoon after classes, and if you would like to join me you can. It will give you the sort of warm you need for the try-out."

"Gee, that sounds great," I responded. "When and where shall we meet?" We then made arrangements, and when the time came I was ready.

"I usually run about three miles," Jack said, "But you can drop out any time."

Now I was in good shape in those days because I played lots of tennis, and also frequently ran so I wouldn't be late for classes. Besides, I had been on my high-school football team. All went well for the first mile, then Jack said, "Are you O.K.? You shouldn't overdo it the first day, but gradually build up to it. Too much will make you stiff. "

I assured him I was O.K., and we proceeded toward the two mile spot. I was getting a little weary then, but my stubborn streak made me again say, "I'm O.K." when he repeated his first advice. I was pleased when we made it the full three miles, and I had kept up with Jack, who was already a track-team member.

As I walking back to my dorm after dinner at the cafeteria, my legs suddenly started feeling funny. I stopped by Jack's room and told him that they were getting very stiff.

"That's what I was warning you about," he said.

I then asked, "How long will it last?

"Oh about a week," he replied. He then added, "Now don't try to run even a short distance, until they feel normal."

Much to my chagrin, Jack was absolutely right. So why was that an embarrassing moment? First, because I missed the track-team tryout, and was too late to try again. That meant my skinny calves remained skinny. Second, because my stubbornness in view of Jack's advice was not only embarrassing, but painful for a week. Third, because I am re-living it again and you readers and listeners will see what a dope I was!

THE INDOOR POOL:

When I was in my sophomore year at N.C. State College of Agriculture and Engineering, I had a classmate who was a good swimmer. His name was Luke Cartwright, and he was a tall, good-looking, athletic guy. Both of us were majoring in Aeronautical Engineering, so we got to know each other quite well. Both of us liked to swim, so Luke and I would go down to the indoor pool at least once a week, and race to see who was the faster swimmer. He usually beat me, but sometimes I beat him, especially after our swimming teacher gave me pointers about my strokes and breathing. We even raced to see who could undress and get to the pool first.

Now the college had very few co-eds, and none of them lived on the campus. It also had a funny rule, which was that we should swim nude. I don't know why they had that rule, unless it was because only male students and faculty, which also were only male, used the pool. It didn't take long for all the guys to adjust to the rule. It was easy for me, since that was what I did in high school when I went to a near by creek for a quick dip with my buddies.

One day it was raining very hard when Luke and I decided to go for a swim. We had our raincoats and hats pulled up tight when we entered the gym and had started to take them off as we entered the locker room. We quickly took off all our clothes, and then raced to see who would get to the pool first.

There were others at the pool, and we were almost ready to dive in when we noticed that they were all girls. I hasten to add that the girls were clad in the bathing suits of the late thirties. Some of them shrieked in surprise and embarrassment, and I thought I detected a few that looked a bit pleased, but maybe that was wishful thinking.

We both had too much momentum to turn back, so we dove into the pool as originally planned. I stayed under water as long as I could, but eventually had to stick my head up and face all the girls staring at us. Some of them didn't want to make eye contact, but others not only looked directly at us, but looked down into the water, which was pretty damn clear. Luke didn't seem to be as embarrassed as I was, because he was grinning from ear to ear. I put one hand over my face and the other one down lower.

One of the lead girls said, "Didn't you see the sign at the entrances? It said: "Meredith College Girls Only-- 2 to 4 pm."

Luke spoke for both of us, saying, "No we didn't." It was raining too hard when we entered the gym, and we were too busy taking off our rain gear when we entered the locker room."

"Well why are you both naked? Don't you have swim suits?"

I answered that one, saying, "Yes we do, but it is a rule of this pool that we don't wear them. You see, it's all male most of the time."

There was dead silence, broken only by a few giggles.

Luke then said, "If you will lend us both a towel, we will get out and go back to the locker room."

"Good idea" their spokes girl replied. "Here, you can have mine," she said as she handed it to Luke. A very pretty girl handed me hers, and after we had wrapped them around ourselves as carefully and as surreptitiously as possible, we went back to the locker room and dressed ourselves. However, on the way back to the locker room, Luke dropped his towel, and glanced back to see if anyone had seen him; most of them did. To this day, I don't know whether dropping the towel was an accident or deliberate, since Luke had a big naughty streak in him.

Then came the second embarrassing moment-- taking the towels back to their owners. Almost begging, I said: "Why don't you take both of them back, Luke?"

"No way," he replied. "I'll take mine back and you take yours back."

When we entered the pool area, the girls were very gracious and even applauded a bit as we bowed to hand them back to their owners. "Tell me your name," I whispered to my towel donor. "Maybe I can come by the college and thank you more properly."

After she gave me her name, Luke and I exited again. Luke then asked, "What were you whispering to her?

"Oh, I just got her name and kind of made a date. Do you want me to fix you up with your towel donor?"

"You bet!" We then parted and went back to our separate dorms.

When we went to Meredith College for our dates, we found that we had become almost famous with the other girls. In fact some of them made advances for us to date them. As Luke said, "It pays to advertise!"

I would tell you about our subsequent dates, both with our towel donors and the others, except they weren't embarrassing moments. They would have to come under the heading of "Delightful Moments!"

Note: Luke was one of my first college buddies to die. Shortly after graduation I learned that he had joined the Air Corp and died in a crash. But I still remember his good looks and sense of humor.

FAMOUS PEOPLE

A mature person would have lived a very sedentary life to have never seen at least one famous person. I suspect that most Americans have seen many famous people, and quite a few have probably talked with them personally. I doubt if many have known them as close friends, but a special few have.

Now when I say "famous people", I mean those whose names are household words in the USA. I even include some who may not be know by most Americans, but are famous within large circles of endeavor. For example, there are many Rock musicians that I may not have heard of, but they have such a large circle of admirers that I classify them as famous. On the other hand, some people are world famous, or perhaps infamous. The latter group usually consists of political or religious leaders, but some become famous for their huge contribution to mankind. (<u>Albert Einstein</u>, <u>Mother Teresa</u>, and <u>Jonas Salk</u> come to mind)

During my 87 years on earth (so far), I have been privileged to see many famous people, talked with a good number, and even been friends with some that were famous in special circles.

Here are some memories about famous people in my own life, grouped alphabetically by their field of endeavor:

1. ACTORS AND ACTRESSES

From 1963 to 1965, we lived in Long Beach California. One evening, we went to see a play dramatizing some of a famous science fiction author's stories. Yes, <u>Ray Bradbury</u> was the author, but I don't think he was present that evening. During intermission, some people spotted <u>Carl Reiner</u> and his <u>wife</u> and there was a small buzz going around. Carl may have been more famous as a TV writer, but he was also a damn good actor. No one seemed to have the courage, or perhaps desire, to approach Carl, so I said to my wife, <u>Betty</u>, "Hey, let's go over and say hello to Mr. Reiner." She agreed, so we ambled over.

After saying "hello," we introduced ourselves, and told him how much we admired his acting, as well as his writing. He was most gracious, introduced his wife and thanked us. I was prepared to leave until he said, "How do you like the writing and acting we are seeing tonight?"

"I like it a lot. I am a long-term admirer of <u>Ray Bradbury</u>, not only his writing but also his vivid imagination."

Carl agreed, and we had a brief discussion about various points in the play we had just seen. When we shook hands and left for the next act, it seemed like we had been talking with an old friend, or at least a new friend. Before that event, I was usually too shy to approach a famous person, but that experience made me realize the truth of the old adage, "Nothing ventured, nothing gained!"

During the second intermission, we spotted another famous actor, and I said look, there's the star of "Rawhide", which was a popular western TV show at the time. He must have heard me, and believe it or not, he came over and said, "Hello, I'm Eric Fleming. Are you enjoying the play?"

"Yes", we both replied, and I added, "and I also enjoy "Rawhide" and your role as Gil Favor."

After he thanked me, I said, " Some of the reasons I like it so much is that each story is interesting, shows life in the old west, and builds up tension when trouble arises. Best of all, I like it because it seldom uses violence to solve the problem, as so many other Westerns do. And of course the acting and scenery are excellent"

Mr. Fleming was pleased by my sincere remarks, and after a bit more talk we all left for the last act of the play. Some years later we were saddened to learn that he had drowned while shooting a scene in a wild river. I, for one, would like to see some re-runs of Rawhide in the near future.

My younger daughter, Rebecca, was first married to a young man whose cousin, Dan Wilcox, was one of the principal writers for the famous TV program, MASH. Sometime around 1980, Rebecca arranged for my wife and me to go with her to see a filming of one of the MASH episodes. There we met the cousin writer and his partner, Thad Mumford. We also met Alan Alda and had a short conversation with him. It was mostly complimentary about the show and his role in it, but he was generous enough to ask about our lives. I think he was impressed when I told him I had been an aerospace engineer and worked seven years on the Lunar Module. Later on, when we were walking on the grounds of the studio, we spotted him headed toward us. He seemed to remember us, and waved hello. Our original meeting was short, but we came away not only admiring Alan as an actor, but also liking him as a person.

During the filming, we also saw, but didn't meet, other famous actors such as Loretta Switt, (Hot Lips); Jamie Pharr (Klinger); Henry Morgan (Colonel Potter); Gary Burgdorf (Radar) and several others. We were intrigued by the number of "takes" to complete one scene, and amused by some of the laughter and strong language the actors used when one of them made a boo-boo. It was an intriguing experience.

On some other occasions I spotted famous actors but didn't have the nerve to approach them. One was Danny Kaye, who was walking around alone in an airport. He seemed rather bored, and I am sorry I didn't make contact, since I had seen him in person during a Broadway musical and later on in many movies.

A similar thing happened one day when I was on vacation and wandering around Jericho Turnpike on Long Island. I spotted <u>Henry Fonda</u> in a store I was browsing around in, and our eyes made contact, but we left it there. My next stop was a baseball hitting range, and just as I started to enter a cage Henry Fonda was leaving the adjacent one. This time our eyes made even longer contact, because it was apparent that we were both idling away time the same way. I was tempted to make contact then and propose that we join forces, but before I could muster up the courage he had passed me. Nothing ventured, nothing gained happened again.

I was somewhat compensated one day when I was giving blood at a Red Cross station in my hometown, Huntington, L.I. I was introduced to one of the assistants who would help during my recovery, who just happened to be <u>Mrs. Henry Fonda</u>! She was a good-looking and kind lady, and I concluded that I had been amply compensated for not talking with Henry.

Another missed opportunity was when <u>Bette Davis</u> rented a beach cottage in Huntington Bay Village, just down a long hill from our home on Upper Drive. I frequently went down to the beach for a swim, and I usually swam past the cottage so I could stay in water that wasn't over my head. I was a good swimmer, having been given tips by my friend <u>Brand Wehle</u>, who had been on the Harvard swim team with <u>John F. Kennedy</u>. On several occasions, I saw Bette looking at me swimming. It may have been my imagination, but I thought she admired my strokes, and maybe my muscular body. Looking back, I wish that my <u>wife</u> and I had called on her as friendly neighbors. I still wonder how someone so famous would have reacted.

When we saw the Broadway play, "A Funny Thing Happened On The Way To The Forum" starring <u>Zero Mostel</u> and <u>Phil Silvers</u>, we had no idea that one day we would meet Zero in person. It happened when we were sailing off the coast of Maine with our friends, <u>Lynn</u> and <u>Jean Radcliffe</u>, in their 35 foot Yawl. We had stopped at Mohegan Island overnight, and the next day we were touring the island on foot, including the small village there. Tourist abounded in the summer, but only a few brave natives stayed there during the harsh winters. My <u>wife</u> and I spotted Zero as he was going into a store to pick up a copy of the N.Y. Times, and agreed to wait for him to come back out.

"May we say hello, Mr. Mostel?", I asked.

"Of course," he replied with a smile. "It's a free country."

We then told him how much we enjoyed his work, telling him we had seen him in the previously mentioned play. He seemed pleased, and then we started discussing the island. He was vacationing there, while it was just a port of call for us. He asked some questions about our sailing cruise, which we happily answered, and after about five minutes of talk we said good by. He was a very pleasant and personable man, and we left with our previously good impression of him intact, which doesn't always happen during some encounters with famous people.

As my friends know, tennis is my favorite sport and when we lived on Long Island my <u>wife</u> and I went to many U.S. Open Tournaments. We not only enjoyed seeing the great players, but hoped to pick up some pointers for our own games. The famous actor/comedian, <u>Alan King</u>, was also a big fan, and we saw him many times but never approached him. We also went to lesser events, and one night we were at a pro match on Long Island when we saw people gathering around the row about three down from ours. A closer look showed us what the excitement was about, because there sat <u>Robert Redford</u>. People wanted his autograph, but some man with him told them that he wanted to watch the tennis matches and preferred not to be distracted. The autograph hunters were disappointed, but took it good-naturedly. We, of course, watched the matches too, but we snuck in a lot of peeks at this famous and good -looking star.

We saw <u>Bill Cosby</u> early in his career at the "Hungry Eye" in San Francisco. He was the comedian with "<u>Peter, Paul and Mary</u>" who were the group that attracted us. We were delighted with his humor, especially his "Noah" and the one making fun of the city's steep hills. Several years later I was attending a tennis camp in the east, and there was Bill playing with our tennis instructors. Once they finished, I introduced myself to Bill (I already knew the instructors) and told him of our San Francisco evening. He was polite, but wasn't very gracious, so I left quickly.

As avid theatergoers, my <u>wife</u> and I have seen many famous actors and actresses on the stage. It is impossible to name them all, but some that stick in my memory are: <u>Helen Hayes</u>; <u>Mary Martin</u>; <u>Carol Channing</u> (We saw her last original Broadway performance of "Hello Dolly" and it was electrifying!); <u>Louis Calhern</u> (whom I also saw walking on the street one day); <u>Jessica Tandy</u> and <u>Hume Cronin</u>; <u>George C. Scott</u>; <u>Rex Harrison</u>; Audrey Hepburn; Julie Andrews; Gertrude Lawrence; Andy Griffith; James Coco;.... What a treat to see all of them!

2. MILITARY OFFICERS AND GOVERNMENT OFFICIALS

When I was growing up in my small hometown, (population 5000) I knew two older boys that became generals. The older one was <u>Milton McCorkle</u>, but I seldom got to talk with him since he was three school grades above me. He became a Major General in the U.S. Army. The second boy was <u>Jim Murray</u>. He was one grade above me so we got to know each other pretty well. Our friendship was never close, but we grew a bit closer when we went to the same college and studied Aeronautical Engineering. He became a Brigadier General in the Air Force, and we saw him socially after he retired and became a Vice-president at Republic Aircraft, which was near my home in Huntington, Long Island, NY. He had changed a bit since our college days, but basically, his personality was the same. He always had a nice bit of self-confidence and drive, which was why he rose so high.

When I was in college, I heard a talk by <u>Sergeant Alvin York</u>, one of the big heroes of WW I. He became even more famous when <u>Gary Cooper</u> played him in the movie, "Sergeant York." During his talk, he made it clear that he didn't want us to get involved with another European war, even though he knew Hitler was a dangerous dictator. I'm not sure if he maintained that attitude after Pearl Harbor, because that came a few years later. I was favorable impressed with him and his speaking ability.

My most impressive contact with high-level Navy officers and the Assistant Secretary of the Navy happened in 1962, so I wrote a story about that experience in the 1960-1970 decade. I also wrote about my contact with a Two-Star German General in the previous decade, so hopefully you have read both by the time you reach this Multi-decade section.

During my seven years work on Grumman's Lunar Module (LM), I met and was in meetings with many high-level NASA people. My first assignment was as Senior representative to North American Aviation, Space and Information Division, in Downey CA. It was there that I met <u>Astronaut Ed White</u> at a cocktail party. Ed was tall and good looking, but more important he was intelligent, personable, and very dedicated. We had a long discussion about the Apollo program, and he asked me a few question about the Lunar Module, which I was able to answer. I was saddened when he was killed in the electric-system fire while he and two other astronauts were in the Command Module during a test, which many think was flawed.

I was in several meetings with <u>Astronaut Pete Conrad</u>, who was very sharp and had a good sense of humor. His looks weren't very impressive because he was bald, had a sharp nose, and was a small guy. To me, it reinforced the adage that looks don't matter if you have great talents, and Pete sure did. I also met many of North American's top managers and engineers, even a Vice president or two, but they don't qualify as famous. I learned early on that there were many really great people in the world, but that fame came only to a select (and sometimes lucky) few.

After my two years at North American, I was assigned to NASA Headquarters, in Clear Lake, Texas as the Test and Operations Manager, I had these responsibilities: 1. To activate the site in preparation to test a full-sized LM in a vacuum chamber that was also outfitted with hot and cold temperature equipment to duplicate the rigors of space. 2. To perform the tests. 3. To oversee the engineers that would support NASA operation personnel during actual flights. Again, I met some very talented, but un-famous people. My tour of duty there was shorted once I became Assistant to the LM Program Director, <u>Vice-President Joe Gavin</u>.

As Joe's assistant, I was privileged to be in many meetings with NASA's top Brass. I worked overtime, sometimes as late as 2am, to get our slide presentations in order. I also ran the slide machine, and occasionally was asked a question. However, as a staff person, I was not anywhere near their level. Top NASA names that I remember are: <u>Major General Sam Phillips</u>; <u>George Low; George Mueller</u>; <u>Bob Gilruth, Joe Shea</u>….

When Grumman was visited by the Congressional Committee on Space, I sat across the table from the <u>Committee Chairman, Congressman Olin Teague</u>, and next to his staff assistant, who sat across from Joe Gavin. Mostly, I kept my mouth shut and listened to their conversation, unless I was asked a question. Later on, when I was in the men's room, I overheard two congressmen say something like this: "It's amazing what these people can do since no one has ever done anything like it before."

"Yes, It's like asking an African Tribal Leader to design and build a car when he's never seen one." Somehow that conversation has stayed with me all these years.

The high level NASA manager that I got to know best was <u>General "Rip" Bolander</u>. His job with NASA was to approve all engineering changes on the LM, and as Assistant Program Manager, Change Control was one of my main duties. We got along well because he had a nice personality, was very thorough in his reviews and I was able to keep him happy with the data I supplied and the answers I gave.

Along with other managers, I had to give a talk to a large assembly of NASA managers and engineers, plus another Congressional delegation. I'm sure there were some famous people there, but I never knew their names. I was pleased when several of our managers said they agreed that my presentations were the best.

When I was Assistant Director of Advanced Civil Systems in the 1970's, I was Project Manager on a gigantic airship system that could carry two million pounds of pay load. The program was associated with a nuclear power plant company, who was having big problems transporting their heavy plants to the final site. Their plants weighed about 800,000 pounds, but they projected they would get to two million.

As part of my duties, I attended an Airship Symposium in California. Among the attendees was Admiral Rosenthal, who was an airship expert and had written a book many years earlier, called "Up Ship!" Now I had read that book when I was a young man, probably in my late teens. I was very impressed with the subject matter and the book, so I was thrilled when I met the Admiral and was able to talk with him about his book and our project. Unfortunately, nuclear power plants soon faced strong opposition, their production was seriously curtailed, and our interesting program never reached even a development stage. However, it was a very interesting program as long as it lasted, and I learned a lot about airships.

Looking back, I realize how fickle and fleeting fame can be; fickle, because the Astronauts, especially the early ones, got the most fame because they were heroic figures. NASA officials and Congressmen were next in line for fame because of their position. Top corporate executives were near the bottom, even though they were much higher paid than the Astronauts and Congressmen, and more essential to the success of the program. As to the engineering mangers and the engineers whose technical skills made it possible, their fame was almost zero.

Fleeting, because the world moves on and the new generation has no inkling about the people who did such an unbelievable task of landing men on the moon and bringing them home safely. Oh well, the history books may preserve their fame, and they certainly will consider the Apollo Program the greatest achievement of the 20th century, at least from a technical viewpoint.

3. MUSICIANS, SINGERS AND DANCERS

When I was a student at North Carolina State College, I played a baritone horn in three bands, and was a member of the honorary musical fraternity, called *Mu Beta Psi*. I was lucky to be asked to usher at the Community Concerts in Raleigh, so was able to attend them free. This was a good deal, because the Great Depression was still going on and I had very little spending money. Among the famous performers I heard were: Marian Anderson (A lovely lady with a great voice); Jeanette McDonald, (Very pretty and charming with a nice voice); Fritz Kreisler (A great violinist but with a scowl on his face); Ignazt Paderewski (A fine composer and pianist, and later Prime Minister of Poland).

Marian Anderson left a big impression for two reasons. First, because a Southern city easily accepted her in the main concert hall in spite of her African Origin. A few years later, Washington, DC wouldn't let her use the concert hall because of her race, so she gave a concert at the Lincoln Memorial. Second, because the balcony of the concert hall was reserved for "colored people" and the next day I saw one of the janitors cleaning up so well that Mr. Selkinhaus, my Metallurgy professor, was puzzled. I had talked with the janitor and he told me how Marian had inspired him to work hard and maybe become more successful. When I told it to the professor, he was amazed.

I also ushered at the <u>San Carlo Opera Company</u> and the <u>Ballet Russe de Monte Carlo</u> concerts. The opera company performed Carmen and Aida, so I got my first taste of opera and was intrigued. In fact, I was hooked, and my wife and I went to the Metropolitan and N. Y. City Operas many times. We also went to operas in San Francisco; Los Angles; London; Vienna; and Istanbul, Turkey. In Vienna, I was shocked by the rudeness of some of the audience. In Istanbul, I was surprised by the high quality of voices during their performance of "Wagner's "Flying Dutchman," especially since we only paid $2 each for nice seats in the first balcony!

During our many years of attendance, we heard most of the famous opera singers and conductors, which are too numerous to name. Some how we missed <u>Pavarotti, Domingo, and Carerres</u>.

I was also intrigued with ballet, and we have attended performances in the U. S. and overseas, but not as many ballets as operas. Again, we have seen some of the great ballet dancers and ballets, including <u>Maria Tallchief, Barisnikoff, and Eglevsky</u>.

I especially recall seeing two of the women dancers looking for a bar after the ballet in Raleigh when I was an usher and was walking back to my bus stop. I was tempted to go in and talk with them, but having very little money I knew I couldn't offer to pay for a drink. Damn Depression!

We have also attended several of the major Symphony Orchestras and seen many of the major conductors. We even saw <u>Toscanini</u> at an airport restaurant sitting about 30 feet away and were thrilled. I was surprised that he was so short in stature, because he was always a giant to me. Other great conductors we have seen conducting include <u>Leonard Bernstein</u>; <u>George Szell; Andre Kostalanitz</u>; and many others. We even saw the composer <u>Percy Grainger</u> conduct a symphony in our home town of Huntington, L. I. We also saw <u>Demitri Shostakovich</u> conducting a symphony in Edinburgh, Scotland, another thrill.

Perhaps my greatest symphonic thrill was when we attended the N. Y. Philharmonic conducted by Bernstein. The program was honoring <u>Igor Stravinsky's</u> effect on American music, and had composers <u>Aaron Copeland, Samuel Barber</u>, and one other American composer. Compositions from each were presented, and just before intermission, Bernstein acknowledged Stravinsky himself, who was sitting in a spot of honor. Once intermission started, I rushed to where he was sitting, hoping to get his autograph. Unfortunately, one of his attendants stopped me, explaining he was too weak to give autographs. However, I was within five feet of him, and could see his double glasses and other features, so I was pleased.

The finale was Stravinsky's Rite of Spring, one of my all time favorites. There must have been eight or ten curtain calls, and we left feeling happy and very fortunate that we had witnessed such a wonderful event and I had come so close to Stravinsky himself.

Both <u>my wife</u> and I were also on the board of the Huntington Community Concert Association for a number of years. I was President for two, and my wife Campaign Chairperson the same two, including the year we more than sold out the house. We had 2000 subscribers for an 1800 seat auditorium, and I was plenty worried until our booking agent told me there was always a ten-percent shrinkage, usually more. We usually had a major symphony once during a season, with solo or small group performers for the remaining concerts. Symphonies I recall are the <u>Cleveland, Pittsburg</u>, and <u>National</u>. Most of the other artists were also well known, and all were very well received. I met many of them after the concert, and recently I met and chatted with <u>Marilyn Horne</u>, the famous opera singer after her Vocal Competition at the Music Academy of the West, in Santa Barbara, CA.

As a former amateur musician, I have always admired the great skill of professionals. And my admiration reaches its zenith when I hear the compositions of such masters as <u>Beethoven, Bizet, Brahms, Chopin, Donnizetti, Dvorak, Liszt, Mahler, Mozart, Mousorgsky, Prokofieff, Puccini, Schubert, Stravinsky</u>, <u>Verdi, Wagner</u>...and many others. They were not only excellent performers, but had the extraordinary genius to think up so many great compositions and leave a wonderful heritage to us lesser mortals. We have also met and knew musicians who composed but not yet become world famous. <u>Bent Myggen</u> and <u>Roe Estep</u> are such two, so look out for them in the future.

We have also seen many Broadway musicals, enjoyed them immensely, and appreciate the musical actors that work so hard to please their audiences. I mentioned most of the famous ones we saw under actors.

I will close this section with an encounter we had with a famous Folk singer. My wife and I had denoted some money to a friend and high school teacher's cause. His name was <u>Clint Marantz</u>, and his cause was to start a local theater in our hometown of Huntington, N.Y. When the new N.Y. Philharmonic auditorium had acoustical problems, there were hundreds of seats being tossed out. Clint found that he could buy them for ten dollars each, so he started collecting money from people he knew so he could buy bargain seats for his hoped for theater. Once the theater opened a year or so later, Clint listed all the people who had donated money for the seats and other things on a board near the entrance.

Some years later, we got a call inviting us to the home of a man who was trying to improve the theater and had read the list of early donors. His house was down the hill from ours, and was waterfront property. When we mentioned his name, <u>Harry Chapin</u>, to our older daughter <u>Tina</u>, and her first husband <u>Kenny</u>, they were flabbergasted. It was then that we learned that Harry was a famous singer and composer.

When we arrived at his house for the meeting, there were about ten others there, and it wasn't long before we had a lively discussion on how to improve the local theater. As we were finishing the meeting, someone said, "Harry, how about a song or two."

Harry then got his guitar and played and sang several of his original compositions, including "60,000 Pounds of Bananas" and "Cats in the Cradle." I was impressed, both with the nice personality of Harry, and his artistry. We met him and his charming <u>wife</u>, who was a poet and lyricist, several more times, mostly at fund raising parties. Once Harry and I were on the same airliner and exchange greetings. I was pleased that he recognized me. I was saddened when I learned that he had been killed in an accident on one of Long Island's expressways.

POLITICAL LEADERS:

Included here are presidential candidates, senators, representatives, governors, and state and local officials. My first encounter was with <u>Senator Bob Reynolds</u>, from North Carolina. I was in my early teens, and one of my friends, <u>Andy Warlick</u>, told me that the Senator was having lunch with a local mill owner, named <u>Zimptbaum</u>, who lived two houses from my <u>Mom and Dad</u>. Andy convinced a couple of other kids and me to go to the Zimptbaums and cheer the senator, which we did. By golly, it worked. The Senator came to the door, waved and thanked us and then returned inside. It was my first glimpse of a congressman, and I started with a senator!

During my freshman year in college, I attended the Eden Street Methodist Church, in Raleigh, N.C., which is the capitol. <u>Governor Clyde Hooey</u>, later a senator, was also a member. I not only got to see him, but meet him several times. He was an impressive looking man, always well dressed, and like most politicians, very friendly. I was a bit amused with his last name, but I guess he proved that he wasn't a lot of hooey!

<u>Elizabeth</u>, my wife, grew up in Poughkeepsie, NY, which was near Hyde Park, <u>President Franklin Roosevelt's</u> hometown. She attended several parties there and square danced with <u>Eleanor</u> while the President watched the dancers while sitting on a chair with his famous cloak around him.

After <u>Harry Truman</u> became president, we went to Central Park in NYC to hear him give a speech. We were too far away to get a close view, but we did see him and hear his speech, Missouri twang and all. While living in California from 1963 to 65, we saw <u>Presidential Candidate Lyndon Johnson</u> ride by in his limousine, and got a closer look than we did with Truman.

We heard and saw <u>Ronald Reagan</u> in the same era in Long beach, CA before he was Governor. His speech was in support of <u>Barry Goldwater</u>, and we were very impressed with Ronald, whom of course we knew as a movie actor. A friend who also heard him said, "I think he'd make a better

President than Barry. Barry never made it, but many years later, Reagan did, and I felt he did a damn good job.

After I retired in 1977 and founded a new business, we were intrigued by third party candidate John Anderson, and went to several of his rallies. He was the first presidential candidate we ever spoke to personally, so it was a thrill for both of us. I was a Democrat in those days, and my wife a Republican, but we were both getting tired of the trend in both parties, so I believe we voted for him. We also got acquainted with the county supervisor and other local politicians, and I was able to arrange some business meetings with them or their staff regarding some projects my new company, the I-Cubed Corporation, were developing. (I-Cubed = Ideas, Innovations, and Inventions.)

We also met our new Congressman, Bob Mrazek at campaign events. I knew his father because he was a fellow engineer at Grumman Aerospace. The events we went to were relatively small, so we got to talk with Bob personally. At the time I-Cubed had a tentative project going with the State University at Stony Brook regarding using Hot Dry Rock (HDR) Geothermal Energy to heat and cool the campus buildings. As I-Cubed President and the principal person on the project, I worked with the Congressman's Senior District representative, Bud Mitzman, to arrange a meeting with: Dr. John Marburger, the President of the university; Dr. Robert H Francis, VP Campus Operations; Burton Krakow, NY State Energy Research and Development Association Representative; Bruce Stevenson, Caithness Corp. (venture capitalist); and Dick Shockley, President, Delta Well.

During my presentation I stated that the University was spending 10 million dollars a year on energy and that our calculations indicated that we could drill the holes and build a plant for between 10 and 20 million dollars, and operate it for a million per year. That would be a saving of 9 million per year, so it would have a quick payoff. However, the next step would be to drill a test well to make sure the thermal gradient was good enough to make the project feasible After my presentation, it was the Congressman's staff man that urged everybody to get behind my program by putting up enough dough to drill the test well.

Caithness and NY ERDA did, and my company was on the brink of great success. Unfortunately, we had big problems with the drilling and ran out of venture capital money. I still believe that HDR geothermal energy is one of the best solutions to our energy and environmental problems and hope our government won't overlook it. I still take pride that I may have been the first commercial pioneer in that promising type of renewable and environmentally friendly energy, and have two notebooks with details of our effort.

In 1986 we moved to Dover NH, the first Political Primary State, which gave us many opportunities to see, hear, and talk directly with famous politicians. We even took pictures of many of them with my wife, friends, or me standing with them. Here are some of the candidates who were:

Governors: Bill Clinton; Michael Dukakis; Lamar Alexander; George W. Bush; Judd Gregg. The two that impressed me the most were Clinton and Alexander.

Senators: Bill Bradley; Bob Dole; Phil Graham; Al Gore; Bob Kerry; John McCain; George McGovern; Bob Smith. Earlier stories in this book give details about Bradley and Gore, and I was privileged to be Bob Smith's Senior Intern for a week when he was a Representative from NH, and before he became a Senator. I meant to write a story about that experience here, but ran out of time. Oh well, maybe in Volume 2. Of the remaining ones, my favorites were Bob Dole and John McCain.

Most of the times we met the above, we were in public buildings or I was at Rotary meetings, but on several occasions, we were invited to parties at friend's homes. Those were the best, and gave us much more chance to get acquainted.

The only Presidential candidate who was a Representative, was Dick Gephardt, whom we met at our friends, Doug and Katie Wheeler's, home.
We also met candidates Alan Keyes and Jessie Jackson, both of whom impressed me. As we were leaving Jessie's meeting in Manchester, NH. I noticed a woman sitting in the room carrying an Anti-Pollution sign puffing away on her cigarette. I asked her how she could smoke in a closed area and still carry the sign, and she gave me a weak excuse. Unknown to me, Jessie was just behind me, overheard our discourse, and backed me up vigorously. In fact his comments were much stronger than mind, so I was especially impressed with him.

RELIGIOUS LEADERS:
Billy Graham was the most famous one of this group, so when he gave a big meeting in N.Y. City, some of the people from my church hired a bus and a group of us attended. Billy was a powerful speaker and quite persuasive, and I nearly went down to be "saved." However, we were sitting far away so I missed the opportunity. I felt a certain closeness to him since he was from my home state, North Carolina, and his home town was fairly close to mine.

Reverend Martin Luther King, Jr. was probably more famous, but his fame was more associated with Civil Rights than Religion. My wife and I saw and heard him in person during a big rally in Los Angeles in 1964. He was a powerful speaker and had a great cause, which we both supported.

Unfortunately, it was a large outdoor arena, and we were too far away to see him up close.

After his tragic death, we attended a meeting in our hometown, Huntington, NY, featuring the man who led his cause, <u>Reverend Abernathy</u>. It was a dinner meeting, so we got a much closer look. He too was a powerful speaker, but not quite in Dr. King's class. Anyway, we were inspired by his talk and supported the cause. I especially remember that night because of an unusual incident, which I have described under "Coincidences" in Multi-decade.

Sometimes we went to NYC and attended some of the large churches. <u>Norman Vincent Peale</u>, <u>Henry Sloan Coffin</u>, and <u>Harry Emerson Fosdick</u> were famous pastors we heard and saw.

SCIENTISTS AND PROFESSORS:

When we lived in California in the sixties, I was privileged to hear a talk by <u>Dr. Edwin Teller</u>, the father of the Hydrogen Bomb. He was a good speaker and his heavy German (?) accent added to his fascination. He gave a good insight into the work needed to create the bomb, and my memory tells me that he had some deep reservations that it had been created, even though he acknowledged that it was a matter of time before someone else would create it.

Perhaps the most famous person in this category is <u>Carl Sagan</u>, who is remembered for his excellent TV talks on the Universe. We heard him at M.I.T. in Boston, and he was even more fascinating live. After his excellent talk, I met with him and discussed a subject where I had some knowledge. I forget the subject, but I believe I told him something with which he was unaware.

Now the last person on my list is <u>Dr. Alexander Klemin</u>, a distinguished professor at N.Y.U. He didn't have national fame as did the first two, but he was famous in engineering and mathematic circles. He was one that I got to know very well, because I was a student in several of his classes. Furthermore, he was a consultant to Grumman Aircraft, and he said "hello" several times when he was there. He was a very smart man and an excellent teacher. I will end my Famous People Stories with this somewhat amusing one.

During one of his classes, he showed us how to analyze a two cell wing structure subject to torsion loads. When he finished, he said, "Unfortunately, there is no way to analyze a three cell structure."

My close friend, <u>Brand Wehle</u>, who was a quiet and somewhat shy person, got the courage to say that he knew how to analyze three cells.

"What's that you say? Tell me how?"

Brand described the procedure and then Dr. Klemin proceded to work the problem on the blackboard. It took about 5 or 6 minutes to do so, and when he finished he said, "Now, Mr. Wehle, do you see how it's done?

We were all astounded by his remark, but <u>John Meirs</u>, a fellow Grumman engineer, said in a loud voice: "Does he see how it's done? Hell, he was the one that told you how to do it!"

Dr. Klemin took it good-naturedly, but it was a story that was told for several days back at work. Somehow, it stuck in my mind all these years.

FANTASTIC GOLF!

Any golfer with a little imagination, and show me one who doesn't qualify, has either prayed for a miracle on certain shots, or fantasized about getting a truly astounding one. Golf is a game that frequently stretches the physical and mental powers of humans to the breaking point, so the above statement shouldn't be surprising to golfers, their friends, or golf "widows".

To illustrate my point, I will use two old golf jokes. If you have heard them before, bear with me and try to get something extra from them. They both deal with Jesus Christ and Saint Peter, and aren't meant to be sacrilegious. After all, Christ himself used parables to illustrate fundamental truths, so consider them modern parables which show that miracles and fantasies are part of the golfing culture. In both stories, they returned to earth to play golf so they could better understand mortals like us. They assumed human forms and identities, and called themselves' "Joe Church" and "Sam Peterson", respectively. Here are the "parables":

Joe and Sam first went out as a twosome when the course was almost empty. Sam had a nice long drive straight down the fairway, but Joe sliced his first shot into the woods, where it disturbed a hawk's nest and then bounced back into the rough. The hawk then fluttered down, picked up the ball and flapped away with it. As he flew over the green it grew heavy, so he "dropped the ball". It then rolled into the cup for a hole-in-one. Sam was a bit dismayed, so he said:

"Are you going to play golf, or perform miracles?"

The next time they played, they were part of a foursome. After their tee shots at the eighth hole, they noticed that the green was protected by a large pond. They were all about two hundred yards away from the green as the hawk flies. Three of them opted to play it safe by staying in the fairway, even though it meant, at least two strokes to reach the green. Joe decided to go directly for the green by using his number three wood to clear the pond. Sam was upset, and cautioned against such a risky shot, but Joe said, "I saw Arnold Palmer make this shot with a three wood, so I can too."

Sam was right, and Joe's ball landed smack dab in the middle of the pond. Unperturbed, Joe strolled to the pond, walked on the water, and chipped his floating ball on the green near the cup. When the others saw him walking on water, they were amazed, saying, "Who does he think he is-- Jesus Christ?"

Sam's reply was short and sweet: "He IS Jesus Christ, but in his fantasy he thinks he's Arnold Palmer!"

I'll bet that most golfers have favorite true stories that confirm that their prayers for a miracle were answered, or perhaps their greatest fantasies were realized. Here are some of my own:

OVERCOMING A BAD HOOK:

The hole was a dogleg to the right. As a leftie who frequently sliced, it was unfavorable for me. I worried about it so much that I hooked my drive sharply and landed way to the right on another fairway. My companions all advised aiming back toward the proper fairway, so my next shot would be lined up for the green, although it would still be far away. But I noticed a narrow passage between the trees from where my ball lay. I told myself, 'All you need is a long, controlled slice through that passage, and you'll be back on the fairway and within chipping distance of the green. You can make this shot and stay up with your buddies.' To the others' surprise and my delight, the ball went just as I had visualized. It missed the trees by a few feet and landed on the fairway within a few yards of the green. Fantasy realized!

A LONG-SHOT PUTT

I was on the apron of the green, about 60 or 70 feet from the pin. "Chip with your nine iron," my partner suggested, "and watch out for those ups and downs in the green." But I was listening to my fantasy brain, which said, 'Use your putter, hit it firmly, and aim it way to the right of the hole so it will weave down one slope, up the next one, and then down again to the hole.' It was a case of mind over matter, or perhaps the answer to a subconscious prayer, because the ball did exactly as I planned and went into the cup! I asked my friend, "Why can't I do that every time instead *of* hitting all those lousy shots that make it hard for me to break a hundred?"

"Putts like that are rare, even for pros," he replied.

"Yes", I agreed, " but they increase my hope that I can become a good golfer some time in the distant future." Alas, it turned out to be another fantasy!

A LONE EAGLE:

One day I was teamed with a father and his two teen-aged sons, all strangers to me. The first hole was a short par four, with the green about 325 yards away. My drive went out over 200 yards, but sliced slightly to the left. The others didn't drive that far, but their shots were straighter. After they had taken their second shots and were near or on the green, the father came over to me and said, "Since the green is hidden from your view by this hill, let me line it up for you. Then after I move away you can shoot."

"Thanks", I replied, and then proceeded to do as he suggested. I used my trusty five iron, caught the ball squarely, and it soared into the air toward where he had lined it up. The father yelled, "Good shot—I think it rolled into the cup,"

That seemed too good to be true, so I looked for my ball as I approached the green, but didn't see it anywhere, not even on the green. 'Damn', I thought, 'I'll bet I overshot.' I then proceeded to cross the green to look for my ball. Soon the father, who was on the green, yelled, "Here it is--right in the cup like I told you!"

I was surprised and delighted, because I had just made the second eagle of my golfing endeavors. I could hear his kids whispering to each other, "That man must be a good golfer—he just made and eagle!"

"Yeah, " the other one replied, "and on the first hole! "

Unfortunately, instead of it boosting my confidence, I silently said to myself, 'Wait 'till the next hole, kids, and then you'll see that I'm not even an average golfer.' My prediction came true, because I shot a six on a par three! Quick result: Two disillusioned kids!

A HOLE-IN-ONE— ALMOST:

We were playing nine holes after work one day, hoping to finish before it got too dark to see. My friend <u>Harvey Gardiner</u>, who was about as poor a golfer as I was, bet me a quarter a stroke after we tallied up our score. That was our standard bet, and we often flipped odds or even with quarters at work. Much to his chagrin, I usually won. But luck seemed to be going his way that day, because by the time we reached the ninth tee, he was three strokes (seventy-five cents) ahead, a comfortable lead. He suggested that we stop the game, and thus the bet, because it was getting too dark to see.

"No way," I replied. "If we loft our balls we can see them against the western sky. Besides, it's a par three, so we don't have to hit far."

He grudgingly complied with my logic. Since he had honors he hit first. He topped the ball and it dribbled off the tee. It went only about ten yards. His excuse was the poor light.

I used a six iron and somehow hit it squarely. Both of us could see it headed straight for the hole against the glowing sky, as I had predicted. He groaned audibly at my good fortune. The men who had just left the green yelled, "Hey. that was a great shot. It went in the cup but bounced out!"

Harvey not only groaned, but also muttered a few curses. He reached the green in five, took three putts and ended up with an eight. I sank my six-inch putt for a birdie two. His comfortable lead of seventy-five cents was reversed-- in my favor!

As we drove home from the south shore of Long Island, it became quite foggy. Harvey complained about the bad luck of the day, but I said, "Don't worry; it will clear by the time we reach Jericho Turnpike."

Ever resourceful, Harvey bet me that it would be foggy all the way to Huntington. "Double or nothing," he bravely offered. I accepted, and just as we crossed the turnpike the fog lifted. He was so amazed at my "ability" to predict the weather that he gladly handed me the buck and a half he had lost. So two of my fantasies came true that evening. Strangely enough, they almost seemed to be preordained!

So you see, even hackers like me can get golf shots that professionals would admire. The big difference is consistency. They make great shots almost all the time, hackers rarely!

A FANTASY GOLF COURSE:

Those reminiscences gave me this inspiration: suppose there was a golf course that would let the hackers of the world live out their wildest fantasies. The answer came to me in a dream. Once I fleshed it out with my imagination, it went something like this:

The course is built on a long, gradually sloping, bare mountain, such as Mauna Loa in Hawaii. You take a shuttle bus to the top and at the pro shop you are given three balls, each one with your name and hometown stamped on it, and a snap-on grip. You then go to the first tee, are given your choice of a high-tech right hand or left hand club, a scorecard and a few tees. The first hole is 5,280 feet away, or 1760 yards. It is rated a par 12 because of the huge distance, and there are five other holes rated par 12, or the usual 72 for the course. New clubs are supplied at the point your ball stops, and all you have to do is snap on your special grip to be ready for the next shot.

Now comes the fantasy part. The first fairway is all down hill, there are no trees, bushes or rocks to impede the ball, and the contour of the ground is shaped such that any shot rolls toward the middle of the fairway. Once it reaches the first green, there is an inverted tent over the green, with a small hole in the tent over the golf cup. Almost any drive will thus roll down the middle of the fairway for a mile, be stopped by the tent, and then funneled toward its hole, where it will softly drop about eight feet into the cup. You have just made a mile long drive on a par 12 hole, and achieved a hole in one! What a fantasy!

The other holes are similar, but designed such that it takes three to five strokes to reach the green. Along the way, the course is contoured so each shot lands in one, two or three places, which adds a little challenge while keeping club supply reasonable. Once you reach the green, it slopes such that no matter where the ball lands, it heads toward the cup. The slope around the cup is even greater, and designed such that any putt that comes within ten feet will spiral into the cup. Two putt greens are almost assured.

When you finish, you have shot somewhere between 26 and 36 on a par 72 course. You have not had to bring heavy, bulky clubs on your vacation, or carry any clubs on the course, just balls, tees and your snap-on grip. All the walking (or cart riding) has been down hill. Best of all, you and your partners' sign each other's cards and the pro validates them to make it very official. He even labels and signs your hole-in-one ball. You have now lived a HUGE FANTASY!

Now I'm not suggesting that "Fantasy Golf" replace regular golf, because the former is much less challenging. But it would give us hackers of the world a rare chance to feel that the cards are stacked in our favor, instead of vice-versa. Furthermore, it would permit us to tell golf tales which seem unbelievable, but are perfectly true and verifiable. How much would that be worth to a frustrated golfer? And how much would the free publicity from the stories be worth to the owners?

Could my "Fantasy Golf Course" become a reality? Of course! (No pun intended). **If any of you readers are wealthy and have a strong entrepreneurial spirit, I would be glad to form a fifty-fifty partnership; you supply the dough and business acumen, and I'll contribute this concept, and help design the course using my outlandish, but fantastic, ideas!**

It may not result in "miraculous" golf, but it's certain to become FANTASTIC GOLF!

GLOWING IN THE DARK

Most households contain things that glow in the dark. Now I'm not: talking about the occasional lightning bug that slips in and glows softly until it reaches its fascinating flash point. And I don't mean the kid's collection of "fox fire" gathered from decaying wood during the last scout camping trip. Nor do I mean Saint Elmo's fire, the strange, ethereal wisps of bluish fire that sailors and others see floating around in mysterious ways when atmospheric conditions charge the air with electricity. Truth to tell, most households don't contain any of the above.

What they do contain are light emitting diodes, and they can be found in several rooms– anywhere there 's a digital clock or other electronic devices. In my own home there's one in the living room—my Hi-Fi music system; two in the kitchen– the microwave oven and the clock radio; and four in the bedroom—the video tape recorder; the DVD player; the clock radio; and a tiny one in our rechargeable hand vacuum in the corner. Oh, and there's also two tiny ones in our rechargeable Sonicare dental appliances in the bathroom.

Of course, all of these "glow-in-the-dark" items are man-made. Like other human products, they have their flaws, mostly when there's a power interruption. The most frustrating part is that even a microsecond interruption disrupts all the digital clocks, and they start blinking until either my wife or I reset the damn things, I usually wait a few hours to reset some of them in case the power fluctuates again. Somehow, it holds steady until I have done so, and then, bingo–it goes off again!

The other night my bedside digital-clock radio seemed to be sending me messages. I had gone to bed early, at least for me, and as I crawled under the cover I noticed that it was 11:11. I took it as a good omen by translating it as "won-won: won-won". Maybe I would be victorious in next morning's tennis game, which was the reason for my early bedtime. And I was!

Now men my age seldom sleep through the night without having to arise, so I got up at. 1:11 and 4:44 a.m. I had deciphered the 1:11 earlier, but what was the significance of the 4:44? Other than the fact that they were repeating digits and that I was playing men's doubles, consisting of four players, I was baffled. Alas, I never did discover a sensible meaning. (Do you have one?) When I woke up for good a few minutes before the clock-radio alarm went off, it was 7:47. Wow, I thought, it's the number of my favorite airliner, the Boeing 747. What more appropriate wake-up "sound" than a "BIG BOEING!"

There are times when the human spirit "glows" in the dark. Parents will recognize such "glows" when they see their first baby smile in its sleep; or when their young son hits his first home run during night baseball; or their daughter performs flawlessly during her first piano recital. I suspect that most of the world "glowed" in the dark when glued to their television sets as Neil Armstrong first set foot on the moon. I know I did, and as one of the Lunar Module managers for my company, I glowed even more when our craft made it back to the mother ship safely. My ultimate glow came when all the astronauts returned to the good earth triumphantly and intact!

On one occasion I had a remarkable coincidence with a digital-clock glow, or perhaps it was a divine experience. I was in my late thirties and working at Grumman Aerospace Corporation, when our well-liked engineering manager, Warren Allen, contracted cancer. He was only a few years older than I, and everyone hoped his relative youth would help him conquer the dread disease. I remembered him in my prayers frequently, but on this particular night I saw him active and healthy in one of my dreams.

In those days, I usually slept through the night; but during this one I woke up right after the dream at 3:21 a.m. I wondered what its significance was, and all I could think of was the last seconds of countdown for a rocket launch: ...3-2-1– blast off! As an aerospace engineer, that seemed a logical explanation, except I wondered; "What blast-off?"

Next day, another engineer stopped by my office and said: "Did you hear the bad news about Warren? He died last night at 3:21." We conversed for a minute or two, and after he left I realized the significance of the "glow-in-the-dark" message.

It was Warren's "count down" as he blasted off to eternity!

A LETTER TO SHAKESPEARE

Mr. William Shakespeare: April 17, 2003
Somewhere in Eternity

Dear Will:

Please forgive the first name familiarity, but I have known and admired your work for over 65 years. At age 83, I think I deserve the privilege of familiarity, even with someone who has left such a great legacy to his fellow humans. In addition, I belong to the great brotherhood of writers and poets. As you probably know, the chief reward for most of us is the fun we have in coming up with new ideas, or playing around with existing ones.

Although I admire your work, I am by no means an expert in it. In fact, I am still puzzled by many aspects of it. In the spirit of fun, here are some questions it has raised in my mind:

o While I admired Juliet I always wondered: 'Just what was it that Julie et?' Also: 'How far did Romeo roam, and was the deep-sleep drug that Juliet took a pill or a capulet?'

o Your principal character, "Hamlet", also confused me. I kept wondering: 'Was he named for a small village, or a contraction of Ham Omelet?

o Who made Desdemona moan, and who's gonna have the nerve to tell Othello?

o When comely courtiers enter the royal chambers, at which one will King Lear leer?

o After seeing "The Taming of the Shrew", I concluded that it took a shrewd man to do it. OK?

o If the "Two Gentlemen from Verona" meet the "Merry Wives of Windsor," what happens? Hopefully, it won't be "Love's Labor Lost"!

o When Antony met Cleopatra, where did he pat her? And how about Julius-- did he Caesar?

o Have you heard the rumor that one of King Duncan of Scotland's heirs started a successful business in America? He called it "Duncan Doughnuts", or something like that.

o And you, dear Will, what kind of a spear did your ancestor's shake?

Well, I guess I've reached the bottom of my list. Some may say that this epistle is the 'bottom", but as your character in "Midsummer Night's Dream" proved, Bottom can be lots of fun.

Your devoted servant,

L. Macon Epps

P.S. I am enclosing a poem, inspired by Macbeth's soliloquy on sleep, for your amusement.

P.P.S. I haven't given my address, but I hope we'll meet somewhere in eternity

SLEEP

*Me thought I heard a voice say: Macbeth's sleep soliloquy
has half truths! For instance:
Sleep isn't always "innocent"; sometimes its violent,
rapacious—even murderous-
especial after watching late night T.V.*

*It doesn't always "knit the raveled sleeve of care."
If too many nightmares rob you of rest, sleep doesn't
attend to it knitting!*

As to the "death of each day's life," methinks Macbeth wasn't referring to dream sleep. Dreaming is not death, but a life unto itself, and perhaps more interesting than life when we're wide awake!

Yes, sleep can be "sore labor's bath" or, in today's lingo, a hot tub or Jacuzzi;
But, if you sleep in the wrong position, or encounter busy dreams, it seems like you have worked all night!

"Balm of hurt minds?" Well, maybe— but some hurts are so painful that they take months to fully heal. And some are so penetrating that they drive you BALMY!

Now sleep is surely "Great nature's second course ." That's why I said, "It's a life unto itself." If conscious life is the first course, it follows, like night does day, that subconscious life is the second course!

"Chief nourisher in life's feast[1]? Not for me—good food's more enjoyable when awake than asleep, although punishment for over indulgence can occur during r.e.m. sleep!

Macbeth was a flawed character; a product of the immortal bard's creative mind, which surely knew that dream sleep, with all its faults and unreality, is a special time. A time when the impossible becomes possible; the imagination leap frogs over reality; and our finite minds come face to face with our:

IMMORTAL SOULS!

LIFE IS D.E.A.R.

Yes, life is dear! It is also D.E.A.R. - Dreams, Expectations, Ambitions and Reality.

Everyone has dreams. Some occur when we are asleep, some when we are awake, and all are important. The stronger your imagination, the more powerful your dream. Martin Luther King's famous speech, "I Have a Dream," illustrates how important one man's dream can become. It wasn't his expectation, certainly not for his lifetime. It wasn't even his ambition, although others who followed him made it theirs. It certainly wasn't his reality in the usual meaning of that word, but in a curious way, it became a reality for millions of people, both black and white.

My own life has followed the D.E.A.R. sequence. First, I dream of achieving something wonderful, but my practical self soon convinces me that it is way beyond my capability.

Then I discover that certain dreams are achievable and they become expectations that sharpens my ambition to work hard so that they may become a reality.

Some expectations are inborn. When I was a baby I expected someone to feed me when hungry, change me when messy and cuddle me when insecure. I was blessed with good parents, so I was seldom disappointed.

Some expectations are cultivated or learned slowly! Day follows night; Spring, Winter; Fall, Summer; plants, seeds; marriage, love;....

Some expectations are a matter of faith: the surgeon will fix my ailing heart, the enemy's shells won't find my foxhole, God won't let my plane crash...

Expectations frequently change and the reality changes with them, especially if the ambition, and how hard you work, changes. Let me illustrate by some scenes from my own life:

When I was 6 or 7, the most important man in my small town was the preacher. All those people listened to him every Sunday and he could raise and lower his voice beautifully. He could make you laugh or cry, hate injustice and love goodness. Your thoughts and emotions became a yo-yo in his hands. Naturally, I expected to become a preacher. I was ambitious and worked at it in my childish way—even read scripture and gave little sermons from a living room chair, which my father placed backward to simulate a pulpit.

I never became a preacher, but I did become a church-school teacher and superintendent. In the latter role, I conducted mini-church services, including mini-sermons. My early expectations became a reality, but not in the way I had dreamed.

One day my Dad took me to the local railroad station and the engineer took me aboard his great huffing and puffing machine. Wow! I was impressed—his job looked more important than preaching and I dreamed of becoming a railroad engineer. But it was only a dream. A railroad job wasn't in my future, but the word engineer hibernated in my mind.

When I learned about the great missionary to Africa, Robert Livingston, my preacher expectation changed to this new and exciting field. I would still be a preacher, but instead of serving a small town congregation, I would preach to all those poor, unsaved souls in some exotic, far away place.

From time to time an airplane would fly over my small, western North Carolina town. If I was inside, I would run out into the yard and watch it until it faded from sight and sound. My imagination soared skyward and I felt my missionary zeal waning. A few WWI movies like "Wings" and "Hell's Angels" intensified the tug of aviation and I oscillated between the two fields.

Then I had a happy thought—I would become a FLYING MISSSIONARY!

I never became a missionary, but again, church membership let me experience mission work vicariously. As an elder, I became Chairman of the Mission Council and started an active program of bringing missionaries and foreign Christians to talk to the kids and sometimes the adults. The visitors usually stayed at my home so my family and I really benefited.

During my early teens, a barnstorming flying group came to my hometown. The pilots did stunts over the middle of town to attract a crowd, while some of their ground crew passed out circulars. I eagerly took a circular and learned where and when the free air shows would be held and that rides would be two dollars.

Somehow, I raised the two bucks (no mean feat in the middle of the great depression) and found a ride to the farm airfield. At my request, the pilot made sharp banks and turns and buzzed the airfield before landing. What a thrill!

The friend who joined me in the front cockpit almost became ill, but not me. Although the flight lasted only about five minutes, I was in seventh heaven. My dreams/expectations of being a flying missionary was replaced by a strong desire to become a full-time pilot and go barnstorming.

The barnstorming dream changed to one in which I would become a test pilot. Some of the movies of that era really glamorized test piloting and my youthful mind swallowed it—hook, line and sinker. One night I saw another test pilot movie and one scene changed my life forever. No, it wasn't a crash scene, but one in which two test pilots were chatting inside. "Who's that guy sweeping up the office," one said. "Oh, that's old Jake," the other pilot responded. "He used to be a test pilot, but he got too old to fly."

The "old boy" didn't look a day over forty, so the wheels in my head started whirring and clicking. A serious impediment to my test pilot dreams had surfaced. After a bit of "noodling," I decided to become an aeronautical engineer. That way, could be a pilot during my younger years and fall back on engineering as I aged. I was determined to avoid those unpleasant sweeping chores!

A year or two later I enrolled in the Mechanical Engineering School at North Caroline State, taking the Aeronautical option. Four tough years later I got my B. Mech. Eng. degree. I wasn't a railroad engineer as I had earlier dreamed, but a graduate engineer! A major expectation had finally become reality.

But how about the flying part? Well, during my junior year at N.C. State, Uncle Sam started the Civilian Pilots Training Program—C.P.T.P. for short. The student paid $50 and the government paid the rest—all the way to a private pilots license. I didn't have the 50 bucks that year, but by my senior year I not only had the money, but even more important, my parents consent.

My instructor was tough but thorough, and by late spring of 1940 I had my license and zero accidents. Hooray, another expectation reached!

Just before I got my license or graduated, the Army Air Corp visited the campus seeking new air cadets. Boy, was I excited. Here was my chance to fly the latest military craft, serve my country and start an exciting career. I had taken four years of R.O.T.C. and was a cadet first lieutenant. That experience, coupled with my upcoming engineering degree and pilots license made me feel that I was a "shoo-in."

But fate intervened. Although I passed most of my exams with "flying" colors, the final physical revealed a slight hernia. The doctor said it would never bother me unless I performed the high "g" maneuvers required of military pilots.

To console my disappointment he said I would be accepted if I got if fixed—at my own expense. Some consolation! I was barely making it through college and couldn't afford the necessary operation, so that great expectation never materialized.

After graduation, I started working for the Grumman Aircraft Engineering

Corporation on Long Island, New York. When WWII started on December 7, 1941, I was a design engineer and a member of the local flying club. I remember that day of "infamy" well. In the morning I played in the Grumman band for the dedication of plant 2. In the afternoon I went flying and heard the awful news about Pearl Harbor on the way back to my room.

That major external conflict aroused a strong internal one in me: Should I try to join the Air Corp (their standards my be less severe now) or stay at Grumman and help design airplanes for the war effort? After much soul searching, I heeded Grumman's advice and left the awesome decision to the draft board. It decided that my work at Grumman was more vital to the war effort than military service. I not only stayed at Grumman for the rest of the war, but for 37-1/2 years!

I often wonder what would have happened if my Air Corp expectations had been realized. Would I have won my wings or washed out, like many did? Would I have become a war hero or another casualty? Would I have met my future wife in some foreign country or at a stateside training base? There are more questions than answers.

On the other hand, I now knew the reality of my engineering expectations. I had a satisfying career that reached its zenith when I became assistant program manager for the Lunar Module. Little did I imagine during my college days that men would land on the moon and that I would play an important role in it.

Then it was at Grumman that I met many of my life-long friends and my life-long mate. In a few years, my <u>wife</u> and I will celebrate our 50th anniversary, hopefully with our children, grandchildren and friends.

That's an expectation that I devoutly hope will become a reality.

P.S. It became a reality with a trip to a resort in Canada in 1995.

MEMORABLE WEATHER

Let's face it—weather is one of the most talked about subjects of daily life, so writing about it is a real challenge. Why? Because every day conversation about weather is usually dull, Dull, DULL!

So let me begin by quoting some "Weather Song" words I heard about 75 years ago, that still stay in my memory. Here they are:

"Don't know why, there's no sun up in the sky—Stormy Weather—since my gal and I aren't together—it keeps raining all the time."

Of course there are more memorable words in the song, but those above make my point: Someone wrote about the weather in a creative way, and it made its mark in the world for many years, especially in our memories.

So the rest of this composition will tell about my most memorable experiences with the weather, both foul and fair.

STORMY WEATHER:

It was late spring in 1939, and I was walking back to my dorm on my college campus. As I looked up, I could see storm clouds and hear distant rumbles of thunder. I was in regular clothes and sensed that pouring rain was imminent, so I decided to go into the YMCA building and relax a bit. There were lots of trees on the campus, and I knew enough not to get too close, in case lightning struck. Just as I started rushing up the first steps of the building, lightning struck a tree about 25 feet away.

Not only did the loud crash of sound scare me, but the brilliant flash of light was almost as scary. Joined together, they scared the Devil out of me. Yes, I had a bit of the Devil in me in those youthful days, and he still tempts me now and then in spite of my 89 years. It makes me wonder; how old must we get before he has either given up or considered us a shoo-in to his evil realm?

But wait, there's a bit more to my story. The lightning hit a large limb, and it came crashing to the ground where I had been scampering about 3 seconds ago. Once I was safely inside and had calmed my nerves, I was grateful that Thor had waited those extra 3 seconds before unleashing his awesome power!

FREEZING WEATHER:

Snow skiing was a hobby of my family for years, so sometime in the late sixties, my wife, Elizabeth, and I decided to spend a week at Mt. Killington, Vermont. We drove there from Long Island and arrived too late to ski, but the weather looked good for the rest of the week. When we woke up the next morning, we learned that the temperature had fallen to about –30 degrees. We debated whether or not to ski, but decided that if we put on all of our warm clothing, including a facemask, that we could try it. Elizabeth decided to take the low lift, but my male ego said, "Take the chair lift to the top." Before I boarded it, the attendant showed me the fur comforters on the seat and the one he draped over skiers, explaining that it was –100 degrees with the wind chill factor on the top. He even suggested that maybe I should re-think my trip. I told him I was dressed very warmly and wanted to give it a shot. There were other men going up, so I wasn't the only damn fool.

Once I got to the top and the peak wind hit me, I realized that all of my clothing wasn't enough. I decided to ski down as fast as I could safely, realizing that if I fell I could be in very big trouble. Somehow, I made it down. I quickly took of my skis and headed for the warm interior of the base hut. There I found my wife, and many of the other skiers. She told me that it wasn't too bad if we stayed at lower altitudes, so we did a bit more skiing that day; one quick trip up the lower lift, a quick run down the slope, and about an hour in the hut to warm up and rest.

As an Aerospace engineer, I had learned that absolute zero was –473 degrees F, considerably colder than my meager −100 degrees. Later on, when I was working on the Lunar Module, I learned that the astronauts had to be protected from about −250 degrees at night and +250 during the day <u>plus</u> a pure vacuum. Overcoming those challenges were big technical accomplishments in a program full of many accomplishments.

ICY WEATHER

I was fortunate to have a friend, <u>Brand Wehle</u>, teach me how to navigate a car in icy weather. I had moved from North Carolina to New York State, so driving in icy weather was relatively unknown to me. Because of Brand's lessons, I was able to avoid pitfalls that overwhelmed less knowledgeable drivers. Even so, there were certain circumstances that trapped me.

One happened in Pennsylvania when I was approaching a stoplight on a steep icy grade. Although I used all my training, I couldn't stop before I hit the car in front of me. Fortunately, I used my head and didn't try to avoid it by swerving, but decided to hit it squarely to get the maximum benefit of our bumpers. We both hopped out of our cars to assess the damage, and I almost fell on the slippery ice. The damage was so minor that the driver of the other car said, "Drive on, I will blame it on the ice rather than you!"

FOGGY WEATHER

Whenever I encountered fog while driving, my instinct told me, "Slow down, and if it gets too bad, pull over and wait until it clears." The last solution is not always practical, because it may take so long that you run greater risk while waiting. After attending a Christmas Party in L.A. in the sixties, we ran into a terrible fog on the way home. I had planned to drive back to Long Beach on the freeway, but I decided it might be safer to take local streets. This I did, and although it was slow going, we made it back home safely. The papers next day were full of accidents on the freeway, so I felt both lucky and smart.

GORGEOUS WEATHER:

As I look back on my long life, I am pleased to say that gorgeous weather has been much more available than bad weather. Sometimes we take if for granted, but at other times it is so gorgeous, and the circumstance so favorable, that such times become frozen in our memories. One such time happened when two buddies, <u>Lynn Radcliffe</u> and <u>Ray Korndorfer</u>, and I climbed Mt, Washington, in New Hampshire.

Now it is a 6200-foot mountain, and the trail is tough, so we spent most of the day getting to the summit. Ray was the novice of our threesome, and Lynn the expert, so we went slower than usual because of Ray. Once we left the tree line, we ran into low clouds all the way to the top. Now a cloud up there is like a deep fog on the ground. To make matters worse, the trail to the top is hard to follow because there is not an easy path through trees, only rock Cairns about every 100 yards.

We wondered whether we should go back, but Lynn came up with a brilliant idea. Ray would stay put, Lynn and I would go about half way in the direction of the next Cairn, and Lynn would wander around until he found it. He would them yell to me, I would yell to Ray, and Ray would follow my voice until we met. We would then follow Lynn's voice until we met him at the Cairn. We would repeat the process, Cairn to Cairn, until we found the manned building at the top.

It worked like a charm, and once we reached the building, we made arrangements to have supper and spend the night, as hoped. We used our sleeping bags on the bunks provided, and had a great nights sleep. Ray was the first to wake up, and when he looked out the window at the dawn, he woke both of us. We quickly dressed and went outside to see a gorgeous sight.

The sun was creating brilliant colors in the east and the clouds had fallen about a thousand feet. They were the stunning base for all the peaks that rose above them. I have only seen such a sight a few times in my life, and this one was perhaps the finest. We watched in awe for about 15 minutes, at which time the clouds rose and blocked our view. However, the fifteen minutes were so perfect that I can see it in my mind to this minute.

Then there was another time, in the New Hampshire Mountains, when rain had ceased around five pm, and there were two brilliant rainbows in the sky. My <u>wife</u> and I left our car, climbed up a small knoll, and watched them sparkle and glow until they started fading. Another glorious sight created by friend weather!

I could describe many more glorious and dangerous weather-created scenes that have blessed my life, and I suspect so could many others. Those of us who appreciate and can recall them are the lucky ones. Unfortunately, many of our fellow humans pay little attention to them, except perhaps the dangerous ones. Which group are you in?

MEMORY

"What is the most important thing in your life? Ask that question and I doubt if many will answer "Memory," so I guess I have lots of convincing to do when I say: "For me, it is memory!"

Before I explain my reasons, I will make the following bold statements: 1. Without memory, we would not exist. 2. Without memory, life would be almost meaningless. 3. Without memory, our accomplishments would be minimized. 4. Without memory, there would be very little intelligence. 5. Of all human traits, memory is the most perplexing to science. 6. Without memory, I would not write this essay and you would not read or listen to it.

I will now try to convince you of statements 1 through 6, but in reverse order. Here goes:

6. Without memory, I would not write this essay and you would not read or listen to it.

This is a fairly simple statement to explain. When we both learned to listen and speak, then read and write, we had to memorize many things: thousands of words, and their pronunciation, meaning and spelling; rules of grammar, which helped us organize and understand the thoughts and concepts behind spoken and written words; where we stored the written words, or recalling spoken words we heard. The latter two are still a big challenge as time goes by—even with our marvelous memories.

If you go back to your childhood, you should remember how difficult it was to learn all the tasks listed above and then keep them in your memory for a lifetime. But somehow, most of us have done it, and it has been one of life's great blessings.

5. Memory still perplexes science.

Recently, I did a Google search of the brain and how it works. I wont go into details, because it is very complicated and not in my field. But I came away with admiration for the knowledge of many scientists and how they have slowly learned how the brain functions. They seem to know the mechanism by which our minds acquire and process sights, sounds, odors, touches, feelings, and other things. I was surprised that even the best minds are still uncertain how things are stored in our memory, and they are really puzzled at how all the stored things can be recalled so easily and quickly.

To check out the recall speed, I thought of my school teachers. I could quickly recall what they looked like and their names; some of the things they did, both pleasant and unpleasant; even which ones wore glasses or had funny features. I especially remember <u>Miss Bridger</u>, my very pretty first grade teacher. Even though I was only six years old when she was my teacher, I was sad when she got married and moved away the next year.

However, I couldn't recall specific lessons, probably because they have been blended into my general pool of knowledge, which I can still recall in some detail. Try remembering your teachers yourself—you may be surprised.

4. Without memory, there would be very little intelligence.

When <u>Albert</u> <u>Einstein</u> conceived the theory of relativity, and his famous equation, $E = MC^2$ (Energy equals the change of mass times the speed of light squared), I suspect he dug very deeply into his memory base before he came up with his brilliant theories, which other scientist confirmed as true.

When <u>Thomas Jefferson</u> wrote the Declaration of Independence, I'm sure he relied deeply on his memory base, not only concerning words, grammar, etc., but also on his many experiences and conversations with others.

When <u>Thomas Edison</u> and other inventors came up with all the products and services we now take for granted, could they have done it without damn good memories and the lessons and knowledge they stored therein? I think not, and that's why I believe that without memory our amazing intelligence would soon diminish greatly.

3. Without memory, our accomplishments would be minimized.

A tree or plant lives and accomplishes a few things. It grows, produces seeds so its species can survive, and it gives off oxygen, which is necessary for humans and the rest of the animal kingdom. But does it have a memory? Not to my knowledge, and certainly nowhere near our own memories. So what do you think we humans could accomplish if we didn't have our marvelous memories. Damn little, I think, and points 6, 5, and 4 tend to support this conclusion. If anyone disagrees, I would like to review your logic. But if you agree, think of all the wonderful things that happen in your life that would be non-existent without memory.

2. Without memory, life would be almost meaningless.

Even if we could accomplish a few minor things, would we appreciate them without memory? Does a tree have a sense of meaning when its leaves turn into brilliant colors and we humans admire them audibly? Does it feel proud when one of its seeds grows and thrives? Does it have a feeling of love because the oxygen it produces helps all the animals?

Again, I think not, and I believe the reason lies in its lack of memory. I suspect that the things humans most cherish, such as family, friends, love, forgiveness, accomplishment, etc., would fade into oblivion without all the things our memories let us do.

1. Without memory we would not exist.

I have saved the toughest belief for last. Let me explain my reasoning. Without memory, would we acquire the knowledge, or have the intelligence, to procreate? Probably not, but even if we did, would we be able to stay alive in a world that demands we learn to take care of ourselves? I have already explained the vital role of memory in the learning process, so that reinforces the answers to the above questions. Even with our current memories, humans have a difficult time existing, especially when nature or evil humans do great harm to us. I think most would agree that without memory we would not exist as humans, or even as other animals.   At age 88, I have observed many things about life. Time flows swiftly by, and without memory all we could do is live in the present. The past, and all its lessons and pleasures, would not exist. Even the future would be blurred, because we would lack the intelligence and insight to foresee and plan for it. I believe that I keep enjoying life because of the wonderful memories of my past, plus the lessons and knowledge that I accumulated that let me look forward to my future, even if it is uncertain.

So, dear readers, cherish your memory, and do all in your power to keep it strong, active and useful. You may find it the key element in all the other things that make your life worthwhile.

© 2009 L. Macon Epps (8-4-08)

MUSIC AND ME

Music has always been an important part of my life. I guess it was in my genes, since my maternal grandmother, <u>Lavinia Rudisill Schrum</u>, played the organ at her church, and so did two of my aunts, <u>Vera Schrum Hinson</u>, and <u>Irene Schrum Hammil</u>. My aunts also played the piano.

More important, my mother, <u>Mittie Schrum Epps</u>, played the piano and sang in the choir, so I not only heard her piano tunes but her sweet voice in the choir. I probably heard her crooning to me as a baby and toddler, but my memory doesn't go back that far. My <u>Dad</u>, whose name I was given, also sang in the choir, and I still have a large photo of him in the Trinity College Glee Club. He sang baritone, or bass, because I remember his deep voice, especially when he was lecturing me for being naughty.

My two sisters, <u>Ruth Epps Hunter</u> and <u>Louise Epps Greer</u>, both played the piano, and both were very good at it. Ruth also sang in the choir, and when she went to college, she majored in music, even taking graduate courses in it. Ruth made a life-long career in music as a piano teacher, church organist, choir director, and director of a community chorus.

As her younger brother, I used to sit on the piano bench while she played some of my favorite pieces, which became so because I heard them from her or mother. <u>Beethoven's</u> "Moonlight Sonata" was my youthful favorite, and still is among my adult favorites. <u>Rachmaninoff's</u> "Prelude in C-sharp minor" and "Polichinelle," plus <u>Schubert's</u> Serenade, were also at the top of my list of pieces Ruth played for me, not just once, but many times.

When I was ten years old, my folks let me take piano lessons from <u>Mrs. Cochran</u>, who lived directly across our street in Newton, NC. I enjoyed them and was catching on well. However, she also gave lessons at our grammar school, and I felt embarrassed when she came to the class during study time and said, "It's time for Macon's music lesson." Some of the other boys teased me about it, because in those day's boys my age felt it was a sissy thing to do.

It wasn't long before I was ready to participate in Mrs. Cochran's recital, which was held in the school auditorium. My piece was called "My Papa's Waltz," and I had it memorized pretty well. Naturally, I was a little nervous about playing in front of all those people, but I planned to do so until I spotted <u>Big Jim Cochran</u>, a nephew of our teacher, shooting spitballs at the bare legs of students while they were playing.

I was still wearing short pants, and I decided NOT to play because of Jim and his damn spitballs. Although I was only ten years old, I was stubborn and resisted Mrs. Cochran's pleas and promise of an ice cream cone. I didn't explain why I wouldn't play, because I didn't want to be a tattletale on Jim. In short, I didn't play, even though my parents and several relatives had come to hear my sister Ruth and me tickle the ivories.

The next day, my dad talked with me about my failure to play, and again I didn't tell why. It was 1930, and the "Great Depression" was in its early stages, so Dad said, "Well, if you aren't going to play in recitals, I think you should give up the piano. It costs 50 cents per lesson, and there's no use wasting money if you behave that way."

I agreed with him, and stopped my piano lessons until I was an adult.

Although I never took voice lessons, I liked to sing. I had a nice boy-soprano voice, and sang mostly around my folk's house. One night I was singing the "Indian Love Call" and some neighbors heard it and complemented me the next day. More about my singing later.

Once I entered my teen years, I became interested in playing in the high school band. I wanted to play a trombone, because I had heard one featured in a rendition of the "Saint Louis Blues." Dad looked for one when he was soliciting orders in nearby towns for his printing business, but he never found one. He did buy me a baritone horn, which was first cousin to a trombone. I took lessons, and by the time I was fifteen I got to play in the band. When I was sixteen, I played a solo in the North Carolina music competition, and was graded a "B".

I entered North Carolina State College in 1936 at the age of sixteen, and became a member of three bands: The ROTC Military Band, the Red Coat Marching Band (Mostly for football games), and the Concert Band. I especially liked the concert band because we played classical pieces such as, "Morning, Night I Vienna," by <u>von Weber</u>, and the final movement of <u>Tschaikowsky's</u> Fourth Symphony. Our Music Director, <u>Major Christian Kutchinski</u>, lent me a double-barreled euphonium, which is a fancy baritone horn with a fourth valve that lets the player simulate a trombone, so my early trombone desire was partly fulfilled.

Later, Major Kutchinski wanted me to play in the Concert Orchestra, so he gave me lessons on the bassoon, which was the orchestral equivalent of a baritone horn. Sadly, I had to give it up because there were no practice rooms, and my dormitory mates yelled when I practiced in my room.

When I started work as an aeronautical engineer in 1940, at the age of twenty, I joined the company band, and played with it for several years. I also took piano lessons and was doing well, but since I lived in a private house as a roomer, it was difficult to find time to practice on my landlord's piano when no one was present. I gave up the piano again, but not before I had started composing a piece, which I titled "Theme and Variations."

Some years went by, and after I was married and had two kids, I bought a Chord Organ and taught myself to play it. I became pretty good, and played many classical pieces, mostly for the family, but sometimes for guests.

My <u>wife</u> and I subscribed to several local symphony orchestras, went to hear major orchestras and operas in NY City and elsewhere. We also attended many Broadway and Off-Broadway musicals, so my musical life was quite full. Once our hometown of Huntington, NY started having Community Concerts, my wife, <u>Elizabeth</u>, and I were asked to be on the Board of Directors. We served on it for many years, and I was Vice-President for four years and President for two. During my term as President, Elizabeth was Campaign Chairman, and for the first time we sold out the house. We had about 2000 subscribers for an 1800 seat auditorium, but our advisor told us it was OK since at least 10 percent never showed up. He was right, but we almost ran into trouble when the Cleveland Symphony performed for us.

The most fun I had with music was when I became guest conductor for several major orchestras. I had my own baton, and it was thrilling to raise it and conduct some of the greatest symphonic music ever composed. I enjoyed the thunderous applause, and always bowed gracefully. I even conducted an encore on some occasions.

I was tired but happy when the concert was over, but either I had to change the radio station, or change the record in my hi-fi system. Yes, I was guest conductor in my imagination, but my physical movements were damn good, and my timing was just about right. I even conducted in front of my friends, and some made favorable comments after they finished grinning. One couple even gave me a record that included a baton, which was entitled: "Music for frustrated Conductors."

One year we went to Disney World in Florida, and it had a feature, which let patrons conduct classical music. It was a clever device, and followed the "guest conductor's" movements electronically, making the music louder or softer, and faster or slower, depending on the conductor's movements. I watched several people try this new device, and then tried it myself. My previous at-home conducting paid off, because I was the only "conductor" that got applause from the crowd.

My closest experience to real conducting happened on the Queen Mary, which is on display in Long Beach CA. There was a small ensemble of musicians playing on deck, and it had no conductor. Much to my wife's chagrin, I stood in a conductor's place, raised my hands and conducted several of their pieces. The ensemble didn't protest, the crowd applauded, I bowed, and many of them thought I was the real conductor.

As promised earlier, I will now tell about my singing. Now this may sound far-fetched, but I actually sang a solo at the La Scala Opera, in Milan, Italy. I sang <u>Verdi's</u> "La Donna Mobile" there one afternoon. Impressed?

Don't be, because I sang the solo while taking a tour of La Scala. I was standing in an upscale box when I sang it, and there was no orchestra, no other singers, and no audience except other tourists, but I still had a good time singing.

I will close with a true, and very exciting story, at least for me: Some months before I was going to my 50th college reunion, I heard a duet from one of <u>Donizetti's</u> great operas. Since I don't speak much Italian, I decided to compose words to the duet. I then wrote words toasting my Alma Mater. Now my university has a special club for alumni who are celebrating their 50th anniversary and beyond, called the "Forever Club." Naturally, I titled my composition "The Forever Club Song." I played the treble clef notes on my sister Ruth's piano, and she wrote them down on a score sheet. I then wrote my words down on the sheet and she added the bass notes. Voila, a new composition!

Once my wife and I attended my reunion, I made arrangements to have it sung by the men's Glee Club, with ME conducting. I rehearsed it once with them, making sure that the each singer had glasses to raise in a toast, and then we performed it at the final banquet. It was received so well that the club members decided to make it their "Official Song." Not only was I pleased, I was exhilarated! Here are the words to "The Forever Club Song:

First Verse:

Here's to the days of yesteryear, and to the school we hold so dear.
Here's to the day we forged our fate, and enrolled at N. C. State!
Here's to the guys and gals we met, and to the Profs we cant forget.
Here's to the homework we all prepared, and the good times that we shared!

Second verse:

Here's to the fifty years gone by; so swiftly that we laugh and sigh.
Here's to the struggles each one had; looking bad they don't seem bad.
Here's to the life-long friends we made, and to those memories that never fade.
Here's to the future years we'll tread, and to the Forever Club—Full Speed Ahead!

Well, those are some of the highlights of my encounters with the wonderful world of music. If there is a reincarnation, or afterlife, I think I may become a full-time musician/conductor/pianist/ singer/ and composer. Wish me luck!

MY HAPPIEST MOMENT

Looking back on 89 years of a wonderful life, it is extremely difficult to pick the happiest moment. Why? Because there were so many happy moments. As I go down the list of some of the most memorable ones, I think of some that were minor, and some that were major-- at least at that time of my life. For example:

The silver dollar I found on a path when I was about 9 years old, and the fun I had spending it without telling anyone I had found it.

The day I was confirmed at my church, at the prevailing age of 12, and the brand new bible they gave me and the other confirmers .

My first sustained swim, and later my first successful dive from a high diving board.

My first kiss, which I coaxed from a pretty girl at a party when I was only 15.

The day I made the first team on the Newton, NC football team, and our subsequent winning the Western North Carolina Championship, even though I was too injured to play.

The day I got my driver's license, and my Dad's generosity in lending me the family car to date some of the local girls.

My first watermelon feast at the farm of a friend of my Dad. For once, I got to eat more watermelon than I could hold.

Graduation from high school, and more importantly from college at age 20. All made possible by the love and support from my parents and relatives during those tough, uncertain years.

Making the Dean's list my junior and senior year at college, especially after a weak beginning my first two years.

My first flying lesson, my first solo flight and the exhilaration I felt when my instructor wasn't present to correct my errors. More importantly, the day I was awarded my private pilot's license.

A few honors and successes during my college years, which modesty prevent me explaining, because they were modest successes.

My first girly show at the North Carolina State fair, where I got to see a nearly- nude, pretty girl-- and from the front row!

My long-range hitchhiking successes. First to R.O.T.C. camp in Alabama, and then to the New York, 1939 World's fair-- and my stay in N.Y. City.

My first day as a newly hired Aeronautical engineer at a leading East Coast company, Grumman Aircraft Engineering Corporation.

My first car-- a 1941 Chevrolet Club Coupe, which cost all of $750, with seat covers thrown in to boot!

Some of the successes I had at work during my first few years, which led to nice raises in pay, promotions and a bit of recognition and prestige.

But my real Happiest Moment was when I saw my beautiful bride coming down the aisle to say "I do!", and we kissed as husband and wife. Why was that the Happiest Moment? Because it was the beginning of more happy moments that I can ever list, such as: the joy and responsibility of children; a house of our own; a garden and orchard on our one acre plot; a host of good friends and social events; an honored place in the community and our church; and a lifetime of real happiness!

Looking back at my advanced age, and with the perspective caused by the swift flow of time, they all seem to be one big happy moment. Best of all, I am hopeful that there will be many more happy moments before I say goodbye!

MY FRIEND (?) JACK
VERSUS
MY GUARDIAN ANGEL

Someone once said that drunks, sailors and little boys have special guardian angels. Their task, and frequently it is a formidable one, is to keep them safe during very dangerous situations. I don't know about the drunks and sailors, but I can testify that I survived more dangerous situations as a boy than I had a right to survive. (Thanks, Guardian Angel.)

It has been over fifty years since I left my boyhood. In spite of its remoteness, many boyhood memories remain strong, especially for those events where my guardian angel watched out for me.

One of my boyhood friends, named <u>Jack Barringer</u>, was the principal architect of some of my most dangerous adventures. We both grew up in a small North Carolina town called Newton. A large field separated our houses and we often met there to play. Jack was a year or so older than I and was bigger and stronger. He had straight brown hair and a mischievous, plump face. He also had an engaging smile with cheek dimples that disarmed even the adults. The comedian, <u>Benny Hill</u>, is a modern look-alike.

Jack was very adventurous and pulled me into many dangerous adventures with his great gift of gab and his devilish persuasiveness. Instinctively, he knew that food could be used as a bribe, especially with a constantly hungry kid like me. He used it frequently to get me to do things that normally I resisted.

Furthermore, Jack didn't hesitate to stoop to threats and blackmail. We didn't call it that in those early days, but the results were the same. "If you don't do this I'll beat ya up", or, "if you don't do that I'll tell your folks about the apples we swiped!"

<u>A Swig of Poison</u>

The first dangerous incident in which Jack tested my guardian angel's mettle occurred when I was about 5 years old. Usually, Jack was imaginative and fun to play with, but one rainy day when we were confined inside, he went astray. He got a bottle of iodine and told me it was good to drink. He removed the cap, held his thumb over the opening and pretended to take a swig.

He then insisted that I take a drink, so I emulated him completely, including the thumb over the opening. He became annoyed that I had caught on to his trick, so he held my nose and forced some into my mouth.

I spit out as much as I could, started crying and ran home to my <u>Mother</u>. She was horrified when I blurted out what had happened and telephoned the doctor immediately. He told her to make me swallow two raw eggs and that he would be right over. The eggs were almost as bad as the iodine, so mother held my nose (like Jack had) to get me to swallow them. Between throwing up and the neutralizing effect of the eggs that stayed in, I didn't suffer any serious damage and the doctor pronounced me safe. (Thanks Mom, <u>Dr. Long</u> and Guardian Angel.)

<u>Underground Adventure</u>

I stayed away from Jack for a month or so, but gradually started playing with him again. A few years later we were playing in a ditch near the <u>Cochran</u> house. We could see the opening of an underground storm sewer from the ditch. It reminded Jack of a cave, so his fertile imagination concocted a new adventure. The dialogue went something like this:

Jack: "Hey, let's get some candles and crawl in there and go exploring."

Me: "What if there are snakes, or lizards or something bad in there?"

Jack: "Oh, there won't be anything in there—besides it will be a good adventure."

Me: "I dunno, suppose the candles go out?"

Jack: "Both of them won't—if they do we'll come right back out."

Me: "I dunno."

Jack: "Come on, let's try it—I'll bet we'll be the first boys in Newton to do something that brave."

The last statement convinced me, so I agreed. We then proceeded to get and light the candles and entered the storm sewer. It was about three feet in diameter at first, but soon turned into two smaller branches about 2 or 2 1/2 ft in diameter. It was pretty tight even for our small bodies. The candles stayed lit and we could see faint daylight in the right branch about 250 feet away. After a brief discussion, we crawled on to continue our adventure.

Somehow we managed to crawl through this small, circular pipe all the way to the end without suffocating or panicking. When we got there we saw plenty of daylight, but much to our dismay, it was a small catch basin with a heavy cast iron grate over it. Try as we might, we couldn't budge it.

We discussed our situation about like this:

Me: "What'll we do now?

Jack: "Beats me. I sure don't want to crawl back, do you?"

Me: "Heck no, but I don't like being cooped up here. Maybe if we yell some one will hear us."

Jack: "Good idea—let's yell."

Both: "Help! Help! Help!"

Pretty soon three older boys came along.

1st Boy: "What're you kids doing in there?"

Jack: "We crawled in here from Cochran's ditch."

1st Boy: "I don't believe you—it's too far away."

Jack: "Please lift the grate and let us out."

2nd Boy: "Let's leave 'em in—they can darn well crawl back the way they came!"

Jack: "Please don't—just let us out and we'll never do it again." (I was with Jack 100% and nodded my head vigorously.)

3rd Boy: "They're just kids, maybe we oughta let 'em out."

1st Boy: "Guess you're right—o.k. kids, you push and we'll lift."

The grate lifted and the three boys slid it to one side. They then helped us out and the second boy admonished us: "Don't ever do such a fool thing again." We swore we wouldn't and that's one oath we both kept!

To this day, I get a creepy feeling whenever I think of this foolish adventure. With my adult mind I think of a few "what ifs:"

What if a sudden, violent rainstorm had sprung up and we drowned and became wedged in?

What if the candles or a pocket of sewer gas had asphyxiated us?

What if we had encountered a den of rattlesnakes, or copperheads and got too dizzy from the venom to get out?

I can see the headlines in the local paper now: "Two Lads Mysteriously Disappear - Police and Parents Baffled." And perhaps some time later: "Missing Lads' Bodies Found - Washed Out of Sewer by Flash Flood" (Big thanks, Guardian Angel, for getting me safely out of that one.)

A Greek Near Tragedy:

When I was around ten, Jack's class studied Greek history. Jack was very impressed with the Spartans because they were very brave and could endure incredible discomfort and pain. Once I was duly impressed, he suggested we take off our jackets, sweaters and shirts and see who could stand the raw December weather the longest.

We were both stubborn and neither of us wanted to give up first. Soon we were shaking like leaves in a hurricane. Finally, we agreed to put our clothes on at the same time and then ran to our respective homes to get warm.

A day or so later he had influenza and I had pneumonia. To make matters worse, it was the last day of school before the Christmas break. Unlucky kids, we spent the next two weeks coughing, sneezing and feeling really miserable. Needless to say, we missed all the holiday fun, which was awful for a kid.

I acquired a very high fever, somewhere around 105°F, and nearly died. On Christmas Eve, Dr. Long told my folks that I was near death but if I could hold on until morning he thought the fever would break and I would live. I was unaware of this trying drama at the time since the fever made me delirious. I hate to think of the anguish that my foolish adventure caused my parents.

Miraculously, the fever broke during the night and I woke up on Christmas day feeling much better, but very weak. My folks knew I was going to recover because I regained my appetite and asked for food. Once I realized it was Christmas day I even asked if Santa had brought me anything!

That was a real close call and again I was indebted to my folks, Dr. Long and my ever present Guardian Angel — but not to Jack!

A Blessing in Disguise:

Some of the adventures that Jack got me into turned out to be blessings in disguise. The next summer he said it was time for us to learn to smoke. He produced a whole pack of cigarettes that he had swiped from his uncle Clyde Wagner and we snuck into my dad's unused chicken house for privacy.

The first few puffs made me cough, but gradually I got used to them and finished my cigarette. I thought Jack would be pleased, but he was a boy who believed in pursuing a task to the bitter end. He persuaded himself (and me) that we should smoke the whole damn pack! His reasoning was simple: "We'll really learn to smoke if we smoke 10 cigarettes apiece."

I don't remember how many we actually smoked. All I remember is that we both got incredibly ill and went home. It was mid-afternoon, so I quietly sneaked into my room and crawled into my bed to die in peace. When my mother found me a few hours later, I was moaning and tossing uncontrollably and wouldn't answer her questions. She worried that I had caught some dread disease. Her worry turned to panic when I refused to come to supper, so she called Dad in to talk to me.

Dad checked me over and since I didn't have a fever he said, "Let him sleep—whatever it is, it'll probably be better by morning."

Mother said, "Shouldn't we call Dr. Long tonight--he seems awfully sick?"

"Let's wait 'til morning before we call the doctor. No point in wasting three dollars if it's something temporary."

Dad was right. By 7 AM the next morning I was right as rain. I never told them what had caused the sudden illness. I suppose they figured it was some passing childhood disease.

Why was that a blessing in disguise? Because it taught me the hard way that smoking wasn't such a hot idea. In fact, I was able to resist other temptations to start smoking, as I grew older. To this day, I have never acquired that unhealthy, expensive and foolish habit. (Thanks Jack, for the important lesson; thanks, Guardian Angel, for letting that lesson last a lifetime.)

Local Fame:

During our early teens, the Great Depression started getting really serious. The worse it got, the sillier the fads became: eating live gold fish; overcrowding a telephone booth; flagpole sitting; even tree sitting for those who couldn't manage a flag pole. Jack and I had read of people in other towns who had broken tree- sitting records, but I never personalized it. Jack did, and one day he proposed that we tree sit and try to break the record. I was an excellent tree climber so I quickly accepted.

When I broached the subject to my parents, Mother said it was too dangerous, but Dad said he could make it safe. So around 12:30 P.M., right after lunch, we met at the tree we had selected and climbed aboard. We had made arrangements to have supper and breakfast brought to us and any other meals if we lasted that long. We filled our pockets with raw peanuts and took apples and water up our tree to sustain us 'til supper. It wasn't long before people passing by noticed us and we of course told them we were trying to set a record.

It was a small town and word spread quickly. Soon, people walked or drove out of their way to see the two foolish kids. Some admired us, some laughed with us, some laughed at us and a few tried to persuade us to come down before we "broke our fool necks." Some even suggested that we would cheat and come down during the night. We swore we wouldn't, but deep down that was part of our plan, especially if we had to have a B.M.

Urinating, of course, was easy; we waited 'til no one was in sight, climbed to an adjacent limb and let fly. We were both delighted at the great distance it fell and wondered who had the world's height records. Of course, such events weren't published in these semi-Victorian times, but it didn't keep us from speculating. (Are they published today?)

Dad brought supper for both of us and Jack's folks were scheduled to bring breakfast. Dad stayed and chatted and we had plenty of other visitors. Dad said he would come back around 9:30 and bring blankets and two ropes to tie us in. After the visitations slowed down he secured us for the night and we finally fell asleep.

Around 1 AM, Jack woke me and told me he had seen a huge dog sniffing at our tree. Although the bottom of my limb was six or seven feet off the ground, Jack swore that the dog was so big he could easily reach me. I untied the rope and moved higher in the tree and so did Jack. Unfortunately, the limbs were too small for reclining, so we tied ourselves in a sitting position. Our plans to descend to the ground when it was dark and no one would catch us evaporated because of the huge dog. After chatting awhile, we both fell asleep.

Next morning we woke up early and debated how long we should stay up in the tree. Around seven o'clock we smelled the bacon and eggs that Jack's folks were cooking, and that did it. We decided to descend, eat breakfast, go to the John and then to bed to catch up on some of the sleep we had missed. All told, we had stayed in the tree for eighteen and a half hours. It was nowhere near the national record, but it did establish the Newton record. As far as I know, it still stands.

The local paper got wind of our accomplishment and we made the front page. No photos, but a nice article with our names spelled right. Finally, one of Jack's adventures had brought us local fame, which we basked in for at least a week.

On the surface, it looked like my Guardian Angel had an easy time. But the old "what ifs" keep coming up.

—What if the huge dog had bitten me? (Later on Jack pointed him out and the "huge" was a gross exaggeration.)

—What if one of us had gotten entangled in the ropes and strangled in our sleep?

—What if the ropes came loose and we fell?

—What if a sudden thunderstorm had arisen during the night and our tree had been struck by lightening? (Thanks, Guardian Angel, for keeping those damn "what-ifs" away!)

Rock Stars!

Although it was several decades before "rock and roll" was invented, Jack and I saw rock stars. One day we were playing "Capture the Flag" with some other kids and Jack refused to play by the rules.

One team defended the flag and could capture any boy that came into the pre-described flag territory just by touching him. A captive could be released by a teammate who reached him before he was touched by the defenders. If the teammate penetrated all the way to the flag before being touched, his side won. In a more difficult version, the aggressor had to take the captured flag back into his own territory without being captured. If a defender ran into aggressor territory, he could be captured. Defenders tried to capture as many boys as possible because if they captured them all, they won. Aggressors tried to capture the flag, rescue their own captives and capture a defender that ran into his territory in hot pursuit. It was an exciting game with lots of running.

Jack broke the rules by pulling me into his defender territory in order to capture me. I argued that it wasn't fair, but he paid no attention to my argument. After the second time, I warned him that I would hit him with a rock if he did it again. However, he had been dominating me so long he ignored my warning.

After the third violation, I picked up a one-inch rock and threw it briskly at him. Unfortunately (for him) it hit him smack in the head—right where he parted his hair. The wound bled profusely and Jack fell to his knees moaning that I had killed him.

I was a bit shook-up that I had done so much damage and decided that I had better leave before he recovered enough to retaliate. I slowly walked away while the other boys were helping Jack, and went home. I was safe there, but I worried plenty about what Jack would do when he saw me again. I dodged him for about a week.

One day he caught up with me and I decided to brazen it out. Our conversation went something like this:

Jack: "You really hurt me when ya hit me in the head with that ole rock. I saw <u>stars</u> for a while. Here, look at the scar!"

Me: "I didn't mean to hurt ya so much, but I warned ya, didn't I?"

Jack: "Yeah, I guess so, but I think I'll punish ya 'cause ya messed up my parting place."

Me: "You'd better not—I don't want to hit ya with another rock."

Jack: "You wouldn't do that, would ya?"

Me: "Well, you're bigger than me and I've got a right to defend myself."

Jack: "Promise ya'll never do it again?"

Me: "Yep, if ya promise to quit bullying me like ya did t'other day."

Jack: "I guess so."

We parted friends and it wasn't long before we were on good terms again. However, a year or so later I got hit in the head with a rock by an unknown assailant. I was finishing my paper route and passed beneath a big cedar tree near a corner. Suddenly, I felt a sharp blow on my head right through my wool cap. I too saw stars and got very dizzy and fell to the ground. When I arose I staggered home and told my folks.

They of course wanted to know who did it, but I hadn't seen anyone in the tree. Fortunately, my cap and the size and roundness of the rock kept my head from bleeding, but a big bump rose on it. When Dr. Long saw it he said I had a mild concussion and should stay out of school the next day. That pleased me and I started having less harsh thoughts about my assailant.

I never did find out who did it and never suspected Jack, because it occurred out of his usual territory. Years later, when we were in high school, he told me he had done it to get even for messing up his parting place. To this day, I don't know whether he really did it or just claimed credit for someone else's bad deed. (Thanks, Guardian Angel, for not letting those "Rock Stars" start us on a journey to the real stars!)

What Else?

Jack led me into many other adventures too numerous to cover in detail. For example:

– Before I leaned to swim, he tricked me into a spot in the creek that was over my head. He laughed as I gasped for breath and nearly drowned, but pulled me to safety at the last minute,

– He pointed an "empty" 45-caliber pistol at me and clicked the trigger several times. Fortunately, it was really empty,

–He tried to play some practical jokes on me—he took me on a hunt for an imaginary critter called a "snipe," in which I was supposed to hold a bag for hours in a lonely spot in the woods. Later on, when I was about sixteen, he took me on a "date with two loose girls" whose overly protective father was away. (But always showed up with his shotgun.) Luckily I was wise to both tricks. Jack taught me many things that today we would call street smarts or worldly wisdom.

For example, when I was around twelve he showed me a medical book that graphically displayed where babies came from. In those days, kids heard all sorts of false information about sex and reproduction, so I avoided the usual misinformation.

Jack was held back a year in school so we graduated the same year—1936. I went on to college and Jack moved away, so I lost track of him for many years. I saw him at our twenty-fifth high school reunion and learned that he was a successful building contractor in Atlanta, Georgia. He still had the gift of gab and the dimpled, mischievous grin. I surmised that his dangerous adventure days were over, but I'd bet my bottom dollar that he still has some sort of adventures.

Today people would call the young Jack a hyperactive, somewhat mean kid that needed strong counseling. I see him as a sort of juvenile Dr. Jeckyl and Mr. Hyde. Most of the time he was fun to be with and his dangerous adventures and bullying could have been caused by a chemical unbalance, or perhaps just a product of his very active imagination.

In retrospect, I guess I was fortunate to have survived Jack's dangerous adventures, plus many I encountered on my own or with other boys. Except for our Guardian Angels (Jack must have had one too), neither of us may have made it to manhood.

But having survived Jack, I consider myself lucky to have had a friend as interesting and as much fun as he was. I consider myself even luckier that my Guardian Angel never deserted me, even though Jack caused him/her to work many hours of overtime.

Jack and Guardian Angel, wherever you are, I salute you!

AN OLD MAN'S DREAMS

INTRODUCTION:

During my long life, I have had thousands of dreams, most of which were so entertaining that they seemed to form a second life. Some were repetitious, or too complicated to describe, so they are not included herein. The complicated ones remain a mystery, even to me. A few put me in dangerous or frustrating positions, but I was usually able to find a solution during the dream. When I couldn't find a solution, I saved myself by waking up, sometimes in a cold sweat.

Many of them were in full color and sound, and also involved my sense of touch. A few involved my senses of taste and smell. It was rare when all five senses were involved, but it happened on a few occasions. Fortunately, most of my dreams were so vivid that I was able to recall them the next morning, and a few have remained in my memory for many years. Some were inspirations for my writings, a few of which were published in small media, and I have included most of them in my book. Senior Short Stories." Some helped me solve problems which were still on my mind when I fell asleep, and some gave me innovative ideas which I was able to use during my working years as an aerospace engineer/manager and there after.

I have been so intrigued with dreams in general, that I have also written poems and essays about them.

As I write this introduction, my wife, <u>Elizabeth</u>, is the principal one I have shared them with. Although she too has dreams, it is rare when she can recall them the next morning, so the sharing is a one-way street. I am writing a number of them down now in the hope that I can share them with others, such as my family and close friends. I don't plan to send them to editors or scientists, but if they should come across them I would be pleased if they found a use for them. At age 87, my primary reason for compiling them is for the pleasure of writing them down and sharing them, with the hope they won't be lost forever.

Given below are some of my recent most memorable and interesting dreams in chronological order. Although I dream most every night, I have not had the time or inclination to compile all of them herein, so some very interesting ones may have been lost forever because I was too busy to write them down before they faded from my memory. Most of them occurred when I was in my 70's and 80's, so they represent the dreams of an old man, hence the title.

I admit that I have embellished some of them for clarity or interest; but, on the other hand, there are no words that can describe adequately their astounding visual and other effects. I welcome comments from any readers, be they your analysis of the dream, (which I frequently did myself), comments that you had similar dreams, or other things that pop into your head.

A SKYSCRAPER TRAGEDY (11/27/91)

It was the world's tallest building. It was also the largest in floor area, so it was the biggest building ever. Some fellow aerospace managers and I were on the observation roof, which covered several acres. As we walked around the periphery to enjoy the wonderful views, a man being chased by a police officer interrupted us.

It was then that we saw the awful fire that the man had started. He had opened the drain valve on several huge rooftop fuel storage tanks, and inflammable liquid was gushing out by the hundreds of gallons. It was flooding the roof and running down to lower floors through the stairwells. It had ignited huge fires on some lower stories and the flames soon reached the roof, cutting off the stairs and elevator we had recently ascended.

Surprisingly, the man reached the edge near us and promptly flung himself off. After a short pause, so did the officer. It wasn't long before the man pulled a ripcord and a parachute opened part way. Fortunately, he had a backup 'chute, so it opened and blossomed out like a giant carnation. Meanwhile, the officer stayed in free fall until he landed on the other man's 'chute, which partially collapsed. The officer then opened his own parachute while hanging on to the other one, so it was clear that he was in control of the situation.

But we weren't in control of our situation. We were trapped high above the city streets with a roaring inferno getting closer and closer. I asked the flight-test guys in our group if they had any parachutes, but none did. It looked like the end, so I told several of my buddies, "Rather than die in the flames, I'll jump off. A 2000-foot fall will be fun while it lasts, and maybe some miracle will save me on the way down-- like learning to fly."

Paul Butler, our leader, said there might be another way down, so we started scurrying around the non-flame periphery to look for it. None was found, until I peered over the edge and spotted a column about 2 feet in diameter and about 80 feet long. I showed it to Paul, saying, "If we lock our arms and legs tightly around the column, we may be able to slowly slide down it to a safer level. I'll go first, and if I make it, send the rest of the guys."

Paul said, "OK, and good luck!"

I climbed over, held on to the column, and started sliding down. When I was about half way down, another man blocked me. He had tried it earlier, but seemed to have lost his nerve. "Hang on to me," I yelled, "and I'll get you down." He quickly grabbed me, and relaxed enough so we could continue sliding. Once we were safely down, the rest of our group did the same.

After we assembled, our problems weren't over. There was still fire on that floor, but we were up-wind of it. Paul then said to the group, " Stay here where it's safe. Macon and I will look for a safe stairway, and if we do, we'll come back for you." They agreed.

We soon found a small stairway and descended two stories. It stopped on that floor, so we looked for another one. We found it near the main elevator, where there was a large group of people waiting for a ride down. I asked, "Why don't you folks walk down the stairs."

Several had the same answer. "We'll never be able to walk all the way down, so why start?"

Paul said, "One of us should go get the group, while the other explores these new stairs." We matched to see who would go back, and I lost. When I got to the stairs we came down, it was impossible to use-- too many people were rushing down it in near panic. I then started looking for another way.

Suddenly, I heard music--dance music; apparently, some people on this level were oblivious to the raging inferno above. I decided to head toward the music in case there was another safe stairway. Finding none, I entered a large, dimly lit room filled with people sitting around tables and dancing. It must be the nightclub part, I thought, because there were performers and a band going full swing. They were playing golden oldies, and the dancers were holding each other tightly, as we used to do when the music was fresh and new. I thought, 'This is like the dance band on the Titanic.'

I realized that it would be difficult to get safely through the crowd, so I prayed for a miracle. It was immediately answered-- not by the dancers parting like the Red Sea did for Moses, but by the unmistakable feeling that I could fly. I spread my arms, flapped them gently, and flew above the astonished dancers. I yelled, "Get out of here; the upper stories are on fire!" They ceased being astonished at my ability to fly when some cynic yelled, "Hey, it's all part of the entertainment-- can't you see the wires holding him up?"

"Of course we see the wires," several responded, and continued dancing. When I got beyond the dance floor, I kept flying and looked for another stairwell. I found an unoccupied one and immediately went up to look for the guys we told to wait. They were nowhere in sight, so I wondered whether they had gone back up or down. On a hunch, I went back to the observation roof and they were all there, including Paul. Except for them, the roof was deserted.

Paul told me the sad news. "I went down two flights only to find that the fuel had accumulated there and the whole floor was burning like hell. I came back up, got the guys, and we all came up here. I figured it would be a good place to jump off, as you suggested, or wait for a miracle."

"Hold on fellows," I shouted. "You don't have to jump or wait for a miracle, because I found a miracle on the way back. If you have faith, we can all fly off the edge and descend safely to the street." They looked at me as if I had flipped my lid.

"You really can," I said in a calmer tone. "Here, let me show you." I raised my arms and flew around them. I even flew off the edge to show that height was no problem. Their disbelief was not completely erased, but I saw big rays of hope light up their worried faces. One by one, I taught them to fly, mostly by example and by telling them to pray and believe. Once they all succeeded, we flew over the edge in unison, flew around for the pure joy of it, and then descended to the street to see if we could help others in the bewildered mob.

I learned later that many of the other people on the roof had either descended or jumped off. Either way, they were doomed. I woke up shortly after we landed, marveling at the realism of the dream and its amazing conclusion. For a while I wondered if I should have tried to save some of the others with my newfound ability to fly and teach others. To assuage my growing feeling of guilt, my conscious mind had two rational thoughts. 1. I had warned the people in the nightclub about the fire, and they were skeptical and unbelieving about that; so how could I ever convince them to fly? 2. I remembered the words of St Augustine, who said something like this: "Lord, I thank you for not holding me responsible for what I do in my dreams!"

Analysis: I have been on the observation deck of several skyscrapers, including the World Trade Center. (WTC) When I was on the WTC, there was a nice breeze, so I went near the edge, held my arms out as if I were flying, and looked below at the distant view. An officer said, jokingly, "Don't flyaway from us, mister!" That sort of explains my flight off the edge, but then I have flown in many, many other dreams. I also had a pilot's license in my youth; so flying under my own control is easily explained. I have no explanation for the huge fire, but recall a business visit to an upper WTC story office when the wind was so strong that the building moved visibly. In fact, it moved so much that I felt it was dangerous and wanted to descend, but my host convinced me that it was a common occurrence. I might have substituted my real life dangerous feeling for the fire in my dream. Please note that my dream preceded the 9/11/01 World Trade Center catastrophe by almost ten years, and happened in the same month-- September. That raises the question, "Was my dream a prophesy, or just pure coincident?

CHRISTMAS STORY (4/19/06)

It was Christmas time, and I was in Bethlehem-- Bethlehem, Pennsylvania. I was delivering a car as a Christmas present from a husband to his wife. Since it was a dream, I wasn't driving it, as I would do in the real world, but was carrying it on my back! Yes, it was a full size car and was heavy.

When I got to the proper address, there was a crowd of people near the spot watching a TV program in a store window. As I deposited the car in the right spot, a policeman came over and said, "You can't park there--this is a holiday and parking is forbidden."

"But officer," I said respectfully, "I'm so tired carrying it this far that I can't move it. Besides, the owner is supposed to come here in about thirty minutes to take it to his wife as a present."

Fortunately, he was a kind and reasonable man, so he said, "O.K., you can leave it for now, but I hope the owner will pick it up soon."

I then joined the crowd to watch the TV. Program. I guess we were in the wrong part of the city, since the program was showing an exciting celebration in the main part. It was then that I decided to walk to the celebration in spite of my tired feeling.

Suddenly, I could no longer walk, but found myself in a wheel chair. I found it easy to propel, because my arms seemed unusually strong. I concluded that I must have been using a wheelchair a long time; otherwise my arms would not be so strong. I ignored the strength I had carrying the car, which was illogical, but who said dreams have to be logical?

Several people joined me in my search for a route to the celebration. Although we went many blocks, all the alleys and streets were blocked. Apparently, there had been a recent blizzard, and the city had piled the snow, fallen trees, etc. in those places so more important streets could be opened. We knew that the street we were on didn't lead to the celebration, and the only way to it was to find a cross one that we could negotiate. We finally found one that, even though blocked, had a gentle slope that seemed negotiable. Meanwhile, my wheel chair had turned into an electric one, so I easily climbed the gentle slope. Eventually, it got steeper, so some of the kind people pushed me up it, but not for long. The snow and debris pile ended precipitously, and was too dangerous to proceed farther. Someone shouted, "Look, there's a large conveyor belt that might let us keep going." It rose at about a 30-degree angle and seemed climbable, since it had handrails. It was not operating, so it seemed like a safe bet,

We proceeded to go up it, and since my arms were again stronger, I was able to stay close to the others. One woman was the best climber, so she reached the top first, hoping to see the descending part of the belt. She was horrified at what she saw, and yelled to us," The conveyor belt has stopped, and there's only about 12 feet left on the other side; it's dangling way above the earth so we can't go any farther."

We soon figured that we were too much weight for the belt and that for every two feet we climbed, the belt went one foot the other way. That was why there was only 12 feet left on the down side. Worse yet, if we went back down, the belt would reach the top and we would all fall to our deaths because we were still high in the air. If we stayed put, we would either freeze or starve to death. What a rotten dilemma!

After a few worrisome minutes, I had a possible solution. I yelled to the woman at the top, "Do you have anything you can wedge between the top rollers-- maybe something from your backpack?"

"Good idea," she replied. "I'll take a look."

The wait seemed interminable, and those of us waiting below, who were hanging on for dear life, grew more and more frustrated. Now this was an interesting and exciting dream, which was about to end either in catastrophe, or in salvation if the woman could wedge the belt firmly. My other dreams have taught me that there are at least three ways to solve such a frightening dilemma. One is to wait for salvation, which is not in my nature while dreaming; another one is to flap my arms and fly away from danger; the third one is to wake up.

This time, I used the "Wake-up" method!

OSAMA BIN LADEN (7/05/06)

I was walking on a beach on Long Island near my former house, which I had left in 1986. I was near an empty lot close to a village road when I spotted Osama and a large contingent of followers, all armed with various weapons. I surmised that they were going to attack all beach clubs, and thus strike a blow to their upper-class members. Osama spotted me and ordered me to be shot, which one of his henchmen did. I staggered toward the empty lot and fell to the ground wounded, but pretended to be dead.

One of Osama's men ran toward me to make sure, and poked me with the butt of his gun. I seized the gun, knocked him out with it, and quickly put on his turban and flowing gown. I then ran back to the beach and waved victory to Osama. As the group came closer, I shot him and several of his followers, expecting to die when they returned my fire.

However, they were so concerned about their fallen leader that they gathered around to help him, and when they found him dead they started weeping and wailing. I slowly snuck away, went into a nearby house and the owner let me call the police. I woke up before they came, my wound had healed, and I again marveled at the power of dreams. I also wondered what would happen if it had been a true event. Would I be hailed as a hero, or prosecuted for murder, or perhaps both in our highly legalistic and news conscious society. As to Divine judgment, I agree with St Augustine, as quoted in the Skyscraper dream.

Analysis: Osama's frequent appearance in the news obviously made a strong impression in both my active and subconscious mind, and going back to a familiar locale is what the subconscious frequently does. Why a gentle person, like I usually am, decided to be violent was a surprise to me, but I suppose we all have some prehistoric remnants of violence in our genes. Also, all the violence in movies and TV could have played its role, so this one is not difficult to diagnose. Come to think of it, I suspect most Americans, including some women, would shoot Osama if they got the chance. Perhaps a psychiatrist could give better insights.

SADAM HUSAIN (8/2/06)

I was on the staff of the Ambassador to Iraq and Sadam was still in power, since it was pre- 9/11 but after the first Gulf War. I was attending a social event in the Ambassador's home, and heard some un-diplomatic comments from an American ex-general, who knew Sadam's brother. Sadam was obviously upset by the General's remarks.

I don't know whether it was training or part of my nature, but I asked Sadam if he would like to give his viewpoint, especially since the Iraqi culture is quite different from the American one. After he made his points successfully, he was obviously grateful. He then invited me to come to one of his palaces the next day, so he could give me a better picture of himself and his rule. Time passes quickly in a dream, and the next thing I knew we were there.

He then launched into a long story about his humble beginnings, his long struggle for recognition and his ascendancy to power. He explained that their culture required strong leaders; otherwise the nation would fall into much infighting and chaos. From his vantage point, intimidation, torture, and killing were necessary to keep the nation viable and promoted the greater good. He also said that many other nations were faced with the same situation, and that Americans seemed to recognize it better in the past than they did in the present.

I never got to offer the American perspective because I woke up. I will not go into what I might have said, but I will ask the reader, "What would you have said?" Pretty tough question, isn't it?

Analysis: This dream may have been triggered by a suggestion from the leader of a class on understanding other religions and cultures, given By Dr. Bill Garlington, Director of Adult Education at the Camarillo United Methodist Church. One of his assignments was to write an essay on a current problem, but take a viewpoint that was opposed to your own. This I did via an essay, *Iraq War Options*.

COMMUNITY SERVICE REWARD? (8/20/06)

I was standing on top of a steep bank with a slope of about 45 degrees. It was overlooking the ocean, and I was admiring the surf and a hazy sunset, which was in full color. As I drew nearer the edge, I noticed that people had deposited many piles of lawn clippings on the bank, and they were in such a jumbled mess that I figured I should straighten them out. I picked up a nearby broom rake, scrambled down the bank, and worked diligently. After a while, I made the clippings in an even, spread out pattern, which I figured would be more aesthetic, and perhaps better for erosion or new plant growth.

I was pleased with the community service job I had done, and started to go back to the top of the bank. That was when the trouble started. Try as I might, I could not climb up the bank. It may have been because I was too tired, or perhaps I had reverted from the younger man who did the raking, back to my current age of 86.

I felt a bit of panic, so started to call for help, but my voice was weak and a bit garbled. Worse yet, no one heard me or came to my rescue. I had hoped someone would throw a rope to me and then pull on it while I did my part climbing back up, but no such luck. My voice was getting weaker and weaker, and I feared I might have to stay there all night, which was getting colder than my clothing could support.

Than a bright idea dawned on me-- I would send the Morse code S.O.S. by clapping my hands. Surely some one would hear that and I would be rescued. I never got to clap my hands, because I woke up and was safe in my bed. I then made my usual visit to the bathroom and went back to sleep wondering what triggered the dream, and perhaps more important, what triggered my waking up. The latter could have been my need to visit the bathroom, or perhaps my survival instincts came into play. Either answer is OK, but the former is still a mystery. Any ideas?

P.S. When I described the dream to my wife at breakfast, <u>Elizabeth</u> said she had heard me mumbling something in my sleep. It was a bit incoherent and could have been "Help." It also had a bit of emergency in its tone. She was tempted to awaken me, but didn't.

EVOLUTION, DANGER, MAGIC, ENTERTAINMENT, AND MORE... (9/1/06)

My cousin, <u>David Schrum</u>, and I had rented a waterfront cottage on a peaceful bay. It may have been somewhere on Long Island, NY, since my wife and I lived within walking distance of Huntington Bay during 36 years of our married life. Both <u>our wives</u> were in the cottage, and David and I were standing on the beach in our regular clothing. The water was so clear and calm that we could see some of the fish swimming by.

Suddenly, a small fish, perhaps 6 inches long, swam by that had four legs and feet growing underneath its body. I immediately called it to David's attention, and he came over to see it. He then spotted another one just like it coming toward the first one. I reached my hand into the water, and the fish started coming toward me, as if it wanted to be picked up.

'What a find,' I thought. 'It could be a recurrence of evolutionary theory when sea creatures first sprouted limbs and started crawling on dry land.'

Somehow, we both knew that it was an important discovery that would please the scientific community.

Before I could pick the fish up, the tide started coming in quickly and the water got too deep for me to catch the strange fish with my hands. In fact, the tide was rising so fast that it soaked our shoes and we started retreating toward the cottage. We both grew alarmed as it kept rising, and we barely made it to the front door before it did. Clearly, it was an unusual tide, because it was obvious that it would soon engulf the cottage. We entered the door yelling to our wives to evacuate out the back door immediately, and went looking for them.

It was then that another amazing thing happened. We hadn't really entered the cottage, because it had magically turned into to a large warehouse. It was almost empty except for a few machine tools stuck here and there. We spotted a worker in a nearby corner and started approaching him, but when he saw us he started singing and dancing in a strange way. We both felt he may be a bit out of his mind, so we applauded his performance, hoping it would please him.

He stopped, and said, "Did you really like it, or are you making fun of me?"

We assured him we were sincere and asked him where the exit was. It took a while to convince him, but once he was, he pointed in the direction of the exit. Although we couldn't see an exit, we started walking the way he pointed. We soon spotted several other men coming in our direction. They didn't look very friendly, so David decided to separate from me in case they ganged up on us. That way one of us could go for help if the other one got trapped.

They kept coming only toward me, so his plan was working. However, I had to find a way out of the incipient danger.

'Look important,' I said to myself, 'and tell them you want to see the manager.'

Now I have never been a magician, but somehow I outfitted myself with a suit and tie, plus a hat and expensive overcoat. By golly, my plan worked and they pointed me toward the manager's office, which was near the entrance. Once I saw it, I bypassed the manager and immediately left the building.

'Hooray,' I thought, 'I'm free. But where the hell am I now?'

David had exited my dream, and was nowhere in sight. I soon found myself in a shallow, narrow canyon with several other people. They were crowding behind me so all I could do was go forward. Unfortunately, the canyon grew narrower and narrower, and I got that old feeling of claustrophobia. I picked up a trumpet, which conveniently was nearby, and started tooting it. People behind me were annoyed, and started retreating. I kept tooting until they went back to the canyon's entrance.

Once again, I was free, but now I was sitting at my computer. Its hard drive had gotten overcrowded, so I was using the clean-up program; or should I say clean-out program because it gets rid of all unnecessary stuff? When Elizabeth saw what I was doing, she told me to come to our big walk-in closet and see the clean-out job she had done. Sure enough, she had gotten rid of about half of her clothes and her 60% of the space was now un-crowded and less than 50%. When we looked at my 40% of the space, it was completely empty. She said I had gone too far and was displeased. I pleaded "not guilty" since I hadn't done the job myself. The person, or evil spirit, that did it was very thorough, since not only were all my clothes missing, but also the clothes rods and shelves. All we could see was a bare wall! We never solved the puzzle, because I woke up and marveled at these fascinating dreams. I repeated them to myself several times so I could remember when I finally got up. Immediately after breakfast, I sat at my "cleaned-out" computer and typed the story as shown above.

Analysis: David and I have never rented a cottage together so its origin is a mystery. Disney's movie, "Fantasia", did show a sea creature with limbs crawling out of the water and onto dry land, which my memory could have stored and released in a different form for my dream. The fast rising tide could have been triggered by the recent news about the Indonesia Tsunami, but mine was very gentle and had no crashing waves and no loss of life. Was that caused by my optimistic nature or in sympathy to the victims of the Tsunami?

The empty warehouse scenario may have been triggered by a movie I saw years ago, in which evil men used a warehouse, which was empty when the good guys came. I have run into "nutty" singers and dancers before, and usually treat them with respect, or walk away. I have frequently asked for the manager whenever I am displeased with the service, but never to get myself out of trouble.

While I have been in narrow canyons and gullies, I don't recall having feelings of claustrophobia there. In caves and other tight spots, yes, but not when I can see the sky overhead.

The clean-out part is easily explained, not only because of the computer, but because we have actually done some cleaning out and have recently talked about doing it again once we find some spare time and energy.

A psychiatrist could probably make a good analysis of this series of dreams, but I am still awed by what the sub-conscious mind can produce. I recently heard on TV that science is still baffled as to how the human memory works. Brain functions they understand pretty well, but memory is still a big puzzle.

DELAYED VENGEANCE (9/8/06)

Preamble: When big Jim Cochran appeared in my dream, I knew he was going to be mean and physically abuse me, as he had done so many times when I was in my pre- and early teens. Perhaps the worst abuse happened when we were at the same summer camp for boys. Along with the other kids, I was swimming in the camp's pond, having a good time until big Jim snuck up on me. He grabbed me with his powerful arms, and said, "It's time for your ducking, so don't even try to resist."

I reluctantly obeyed, and he shoved me completely under the water and held me until I started struggling to come up. He let me come up, but just as I was gasping desperately for air, he shoved me under again and I damn near drowned. Fortunately, he let me come up sooner than before, and when I surfaced I was really gasping, coughing up water, and in a terrible state of mind. Sadist that he was, he roared with laughter, thinking it funny to see a kid half his size in agony. Incidentally, he became a dentist when he grew up, so he had a legitimate outlet for his sadism.

As I grew older and stronger, he continued the abuse; but one day after he was doing it again, I slipped loose, grabbed a long pole, which we had been using for vaulting, and started pounding him with it. He ran away screaming, and from then on he was cautious about abusing me, but still did so when he could catch me. Eventually, I grew so big and strong that he let me alone, but I swore to myself that if he ever harmed me again, I would fight him to the finish.

Now to the dream: Big Jim was young again, and so was I, and that's why I was fearful of him. Just as he started to grab me, I beat him to the draw, grabbed his nose and pinched it sharply. He yelled in pain and struggled loose, so I grabbed his ear and pinched it, using my fingernails to make it more painful. Again he yelled, struggled loose, and stepped back a foot or so. I knew he was preparing to attack me with his massive weight and frame, so as he came toward me I lifted my right knee and kicked him where it hurts most for a male.

He grabbed his groin, bent over in pain, and started moaning. It may have been a mean streak in me, but I kicked his rear so hard that he fell to the ground in even more pain.

It took over 70 years to repay him for his earlier abuses, but delayed vengeance, even in a dream, is better than no vengeance. I know that the Good Book says, "Vengeance is mine, saith the Lord", but since this was only a dream I don't think I violated the scripture. Why? Because I again quote St Augustine, who said, "I thank you Lord that you don't hold me responsible for what I do in my dreams."

LEVITATION (12/3/06)

I was standing on a steep hill looking at a beautiful scene. Below me were fertile farm fields with bumper crops about ready for harvesting. Beyond the fields was a gorgeous lake, with sparkling blue waters glistening in the late afternoon sun. Beyond the lake were mountains, beyond mountains, beyond mountains. The first mountains seemed to be about 3 or 4 thousand feet high and are covered with trees. The second group was very rugged, about 8 to 10 thousand feet high, and some had snowy peaks. The final group was between 20 and 24 thousand-feet high, were extremely rugged and completely covered with snow.

As I stood there, I marveled at the wonders of nature and the productivity of mankind. The farm fields would supply bountiful and healthy food; the lake plenty of fresh, tasty water; and the mountains something for the human spirit to contemplate, and be thankful for-- the majestic symbols of the Creator's power and goodness.

I don't know how long I stood there in awe of the scene, but once the sun started setting it grew more amazing. The brilliant and varied hues of the setting sun changed everything I had been admiring-- and for the better. It was as if nature had changed from her working clothes to her finest social-event garb. I knew it wouldn't last, and I desperately wanted to keep it from disappearing from sight. Knowing it was a dream, I unleashed one of my dreamland powers-- I levitated myself up about 600 feet into the air and saw an even more spectacular scene, which I gloried in for several minutes.

A gentle breeze slowly drifted me over the lake, and as I glanced down I saw a frightening sight. It was a shapely young woman in a bathing suit, about to be swallowed up by the waves from the lake. She was supine in the water, and I could see that it covered her head for an extended period, until the wave subsided. I wanted to descend and help her, but some how I was unable to de-levitate. Yes, I was stuck at the 600 feet elevation, and powerless to help.

Then a strange, but amazing thing, happened. She started breathing while submerged under the water, and I knew that she would not drown. In fact, it seemed to be part of her plan, because she seemed to be enjoying it immensely. I was so relieved that I stopped admiring the gorgeous sunset scene and WOKE UP!

Analysis: I have seen some spectacular scenes during my lifetime, and some gorgeous sunsets, especially while in the mountains. I have even climbed higher up a hill, or in a building to extend my sunset viewing time, so levitating while dreaming to do so is no surprise. Here's what surprised me: the young woman who seemed destined to drown; my inability to help; and her saving herself. I have seen people close to drowning, but I don't know why I was unable to descend and help her. Perhaps former visions of myself standing on a cliff prevailed, because even though I sometime wanted to jump, common sense told me "no!" As to her breathing while submerged, my best explanation is that I have breathed while underwater in a few other dreams. If I can do it, who am I to say she can't do likewise, especially in my own dream!

A SEXUAL ENCOUNTER (2/27/07)

I was walking along a lovely beach, enjoying the sound of waves crashing on the sandy shore, watching the slowly setting sun, and breathing in the cool ocean breeze.

After walking a while and enjoying nature's splendor, I spotted an empty bench. I decided to rest a bit, and continue enjoying the view. After a few minutes, a middle-aged woman that I knew approached the bench and said, "Hi, Macon. May I join you? I've walked several miles now and I'm real tired."

"Of course," I replied. "There's plenty of room, so sit down and have a good rest. Isn't the sunset gorgeous? It will soon be over, so we may as well enjoy it fully now."

"Yes it is, but I'm so tired that I need to rest. Would you mind if I stretch out and lie down?"

" Please do", I replied. Do you have enough room?"

"Yes, if you don't mind me putting my feet on your lap."

I nodded OK, and she put both of them on my legs. Although I said nothing, I wished she had put her head on my lap, but she was already stretched out, sighing with contentment, and seemed about ready to go to sleep. She wiggled around to get more comfortable, and her feet ended up on my crotch. I could see her bare legs way up high, and the sight and the motion of her feet sent blood to you know where. I was powerless to stop it, and felt a bit embarrassed.

She sensed it too, but didn't remove her feet. In fact, she wiggled them mischievously to see if she could make my erection even bigger, which she did. She then said, "Let me sleep until it gets dark, and then we can make love. How does that sound to you?"

I said nothing, but I did send a yes signal by moving my erection several times. She smiled and laughed softly. Encouraged, I started caressing her legs, and when she didn't complain I went all the way up. I used the back of my hand to stimulate her clitoris, and my finger to try and find her "G spot." But she was too tired to respond properly. I decided to let her get more rest, and then see if she was ready for action. It was now completely dark, my dream faded away, and we never made love.

Analysis: At 87, and with almost 62 years of a happy marriage, I was a bit surprised by this dream. The fact that I didn't go all the way may be because of my loyalty to my dear wife. I was even more surprised by the woman in my dream, because she was not a tempting, sexy, beauty. She was a nice looking and pleasant woman that I have known, but I don't remember ever feeling any lust for her, as I sometimes still do for a few outstanding beauties. I suppose some of my youthful, horny memory cells came into play, and perhaps my analytic brain picked a pleasant but somewhat plain middle-aged woman because of my age. What young, sexy, beauty would want an old geezer like me?

THE GOLF FAIRWAY (3/1/07)

I was on a par five fairway with five other men, and it was still a long way to the green. We all made good, long, second shots, and could see that our balls went to the same fairway area, but at least 50 yards from the green. As we all ambled to or balls, we were completely surprised at how close together they were. In fact, they were almost touching each other, and it seemed a miracle that six balls, hit from between 160 and 200 yards away, and from different places, could end up that way. As we examined them more closely, we began to understand their miraculous nature. Here is what they looked like:

```
        O
     OO O
        O
        O
```

Analysis: Six men on a fairway is unusual, but unusual things happen during dreams. Could golf balls hit from far away end up almost touching each other in the real world? Well, I have actually seen two balls end up almost touching under those circumstances, so it is possible that six could do so, although it is highly improbable. The fact that they formed a "Cross" and I am a strong Christian made it seem very possible for a dream, and perhaps there was even a divine message there, such as "Keep your faith, old guy, your days on earth are almost over!" Suggestions as to what other message was there will be appreciated.

A LOST LOVE (3/3/07)

Preamble: During my bachelorhood, I dated many different girls. All of them were attractive, most still stay in my memory, and a few surface occasionally in my dreams. However, there were only two that I seriously contemplated marrying. Their names were <u>Lois</u> and <u>Betty</u>. Both were beautiful, talented, and had pleasing personalities. In fact, I proposed to both. Although both seemed fond of me, they turned me down. However, with Betty I didn't take no for an answer, and persevered until she said, "Yes!" In May of this year we will celebrate our 62nd anniversary, so I guess I did a good thing. No, make that a magnificent thing.

Now Lois has entered my dreams more than any other girl except my wife, so now that I know how to use the Internet, I decided about a week ago to see what had happened to her. I knew early on that she had married, been widowed once, and then remarried, but lost track of her for decades. She had been a concert harpist, so I found something about her career. Unfortunately, my search showed that she had died in 1992, at about age 72. I was saddened, but didn't feel a personal loss since so many years had flown by since I even saw her.

My mind then went into the "What if " mode, and I wondered how I would have handled her death if she had been my wife. Perhaps I would have died first, because I had a few close calls, and Betty was very helpful in keeping me alive. Would I have re-married at 72? (Lois and I were about the same age) Or would the life-style she would have had with me have kept her healthier and still alive? And what sort of life would I have had being married to a concert harpist? I know that "what if's" are futile, but they invade your mind anyway.

Now let's get to the dream: Lois and I were at some sort of outdoor event, and we kept changing our places to get closer to the action. We were together again, and enjoying each other's company. She seemed to be even happier to be with me than I was with her, because sometimes I went searching and left her behind. In fact, when the event was over she was no-where in sight. My dream then changed, and I was in a beautiful religious building. The floor was marble, and the halls and rooms were large and sumptuous.

I was looking for Lois, since I thought she had been a member. I stopped in several offices to inquire, but no one knew about her. Finally, I asked a man how to get to the sanctuary, and after following his directions I went outside and saw it nearby. But before I could enter it I spotted a small lake, which attracted my attention. In fact, it drew me to itself strongly, and some how I knew that the lake contained Lois's casket. Yes, she and others in that congregation had been buried UNDER WATER!

Analysis: It's not surprising that I would dream of Lois again, especially after I had searched the Internet and found what I did. What is surprising is that I would treat her so casually while we were at the outdoor event. That was very unlike my basic nature or habits. Searching for her at a church is not surprising. Both she and Betty were Presbyterians, and as a Methodist, I joined Betty's denomination once we were married. Burial underwater was a big surprise, and a bit frightening, because I have nearly drowned in real life, and found it very scary. Once I woke up and thought about it, it seemed like a good idea, provided the casket is completely sealed and the corpse doesn't contaminate the water. After all being under ground seems worse, because it is harder to escape from than underwater. (In case you are buried alive, or your soul needs to be rescued.) So maybe this dream ended with a good idea.

COUNTRY CLUB: (3/17/07)

Preamble: During my middle years, my wife and I belong to a prominent country club in Huntington. NY. It was one of those clubs that you had to be sponsored to join, and even then your sponsors had to have a cocktail party at the clubhouse. Purpose: So the Membership Committee could meet you personally and see if you were the sort of couple they wanted to have. We passed the test and became tennis members, since neither of us is good at golf, and being a golf member had much higher annual dues. Tennis was our favorite sport, so we were contented members for many years, resigning only when we moved to NH. Most of those years were full of fun and pleasure, and we made some good new friends there. Unfortunately, there were a few unpleasant incidents, and they may have triggered this dream:

I was having soft drinks with three men friends after a close tennis match. We were sitting on a patio, but it was not one that I ever saw at my former club. Beyond the patio was a parking lot, and a small hedge separated the lot and the patio. However there was a fairly large opening in the hedge that was the beginning of a large path that ended at the patio. We had barely started sipping our drinks, when a gray-haired old man driving a small sports car, with the top down, drove down the path and was headed for the patio.

Two of our friends had their backs to the path and the oncoming car, so I yelled, "Watch out--a car is coming toward you!"

They turned their heads, and scrambled out of the way--and just in time. The little car went onto the patio, smashed their chairs and knocked down the table, then turned and drove back the path to the parking lot, where the old man parked it. I was very disturbed at his dangerous actions, and ran to the parking lot to accost him, almost yelling, "Why did you do that?" Don't you realize that you could have killed several people with your careless driving?

He looked very calm, but a bit surprised, saying, "What are you talking about? All I've done is park my car."

"You just drove down that path," I said, as I pointed, "and drove onto the patio while my friends and I were having a drink. Come and see for yourself. Your tire tracks and some knocked down furniture are still there."

He still pretended to be completely aware of any wrong doings, and told me to stop pestering him. About that time, several of his friends arrived and wanted to know what the ruckus was about. When I explained it to them, they immediately defended the old man, and refused to even go and inspect the evidence, saying, "It's probably something you planted so you could harass our friend. Do you know who he is? He's one of the founders of this club. How long have you been a member?"

"About ten years," I replied, and I would appreciate it if you at least examined the evidence and talk with my friends."

"What friends?" one of them said.

I turned to point to my friends and ask them to join me, but all but one had left. When I motioned him to join me, he shrugged his shoulders and walked away. Apparently, he knew the old man and his friends, realized their power in the club, and decided not to jeopardize his membership.

The old man said, "If you want to stay a member of this club, I suggest you do what your friends did."

"No thanks," I replied. "If I have to kowtow to people like you, I will gladly give up my membership, and I'm sure my <u>wife</u> will agree with me. But I give you this warning: You may have won the battle today, but you have started a war with me whose outcome is uncertain! The dream ended there, even though I didn't wake up at that time.

Analysis: This is a difficult one to analyze, because I never had any such encounter at the club, not even one close to it. Oh, I was sometimes a bit upset at what I thought was discrimination by some members, but after all, it was a private club-- and member selection and controlling behavior is one of the privileges of privacy, even if it is a bit distasteful. Perhaps some other, real-life, unpleasant events emerged from my memory and used the country club as a new background. Dreams can do such things with great ease!

IMPRESSIVE DRIVE: (3/22/07)

In Huntington, N.Y., where my <u>wife</u> and I lived and raised our kids, there's a two-lane road called "Bay Road." It is in an upscale suburban neighborhood, and is a pleasant road, but never so pleasant as during this dream. I was riding in a car driven by a college classmate, <u>Herb Posten</u>, who I haven't seen for over ten years.

We were headed away from the bay end of the road, and suddenly there were millions of blossoms in the trees that lined both sides of the road. They were not only large blossoms, but were a deep pink in color, almost red. Furthermore, they were so plentiful that they made the tree branches droop down so they were about 4 or 5 feet off the ground. My first impulse was that Herb's car would run into them, knock off the blossoms and scratch his car. Somehow, Herb sensed something different, because he actually sped up a bit. To my amazement and pleasure, the upward pressure of the car's motion lifted the branches quickly into the air and we passed without damaging anything-- branches, blossoms or car.

It was a beautiful sight, and it seemed that the branches and blossoms were actually greeting us as we passed. I got the feeling that they were enjoying the event as much as we were, which is saying a lot.

This dream was in full color, and the drive was much longer than a usual trip along Bay Drive. Both Herb and I commented on the unusual motion of the branches and the gorgeous colors of the blossoms. I was sorry when the dream was over, but it was nice to see my friend Herb again under such pleasant circumstances. Actually, I have lost contact with Herb and don't know whether he is still alive. A recent telephone call from me found that his old number was no longer in use, and there was no new number given.

If he __has__ passed on, this was a very beautiful and heart-warming reunion between the hereafter and the here now!

A STRANGE PLAY   (4/5/07)

I had a bit part in a large play. I knew it was a large play because the stage was huge, and the set had several scenes at the same time. I knew I had a bit part because I was laying in a cot along with some other bit part cast members. As the play progressed, I was supposed to be feigning sleep, (which was easy to do since I was really asleep). However, when one of the actors asked a question, I immediately blurted out the answer in a loud voice. Someone walked over and told me to keep my trap shut, as I was not part of the dialogue. The message got through, and I didn't utter a word until I had to do so later.

As the play went on and on, I found that I had to go to the bathroom. I motioned to one of the silent cast members, and whispered my need, adding, "Where IS the bathroom." The member helped me slowly slip out of my cot so that it wasn't too noticeable to the audience, and then took me behind the set and pointed to a door, telling me to bear right until I found it. This I did, even though it was much more complicated than I had been told. Finally, I found it and walked over to the toilet to relieve my self. As I started urinating in the bowl, it became very small in size, so I had to direct my stream carefully. Much to my surprise, the yellow liquid came back, splashing strongly into my face. I was so disgusted with this turn of events that I mumbled a few swear words and then woke up.

Analysis: I have had more than bit parts in several plays, so the play part is easy to explain. Laying on a cot in a play is not as easy, but having to go to the bathroom, and actually going, is very easy. In fact, it is a frequent occurrence, and is caused by the mind trying to keep you asleep longer by creating artificial relief. Usually, I encounter problems during these occasions, such as: finding a suitable bowl; dripping on the floor; having too many people present; or having an endless stream of urine. When such problems arise, I suspect part of the mind is saying to the other part, "You can fool me part of the time, but not all of the time; I'm going to put some problems in this dream so this old guy can wake up before he messes-up the bed."

OUTDOORS AND COMPLETELY NUDE: (4/5/07)

After I woke up in the above dream, I lay awake about an hour. Once I fell back asleep, I found myself walking along a lonesome road at night. Surprisingly, I didn't have any clothes on, not even shoes and socks. It was never clear why I was that way, and I suspected that I was either being punished for a bad deed, or being initiated into some secret society.

Regardless of the reason, I was very uneasy, and started looking for a remedy. After all, if I met people, would they be tolerant of my condition? And even if they were tolerant, I was still concerned that the cold night air would soon freeze me badly, maybe to death. My main concern was to find some warm clothes, or at least some shelter where I could curl up in a ball and stay alive until dawn.

As I started walking toward some woods, a group of people started walking my way. My first reaction was to put my hands in front of my private parts. That caused a few giggles from the women in the group. The men were more understanding, and one of them led me to a house, where he draped a small cloak over my upper torso, promising to find more for the rest of it. (But he never did.)

The cloak helped with the cold, but it didn't quite cover my lower part sufficiently. When I approached more people, I would bend forward to cover my private parts, but once I had passed them I found them laughing, because my rear end was now exposed. I solved this problem quickly by lowering my cloak to the rear once they had passed me. Unfortunately, it didn't work when the crowd grew larger, so I was eager to get some pants. I'm not sure I ever did get any, since I woke up again

Analysis: Most humans have experienced times when they were ether nude or partly nude, and embarrassed by the occasion. Therefore, I suppose I was responding normally. I wonder if members of nudist colonies have solved the nude-embarrassment problem? Also, are there any animals that try to cover up their private parts, and, if not, where did humans get their embarrassed feeling? (Any enlightenment on this subject would be appreciated.)

MY YELLOW CONVERTIBLE: (4/5/ 07)

I had parked my antique Plymouth Barracuda convertible at the end of a long row when I entered an important meeting. I'm not sure what the meeting was about, because I kept changing my seat before it started. My first seat was a very good one. Not only was it in the front row, but also it was one of the three most comfortable ones. I left it to talk with some friends, but when I returned a woman and two small kids were occupying all three of the comfortable ones, and others had now filled up the front row.

Naturally, I started looking for other seats in the auditorium, but most of the good ones were taken. I fond a couple of seats, but they were so uncomfortable I started searching again. Even when I spotted a promising new prospect, someone beat me to it fairly, or when I got closer I found someone had saved it by putting a coat on it. I felt bad that I hadn't used the same tactic on my first great seat. After wandering around looking for a seat, I finally gave up and left before the meeting started.

When I returned to the parking lot and spotted my old yellow convertible, I noticed that the top was down. I didn't remember leaving it down, but concluded that I must be a bit absent-minded. As I drew closer, I discovered that I had NOT been absent minded, because someone had pulled both doors off and left them near by. Also, the trunk had been opened and was still way up in the air, with all the tools and other stuff from the trunk scattered over the ground.

It was a disgusting sight, and I wondered who could have been so mean-spirited as to do such a dastardly deed. I picked up the doors and put them in the back seat, and was starting to pick up the contents when my bedside alarm radio went off. The pleasant music that followed partly made up for all the frustration the dream had caused, but I still wondered what had triggered so much trouble.

Analysis: It has been about twelve years since I sold my convertible for more than I originally paid for it. (It was 28 years old then) Dreaming about it is not hard to explain, but all the trouble I found is. Maybe I was being punished for some evil thoughts, or even a few evil deeds. Finding a good seat at an important meeting has occurred many times during my long life, but I don't remember ever having this much trouble. More punishment?

AN UNUSUAL DREAM: (4/18/07)

This dream was unusual for three reasons:

1. It occurred during my afternoon nap, and I rarely dream then; if I do, they are too fuzzy to remember.

2. It involved both of my younger brothers; Charles, who has been dead for 21 years, and his twin, Joe, who is still alive. Now Charles and I always got along famously, but Joe became upset with me after I loaned him a sizeable amount of money to save his struggling business. Although I

renewed the loan many times when he couldn't (or wouldn't) pay the interest, he seemed to think the loan should be a gift, or at least interest free. After several years, I finally went to a lawyer and made arrangement for him to pay it back, but not all the accumulated interest. Although I sometimes communicate with him, and he is pleasant and friendly on the rare occasions we meet, he never communicates with me. In fact, he won't even answer letters about family business.

   3. We were discussing personal financial matters.

During the dream Charles was asking about my financial position, showing some concern that it might not be as good as it should be. Now he was the wealthy member of the family, becoming a multi-millionaire because he was smart and entrepreneurial in Texas real estate. In fact, he had gotten me to invest in some of his projects, most of which were much better than my limited excursions in the stock market.

While I didn't reveal my net-worth to him, I did say that it, and my steady income, were good enough to last the rest of my and my <u>wife</u>'s lives, barring unforeseen problems or too much longevity. He seemed a bit dubious, mostly because he had a much higher living standard than I did, and probably didn't understand how I could live so well on so much less than he did. Now Charles wasn't rude, just showing concern for my finances. Even so, his probing was starting to get a bit annoying.

When Joe entered the room, I decided to shift the conversation to him, asking, "Joe, how are you doing financially these days?"

"Oh, I'm doing OK", he replied.

Charles then entered the conversation by probing Joe deeper. Although Joe and Charles were fraternal twins, they never got along too well with each other. Call it rivalry, jealousy, different experiences, or whatever you like, but they just didn't see the world the same way. They were usually polite with each other, but if they weren't careful a big argument could surface quickly.

Sensing that a big argument was about to happen, I woke up, and was glad that I did. However, it was good to be together with my two brothers again, especially Charles after so many years after his tragic death. If I meet both brothers again in a dream, I hope it will involve happier days, when Charles was vibrantly alive, and my good relations with Joe hadn't been changed by the loan I made. (Who ever said, "Never loan money to a family member!" was very wise.)

A SINKING BOAT (5-18-07)

I was in a mid-sized sailboat, about 22 feet long and with very little cabin. It wasn't my boat, so a friend of mine was the skipper. Strangely, the skipper never appeared in the dream and I am not even sure who he was. All I remember is that we were sailing with a following sea with high waves. In fact, they were coming over the stern transom, and starting to flood the boat. It didn't take long for me to imagine that the boat was going to sink once it got too much water, so I yelled, "Head for that dock," which was only a few hundred yards away. The skipper started for the dock, but the waves kept flooding over the transom and into the boat.

As a crewmember, I knew I should do something, so my first impulse was to go forward, hoping that would elevate the transom enough to stop the inflow of water. This I did, but as I moved forward, the water started coming in over the bow and was filling the boat even faster. I visualized it sinking completely, which would have been terrible since the water was still fifty feet deep or more. I needed to do something more drastic to keep it afloat until we reached the dock, or at least shallow water.

My next move was to jump overboard and encourage other people who could swim to do likewise. I knew that I was a good enough swimmer to make it to shore, but it seemed wrong to leave the boat as long as it was still afloat. The boats extra buoyancy created by my departure seemed to help, because the inflow of water almost stopped. I then swam to the stern and pushed up on it to try and raise it even more, but that had very little effect. Two other people then jumped into the water, and the inflow of water stopped completely. The skipper made it to the dock, tied it fast, and we all swam to the boat, climbed aboard and started bailing.

I woke up before we had all he water out, but not before we all knew that we had saved the boat, and possibly some poor swimmers who had stayed aboard, from a terrible fate.

Analysis: I once owned a small sailboat and one afternoon in the summer of '56 or '57, my wife, Betty, and I went for a sail. It was very windy, and Betty was concerned that it was too windy, pointing out that there were no other sailboats out in the strong wind, only a few large powerboats. With typical male bravado, I convinced her that we could handle the wind, and that it would be a very exciting sail. Unfortunately, my skill was not as good as my bravado, and before long a big gust almost tipped us over. I moved the tiller fast enough to save us, but not before lots of water came into the boat. By then, we were in the middle of Huntington Bay, on Long Island's north shore, and about a mile from our mooring.

I decided to lower the sail since the boat was getting to hard to handle. We were both bailing when a large powerboat, spotting our plight, approached us and offered to tow us to shore. It was headed to Lloyd harbor, several miles from our mooring, but a much more protected place. We had friends, George and Jane Toumanoff, who had a water front home in the harbor, so we asked to be dropped off there by the power boat. After we thanked them, we rowed our little sailboat to their beach and went up to their house.

They were very gracious, insisted we have supper with them, following which George and I would sail my boat back to our mooring once the wind died down. This we did, and a very dangerous adventure ended up with a pleasant interlude with our good friends. Eventually, I sold my little boat and Betty and I started sailing with some other friends, <u>Lynn</u> and <u>Jean Radcliffe</u>, in their 38-foot yawl. We had a few close calls with them, but none so dangerous. Or were they?

I have now replaced my dream story with a true one that was even more interesting and dangerous. I suspect that somewhere in my subconscious memory, that exciting, but foolish, true adventure surfaced and I relived it. I was probably in the larger boat because of our sailing adventures with the Radcliffe's. The fact that I was in a strange boat, with an unknown skipper and people, and under different circumstances can only be explained by the minds ability to create new stories from old ones. But that ability of the mind is still a mystery to me.

A SUBMARINE IN TURKEY (6-3-07)

I was a crewmember on a small U. S. Submarine in a river in Turkey. It was a spy expedition, so we were careful not to be seen. We had navigated the river submerged, but now we were in a part of the river that was hidden from the general population. Once we surfaced, several other crewmembers and I went on deck to peek through some openings in the wall, using our binoculars to try and spot some WMD activities that would be dangerous to the U. S. and its allies. Poison gas and nuclear bomb plants were uppermost in our search, but none were evident, so the skipper kept moving slowly forward.

It was then that I realized that the river was getting narrower and narrower, and I was concerned that we would run aground. What an embarrassing position, or dangerous one, that would put us in, so I started growing very worried. I wondered if I should go below and tell the skipper, but felt my low rank would not permit it. Then an even greater worry flashed through my mind. Suppose the skipper saw something that would endanger the submarine, and decided to submerge and go backward until he could turn around and head back to international waters. Would he make sure that the deck crew came below, or would he sacrifice us to save the ship? And if he did leave us on deck, would we drown, or be caught by the Turks? Once again I saved myself by waking up, but it took several minutes to quell the fears this dream engendered!

Analysis: My wife and I have visited Turkey, and were very impressed with all of its ancient treasures. I realize that it wants to be part of NATO, so it is probably more of a friend than a foe. I can't explain why I picked it instead of a more dangerous country, like Iran, but that just proves that dreams can be irrational. I have never been a crewmember on a submarine, but I have been below deck on one, and have seen many movies that let me get a strong glimpse of life aboard these fascinating vessels. All of the movies involved dangerous situations, and the news is full of problems with mid-eastern nations, so perhaps my subconscious mind created its own movie, using a mid-east country that I had actually visited.

A TRIPLE PLOT DREAM. (7/2/07)

This dream started in a large auditorium full of people. I don't know what was going on there, because the program never started. While I was waiting, I glanced around to see what sort of an audience was there, and it seemed to be a typical American one. During my survey, I spotted a very pretty woman several rows behind and to the left of me. At first, she didn't notice me, but when I kept staring, she not only saw me, but after a while she came over and wanted to know why I kept staring at her.

"That's easy to explain," I replied. "You see, I am in my late eighties, I'm a man that appreciates feminine beauty, and you are one of the most beautiful women I have ever seen. Since I am getting near the end of my life, I decided to enjoy your beauty while I still can. Believe me when I say I have no bad intentions; I just want to enjoy the visual feast you supply just by being near by."

Her attitude changed quickly, and my words seemed to make a strong impression on her. She then said, "You are very kind, and I like your explanation. Since I am alone tonight, would you mind if I sit next to you? I think I will enjoy your company, and I suppose the feeling is mutual. Is it?"

"I will be pleased and honored," I responded.

Suddenly, the auditorium disappeared and we were strolling along a crystal-clear stream whose banks were filled with gorgeous flowers and trees. We both admired the scenery, so I said, "It is certainly a beautiful spot, but it can't come close to your divine beauty!" She blushed, and we continued walking and talking.

Before long, we saw a very unusual sight. Two men were walking along the bottom of the stream in perfect contentment. What made it unusual was the fact that they were not wearing breathing apparatus, and stayed below for a longer period than I thought possible. They waved to us, and invited us to join them. She declined, but I decided to give it a try. Once I was submerged, I found that I could breathe underwater. Not by gulping in water, but by sort of letting the water near my nostrils change into hydrogen and oxygen, with the oxygen entering my nose and the hydrogen bubbling up to the surface. Why the water disassociated into its two elements was never explained, it just happened. I enjoyed my underwater adventure for a reasonable time, but I kept wishing that my beautiful companion had come along too; then my mind went blank.

Next, I was skiing down a steep mountain slope. All was going well, and I was exhilarated to be back on such a challenging ski trail. As I looked ahead, the trail stopped, as if we were coming to a cliff, or at least a very steep slope. I was going too fast to stop, so I looked carefully at the ski tracks made by other skiers. Normally, I would have stayed on what looked like the main trail, but I noticed that most tracks had gone to the extreme left. It was a split second decision, but it turned out to be a good one.

Once I got to the end of the visible trail, the new one was so steep that I soared high above the descending ground. I took a quick glance ahead and saw that I would land about 300 feet lower, but on a steep slope, thus cushioning my landing. Furthermore, the trail after the landing was going to be quite navigable. I then glanced at what had looked like the main trail, and it was a disaster waiting to happen.

I would not have landed on a steep slope but I would have landed on level ground, or even steeply rising ground. After the 300-foot drop, I would have been killed or seriously injured. I woke up shortly after I landed, and wondered if there was a message in this dream. Suppose I had a stroke, or even died in my sleep; would anyone have guessed that making the wrong decision in this dangerous dream led to my death? Probably not, but now that I have written down some of my dangerous dreams it might explain things if I should die in my sleep in the future.

Analysis: Staring at a beautiful woman is easy to explain, but the subsequent conversation is not. I was surprised at the nice outcome of our conversation, but disappointed that she didn't join me underwater. It just goes to show that we don't have full control of our dreams. If I had full control of this one, I would have her staying with me much longer, perhaps getting very affectionate….

Breathing underwater probably was triggered by a recent TV program, which showed Dolphins swimming for long periods far below the water's surface, and the obvious breathing of regular fish. I have always marveled at this trick of nature-- we drown if we try to breathe underwater, while fish "drown" if they try to breath our life-giving air.

The skiing part also demonstrates that we face dangerous situations in our dreams, but sometimes we control a catastrophic outcome by means other than waking up. Remember this: everything that happened in this triple plot dream was conjured up by my own sub-conscious mind!

LOST ON A MOUNTAIN (7/7/07)

My wife, Elizabeth, and I were traveling through the White Mountains of NH, and had stopped early at a motel. She decided to spruce up and maybe take a nap before dinner, but I decided to walk around the motel grounds and explore a bit. It wasn't long before I came to a sign that said, "MOUNTAIN TRAIL-- Get trail map at motel."

I figured I wouldn't have time to go far on the trail, so I decided not to walk all the way back to get a map. I had walked about 20 minutes up a fairly steep grade, and was about to turn back when I saw an opening in the trees ahead. I figured it was a lookout point, so I proceeded to it and saw a spectacular view of a beautiful valley and distant mountains. As I stood there in awe, a man on a bicycle rode by saying, "There's an even better view up ahead a few hundred yards!"

Naturally, I went the extra distance to see the view. After I finished ogling, some more bicyclers intrigued me. I went a short distance to another viewpoint, and was amazed at their skill in negotiating sharp turns near a rocky cliff that dropped several hundred feet before it hit sloping ground. Somehow I got a bicycle (remember this is a dream) and decided to try and negotiate the sharp turn. Of course I did it much more carefully, but even so it was quite a thrill. I then rode the bike up higher, passing several other trails on the way.

I left the bike and started walking, figuring it was time to return to the motel. As I started to descend, there were several choices of trails, but I didn't remember which one I had previously taken. Every time I tried one, it quickly became obvious that it was the wrong one, and pretty soon I knew I was hopelessly lost. What was worse, there were no more bicyclers from whom I could ask directions. I decided to go back to the intersection of the various trails and hoped some one would come and get me un-lost. After a fairly long wait, with the sun sinking lower and lower, two hikers came by and I said, "Can you help me? I am new here and forget which trail I came up, and my wife is probably starting to worry about me."

"Where did you start from, one of them said?

"At the motel near the trail," I replied.

"Which motel," the other one said. "Most of the motels here have access to trails, so we need to know your motel's name."

"Gee, I don't remember it," I confessed, "but let me think a minute." Try as I might, I couldn't think of its damn name.

The first one then said, "Well I guess we can't help you. Good luck!" He then started to leave.

The second one said, "Are you willing to take a chance?"

"Yes," I responded.

"Well, I'll show you the trail to the nearest motel, and if it's not yours you can either walk or hitchhike back to your motel. If the road is familiar, you should know which direction to go. If not, go back if you can figure which way that is. Oh, another thought. If it's not your motel, ask the manager the names of nearby motels. It might bring your motel's name back to your memory and you can have your wife come and pick you up."

"Those are good suggestions," I replied. "Thank you very much!"

He then showed me the trail and I walked down it just as a gorgeous sunset took my mind off my troubles, but added to them as the sun kept sinking. I woke up before I got back to the motel, and all was well!

Analysis: Although my wife and I have both driven through many mountains and hiked up quite a few, both the road and mountain of my dream were brand new. Also, I have never seen a bicycle on a mountain trail. Oh, I have seen TV scenes of bikes and mountain trails, but none that rode so near a dangerous cliff, so that also was brand new.

I have never been lost on a trail, mostly because I had trail maps. I have been confused on a number of trails, but either or one of my hiking buddies or I, figured how to find our way with out the anxiety and worry of this dream. Some may say that the dream was a substitute for some other worries I had when I fell asleep, but I don't remember having any, and certainly none of that magnitude. Maybe my mind went back to the distant past and started recalling another big anxiety, and took care of it by creating this fascinating dream. If, so, I am ready for another one as long as it is equally fascinating.

LATE RETIREMENT? (7/21-07)

Although I retired from Grumman Aerospace Corporation in 1977 at age 57, in this dream I was still my current age (87) and still working. The main reason I was still working was my dream concern that I wouldn't have enough money to retire, what with inflation rising so steadily and sometimes sharply. Strangely, my old boss, <u>Senior Vice-president Grant Hedrick</u>, hadn't retired either and was meeting with the managers that reported to him, of which I was one.

As the meeting progressed, Grant expressed concern about the validity of some data he recently received from an outside source. I volunteered to track it down and determine its validity, so Grant handed me the data and told me to start immediately. As I left the meeting, I wondered why I had volunteered so quickly, because I wasn't sure where to look. I didn't want to let Grant down, so I started wandering around to look for clues.

I wandered into a large room with some of the other top officers of the company who were entertaining high-level government officials. Several other managers of my rank in the company had also entered, and none of us were asked to leave. However, one other manager and I were the only ones not dressed in a suit. In fact, we were still wearing just a shirt and tie. This bothered me, but it didn't seem to bother the other manager or the officers, so I started mingling with some of the others.

Later, four of us entered a large, fancy restaurant full of people. We started looking for empty seats. Since it seemed to be a banquet put on by the company, we knew we could sit at any table with empty seats. I had hoped to find four seats so we could be together, but before I found them, my friends had taken other seats and left me alone. This bothered me quite a bit, but I continued searching. The others had already been served and were busy eating. Once I smelled the delicious aroma of the food, I increased my search for an empty seat. However, I started admiring the restaurants décor, its enormous size, and its high ceilings, which rose at least 30 feet in the air. My dream then ended. I didn't wake up immediately, but remembered the above details when I woke up later on. I never completed my errand for Grant, nor was I served any food, but I enjoyed my dream anyway.

Analysis: I retired in 1977 (at age 57) because the company gave early retirees a temporary bonus until Social Security kicked in. My main reason for doing so was my desire to start a business of my own, which I did and ran until 1986. My pension and bonus in 1977 was adequate, but not nearly as good as it would have been if had stayed to age 65 or longer, which some of my friends did. The decision was a tough one, because of my concern about slipping into old age with not enough dough, so I suppose I dreamed I was still working because of those concerns resurfacing.

My small business made enough money to let me add a small amount to my assets, but probably not enough to replace the extra amount I would have made if I had not retired. However, I am happy to report that I managed my limited assets so well, which were increased substantially when we sold our large house, that I have not been pressed for money. In fact, my assets have increased more than I visualized or projected, so my earlier concern was futile.

As to entering the high level meeting, this can be explained by the fact that I was privileged to join a few. One involved the Assistant Secretary of the Navy, a Vice-Admiral, a Rear Admiral and one of our Senior VPs. Another one involved several congressmen and the Lunar Module Program. As to my friends leaving me when they found seats, that has happened in the past, so it must have entered my sub-conscious at the time and resurfaced in this dream. What I can't explain is why I wasn't properly dressed in my dream, or the completely new meeting room, the huge restaurant and the large number of new or unfamiliar faces that my mind created.

THE TOO TALL TOWER: (8/22/07)

I was on the top deck of the latest tall tower, which must have been 5000 feet tall, or perhaps 3000 feet tall and built on a 2000 foot cliff. Anyway, the ground was really far below. I didn't get to enjoy the view and the awesome height very long, because the building started leaning toward my view. Obviously, it was collapsing and taking me and other viewers with it. Someone yelled, "This is like the Tower of Babel; man made it too tall and now the Lord is going to destroy it, and us along with it."

I certainly agreed that it was going to destroy us, but instead of panicking, I yelled, "Let's enjoy the long ride down!" I then leaped away from the falling structure and started descending all alone. I stretched my arms out and flattened my body so I would have the most air resistance. This would not only prolong my pleasure and give me a sense of flying, but delay my incipient death. In fact, I was able to move so far away from the building that I could see a city below. Somehow, I seemed to have a little control over where I was going to crash.

It was then that a glimmer of hope rose in my mind. I started looking for a lake, or other body of water, hoping it would cushion my fall and maybe save my life. Alas, there was no lake in sight. I did spot the blue color of a few swimming pools, but they were too far away and too small to save me. My next thought was to find a grassy hill that sloped about 60 degrees. If I could land near its top, I could do like ski jumpers-- use the slope to cushion my fall and save my life. I even figured that my clothes would protect me from harm to my skin from the steady friction. Unfortunately, there were none in sight.

The ground was getting so close that I could see details, so I knew the end was near. It was then that I spotted a big pile of sand at a concrete plant, so I steered my self toward it. These questions then rose in my mind: Could I move close enough to it? If I hit it near the top, would it cushion my fall enough to save my life? Or was this the end for me?

The first two questions were never answered, but the third one was. You see, I woke up before I hit the ground. And just in time!

Analysis: I have always admired tall buildings, and remember the "Tower of Babel" story from my early Sunday school and church attendance. I realize that the tower was never built, because the Lord confused the language and scattered the people before they could build it. This time, mankind did build it and the results seemed even harsher. The scenes of people jumping from the World trade Center on 9/11 may have triggered my mind to jump away from this "Too Tall Tower", but my decision to enjoy the "ride" was something I had thought of earlier. As to searching for soft spots to land, I suspect that is something anyone would do, once they found they had some control over their landing spot. After all, saving our lives is a basic instinct in humans, and it was probably this instinct that woke me up before I hit the sand pile.

Or maybe it was lack of curiosity and my dislike of getting messy by too much sand!

FLYING (9-3-07)

I had stretched out my arms and slowly risen up in the air. I was moving forward along a busy city street at about ten miles per hour, but I was unable to climb toward the sky because there were too many electrical wires crossing the street and the buildings were too near to get from under the wires. I was very concerned about the traffic, especially large trucks, since they left little room between the wires and me. Trucks were especially dangerous when a number of large trailer ones were in both lanes, leaving me very little room too maneuver.

Somehow, I managed to avoid "foreign entanglements" until I reached open country, at which time I maneuvered out from under the wires and then slowly rose up about two hundred feet and away from the damn wires. I was not only greatly relieved, but a bit proud of my accomplishment.

I was soaring along as happy as a lark, but then a new problem arose. I had entered a canyon whose vertical walls were over 300 feet high and rising. Try as I might, I couldn't rise as rapidly as the canyon walls did, which were now at 700 feet and growing higher. As I looked ahead, I discovered that it was a box canyon and the vertical walls on all three sides were well over 1000 feet high.

What a predicament; If I kept flying, I would crash; if I landed, the terrain was very rough and walking out would be very tough. Worse yet, the breeze that helped sustain my flight was dying down, so that could lead to a crash landing.

I decided the best solution to this vexing problem was to reverse direction and exit the canyon. Somehow, I was able to do so without hitting the nearby walls. After a few tense minutes, I reached level ground, found a steady breeze to help my flight, and started soaring to 1000 feet and higher. I had accomplished my mission, so I woke up. I was pleased that it overcame the worrisome part of my dream.

Analysis: Flying with my arms alone and encountering overhead wires is a common dream for me. However, this was the first one in which I had to dodge trucks and enter into a dangerous canyon. Of course I encounter trucks every time I drive on city streets, and especially when I drive on the freeway. Canyons are harder to explain because it has been many years since I was in one. Many years ago, I was sitting in the co-pilots seat of a small multi-passenger airplane flying from Burbank, CA, to Las Vegas, NV. I still remember climbing slowly to reach the mountain pass ahead of us, with even higher ones on each side. I realized at the time that it was a routine flight for the pilot, but I couldn't help wondering what would happen if one engine failed, and if we could miss the mountains on both sides when we had to turn back.

My background as a private pilot and my Aeronautical Engineering degrees explains the flying knowledge I used to escape the canyon, but I still marvel at how the human mind can piece so many ancient, past events into such an exciting and interesting dream.

BUS TRIP (9/28-07)

I'm in the window seat behind the driver, and all alone. The bus is making good time, and I am reasonably contented to be alone, watching the scenery go by and reminiscing about past events. Suddenly, an attractive young woman from the back of the bus sits in the seat next to me and starts some small talk. I am polite, and a bit flattered because she seems to be interested in me.

After a few minutes, her interest changes from talk to action. She gently puts her hand on my crotch, and starts rubbing my private parts through my pants. I say nothing, but quickly remove her hands. She looks startled at first, and then very offended, mumbling something under her breath as she leaves.

Before long, an even more attractive young woman takes the seat by me, and she does the same routine, and so do I. She seems even more offended, and calls me an "ungrateful bastard" as she leaves.

I am now alone again, and start wondering why they started rubbing my crotch. It is especially puzzling since I am 87 years old, and hardly an eager young buck. Were they lonely widows or divorcees seeking an outlet for their loneliness? Were they prostitutes seeking money from a well-to-do old man? Were they psychologists doing a bit of research on human reaction to unusual behavior?

I then start wondering what made me turn them down so quickly. Was it shock of such action in a public place? Was it loyalty to my dear wife of 62 years? Was it because my sexual urges have slowed down with age? Was it just caution and built-in morality?

I reached no conclusions on both sets of questions during my dream, because the bus slowed down to avoid some big holes in the road ahead. Once it stopped, most of the passengers got out to guide it through the narrow path between the holes. Finally, the driver stops the bus, throws out a rope, and asks us to slowly pull him through the narrow path, since it is too dangerous to use the engine because it moves the bus too fast.

We do as he asked, and about 20 passengers start pulling the bus. I do not see the young women who sat by me, but I do see someone that is surprising. It is the Associate Minister of our church, a woman in her seventies, about 5 feet tall and slender, hardly the type for such strenuous action. Even more surprising, she is not only pulling the rope as vigorously as anyone, but has become the leader and is giving directions. In fact, I was so surprised that I woke up, leaving the bus still stranded among the holes in the road!

Analysis. I think I raised enough questions regarding the conduct of the young women and my reaction, so I will leave it to others to pick one or more of my reasons as the best one(s). As to the holes in the road and pulling the bus by rope, I am at a loss for a good explanation, since I can't remember any situation remotely close to that one. As to the leading role of our associate minister, that is partially explainable because of her leadership qualities, but her strength in pulling the rope is still unexplainable to me. Any ideas?

A SLIPPERY SLOPE (10-11-07)

I'm at an important, daylong meeting at the University of New Hampshire. The morning sessions ends at around 11 a.m., and since lunch starts at 12 noon, several of my friends and I decide to shop in some of the nearby stores. We enter an up- scale men's shop and start looking at some dress pants. Most of them are very colorful, and we see some that are pink, lavender and purple. At first I wonder if we are in the ladies section, but conclude that time has marched on and left me a bit behind as far as men's fashions are concerned.

A rather snooty clerk comes in and asks, "May I help you gentlemen?"

I point to a more conservative pair of pants and say, "How much do these cost?"

"Those are only $200 a pair, since they are a bit out of date. The colorful ones are $300. How many would you like?

I am shocked at the price, but play it cool. "Well, we've got to get back for lunch now; perhaps we will come back later and buy some." My friends nod in agreement, and we leave the snooty clerk, hoping in vain that he will make a big sale later.

We leave the store by a different door than the one we entered, and find ourselves on a side street. Since we have a bit of time left before lunch, we decide to explore it. After about five minutes, it becomes a dead end. We are about to reverse direction, but I spot a main road down a steep hill. The others go back, but I stubbornly decide to go down the hill to the road, hoping to beat them back for lunch.

I carefully start going down the hill, but suddenly the terrain changes. The road has disappeared, and I am on a steep mountain slope, with a steep cliff on the left and a narrow, icy path leading down on the right. I figure it will eventually lead to the road, so I take it. It is so slippery that I start skiing down it, using my shoes as skis. It is sort of fun, so before long I am enjoying the ride, but wondering where it will end. As the icy path gets steeper I decide to sit down and slide, using my pants as protection. I am able to negotiate twists and turns easily, and again I start enjoying the exciting ride, which gets faster and faster.

I look ahead and see that the trail leads to a cavern or tunnel. I decide it is too dangerous, even for a fool like me, and find a branch of the trail that avoids the tunnel/cavern. I continue sliding down the new trail, and run into water entering the trail and flowing rapidly down it. I have no choice but to continue, and it works out OK. The water doesn't seem to wet or chill me, and occasionally I even spot a main road. I figure that if can just get to it I will be able get back to my friends, even if I have to hitch hike. Alas, I am never able to reach the road, but continue sliding the slippery slope until I finally wake up.

Analysis: I have been to all day meetings at the University of New Hampshire; I have been in expensive men's clothing stores with snooty clerks; I have skied down narrow mountain trails that were a bit icy; I have seen highways that were hard to reach on foot, so all of the above probably crept into my dream because of subconscious memories. But I have never gone down an icy trail sitting down, and certainly not for such a long time. Nor has a trail led to a tunnel or cavern so its appearance in my dream must have been caused by previous concern about their dangers, or claustrophobia, which most humans have in different degrees. What surprises me is that in spite of the unusual circumstances and the incipient dangers, I still enjoyed the dream, and wouldn't mind a re-run.

MEN'S CHORUS: (11-6-07)

I was in a huge auditorium, but it had no stage. I guessed it was about 500 feet long, 300 feet wide, and 80 feet high, so it was one of the largest I have ever been in. There was a large audience, and grouped around the front of the auditorium was a men's chorus. It was an unusual chorus, because of the size of the men. I was a member of the chorus and the smallest of the lot, even though I am 5' 11" tall. The guy next to me was at least 8 feet tall, and he was one of the shortest of the others. As I looked around they seemed to grow taller and taller, reaching 40 feet in height, with bodies in proportion. It wasn't long before I realized it was mostly a bass chorus, with a few baritones like me sprinkled in for good measure. Once I heard the deep voices of the really big men, it dawned on me that bass voices seem to be proportional to size, with basso profundo voices belong to the really big guys. I know there are exceptions to the rule, but it makes sense that the bigger the person, the lower the voice. I felt a bit insignificant being part of these giants, so I exercised a dream prerogative: I levitated myself up to 40 feet high, and believe it or not, my voice went lower, which seemed to be a contradiction.

The first song we sang was "Old Man River", which everyone knows is usually sung by a solo bass voice. But on this occasion, we all sang it. Likewise the other songs, the next of which was "Many Brave Hearts are Asleep in the Deep." Of course we let our basso profundo sing solo once we got to the really deep notes: "So beware, beware, beware!" I have never heard them reach such a low, earthshaking range. It was marvelous, and sent chills up and down my spine.

Our next song was the familiar hymn, "Amazing Grace." It is one we sing as a congregation in my church, so I felt very much at home with it. It was pure pleasure to hear this men's chorus perform it, because both the words and music are so powerful. For this hymn, I sang with gusto and sincerity, and, for the first time, I felt I was almost equal to the really big guys. They seemed to notice, and gave me encouraging nods.

Throughout the concert, I don't recall any applause from the audience. This seems a bit odd in retrospect, but during the dream it seemed perfectly normal. Perhaps they were too overwhelmed by the music to applaud. The concert then ended, at least for me, because I woke up feeling refreshed, revitalized, and eager to get to my computer to record this strange event.

Analysis: I have heard of "Little-man Syndrome", but since I am medium in height, I have seldom experienced the syndrome. Levitating myself may have been a subconscious way to overcome the 40-foot giants of the dream, but I don't know why they were there in the first place. All of the songs are ones I have enjoyed and admired, and although I have never been in a chorus of any kind, I have sung along under my breath with them. When they are singing on the TV or the radio, and I am alone, I join them with gusto. I suppose my deep appreciation of good music explains this dream, but its largess is hard to explain. Maybe I should have used the term "great" instead of "deep" in describing my appreciation of good music. That way, the largess of the dream is more understandable.

AN OLD GIRLFRIEND: (12-22-07)

I was sitting at a large dinner table with other people, when in came an old girl friend from my teens. I will call her <u>Alice W</u>., because she may still be alive. She sat down some distance from me, so I got her attention and motioned for her to come closer. She seemed surprised to see me, and reluctant to move, but I kept insisting. She moved a bit closer, I kept trying to get her nearer, and finally I got her sitting next to me.

She was no longer in her teens, but seemed to be around fifty. She was still reluctant to talk, so I told her that I remembered the sweet kisses we had together in our youth. That seemed to awake some memories in her, so I followed up by taking her into my arms and kissing her passionately. She responded with equal passion. The other people at the table slowly walked away, and since we were alone, I lifted her skirt and started real love-making. She didn't protest, so I kept going. It was pleasant, but we never reached a climax. After a bit more, I woke up.

Analysis: It has been almost 70 years since I dated Alice, and I don't know why she popped into my dreams last night. She was several years younger than I, and just before Christmas in 1938, I decided to stop dating her. I'm sure she was disappointed, and I felt a bit like a heel. Perhaps guilt feelings entered my subconscious, since my dream occurred about the same time of year when I ditched her. Why it waited so long is a mystery.

Although we did a lot of hugging and kissing during our dating years, we never had sexual intercourse. On one occasion, I spread her legs and pressed my body against hers, but I never went further. Perhaps my subconscious recalled that time and decided to relieve the frustration of not completing my conquest when I had a chance.

Although we never dated again, I knew that she started dating other guys. She finally married a local pastor and I suppose had a happy life. Unfortunately, he died early and she became a widow much too soon. I have lost track of her since his death, which was in my old hometown paper.

MUSLIM EXTREMISTS: (12/31/07)

I am standing in some distant desert, when I see about a dozen armed Muslin extremists. They are not labeled as extremists, but something inside tells me that they are, and that I had better avoid them at all costs; but how and where? The desert has a few scraggly palm trees, but they are hardly safe hiding places. As the extremists get closer, I become desperate.

Suddenly I decide that my only salvation is to levitate myself high in the air. Perhaps they won't see me if I get high enough. I slowly rise several hundred feet and I try to put the palm trees between them and me. But I feel that I am still too low to avoid them seeing me, and of course, once they do, they will probably shoot me. It is a tense and worrisome situation, and all I can do is wait for the outcome.

While waiting, I extend my arms and form the silhouette of a cross, hoping that its religious symbol will help. But then I decide that a cross may make the extremists even more vicious, so I retract them. I am temporarily relieved when most of them keep their eyes on the ground. My fear deepens when one looks up and spots me. He talks to another terrorists, pointing to me. Although I can't understand their language, I deduce that the other guy tells the spotter that it must be an illusion, because no man can float in the air like I was.

They pass, and I am saved, but I remain in the air until I wake up, greatly relieved.

Analysis: With all the news about Muslim extremists, it is not surprising that I had a dream involving them and me. It is not even surprising that I levitated to avoid harm, since both levitation, and flying are frequently in my dreams. What is surprising is that I didn't rise higher, and that I escaped harm by an extremist who logically decided that I was an illusion. Come to think of it, that is exactly what I was, because most of the events in dreams are some sort of illusion. Or are they?

RETURN TO NEW HAMPSHIRE (1-25-08)

I have just returned to Dover, NH, a place where my <u>wife</u> and I lived from 1986 to 2001. I am wandering alone in a large mall, looking at shop windows and hoping I will run into some old friends. When I spot an empty meeting room I wander in, and am pleased that it is the place where the Dover Rotary Club meets. As an ex-member, I feel I will surely see many old friends, so I wait patiently for the members to come in, sign up, and pay their meal fee.

As some approach the registration desk I see some familiar faces, but as they came closer they either morph into someone else or I had not seen them correctly. Although I wait until the meeting begins, I see no old friends, so I leave greatly disappointed. I realize that some may have died or moved away since I left, but why weren't there any there that I had known?

I then leave the room and continue my mall window-shopping, but I see no old friends or anything I want to buy. I feel sad, and a bit rejected, then the dream stops and I stay asleep. It was so strange that I recall it the next morning.

Analysis: I went back to Dover and to a Rotary Meeting in 2004, and saw many old friends, both at the meeting and elsewhere. Why I didn't repeat those pleasant meetings in my dream is a mystery. Was I projecting a distant future in which there would be no old friends still alive? (Time flies, and some day we will all be gone) Was I in the wrong mall or meeting room, and if so why did I go to the wrong one? Was I having indigestion or some other physical problem that made me feel lonely and rejected, even though

I was safe in my bed with my wife near me? I don't know the answer, but I sure hope this dream doesn't repeat itself.

A SENSUOUS WOMAN (2-3-08)

I am by myself at some sort of large social event, perhaps a wedding reception. I eat a few goodies, and sip a glass of red wine, then glance around the room. I see no one I recognize, so again I feel lonely. I then spot a woman standing alone in a deserted part of the room, and no one is paying any attention to her. As I look closer, she looks like someone I had once known, but has put on a few extra pounds. She is still attractive, but she is not a beauty, and wasn't one when I knew her in the distant past.

I approach her and she smiles as if she once knew me. As I get closer, she starts moving her hips in a sensuous way, perhaps in time with the music. I then do something that I would never do when awake. I boldly stick my knee in her groin and wait for a reaction. She looks surprised, perhaps annoyed, and I feel I will be reprimanded or worse. Then the sensation of my moving knee turns her surprise into a big smile, and she starts wiggling in obvious pleasure. We continue the erotic movement until she has an orgasm, but no one else notices.

Once she recovers, she suggests we have regular sex so both of us can enjoy its extreme pleasure. I am about to accept her invitation, but realize that we are still in a large room full of people. I suggest we find a more private place, and we start looking for one. Just as we are about to enter a nearby bedroom, my wife says, "It's seven thirty dear. Time to get up for your tennis game!

Analysis: In spite of 62 years of a happy marriage, my subconscious mind has its own desires. I guess Sigmund Freud could explain it better; however, once we are dreaming, our normal inhibitions seem to either fade away or rise to the surface. I'm sure my wife had no knowledge of my naughty dream, but perhaps her feminine instincts told her she should stop me before I fulfilled my subconscious desire!

A POTPOURRI OF DREAMS: 3/12/08

I am walking on a very soft sidewalk, which seems to be made of foam rubber or foam plastic. It has such a good odor that I pick up a stray piece and hold it to my nose. The odor is so delightful that I take a taste, and it is delicious. As I eat the whole piece, I realize that it is unsanitary, because people have walked on it. I wonder how unsanitary it is from just shoes, but decide it is too dangerous to continue. I then pick up a large piece and start washing it with water from a nearby faucet. The large piece is filled with dirt and grime, and I am disgusted, but still intrigued with its taste. Once it is clean, I start eating it again, hoping it is sanitary and that the previous un-cleaned piece I ate will not harm me. As I keep wondering, my dream changes.

I am with my wife <u>Elizabeth</u>, and my daughter <u>Rebecca</u> and husband <u>James</u>. We have finished shopping and have bought more than we can fit into the car. James suggest that he and I fill the car, drive it home, and come back later for our wives and the rest of the stuff. Everyone agrees, so we start off in the car with James driving.

Suddenly, the road gets very rough and steep. James wants to back up quite a distance to get back to the main road, but I persuade him to wait in the car while I explore the road on foot. As I turn around a bend, I see a huge log blocking the road. I wonder if authorities placed it there to warn people, but as I look ahead I see that the road joins the main road in a few hundred feet.

Somehow, I manage to move the log out of the road, even though it would be impossible in real life. I return to James with the good news, and we start up the road again. As we drive around the bend, I no longer see the main road. In fact, the road is steeper and rougher, and James seems disturbed. I am at a loss to explain the change, so I quickly switch to another dream.

The four of us are now at a wine tasting vineyard, and are sampling some very good wine. I notice that the fancier the bottle, the more expensive the wine, so not being a wine connoisseur I look for a simpler bottle. I spot a cheap plastic bottle that is about half full of red wine, and it is delicious. I offer it to the others, and they all agree. When we ask its price, the owner says, "It is the most rare and valuable wine we have, and it would have a very high price, but we give it away."

We are astounded, and several of us ask "Why is it in such a cheap container?"

"Ah," he responds, "Twenty centuries ago a cheap, wooden cross contained something that was more precious than the best wine. Today, over two billion people are followers of the precious person on the cross, so we donate it to our local churches for their communion services. We put it in the cheap container as a reminder of the cheap, cruel cross. Once they taste the wine, they realize that it was the blood that was shed for them that is priceless-- in spite of the cheap container-- the cross! As I let the power of this dream flow through my mind, the scene changes again.

My wife and I are now looking for a nice resort hotel to stay at for a few days. We check several really great looking ones, but they are very expensive and filled with unfriendly people that look down on our common clothes. Further down the road, and away from the business district, is a boarding house that attracts us. Once we enter, the host and guests greet us warmly, the odor from the kitchen is delightful, and the flower garden is gorgeous. The price is reasonable, so we decide to stay.

A picture of <u>Joseph</u> and <u>Mary</u> floats through my head, and I see the simple stable where <u>Jesus</u> was born. I also see the friendly shepherds coming to see them, and the wise men with their precious gifts. It is an ancient example, but it reminds me that wonderful things can happen in common places, and that meek and loving people will inherit the earth!

Shortly after the above potpourri of dreams, I wake up refreshed and delighted that I had so many vivid and interesting dreams in one night.

Analysis: Eating foam rubber or plastic is hard to explain, especially when it has been walked on and is obviously dirty. Perhaps I went back to my boyhood when I would eat most anything and never worry about washing it or getting sick from it. Even so, this is the hardest one of my multiple dreams to explain.

Being with my wife, daughter, and son-in law on a steep, rough road is easy to explain. They live in Topanga Canyon, CA, and the road to their former house was very steep, windy, narrow, and sometimes rough. And too much stuff is also easy to explain because we spend Christmas with them, and the place is overflowing with all sorts of gifts. Somehow, my sub-conscious mind brought the two together and, voila, the dream was formed. The log is a bit harder to explain, but somewhere in my past there must have been a "log jam" even if it was just a mental one.

The wine tasting can be explained by a recent trip the four of us took to about six wineries north of Los Angeles. Yes, there were some good wines, and the fancier the bottles, the more they cost. And my taste for wine is very non-expert, since my daily dinner wine comes from a box, not even a cheap plastic bottle. Why I made the comparison with the cross could be explained by our regular church going and Judean-Christian faith, but why it popped up here is hard to explain.

Although we have stayed at some fancy resorts and met delightful people there, we have also stayed at Boarding houses, especially when we were young. Why I put them in such contrast in this dream may have been caused by my desire to go back to more simple and youthful days. The world is much more complex now, and my 88 years don't make it easy to overcome. The religious thoughts are explained by the previous comments.

AMAZING EVENTS: (4/12/08)

As usual, someone else won big at poker, so having reached our limit early, we guys decided to cook a meal. Our wives were in the city attending a meeting and wouldn't be back until midnight, so we had plenty of time. We decided to create an original gourmet dish that would surprise our wives. One guy said, let's make it completely white, so we started assembling cauliflower, Irish potatoes, white onions, crabmeat, and chicken breasts.

Once it was mixed and cooked, it was off-white so we wondered what to do to make it whiter. One guy said, "Let's spray some Clorox on it, that'll make it real white!

"Are you kidding", I replied. "Do you want to eat it or just look at it? It will taste terrible and could be deadly!"

We decided to leave it off-white, and for some unknown reason we hopped into a car. We drove through several dark tunnels and by a large lake with large waves and swirling sinkholes. We were so frightened that we went to a church. The others sat in the rear seats, but, since I was well known, I was escorted to a front pew. As I walked down the aisle I realized that something was missing—my shoes and pants! I sat for a tantalizing time before I decided to leave and call my <u>wife</u>. The usher took me to an office with a telephone and I made my call.

She wondered why I was in church without her, and when I told her to bring shoes and a pair of pants, her curiosity changed to concern. "What happened? Her voice was demanding.

I don't know," I replied. "They just disappeared as I walked down the aisle."

"A likely story", she huffed.

After I hung up, I went to a window and looked out. Traffic was heavy and parking places scarce, so I foresaw problems and delay. I wondered if I would need to go to the street without shoes and pants.

As I continued my concern, a young woman entered the office. She wore glasses, was very prim and proper, her hair was in a bun, yet she was very pretty. I remembered Dorothy Parker's famous saying, "Men seldom make passes at girls that wear glasses." In spite of the circumstances, I disregarded Dorothy's advice.

Yes, I made a pass, and after a few choice words she responded by letting her hair down, taking off her glasses, and moving close to me. Her lips were warm and soft as they melded with mine, and I knew more intimacy was about to come.

Guilt flashed through my mind. "Making love to a stranger in a church office, and while waiting for your wife? You must be crazy!" But the intense pleasure over came my guilt. So what happened next? All I have to say is this: The human mind is a wonderful organ, since all the above events happened in an incredible short time. R.E.M. sleep is truly amazing!

OPTIMIZING A FORTUNE

If I got a telephone call saying that I had just won a fortune, my first reaction would probably be surprise and incredulity. Flitting through my mind would be, 'Why couldn't this have happened before I reached age 85.' Next would be a wave of happiness, followed by a question: "Will you repeat the amount, please?" When the caller says, "50 MILLION DOLLARS-- TAX FREE", my head would spin. Then I would think, 'Hmm-Once the money is under my control I must do some serious thinking; after all, the annual income at 10% will be 5 million dollars!'

Of course I would share the news with my <u>wife</u>, our <u>children</u> and their

<u>families</u>, and maybe go on a short binge with them to celebrate. I would then prepare a preliminary plan and discuss it with them. Here's what my plan would be:

1. Find a first-rate financial advisor, or use my current one, to protect the fortune and make it grow safely. Included would be the best way to distribute some of its income to charities and our children and grandchildren, but not enough to tempt them to stop working. This would be followed by the best way to leave everything to them after our death, including safeguards against misuse. (Uncontrolled large sums of money can wreck lives)

2. Find a service that would test and analyze our family health, and then set up a long-term program to extend our longevity. This would include a cook and housekeeper, which I am sure my wife wouldn't mind. Maybe we can overcome some of the disadvantages of getting a fortune so late in life.

3. Purchase, or lease, a home in a place that would fit our new life style, but nothing that would destroy our old values. It might have 4 bedrooms, like we once had, but I would add a roomy, well-equipped office, and something for exercise. Maybe even a tennis court or indoor pool.

4. Establish a small, private business, so I could complete some of the projects I have underway, but may never finish successfully because of time, energy, and money. I would hire a small staff of skilled people, many of whom would be young so they could carry on and learn from the work. I would contract additional work as needed. Here are some of the projects I would try to complete:

a. Finish writing, then publish and promote books currently underway, whose working titles are: *Senior Short Stories; Old Granddad's Children's Stories; Looking Back 90 Years; Poems from Life; The Ultimate <u>Pen</u> Pal, (Letters from Death Row); Senior Perspectives; Capsule Comments; Memoirs of a Common Man.* Once the public knew I had won 50 million dollars, I bet they would be best sellers, because being rich and a little famous seems to attract readers like nothing else.

b. Develop and promote some of my many ideas, innovations, and inventions, which I will not describe here for legal reasons.

c. Write scripts for plays and movies for which I have written short scenarios, and promote production of those that look promising.

d. See if some musical expert can capture some of the original tunes that I hum, or that float in my head, and turn them into compositions, or songs.

5. Take time to attend and support the arts and worthwhile causes, and maybe sneak in a few trips to far away places. I might even take up oil painting and sketching, which I did in my younger days.

In short, I would try to optimize the newfound fortune by working on productive projects that would benefit society, stimulate my mind, and fulfill some of my "Impossible Dreams!"

Would I be able to accomplish so many ambitious projects? Perhaps not, but with all the human help that money could provide I sure would like to give it a try. One thing seems certain-- unless I live past 100, or some really wealthy person comes to my aid by reading this article, most of my projects may be LOST FOREVER!

PAINTINGS FAMOUS ARTISTS SHOULD HAVE DONE

(Here is some word play that might amuse you. Hopefully, you will get the connection. If you have trouble with some of them, mispronounce the artist's name, or think more wildly.)

THE GREAT TRAIN WRECK, Toulouse Lautrec
THE WINNING SUV, Van Gogh
DARKNESS RETURNS, Renoir
THE WEALTHY BANKER, Monet

FROM APOLLO TO ZEUS, El Greco
THE STATE THAT INVENTED ALE, Bierstadt
LAS VAGAS LOSER, Pollack
THE BRAND NAME ADS, Rembrandt

WHAT'S IN THE BOTTLE, De Hooch
THE DIRTY PIG STY, Hogarth
STIOCK BROKERS' VILLAGE, Gainsborough
THE UNDONE BRIDE, Turner

AGAINST HORSE STALLS, Constable
A WELCOMED URINAL, Pissarro
COUNTRY BUMKINS, Hicks
THE QUEEN HAS SPOKEN, Cézanne

THE WINNING BOXER, Duchamp
AN UNEATEN ORANGE, Peale
A GORGEOUS GAL, Whistler
A MUSICAL STORING PLACE, Cassatt

BASEBALL'S M.V.P., Homer
TOP NON-COM SOLDIER, Sargent
I'VE BEEN THINKING, Rubens
THE LEAKY BALLOON, Degas

TRY, TRY, AGAIN, Gauguin
BOUNTIFUL ARMENIAN BOSOMS, Titian
WHERE DID ALL THE PEOPLE GO? Church

THE STRAIGHT AND NARROW, Bellini

YOUR HOUSE OR MINE? Picasso
COULD SHE, SHOULD SHE? Wood
THE SLIPPERY RUG, Matisse
CAROL CHANNING PORTRAIT, Dali

THE MURDERED ANGEL, Michelangelo
LET THE LADY GO! Canaletto
THE DISAPPOINTED BRIDE, Van Der Weyden
AHEAD OF TIME DRIVER, Van Orley

THE TRAVELERS, Van der Goers
THE RAVISHED VIRGIN, Peter Brueghel
SEXY DATE, Hans Holbein
DRUNKEN PAINTER'S RESULTS, Stuart

PRESIDENT EISENHOWER'S LIMO, Van Eyck
PHILLIPINE BATTLE, Correggio
SATISIFIED DINER, Manet
THE TV COMEDY STAR, Van Dyck

NEW COPYING MACHINE, Copley
GEORGE WASHINGTON'S CROSSING, Delacroix
THE BRAZEN HUSSY, Bronzino
LAKESIDE RESORT, Inness

© 2009 L Macon Epps (12-11-06)

POEMS THAT LOOK BACK

LIFE

Life is fun and full of joy,
when you're a little girl or boy.
Life is learning from demanding lessons;
use them often—they'll be blessings!

Life's a game and a pleasant sport
when you date and start to court.
Life is great, but has some strife,
when you become 'man and wife'.

Life is dandy and makes you glad
when you become a mom or dad!
Life is work to earn your pay;
do it well — it'll make your day!

Life is saving, but full of spending;
certain bills are never ending!
Life moves on, your kids grow old;
then their kids become 'pure gold'!

Life is joy and lots of fun
when you retire and 'work' is done.
Life is serious and often sad
when loved ones die, or things turn bad.

Life is fleeting and moves too fast;
our time on earth doesn't last.
Life's a gift from heaven above;
let's honor it with boundless love!

MEMORIES

As we grow older and older,
some memories become bolder and bolder.
Others may dim and disappear
as we pass from year to year?

Most of us have youthful yearnings,
so to early days   we keep returning.
Memories can be a vacillating variety,
so this can happen when we search and see:

Some are vivid and vivacious;
others are cute and capricious.
Some let us re-live flirtatious flings,
which brief pleasure benignly brings.

Some are very bleak and blurry;
others move with haste and hurry.
Some make us worry and wonder
why we made that great big blunder.

Some are sad and super sorrowful;
others are wild and wistfully wonderful.
Now I'll reveal my questionable quest:
I hope they'll last-- 'till my final rest!
© 2009 L. Macon Epps

METAPHORS OF LIFE

Pessimists presume: "Life is a vale of tears"
But laughs outnumber tears, smiles outnumber laughs.

Optimists opine: "Life is a bowl of cherries."
But some cherries are tart, and all have troublesome pits.

Pastors preach: Life is a journey whose destination is heaven or hell.
But science says that dust is our destiny and only our seeds live on.

Philosophers postulate: Life's a menu and our choices determine our fate.
But "fate" implies pre-destination, so it's confusing.

Entrepreneurs entreat: Life is an opportunity, grab all you can.
But long hours and greed seldom lead to happiness.

Politicians pontificate: "Life is the next election, think short-term."
But most problems need long term thinking to find real solutions.

Criminals complain: "Life's too tough to obey the law, so let's break it."
But justice frequently prevails, so they end up in jails

Tyrants think: Life is POWER--lie, cheat, steal, kill to get and keep it.
But tyrants are the ones who promote " the vale of tears."

I believe: Life is a divine blend of the above, justifying the metaphor:
"GOD IS A MYSTERY, AND SO ARE GOD'S WAYS!"
©2009 L. Macon Epps All rights reserved (6/18/06)

ODE TO WOMEN

How can I describe the women of the earth?
Every man already know that:
you are our mothers and grandmothers;
our sisters, daughters and friends;
our aunts, nieces and cousins;

our lovers and wives;
our strongest critics!

Every man also knows that:
you're not angels, but without you
the human race would not survive;
life would be: duller; more violent;
less sensitive to other's needs;
short of inspiration;
barely worth living!

So how can I worthily describe women?
Ah, I have it: You are like fruit trees:
you blossom in the spring of life,
and your beauty and fragrance attract many b..'s.
You grow in life's summer
and produce fruit that not only delights,
but sustains the human race.

Life's autumn may find you in decline, but your
accomplishments and inner beauty make you
lovelier than fall foliage! The chill winds of
winter screech: "the end is near— the end is
near!" And as winter turns the earth white, so
does it your glorious hair, leaving a cool beauty
and quiet dignity.

Eventually, the tree falls and crumbles away;
but all is not lost:
The fruit you bore will have blossomed
and produced its own fruit;
loved ones will have fond memories of you;
If you are a writer, artist, inventor... posterity will know you.
Best of all, your Creator will let your soul bloom
in a way that puts earthly blossoms to shame!

OLD AGE?

As a teenager I thought:
'40 is old, 60 is really old.'

At 40, I was sure that
60 was old, 80 ancient.

When I reached 60, I realized
That 80 was old, 100 improbable.

Too quickly, I became 80;
90 seemed probable, 100 possible.

Soon, I will be 90, and my thoughts are:
My body and short-term memory have slowed down;
My mind is still active, even creative;
My long-term memory is amazing;

100 is now my goal, and if I make it, I'll set a new one.
Someone said, "Age is in the mind!"
To which I say, "This poem supports that thought."

OUR LIVES

Our lives are worrisome, worrisome things.
We're faced with thousands of troublesome things;
they cause overload bells to ring, and ring.
Yes, life is a worrisome, troublesome thing.

Our lives start early each glorious day;
we each have a chance to earn our pay.
There are thousands of jobs we can eagerly fill;
they help us pay those troublesome bills.

Our lives have valleys and precipitous hills;
they create big trouble and wonderful thrills.
Too soon they wane and lose their zest;
'tis then we need peace,l comfort and rest.

Our lives are wonderful, wonderful things;
they're full of millions of marvelous zings.
There are thousands of songs we should joyfully sing;
yes, life is a wonderful, marvelous thing!

Author's note: This verse was inspired by Sibelius' incidental music to Shakespeare's, THE TEMPEST, Ariel's fifth song. It may be sung to that tune, or read as is.

TIME: THE ETERNAL RIVER

Every second of our lives, we must face the upcoming future;
hopefully, it is as we planned or foresaw,
but sometimes it brings surprises, both pleasant and harsh.

The present is always with us; it's where we live;
but each second is fleeting, and all too soon fades into
the near past. Eventually, it slithers into the distant past!

Our bodies meet time's demands;
our hearts beat its incessant rhythm and our minds
store its memories of people, places, thoughts and events.

But time takes its toll on all things.
Our bodies are hard pressed to meet its demands
and slow down just when time starts to accelerate.

Our hearts may become arrhythmic;
clogged and diseased;
eventually, they stop completely and we cease to be!

Our memories seem to remain unimpaired the longest,
but even they fade or are hard to recall;
they can give us pleasure-- or pain.

Occasionally, our minds engender worthy ideas,
and we achieve great accomplishments
that become blessings to others.

Time is like an eternal river that has no source and no terminus.
We are like buoys in this river, anchored to a planet called earth;
we bob and weave with the current and rise or fall with flood or drought.

We see its water rushing toward us from the future;
we feel its tingle in the present, and we watch
as it recedes further and further into the past.

No one can deny these truths:
Time surrounds us, but soon leaves us;
it has little regard for our position;

the company we keep; our wealth, or our dwelling place.
Our lives on earth are finite,
but the great river of time flows forever!

These important questions remain:
When time ceases for our mortal being, do we have an immortal one?
Will it rejoin the eternal river and flow gently forever?

TREASURES OF THE MIND

Deep inside my mortal mind there's a hoard of purest gold!
It's unique—one of a kind-- with stories that should be told:

"What sort of stories?" you may ask, to which I quickly will reply:
"Those which gently will unmask worthy thoughts that should not die!"

"Thoughts of people I have met, be they plain or full of fame;
great events I can't forget, or minute ones that have no name."

"Ideas, concepts—things like that-- created by my busy brain;
thoughts on which too long I sat to reap a million dollar gain!"

Thoughts so gentle, pure and kind they'll accomplish the worthy goal,
of fusing my mortal mind with my immortal soul!

So now in my retirement years, I think and write, and write and think;
mining, from past hopes and fears, thoughts I hope to save with ink!

But some problems have arisen—thoughts outpace my typing skills.
Fingers are a kind of prison; energy faces steep, high hills!

Should I use a tape recorder to make my pile grow very high?
Or should I try to get more order in my life before I die?

Should I be much more focused and concentrate on just a few?
Or should I be hocus-pocused by some sort of witches' brew?

Should I simply shrug my shoulders and work at my usual pace?
Or should I conquer all the boulders that writers every day must face?

One thing almost blows my mind: it's the number of my thoughts;
a million of a thousand kind 77 years to me has brought!

When I begin to write them down, fuzzy thoughts grow very clear.
They even seem much more sound, like sweet music to my ear!

But there is ONE writer's problem that on my door doesn't knock.

Though my sight grows somewhat dim, I never have "writer's block"!

And so, dear reader, I must say: "You, too, have a 'hoard of gold."
Don't be a miser, spend today, by writing stories YOU want told!"

PRACTICAL JOKES

To many people, practical jokes are a form of "sick" humor; however, they do tickle the funny bone of countless others. They are "sick" because they always have a "victim", and they are funny because people seem to get a kick when they see the victim fooled and embarrassed. The latter two words have almost universal appeal when the victim is a "wise guy" or "better than thou" person.

During my long lifetime, I have been a victim, an observer, and an instigator. Here are the ones that come to my memory, some of which are over eighty years old, but still effective.

PART I. VICTIM:

A. Peanut Boy.

When I was about eight years old, my father took the family to Carolina beach. Since we lived in western North Carolina, it was around three hundred miles away, a long day's journey in those ancient, pre-depression days. Some vendor had the bright idea of sending me out to sell bags of roasted peanuts to the people on the boardwalk. If memory is correct, the bags cost a nickel and I got a free bag for every ten sold. One day a voice called out, "Peanut boy, come upstairs."

I looked up to the second floor of some of the buildings, but saw no one. I was about to leave, when the voice repeated the same message, promising to buy two bags. I climbed the stairs where the voice seemed to be coming from, but no one was in sight. As I was descending, the voice called out again: "Come back, you didn't go far enough."

Back I went, covering the whole upstairs, saying, "Here are your peanuts, sir." Much to my dismay, the voice was silent, so I went down stairs a second time. When the voice called out again, I ignored it, which, was pretty smart for a kid my age. I often wondered, as I grew older, what sort of person got a kick out of fooling a young kid likes me. I soon discovered that there were plenty of them around. Subconsciously, I learned an important lesson: "Don't respond to a voice until you connect it with a person." Today, I've also learned: "Fool me once, shame on you; fool me twice, shame on me!"

B. Grab a Prize.

When I was around ten years old, I visited my dear <u>Aunt Vera</u> for a week during summer vacation. Usually, I played with a kid next door named "Pee Dee Hinson", but one afternoon my aunt drove me to visit my second cousin, "Merton York Rudisill", who was several years older than I. He already had some of his friends there, and it wasn't long before they decided, unknown to me, that *I* would make a good victim.

The game was "Grab a Prize", and each boy put a prized possession on a large flat stone. The other boys placed knives, leather pouches full of marbles, etc. on the stone, but all I had was a cheap top. Clearly, I had a chance to win a much more valuable prize if I was quick enough.

Cousin Merton York said, "Let's walk around the house while Billy rearranges the prizes and covers them with this big pot."
Once we came back, Billy counted to ten and lifted the pot, while the rest of us were poised to grab the best prize we could.

When the magic moment came, something told me to be careful.
Fortunately, my instincts were correct; instead of prizes, there was a big chunk of fresh manure from a neighboring barn. I think my nose had detected the odor, so I hesitated, much to the disappointment and chagrin of the other lads. They were good sports about their failure, and we played harmless other games the rest of the afternoon. Not only did I keep my hands clean, but I learned another valuable lesson that day-- "Wait before you grab", or, as the sages say, "Look before you leap!"

C. Catching a Snipe:

When I was twelve, I joined the Boy Scouts for fun, knowledge, and adventure. One of my favorite activities was an overnight camp out in some nearby woods. We played games, worked on merit badges, cooked our own meals, and talked half the night.
Along about the third campout, some of the older scouts decided they would "let me come along" while they caught a "snipe". I didn't know what one was, so one of them said something like, "It's a small, night animal that's real good to eat. It's very gentle and won't hurt'cha. We'll share it with ya for breakfast tomorra mornin'."

"How can I help ya?" My response was eager.

"Well, all ya hav'ta do is sit along the trail in the dark'n hold this big tote sack 'til we drive the snipe towards ya. Just sit very still and remain quiet. Close the bag quickly once the snipe is inside and bring it to us. We'11 be a bit behind the snipe!" They then stationed me out of sight and sound of the camp and left, promising the meat would be "real tasty". 'Real adventure at last,' I thought, hoping that the snipe would be as gentle as I had been told and wouldn't bite me. I must have sat there for an hour or two before it dawned on me that there was no such animal as a "snipe".

When I returned to camp, the whole troop laughed and made fun of me. Now I was chagrined, but I took it good-naturedly and settled for bacon and eggs the next morning. Two valuable lessons learned were: "Don't trust the big boys when they seem to be doing you a favor– it might just be a big joke." The second one was: "Smile and enjoy the fun when you're the butt of a joke!"

D. Double Duck.

The year I was slated to go to Boy Scout camp in Tyron, N.C., I came down with a bad case of poison ivy two days before departure. My 'folks wouldn't let me go, and I suspect the troop was just as happy, since it is a contagious affliction. To ease my disappointment, my dad sent me to a Kiwanis camp later on near Lenoir, N.C. It cost the princely sum of three dollars for a whole week, four dollars less than Boy Scout camp. That was a bargain, even in those depression days, and today I realize that the generous men of Kiwanis subsidized it.

There was a small swimming pond at the site, and we kids took advantage of it daily. Among the campers was a big, fat, overgrown kid from my hometown, Newton. His name was Jim Cochran, and he had a mean streak a mile long. He was several years older than I and easily twice my size, or at least my weight.

One day he said, "Epps, I'm gonna duck ya, so don't try to get away."
I was up to my neck at the time and saw no easy way out of the situation, so I said, "All right, go ahead."

He grabbed me and proceeded to hold me under until I started struggling for air, at which time he let me up. But the mean streak and the practical "joke" surfaced.

He immediately shoved me back under while I was gasping for air. I took in a lot of water in places I disliked, and when he let me up again I was coughing and gasping like I might die. He just stood there laughing his head off. How's that for mean?

He did other sadistic things to me in later years, especially when my guard was down and he got close enough to catch me. I soon learned to stay out of his reach, and, since I was a faster runner, that was easy. As I grew older and stronger, I vowed to beat the daylights out of him if he ever laid hands on me again! I'm happy to report that he tried it before I was a match for him, so I picked up a long pole and whacked him hard several times. Figuratively, I made him yell "uncle" and he never bothered me again. When he grew up, he became a dentist. Some say that his sadistic impulses were legalized, but *I* make no such claim.

The lesson? "It's O.K. to use a weapon on big bullies!" Some see a lesson for Jim: "Find a legal use (Dentistry) for your bad instincts!"

E. Un–Welcomed Baptism:
During my early teens I delivered the "Hickory Daily Record" to about twenty customers. It cost fifteen cents a week, of which I got to keep a nickel. Wow! I was making a whole dollar a week, which easily kept me supplied with soft drinks and other goodies cherished by teenagers to this day. My folks insisted that I put a dime in the collection plate at church; so at least once in my life I tithed.

One hot summer day I passed by the Chief of Police's house, and his three sons were lazying around on the front porch. Earl Robinson was a friend, so he invited me to sit and have a glass of ice water. He seemed to be sympathetic to my obvious sweat caused by carrying my newspaper satchel up the hill near his home. I accepted gladly, sat down on the front steps, and started sipping the delicious water and enjoying a brief respite from my duties.

Suddenly, I felt a warm, smelly liquid on top of my head, followed by loud laughter from Earl's little brother, Horace. He was only about five years old, and the little imp had decided to relieve himself on my head. I rinsed my head with the water remaining in my glass, and started scolding Horace. He just giggled even more, realizing that I wouldn't spank him with two older brothers present.

Earl swore he hadn't put Horace up to the trick, but to this day I think his middle brother did. Why? Because he laughed even louder than little Horace, while Earl seemed genuinely embarrassed.

I'm not sure I could have avoided this joke because it was so unexpected, but it made me realize that even the Chief's kids can get into mischief!

F. Hot Numbers.

When I was around sixteen I started dating some of the local southern beauties. They were all "nice" girls, and our evenings together consisted mostly of conversation, occasional dancing and maybe a goodnight kiss or two. One Saturday night I didn't have a date, so I was wandering around the downtown area with my friend, Fred Amos. We were both looking for a bit of excitement, and our hopes soared when my friend Jack Barringer and another boy spotted us and said: "How'd you boys like to meet some good-looking girls tonight? They' re hot numbers and will put out for you!"

"What do you mean by 'put out'?" My curiosity overcame my fear of appearing ignorant.

"I mean they'll let'cha climb inta bed with'em, that's what!"

Being normal, red-blooded youths, we accepted and the older guys drove us to a darkened house in the country. On the way, they said, "You boys are really gonna enjoy this, 'cause it's probably your first time."

We admitted as much, asking, "Are ya sure it's safe, and will the girls' be willin'?"

"Sure it's safe– their mother's visitin' kin folk in Virginia, and their father's in town getting' drunk. He never returns home 'til after midnight, and it' s only nine o'clock now. You'll have plenty of time to have fun!"

"But will they like US?" Fred seemed uncertain.

"Sure they will, " one of them reassured him. "They like to meet new fellows, and both of you are good lookin', so it's a cinch."

I'll admit that we were both eager for this new experience, but the snipe episode rose in my mind. 'Suppose it's another practical joke[1], I thought to myself. 'Better be careful.'

The house had a wrap-around porch and was very run down. The two older boys led the way, saying, "We'll go first and make sure the girls are ready and willing. We'll yell ' come on' when it' s O.K. "

Soon one yelled. "Come on-- everything's fine!"

I let Fred go first and held back a bit. As he approached the rear of the house, an angry male voice from the back yard yelled out, "Get outa here you damned horny bastards, and leave my daughters alone!"

He then fired a shotgun in the air twice. Poor Fred ran like blazes, and the older boys pretended to be surprised and ran a bit themselves. Then a side door opened and several other guys came out of the deserted house with their dates, laughing and giggling because they had frightened poor Fred out of his wits. When they spotted me safe and calm, they wanted to know why I hadn't run, too, so I told them the snipe story. We all had a good laugh and I think I rose a bit in their estimation. I never learned what the guys and gals did in the house while they were waiting for us suckers, but I did learn this lesson: "Use past mistakes to avoid future ones."

G. Yellow Dogs.

When I became a freshman at N.C. State College (now "University"), I joined three bands: the R.O.T.C. Military Marching Band, the Concert Band, and the Red Coat Football Band, (marching and playing at half time, and playing in the stands on the fifty yard line during time outs). My instrument was the baritone horn, but later I switched to a college-owned double barrel euphonium. That's a fancy name for a baritone horn with an extra bell and an extra valve. When the extra valve is depressed, "the music goes round and round", as a popular song of that era said, "and comes out here!" (The small bell). It gives a higher pitch and sounds like a valve trombone, so I played the score of either instrument when the occasion arose.

Toward the end of my junior year, I was inducted into a band club known as the "Yellow Dogs". One of the members said, "The initiation won't hurt ya, but'cha hafta be blindfolded during it."

They took me though some sort of maze with frightening sounds and hot and cold breezes hitting my face. True to their word, no harm befell me. Still blindfolded, they congratulated me on running the maze successfully.

The leader then said, "Now you haft'a take the secret oath of membership."

Someone pulled my pants and underpants down, and the leader proceeded to give me the oath. I was uneasy and felt vulnerable at being exposed. I have forgotten all the words of the oath except the ending ones. They were: "and I promise", repeat, "to never tell the secret", repeat, "of the little dog", repeat, "that pee'd on me!"

Immediately thereafter, a warm liquid was squirted on my exposed flesh. For a brief moment I thought that the promise had come true, but I realized quickly that it was just warm water. When the blindfold was removed, they let me watch the reaction of the next few Boys to enter the oath room. I was pleased when they seemed more nervous and upset than I.

Lesson? "The boys in the band are a fine group." They didn't hurt me and even let me join in the harmless fun. Furthermore, most of our club meetings were followed by classical-record listening sessions at the "Y", accompanied by cigars and light refreshments. I never liked the cigars, but my appreciation of great music took a quantum leap during my college years, and has grown ever deeper with age. Our beloved band director, <u>Christian D. Kutchinski</u>, and the "Yellow Dogs" deserve much of the credit.

H. The Great Train Wreck:

The Southern Railroad came through our campus and we had to cross a bridge or slip over the track almost daily. As a practical joke, some of the students would put grease on the up-hill tracks and watch the engine spin its wheels, listen to the engineer curse, and observe the fireman opening the sand valve to give the train traction. The authorities told us repeatedly at assembly how dangerous it was to cross the tracks when trains were near, and that grease on the tracks could cause a bad accident. Somehow, there always seemed to be a lot of boys who took chances with oncoming trains, some missing them by only a few yards. A few boys couldn't resist the temptation to grease the tracks and defy the authorities.

One night, when, I was studying in my second floor, Wautauga dorm room, the door burst open and in came a close friend and fellow Aero- Engineering classmate-- <u>Dan Belvin</u>.

Dan yelled, "Come on down to the tracks-- there's been a big train wreck! Hurry up and put cha coats on. I'll meet 'cha there!" He then left as quickly as he entered.

My roommate, <u>Roscoe Franck</u>, and I grabbed our overcoats to ward off the cold night air and rushed down the stairs, taking two or three steps with each stride. On the way down it flashed through my mind that boys and grease had been the cause of the wreck. I visualized a fast train ramming into a stalled one, with cars and an engine scattered here and there. It was something I didn't want to miss!

Once outside, we paused to see if we could see signs of the big wreck. Seeing no lights and hearing no commotion, we said to each other, "Do you suppose Dan is kidding us?"

Loud laughter from behind a bush answered the question perfectly. Dan emerged and said, "I sure fooled you two, didn't I?" His smile was as big as a crescent moon, and he chuckled for another minute or so. We agreed that he fooled us, but it didn't mean we didn't scold him for disturbing our study. We went back to our books invigorated by the cool air and fake excitement, but a bit wiser.

I. Courthouse Case.

One hot summer night, when I was with two other young men and three girls, we decided that a big juicy watermelon would assuage our thirst and hunger. First, the guys pooled our meager supply of money and went to a nearby stand and bought one. However, even the girls felt it wasn't enough, so one of them suggested we go to a nearby watermelon patch and swipe one. We all agreed, except I told them that I had been shot at trying to steal a watermelon the previous summer, and that I wouldn't go into the patch. Nobody objected, so off we went.

As we approached the patch, the girls said they couldn't go into it because of their dresses and high heels. The guy driving the car said he had to stay with it so we could make our getaway. This prompted the other guy to protest that it wasn't fair, and that he and I should match coins to see who would go into the patch. I lost, and even though I looked carefully for the farmer, he caught me with his loaded shotgun and made me come to his house to discuss the situation.

He wanted to know the names of the people in the car, threatening to prosecute all of us if I didn't tell him. I told the names of the guys, but refused to tell the girl's names. When he learned who we were, he was surprised, because he knew our parents. I then explained the circumstances and he said he would like a few days to decide whether or not to have us arrested.

When I went back to where the car was supposed to pick me up, it wasn't there. I remembered that Bill, our driver, was low on gas and figured I was doomed to walk the three miles back to town. When I got back to my friends, they were all worried and I told my story, including that he might not prosecute us. We all agreed not to tell anyone about the situation, and the two guys and I worried while we waited for the farmer to make a decision.

My worry turned to near panic when I got a telephone call from one or the girls' mother. She worked at the courthouse, and she said the farmer had just been there and filed a warranty to have me and the other guys arrested for attempted theft. I, of course, told the other guys and gals, and the guys were more panicky than I was, but the girls seemed calm. It was then that one of them confessed that she had told her mother, and her mother was the one who had called me from the courthouse. This was a great practical joke since it was the longest lasting and most worrisome one I ever encountered, so <u>Mrs. Sigmon</u>. you are the champ in my book!

P.S. The farmer decided that if we bought a watermelon from him, he would let us go free. We pooled our money again, and had another watermelon feast with the girls, with lots of laughter and good fun, but sans worries.

J. Navy Lung Test.

When I started my thirty-seven year career with the Grumman Aircraft Engineering Corporation, in Bethpage, N.Y., I was required to spend six months in the shop working on the Navy aircraft for which Grumman became famous. This duty would let me become acquainted with the company's manufacturing tools, equipment and methods, so when I started designing components and assemblies as an engineer, I wouldn't make a fool of myself.

It was a wise move on the part of management and saved me much embarrassment later on. It also got me acquainted with the guys in the shop, and gave me more respect for their role and their skills.

Sometime during my first week, a young man approached me with a clipboard and a strange instrument in his hands.

"Are you Macon Epps?" he inquired.

"Yes", I replied.

"I'm here to give you the Navy Lung test. All new employees are required to take it." He then demonstrated the device by blowing until the fan spun rapidly to prove lungs met Navy requirements.

I thought to myself: 'This should be easy. Not only am I athletic, but playing a baritone horn so many years has given me above average wind power.' I took the instrument in my hands, closed my eyes, and blew real hard. When *I* opened them the fan on the instrument was spinning very fast and I knew I had passed. I was surprised to hear laughter from all the shop guys near me, but when the tester held a mirror to my face I discovered the reason. He had quietly opened a valve that sent black soot all over my lower face and neck!

Once again I was a victim, but this joke was so cleverly done and seemed so official, that I think <u>Einstein</u> himself would have been duped. The only lesson I learned that day was: "Watch for the lung-test guy in the future so I can join in the fun!"

K. Pin the Tail On the Donkey:

During my bachelor years, a girl I was dating, <u>Ann Rozzi</u>, invited me to a party. Since I was new to the group of friends, I was the victim for one of their practical jokes. They were playing the title game, and it was being done in the usual way. But when it came my turn, they made the blindfold extra tight, and suggested that I find the rear end of the donkey first by sticking my index finger out. They guided me to the rear end of the donkey, and, just as I was getting near the tail region, I put my finger in something that was warm and gooey. I immediately withdrew my finger, and wondered what I had stuck it in. Of course you readers know what it was supposed to be, and it was a damn good substitute. Everyone roared with laughter and someone took the blindfold off me. When I saw the warm, gooey stuff was Vaseline, I joined in the laughter!

I was the victim a few more times and the incidents were so memorable that I wrote separate pieces for them that are in this book. One is entitled, "My Friend Jack vs. My Guardian Angel" and the other one "Dracula", which told what befell me when a college classmate discovered I had checked the book out of the library. Any other ones in which I was a victim have now faded from my memory.

PART II OBSERVER

A. Double Sheeting:

When I entered college in 1936, I saw some new practical jokes. We all had two-level bunk beds in the dormitory, and one night some one re-made the lower bunk, taking the top sheet off and bringing the foot part of the bottom sheet so that it looked like the top sheet. The blanket and counterpane were put back as usual, so the bed looked normal.

I was visiting the victim's roommate when it happened, and the victim decided to hit the sack early. When he crawled into bed, his feet hit the folded over bottom sheet, and he said, "What the hell is going on here?" He then hopped out of bed and pulled the covers down and discovered "what was going on." He wanted to know who had done this trick on him, but his roommate and I swore it wasn't either of us, suggesting some one else had enter the room when no one was there to fix the sheets.

The victim accepted our explanation, which was true, and then remade his bed. We heard a few more curses as he pulled the bed apart and carefully put the bottom sheet in its proper place.

B. A Warm Bed:

This joke happened during a trip with the band that played at football games. (I played the baritone horn.) Sometimes we accompanied the team and spent the night in a special group room that had a number of double-deck bunk beds. Naturally, some of the guys went to bed earlier than the rest of us, so when we returned and saw them sleeping peacefully, one of the guys decided to take blankets from adjoining beds and slowly put them on the sleepers. He was clever, and put them on one at a time, waiting a bit so each sleeper would get used to the new blanket. After three or four blankets, the sleepers would wake up, but not at the same time.

Some wondered what had happened to make them sweat so much; others wondered why the blanket had gotten so heavy. One look at all the blankets told each guy what had happened. The reaction of the victims varied: some would get mad and curse, others would laugh and take it good-naturedly. Since there were three or four guys still up, they never knew who had pulled the joke on them, and of course the guilty ones played as innocent as those of us who were innocent.

C. Messy Bunk:

One of the most annoying jokes happened when one of the dorm guys bought a plastic piece that look like a pile of feces. He would slip into the victim's room when he went to the john down the hall, put the plastic piece in the middle of the bed, and then leave the room until he heard the loud yelling from the victim. Guys from adjacent rooms also went into the room to see what caused the yelling, so the victim never knew who was the guilty joker.

When I first saw this joke, the victim was so mad that he kept cursing and vowing to get the S.O.B. who had done it. He also insisted that some one clean the mess off his bunk, but volunteers were rare.

Finally, one guy decided to help because he had figured it was a fake; he then went to the bed, reached down and picked it up. Much to everyone's surprise he handed it to the victim, who then yelled and backed away. When he showed everyone that it was plastic, everyone laughed, and even the victim started feeling less angry. I don't remember what happened to the plastic piece, but I doubt if the joker got it back. If so, there was a wee bit of justice in the outcome.

D. Foot Jokes and Elevated Cannon.

I also learned two jokes involving feet while in college. One was to tie the shoelaces of a guy while he was concentrating on something else. When he got up to walk, the shoelaces made him stumble and say, "What the hell is going on?" The jokesters then had their big laugh. Sometimes the jokester stuck a match in the victim's shoe, and then lit it. Before long the victim felt the heat, stamped his foot and put it out. The reaction was similar.

The cannon one was usually done Halloween night, probably by engineering students because it involved moving a large cannon from its usually place to the roof above the entrance of my dorm. The officials were perturbed, because it took a crane to bring it down, but they admired the talent of the guys that got something so heavy and welded together up on the roof without a crane. I never learned how they did it, but it must have been very clever. I was especially perplexed because I could see the roof from my window.

E. Messy Drawing:

This joke was similar to the messy bunk one, except the plastic piece was made to look like a big spot of black ink. To make it even more realistic, it came with an empty bottle that was on its side and with the top off. This joke happened in the Engineering Department where I worked, and I saw the whole affair from my drafting table. One of the guys, <u>Joe Federowski</u>, had just finished a large drawing using black ink so the blueprints would look good, as was the custom in those days.

He then left his drafting table to do something else, and when he came back he saw the big mess of ink on his drawing. He had taken about a week to do the drawing, so he was enraged when he saw all his careful work go up in smoke, or should I say get drowned in ink. In fact, he was so disgusted that he ripped the drawing in two or three pieces before he realized the ink was fake. Of course, he was sorry that he had lost his temper, but the practical joker was even sorrier for the awful outcome.

I don't remember whether the drawing was put back together with scotch tape, or whether he had to do it again. I do know that the Chief draftsman, <u>Walter Novak</u> was damned annoyed, and told the guys that it should never happen again. I spent 37 years with that company, and it was the only time I ever saw, or even heard of it happening again.

F. The Derby Hat:

One day one of the engineers came to work with a derby hat, which, as was the custom, he placed on a shelf in the cloakroom. Naturally, he got a lot of kidding about his new hat, but he took it good-naturedly. Another engineer then cooked up a very clever scheme. He got some of the other guys to donate money, and then bought two derby hats just like the one the first one. However, the two new hats were a size smaller, and a size larger. He then removed the size labels inside all three hats and enlisted the help of the derby owner's wife so his scheme would work.

Here's what he did: At the end of the day, he would replace the original derby with the smaller one. Then he would get the derby guy's wife to swap the small one for the larger one before he went to work. The victim was puzzled by the mysterious change in his hat, so he discussed it with the guys near him, which included the practical joker.

The conversation went something like this:

Victim: "I don't understand what's happening to my hat. When I go home at night it's too tight, and when I come to work it's too loose. Yet it's the same hat, because I checked the brand name."

Joker: "I think I have an explanation."

Victim: "What is it? It's a mystery to me."

Joker: "Well, you use your brain all day, so that may make your head a bit larger, so the hat becomes tighter Then after a good nights rest, your head probably shrinks a blt, so the hat becomes too loosc."

Victim: "I didn't know the head could change size. It never happened with my other hats."

Joker: "Well, derby hats are different. They don't have nearly as much give as regular hats."

Victim: "I guess you are right, but it sure is a strange thing."

Several weeks later, the joker confessed to his friend, and everyone got a good laugh at this clever joke!

G. Automobile Jokes:

One of our managers bought a new MG, two-seat sport car, and placed it in his usual parking spot. Several of his friends noticed the new car, and made the usual admiring comments, plus a few teasing ones. One of them devised this clever joke: He got some of his shop friends to jack the car up in the rear so the tires just missed the ground. They used axle jacks, so the owner wouldn't notice them.

When he left work for home, he hopped into his new car, started the engine, and put it in reverse. Much to his surprise, the car didn't move, and he heard a strange noise. (The spinning wheels) He wondered if he had bought a "lemon", so he tried to back up several more times before he got out to look at the tires, and even then it took him a bit of time to spot the trouble.

By then, his friends showed up laughing and joking, and the shop guys removed the jacks so the victim could go home. The story went around the Engineering Department, which is how I heard it.

When another top engineer bought a similar car, the jokesters didn't make the wheels spin, they brought it to the third floor and left it there for the victim to figure how to get it down.

Then there was the guy who bought a new car that was advertised as having very good mileage. Naturally, he bragged about it to his neighbor, so the neighbor concocted this joke: About once a week, he would slip into the owner's carport at night and put more gas in the tank. When he checked his mileage, it was even better than before, and he bragged even more to his neighbor. His neighbor went long, by saying, "Well, its now broken in, so the mileage is better."

After a few weeks of slipping extra gas in his tank, he decided to reverse the joke by siphoning gas out of the tank. The owner was puzzled and worried, and told his neighbor the bad news. The neighbor was sympathetic, and acted as perplexed as the victim. Eventually the neighbor quit his joke and the car went back to its original good mileage. I don't know whether he told the owner about his joke, so the poor guy is probably still perplexed.

H. Fake Telephone Calls:

Sometimes when kids got tired of the regular games, someone thought about making funny telephone calls. Some that I remember went like this:

Caller: (to tobacco store) "Do you have Prince Albert* in the can?"
Clerk: "Yes we do. How many cans do you want?"
Caller: "We don't want any cans—we just want you to let him out!"

*Prince Albert was a popular brand name for pipe tobacco in the thirties and forties

Caller: (to a carnival manager) "We would like to speak to Mr. Ferris."
Manager: "I don't know a Mr. Ferris—who is he?"
Caller: "Oh, he's a big wheel at the carnival!"

PART III INSTIGATOR

A. Doorbell Fun:

Someone taught me this joke and I used it on many occasions, especially on Halloween night. I almost always did it with one or more friends, so we could share in the fun. We would select a victim's house, usually someone we thought was crabby and unfriendly, go to his front door and ring the doorbell. Sometimes we would stick a small straight pin near the bell in a manner that kept it ringing steadily.

We would then run and hide in bushes near the side of his house, and wait for him to come to the door. We laughed silently as he looked around to see who was visiting, sometimes calling out "Who's there." After a while he would go back in looking perplexed, because he didn't know it was some kids having fun.

If we had placed the pin correctly, the bell would keep ringing and he would look even more perplexed. Eventually, he would find the pin, and either utter a few curses or laugh at the joke that had been played on him. We never got caught doing this joke, so it became a favorite one.

B. High-Level Calling:

My hometown of Newton, NC, had a six-story hotel. Well, it was really three stories, with a three-story tower. The tower had an open space on top with wooden guardrails all around it. Sometimes a buddy and I would slip into the hotel and go quietly to the tower. It was a good place to discuss current events, plans for our future, and the meaning of life.

It was also a good place to look down at the pedestrians that walked by, and sometimes play a practical joke on ones we knew. We would yell down their name, and say something else to get their attention. Inevitably, they would look all around to see who was calling them, and were baffled when they saw no one calling.

They seldom looked up to the tower, and even if they did, we would hide behind the wooden guardrails. I don't think we ever told anyone what we were doing, so if any of our victims still remember those strange, invisible voices, it is probably still a big mystery.

It was a harmless practical joke, but we had lots of fun seeing their puzzled faces from our lofty perch!

C. Pumpkin Smashing

This was a Halloween joke that, in hindsight, I am ashamed of. Trick or treat had not been started during my early teens, so Halloween was a time for tricks like the doorbell ringing, and this one. Some folks carved funny, or scary faces, on pumpkins; placed a lighted candle in them; and put them on their front porches to enter into the Halloween spirit.

My buddies and I would go up to the porch; take the pumpkin and smash it on the concrete-walk; ring the doorbell; hide in the bushes and then watch the reaction of the homeowner. One night, the owner didn't come out and fuss, or curse, as was the usual reaction. Instead, a pre-teen kid came out, and when he saw his pumpkin smashed to smithereens, he started crying audibly, wondering who would be so mean as to smash a kids pumpkin.

We felt terrible, and that was the last pumpkin I ever smashed!

D. Office Lust:

When I was in my early twenties, I knew some of the pretty girls that worked in the same engineering department. There was an older, married engineer, <u>Grant Hedrick</u>, who later became my boss and a senior vice-president. One day he admired one of the full-breasted girls; "Macon," he said, "you ought to date that girl—she sure has big breasts."

"I'm already dating one of her housemates," I replied. Would you like to meet her?"

"Not now," he said, with an embarrassed look on his face.

I then concocted this practical joke: First, I wrote a note to him that said, "Dear Grant: I thought you'd like to get a closer look of the breasts you admired so much. Macon."

I then went to the girl, whose name was <u>Ann Lilly</u>, and asked if she would deliver my note to Grant, and wait for his reply. She was very obliging and took it straight to him.

When he read the note, his face grew red. When she asked for a reply, he said, "Tell Macon I'll talk to him later."

Once he talked to me, he scolded me for playing the joke on him; but he did admit he enjoyed the close-up look of the pretty girl with the big breasts!

E. Dark Encounter:

The girl in the above story lived with seven other single girls in a triple unit, waterfront apartment building, on an estate called Point Siesta. We bachelors nicknamed it "Passion Point," more in hope than realization.

One weekend, while I was dating my future wife, the lights went out for an extended period. Naturally, the girls brought out their candles, including ones they could carry when they went from room to room. It was then that I had an idea for a scary joke. I went into the hallway and waited for one of the girls to walk toward me. I decided to say nothing, just let her see my shadowy self lurking there. It worked well, because when she spotted me she let out a big scream and damn near dropped her candle. She then ran back to her end of the hall, and I had to apologize for scaring her so much.

Another practical joke that worked very well, but it backfired on my conscience.

F. Nosey Hotel Clerk

When one of the "passion Point" girls named "Jane Tennant" married a bachelor friend named "Paul Anbro", I was engaged to my future wife, "Betty Warren." Their wedding was in Rochester, NY, so we took a train to attend their wedding. WWII was going on, and it just happened that the newly weds spent their wedding night at the same hotel where Betty and I were staying—in separate rooms, of course.

Once I learned they were in the same hotel, I found their room number and placed a call to them around 8 P.M. Jane answered the telephone, so I disguised my voice and said, "This is the front desk; I'm sorry to disturb you, but we don't seem to have your marriage certificate on file. You know we are required by law to have one for young couples, don't you?"

"She sounded very flustered, and said, "We just got married today. Will it be OK if my husband brings our license to the desk?"

I then burst out laughing and said, "That'll be fine, Jane," in my normal voice. She recognized me immediately, scolded me a bit, and then told Paul about the trick I had played on her.

I then said goodnight, because I knew they had more important business to do!

G. Double-Mask Halloween:

When my daughters were young, Betty would outfit them with Halloween costumes, and I would take them around the neighborhood for "Trick or

Treat." I decided to wear <u>two</u> funny-face masks, and the neighbor that gave my daughters their goodies, always said take off that funny mask so I can see your real face. Now the second mask was even sillier than the first one, so when I took the first one off, the neighbors got a big laugh, because my "real face" was funnier than the first mask.

That was a mutually enjoyable practical joke that I used for several years, changing masks to make it fresh and new every year.

H. Bearded Tramp:

In 1993, my son-in-law, <u>James Catterall</u>, got a position on the faculty at the University of Southern Maine. My daughter, <u>Rebecca</u>, flew her <u>two kids</u> there to find a place to live while James completed his work at UCLA. Their SUV was transported to Maine a week later. My wife and I were delighted that they would be only an hour from our home in Dover, NH, instead of a whole continent away in California.

Fate intervened when UCLA made a better offer, and James decided to stay with it. That meant that Rebecca and the kids would have to drive the SUV across the U.S., so I decided to help Rebecca with the long trip and then fly back to NH. Since it would take a week or so, I decided to grow a beard. My grandkids enjoyed seeing it grow fuller and fuller, but when I returned home, <u>Betty</u> was displeased. Now it was an experience I wanted to have, so I convinced Betty to let me keep it for a year or so.

I had many reactions to my beard from NH friends, but decided not to tell my North Carolina relatives. Instead, I would let them see it during my next visit. When I visited my sister, <u>Ruth</u>, and her retired husband, <u>Duncan Hunter</u>, in Brevard, NC, I decided to play a joke on them. It was a rainy day, so I had a hat and raincoat on, so I could further disguise myself. I then parked my car away from their house and left Betty in the car. I then walked to the front door, rang the doorbell, and Duncan soon came to the door. I disguised my voice, and in a low tone said, "Can you help a poor homeless man by giving me some money or some food?"

Duncan was a bit flabbergasted, and before he could collect his wits, Ruth said, from inside the house, "Is that you Macon? Come on in and quit joking around."

Somehow she recognized my disguised voice, partly because she knew that I like to play jokes on them. She got a big laugh when she saw my beard and disheveled hat and coat, and understood why Duncan had been fooled. Both Ruth and Duncan weren't fond of my beard, and neither did my other NC relatives or friends. Betty and both my daughters were pleased when I shaved it off during a visit with Rebecca and James, but there were a few NH friends, who liked my beard, became disappointed.

I. Spilled Whisky.

One day I saw a fake bottle of whiskey made of plastic in a novelty shop. I bought it, and had lots of fun with it when we were serving cocktails to our friends. I would put the bottle on a tray with a few plastic glasses, enter the room and say, "Who would like a shot of this bourbon? I would then pretend to trip, and the bottle and glasses would fall on the floor. Everyone would then gasp, and some would try to get out of the way if it was headed toward them. When I picked it up and showed it was plastic, they either laughed or fussed at me for playing this joke on them. Eventually, everyone had a good laugh and something special to remember.

Now that I've written down the practical jokes that gave me some pleasure, and a bit of sadness, I hope they will bring a few laughs and a few memories to my readers. I also hope some of you will be inspired to write down some of the practical jokes that made your own life more interesting.

SPACE

Of all the things in the universe, space is the most abundant. There is a tremendous amount of it between the planets, stars, nebula, galaxies, and even in globular clusters. Beyond the known universe, space is truly infinite. Even when we enter the sub-microscopic world, there is a lot of space. For example, the simplest element, a hydrogen atom, is composed of a proton and an electron. If we imagine the proton is the size of a basketball and the electron the size of a marble, the electron would be circulating in an orbit several hundred yards from the proton. So even the atom, from which we and all other matter are made, is mostly space!

Now that I have described the big picture—no, it's the amazing picture, I will come back to human terms and describe space as it affects us. Let us start at the beginning of human life. How much space did we need? Hardly any, because the fertilized "egg" in our mother's womb was microscopic, or close to it. Our father's sperm was truly microscopic, since there are about 300 million in each ejaculation.

Yes, the space was so small that it was truly un-noticeable; but in a month or so, it became noticeable to the mother, and in a few more months to family and friends. Not only did we need more space, but we started causing problems for our mother. The big one was when we decide we needed more space, and wanted out of the womb. Labor pains can be a big problem, as most mothers know.

Although we were no longer confined in the limited space of the womb, it was a mixed blessing. We were no longer warm and secure, and on automatic feeding, as we had been for about nine months. On the other hand, we were experiencing some brand new things, such as sight, sound, touch, and feeding by mouth, which pleased our taste buds. We were quick to cry when we needed something, and cooed or smiled when we were satisfied. We were making our first efforts to adjust to the new world we had just entered.

Although we now had much more space, it was limited. Most of the time we were in a small crib, or in our mother's arms. Both were roomier than the womb, but not much more. When our mother showed us off to family and friends, we really expanded our view of the world. There were other creatures out there, and they were all huge compared to us. They made pleasant sounds and touched us in a pleasing way, except for one of the creatures. Yes, it was the doctor, who sometimes did unpleasant things to make sure we were O.K.

Eventually we learned to crawl and walk, which let us use a lot more space. Of course it was limited, because our mom or dad watched us carefully so we didn't encounter trouble, such as steps, electric outlets, breakable objects, etc. Sometimes we were placed in a playpen when left alone, which gave us much more space than a crib. Some of us were even left alone in an outdoor pen, which had a lot more space.

As the years went by, we expanded our space to the neighborhood; our section of town; our school; our town or city; and our state. If we were lucky, we expanded it to other states, other countries, and even other continents. A few humans even expanded it to the moon, and I am pleased that I had an important role in that gigantic effort. Future generations will probably expand their space by visits to other planets in our solar system, and maybe far beyond it. This may happen sooner than we think, if the reports of extra-terrestrial beings are true, as my nephew, Steven Greer, has reported in several documented books and much data.

Now each of not only had access to increasing amounts of space, but had space that sort of belonged to us exclusively. Our mother's womb was certainly our special space for a short period, and so was our crib; our playpen; our bed; and our room. Eventually, we had our own apartment. If we were lucky and productive, we acquired our own house and land, and expanded it as our families grew. For a number of years, my wife and I owned a house with about 4500 square-feet of floor space, and 44,000 square feet of land. Furthermore, it was within walking distance of a beach on Huntington Bay, Long Island, NY.

Eventually, most of us retire, and decide we no longer need all that space. For example, when we bought a condominium in New Hampshire in 1986, our space was reduced to about 2400 square feet, but it was plenty for frequent guests and us. Our yard was also smaller, but the association did all the mowing and raking. It also shoveled our driveway and walks, so we were pleased, because it let us get to local skiing quicker.

As we grow older, most of us need less and less space of our own. When we moved to Leisure Village, Camarillo CA, in 2001, our duplex house had only about 1600 square feet, compared to 2400 in NH, and 4500 on Long Island. Some of our friends have moved to Assisted Care Homes, with less than 1000 square feet of space. Others have gone to nursing homes, with their space limited to a single bedroom, perhaps with a roommate.

Eventually, we will all die, and our space will be limited to a casket that barely has room for our body. Some, including my wife and me, will be cremated, and our remains will be placed in a small urn, probably with less space than our mother's womb. It sounds like a sad situation, doesn't it? But it doesn't bother this old guy, as shown by these verses I wrote in 1993:

Don't embalm me and plant me deep in mother earth;
let fierce flames thwart slow decay and keep me ready for new birth.
Let my vapors and gasses rise up to the playful wind,
and let my ashes be scattered on a mountain trail or river bend.
My spirit, I trust, will return to God, for forgiveness and love,
and I will dwell, forever new, in His glorious realm above!

SUPERLATIVE MOMENTS

If you have lived as long, been as many places, done as many things, and met as many people as I have, you probably have a lot of moments which qualify as superlative ones. Here are some of mine:

The day I was elected captain of my High School football team, which won the Western North Carolina Conference Championship my senior year.

The night I took the Senior Prom Queen to the ball, with a live orchestra playing music of the thirties.

My election as Vice President of my senior class in college, which led to my becoming President a month later when the President had to resign for health reasons.

Becoming the number one player on my college tennis team, which qualified me to play an exhibition set with Grand Slam Champion Donald Budge. (He won 6 to 2. The two was because of his kindness, although I did win a modest number of honest points)

My first aircraft carrier landing as a U.S. Navy fighter pilot, even though I had to take a wave-off the first two attempts.

Finishing near the top of my surfing class while vacationing in Hawaii, and being one of three students who surfed 12-foot waves off the Kona Coast. Not just once, but five times, although I nearly drowned when I crashed the third time.

Sailing through the air 93 feet on my third ski jump in New Hampshire. Talk about a thrill, this one was hard to beat!

The day I was awarded my Doctor of Aeronautical Engineering degree from New York University at age 38.

The night my neighbor's house caught on fire, and I spotted it while going to the bathroom. My call to the fire department and my running to his house saved his family and minimized damage to the house.

The time my wife and I called on our new neighbor, famous movie star Bette Davis, who had rented a waterfront cottage at the end of our street.

My "conquest" of Mt. Everest, even though I only got to 19,000 feet before my oxygen got too low to continue. The wonderful sights and the comradeship were worth all the effort and pain.

Testifying before the Congressional Space Committee on why there were so many changes on Grumman Aerospace's Lunar Module Program.

Becoming First Violinist of the Long Island Symphony, and conducting Beethoven's great Ninth Symphony when the conductor fell ill.

My one and only trip to Antarctica, and the unbelievable sights I saw. Not only emperor penguins, but huge, snow covered peaks and floating icebergs.

The day I was elected to the Huntington, N. Y. Town Council, especially the moment a year later when I decided that politics was not for me;

Becoming Al Gore's chief New Hampshire advisor during his Presidential campaign.

The day I saw wild mountain gorillas, and the close call when the silverback male charged our group leader. It was worth the long trek to their dwelling place in this fascinating world.

The business trip to St. Louis, where my hotel room was adjacent to famous Hollywood actress Linda Darnell, who was making a location movie. She had just been divorced and sought comfort in my room that night. Wow!

Finally, my most superlative moment was when I got the Pulitzer Prize for being the best teller-of-tall-tales since Baron Von Munchausen!

Authors note: Although all of the above were tall tales, some were just embellishments of true experiences. For example: I was right guard on my championship high school football team; I took our class salutatorian to the Senior Banquet; I was V.P. of my dorm in college and V.P. of the Aero Society; I played tennis in college, but never tried to make the team. However I saw Don Budge in an exhibition match at my tennis club, and he played with some of the members; I earned my private pilots license my senior year in college, and later was aboard an aircraft carrier as an engineer for Grumman Aircraft; I took surfing lessons in Hawaii, and made a successful ride on my third attempt; I have jumped off ski mounds a distance of about 12-14 feet, and I watched real jumpers in NH go over 100 feet; I got a Master of Aero engineering degree from NYU at age 27; Bette Davis rented a cottage at the end of our road, but I never got the courage to call on her. (I did see her looking at me as I swam in front of her waterfront cottage, and I have talked personally with actors Carl Reiner, Alan Alda and a few others); I have climbed many U.S. mountains, but none over 8000 feet; I did deliver a Lunar Module talk (along with other managers) to the Congressional Space Committee when they visited Grumman, and I sat directly across from the Chairman of the committee at lunch; I never played a violin, but I did play a baritone horn in five bands and I like to "conduct" major orchestras when I play them on my hi-fi set or TV; I have never been to Antarctica or Gorilla Territory except via TV; I was a committee member of the Huntington Fusion-Economy Party and was asked to run for Town Council until the chairman learned I was a Democrat; during his first presidential campaign, I gave Al Gore some advice, which he took and thanked me for;

However, I never saved my neighbor from a fire, or had a hotel room near Linda Darnell; they were the biggest tall tales of my story. L.M.E.

TENNIS

I'll admit it--I love tennis! I belong to an indoor club where the modest annual fee permits unlimited play. Furthermore, many outdoor courts in my hometown of Dover, N.H., are plentiful, uncrowded and free, so I play about four times a week—winter, spring, summer and fall. If you think I'm lucky, think again! You see, I pretty much planned it that way and looked for a small city with the above qualities when I retired. Yes, I love tennis--its not only lots of fun, but it helps me keep fit, young at heart and is great for relieving pent up frustrations, (you can pound that little ball instead of the object of your frustration).

When I'm not playing, I like to watch tennis tournaments on T.V., or actually attend them. While living on Long Island, N.Y., my <u>wife</u> and I went to the U.S. Open and other tournaments whenever feasible, so we have seen many of the great and near-great players in person—and in action! Men like <u>Budge, Kramer, Emerson, Gonzales, Laver, Rosewall, Roche, Hoad, Newcombe, Smith, Conners, Ashe, Nastase, McEnroe, Borg, Noah, Villas, Lendl, Edberg, Chang,</u>...! Also women like <u>Connelly, Betz, Moran, Court, King, Goolagong, Wade, Casal, Durr, Evert, Navratilova, Austin, Graf, Seles,</u>...!

You may not recognize some of the names, but tennis buffs will. I even took some of their pictures on my camera, and talked with Budge, Kramer and Laver briefly. Furthermore, I have served as a line judge and chair umpire at club tournaments, organized and managed regional tournaments for my Rotary Club, and attended several tennis camps, two of which were run by <u>Frank Brennan, Billy Jean King's</u> coach. I carry two rackets when I travel and usually find (or take along) another player or three.

As I contemplate my long association with tennis (I started playing around age 13), I find that tennis terms have permeated my other activities. For example: o My favorite card is an ACE! o Fishing is more fun when I have a LINE and a NET. o I like JUDGES because they spend lots of time in COURTS! (I don't like to spend it in courts, but on courts) o My favorite toy is a top—I like TOP SPIN! o I like my bread SLICED, o I wish politicians would UNDERSPIN more issues and excuses, o When I go to a restaurant, I want fast SERVICE and a good SERVER! o When I play poker, I usually make DEUCEs wild, o My favorite age—and tennis score-- is 40. I "LOVE 40" when I'm receiving! o Although I'm getting old, I'm not SET in my ways (I hope), o I will be married 52 years in May, 1997, so I guess my wife and I made a good MATCH way back! When I was a bachelor, I slept in a SINGLE bed. After I married, a DOUBLE one—and a MIXED DOUBLE one at that! o I seldom minded when my kids made a RACKET—it meant they were healthy and having fun! o I sympathize with defendants who have been FRAMEd, and don't like it when someone STRINGS them along,

o People with a firm GRIP are more attractive; they can HANDLE things better! o I don't like movies where the villain CHOKES someone in the THROAT, o Don't FENCE me in—unless it's a tennis fence, and spare me those BACKHAND remarks! o I seldom play VOLLEY ball, but I "volley" a lot on court, o I enjoy a long RALLY—tennis, not political! My favorite Christmas flower is a POINTSETtia! (Sp.?) o I've had my share of CLOSE CALLS, but some of the worst ones were when my shot hit the line and my opponent yelled, "Just out!" o People who "hit the OVERHEAD" annoy me. o I like good STROKING—on the court and off!

o When I go to the theater, I hope to see a SMASH HIT! o Theaters and indoor courts have two things in common: CURTAINS and SCREENS o When it comes to poetry, I favor TENNYSon.(ouch!) o I like Robert Frost's comment: "Poetry without rhyme, is like playing TENNIS without a NET!" o When I go to the races, I can't help thinking that a DROP SHOT is better than a LONGSHOT, o I 'm glad Goldwater wasn't President, because he threatened to LOB a nuclear missile into the men's room at the Kremlin, o Normally, I don't like TICKS, but when my opponent "ticks" the ball, I do. o When my shot hits the middle of the net and my partner says "GET IT UP" , it reminds me that I 'm getting old. o When I was young I wanted to SCORE. Now I'm lucky if I remember the score!

THANKSGIVING

When the Pilgrims started Thanksgiving Day, several centuries ago, I doubt if they dreamed it would be celebrated so far into the future. It is now 2006, and the national holiday is still here. During this special day most Americans will pause to give thanks for the many blessings in their lives. Although some may have been overwhelmed by current tragic problems and don't feel very blessed, I suspect that even they could find blessings if they contemplate their total life experiences. Even though I have no current tragic problems, I thought it might be useful if I described some of the people and institutions for which I am thankful. Here goes:

PEOPLE:

My parents, <u>Luther Macon Epps</u> and <u>Mittie Euretta Schrum Epps</u>, were my earliest blessing, not only because they brought me into the world, but because they supported me for twenty years, taught me many things themselves, and sent me through school and college. They were the guiding lights that steered me into self-supporting manhood. And they did it with love and care, in sickness and health. Even when I was naughty and they gave me corporal punishment, it was a blessing because it taught me the invaluable lesson that actions have consequences.

My siblings, of which I had two sisters and two brothers, were also early blessings. My older sister, <u>Ruth</u>, was a special blessing because she taught me so many things that were part of our youthful culture and gave me so much love, fun, and support. <u>Louise</u>, who was 5 years younger than I, and my twin brothers, <u>Charles</u> and <u>Joe</u>, who were 10 years younger, were also blessings. Through them I learned the role of a big brother, and it taught me that life was not only receiving, but giving to others. They were also lots of fun, and as they grew older they partially repaid me for my big brother giving.

My many aunts and uncles were there from my beginning, and were my first glimpse of my extended family. Those on my mother's side were very close, and greatly influenced my life. My <u>Aunts, Vera Hinson, Irene Hamel</u> and <u>Mary Mauney</u>, were almost like second mothers, and were unusually kind and generous to my siblings and me. Unlike my other aunts and uncles, they were childless, which might have been the reason they could devote so much love and affection toward us. My father's siblings were not as close, but when we did get together, they too were warm and caring. It was through all of them that I learned the meaning, and the wonderful gift, of an extended family.

My cousins were also part of my life, and I had them by the dozen. Not all of them were close because of distance and age gaps, but I knew they were there and I guess they knew I was there. Some were very close, and one, <u>David Schrum</u>, has been my very close friend since I was five years old. Once his parents moved to the same block as my parents, David became my best friend and has remained in that special position to this day. Believe me when I say that we have shared more experiences and learned more from each other than any other friend, although a few outside our family have come close. I also have fond memories of <u>David's siblings</u>; <u>Uncle John Schrum's daughters</u>; <u>Uncle Grady Schrum's son Billy</u>, who died in an auto accident at an early age; <u>Uncle Charlie's nephew, Pee Dee Hinson</u>, who was a boyhood playmate whenever I stayed with Uncle Charlie and Aunt Vera. It was through my cousins that my understanding of how the branches of the family tree grew larger and larger. Now they and my siblings have their own kids, grandkids, and maybe great-grand ones, so the tree in now much larger than when I was kid, and is one of life's big blessings. Fortunately, I am still close to most of my nephews and nieces.

Of course there were relatives from my father's side, but as I said earlier, they were not as close as those from my mother's side. I never knew my paternal <u>Grandfather</u>, because he died five years to the day before I was born. However, I met my paternal grandmother, <u>Ellen Epps</u>, on many occasions, usually when my father would take me along. She lived in Lincolnton with my widowed <u>Aunt Kate Henderson</u> and her three <u>daughters</u>. I would usually talk with the daughters after I had said hello, etc to Grandma Epps, and I enjoyed their company. My <u>Aunt Sue Laws</u> and her husband <u>Sherman</u> were fairly close, and I especially enjoyed their sons, <u>Oscar</u> and <u>James</u> during my youth. Both boys died fairly early in life, so I was unable to develop long-term relationships.

My earliest non-relative friend was one who lived in my College Avenue neighborhood in Newton, NC. <u>Bobby Cochran</u> lived across the street and we played, (and got into trouble) starting at age three. We stayed friends through high school, but lost the early closeness once my family moved to another part of town when I was about four. In my new neighborhood, I had a girl, <u>Dorothy Long</u>, as a playmate for a while, but once I found some boy playmates, I soon learned that girls were not as much fun at that age. That of course changed as the years flowed by.

My new play mates were the <u>Sigmon twins, John and William; Francis Self; Billy Mac Cochran; Juny Yount; and Jack Barringer</u>. I was the youngest of the group by a year or more, so I learned a lot from each one.

The twins taught me how to build a house from cardboard and wooden boxes; how to make a slide down a fence; how to pitch a tent and camp out in a backyard, and other things. Francis Self taught me how to bat a ball, convincing me to learn left-handed because all the big hitters were lefties. Billy Mac taught me how to build dams in the gully near his home; how to use big words because he was a studious lad; and other intellectual things. His mother even taught me how to play the piano. Although piano playing didn't stick, my love of music has lasted a lifetime and is one of my unanticipated blessings. Juny introduced me to soft drinks; taught me how to jump off a garage roof into a sand pile; play tag football; make root beer, and other things. Jack was the most influential of the lot, and I had many adventures with him, some of which were life threatening. I have written a long piece about him, titled: "My Friend (?) Jack vs. My Guardian Angel," which is included in this book.

Once I entered first grade at age 5, some of my classmates became my friends, and those relationships grew with the years. Although some of my early playmates became more distant because of age differences and their new friends, my circle of friends widened. High school friends that blessed my life were <u>Bill and Ken Price; Robert Cochran; Charles Turner; Gus Arndt; John Cantrell; Twins Ralph and Roger Neil; Milton Sharpe; Virgil Martin; Charlie Brady</u>; and others too numerous to name. And there were my girl friends, which I will not name but helped me grow up, emotionally, not sexually. Believe it or not, all I have to do is close my eyes and I can see all of those early friends and remember things we did together.

Time moved slowly in those days, and it seemed that my Newton friends would last my whole life. Alas, I soon learned that they would fade away after graduation, in spite of sincere attempts to stay in touch. Distance and the busyness of life meant that our contacts would be infrequent letters; visits back home; and our class reunions. Early death took a few away prematurely, and my own longevity means that I outlived many others.

I will not try to name all the friends, both male and female that blessed my life during my college and working years because they are too numerous. Ditto for the fiends that blessed my retirement years. But I can see them and recall events just by closing my eyes and meditating about them, and I am grateful for each one. I mentioned my earlier friends in more detail because they were there during my formative years and I am running out of time to type. However, if you were or are a friend and are reading this book, realize that you frequently come into my memory and I recall many pleasant hours with you. Some of you are even in the other stories in this book, so you were not neglected.

I have saved the best blessing for last—my own dear family. <u>Elizabeth</u> and I have been married since 1945, and we had two precious daughters, <u>Tina</u> and <u>Rebecca</u>. Both of their husbands are blessings, but our grandchildren <u>Hannah, Grady, and Lisa</u> are special blessings, as is our great grandson, <u>Addison</u>.

INSTITUTIONS:

During my life in Newton, N.C., there were two institutions that were a blessing: the school system (of which my <u>Dad</u> was Superintendent for a few years) and the Methodist Church. I have so many fond (and a few not so fond) memories of both that it would take a book to recall them. Some are included in this book.

During my college years, there were more institutions that were blessings, the chief of which was North Carolina State College (Now university). It was there that I got my advanced education, which made it possible to work as a graduate engineer and do so many of the things described in this book. I now contribute to it annually and have remembered it in my trust as partial payback. It also introduced me to the U.S. Army through its Reserved Officers Training Program, (ROTC), Roosevelt's National Youth Administration, (NYA) and his Civilian Pilots Training Administration (CPTA). Not only did I get academic training in Military science, but field training during my 6 weeks at R.O.T.C. camp in Anniston, Alabama.

The NYA. help fund my college education via part time jobs. My first one was in the Wood Shop, where I made 25 cents per hour, mostly for clean up work. The second one was in the Foundry, where I made 40 cents per hour for doing heavy and dirty work that only a foundry person can understand. The third, and longest lasting, was in the Music Department, where I made

35 cents per hour for keeping the music files in order and drafting letters for the Director. Now the pay doesn't seem like much today, but it helped me get an education and live well, which in those depression times cost about $500 per year. (That's right—per year!)

Roosevelt's CPTA let me earn a private pilot's license and fly for several years. Other stories in this book tell even more.

Perhaps the most enjoyable work I had during my college years was being an usher for the Raleigh Music Association. This job didn't pay any money, but something much more valuable—free admission to their wonderful concerts. It was there that I saw and heard many famous classical artists and orchestras, including my first two opera. I also got lots of exercise, not only by ushering people to their seats, but also by walking three miles each way to get there and back.

I suppose the most important institution in my life was the Grumman Aircraft Engineering Corporation. It has changed its name several times—Grumman Aerospace Corporation; the Grumman Corporation; and now Northrop-Grumman Corporation following the merger, which took place after my retirement. Grumman was a wonderful blessing for many reasons. Not only did it provide interesting and useful work, but it paid me reasonably well and opened up many opportunities. I had some great bosses and great fellow workers, some of which I still communicate with. Its biggest blessing happened when I met a pretty redheaded girl there that became my lifelong <u>wife</u> and mother of our children. That one is hard to top!

Huntington, NY institutions that were blessings were:

Old First Presbyterian Church, where we obtained spiritual growth and many friends. It was there that I became: a Ruling Elder at age thirty, (the youngest at that time); a Sunday-School teacher and superintendent; President of The Samuel T. Carter Club; and member and chairman of many committees. My wife was a deacon, a teacher, and on many committees. Needless to say, we made many friends and had many wonderful times there.

The Huntington Concert Association was where my wife and I were on the Board and served time as officers. In addition to the new friends we made, its blessings were all the many classical concerts we attended and the great musicians we heard and sometimes met. It was a long extension of my Concert days in college, and helped me grow in my appreciation of great music.

There were several institutions involving tennis and social activities that were also blessings. I have played tennis since age 13, and still play it today at age 89. I don't play as well as I did during my middle years, but I am better than when I was in my early teens. I taught my wife how to play when she was around 40, and her cross-court shots were usually better than mine. Tennis has surely been one of my major blessings.

I also served on committees for the Boy Scouts and a new Political

Party. These were short-term activities, but were still blessings because they let me learn more and serve others.

Perhaps the most interesting institution during my post-retirement working years was the I-Cubed Corporation. I was the founding president, and really enjoyed conceiving and working on some of the new ideas that we tried to promote. It was never the big success I had envisioned, but we had some small successes and some major near misses that would have changed our life and made big contributions to our country and the world. It also improved our living standard because it supplemented our retirement income. It gave me some of the most interesting opportunities of my life, so it was a big blessing.

After my second retirement in 1986, we moved to Dover, N.H. Institutions that were blessings were: Community church of Durham; Dover Rotary Club; The Tennis Coop; Dover Athletic Club; and the University Of NH, for many learning activities. We were also blessed with many good friends and neighbors.

In 2001, we moved to Camarillo, CA to be near our daughter, <u>Rebecca</u>, her husband <u>James Catterall</u> and our <u>grand children</u>. We live in a retirement village called, "Leisure Village," where there are more clubs and activities than we can join. We have joined quite a few, and I am or have been an officer in four. We have also made some new and delightful friends, so the blessings continue to flow.

Of course there were difficult times during all those years, but looking back, some of them may have been blessings in disguise. What will happen next is a mystery, but we hope that the proper mix of blessing and trouble will continue. If not, we should have no complaints because the blessings in our live have greatly out weighed our troubles!

WHAT'S IN A NAME?

When <u>William Shakespeare</u> asked the above question, he wisely answered, "A rose by any other name would smell as sweet." I agree with the "Immortal Bard", but I sometimes wonder if humans haven't abused his sage comment. Here are some examples:

o Many in my generation have heard about a Texas family named <u>Hogg</u>, who called their daughter "<u>Ima</u>". Imagine going through life with a moniker like that. Think of the teasing she must have suffered in her school years when the teacher called the roll. Consider the snickers she endured anytime her full name was said at public meetings. But she must have been some sort of "rose", because she became a well-known public figure on her merits in spite of her amusing name.

o Not all peculiar names are as hard to bear as Ima's was. Consider two daughters of friends of mine, whose names were "<u>Melody</u>" and "<u>Memory</u>". Not ordinary names, are they? But when you realize that their parent's last name was "Lane", they certainly become extraordinary.

o My wife, Elizabeth, knew an upper-classman at Vassar named "U.T. Miller. Everyone thought it an odd name, to say the least, but when they realized that her full name was "University of Tennessee Miller", they had to learn "the rest of the story". It seems that her parents met at the University, and in honor of their Alma Mater they decided to give their first born that unusual name. If my father had named me after his college, I would be "Trinity College" Epps, or "T.C." for short. Like Trinity, I would have changed my name to "Duke University." I can think of many worse names to be called than "D.U." (Initials D.U.E.) or maybe I could have been called "Duke"

o Speaking of college years, I had a classmate at N. C. State named B. R. Hood. He always went by his initials, and for four years his classmates and I called him "B.R." I thought it was appropriate for cold weather, since I often said "Hi Brrrr." Imagine my surprise when the senior annual came out, and below his picture was his full name: "Bold Robin Hood."

o Then there was a lab assistant whose last name was "Lipshitz" and a classmate named "George Sheets." You can imagine what fun some of the coarser guys had with those names.

o During my working years I made business trips to the Navy's Bureau of Aeronautics for my employer, the Grumman Aerospace Corporation. During one of he visits I was introduced to a new secretary. She was a real hillbilly type, with long stringy hair and buckteeth. Somehow I remained polite and stifled laughter when they said her name: IDA MAY GOOTCH!

o Tennis friends had a daughter named "Kandy Keene." She voluntarily compounded her problem when she married a young man named "Kane," so her initials were "KKK!"

o At one time we had a dentist named George O'Donnell." Now you may ask "What's wrong with a good Irish name like that?" "Nothing," I reply, unless you abbreviate it the way my wife did on our appointment calendar, which was "G.O.D." I told the story during "Happy Buck Time" at a Rotary meeting, and the name stuck, because I frequently heard other Rotarians say, "Good morning GOD!"

Then there are nicknames that can be as strange and even more unkind than real names. How about these:

o I have a close friend who was named after his uncle, Justice Louis Brandeis. Most of us called him "Brand", but some of the fellows at work called him "Brandy Eyes", and "Screwy Louie". Of course he was neither, but he endured the unkInd names in good humor.

o When my deceased brother, Charles, was in grade school, he referred to number two as "Pooh-Pooh". He was ten years younger than I, so I first learned about his nickname when he showed me his Senior Class Annual. As was their custom, the editors had put that awful nickname under his name for the entire world to see, including his big brother.

o My own name, "Macon", has caused me problems from time to time. Some of the kids in high school called me "Make", but it didn't stick. "Eppsy" stuck a little better, but eventually died out. Northerners always associated it with Macon Ga., and I had a hard time convincing them that I was from North Carolina, not Georgia.

Although "Macon" was more common in the South (I knew 4 or 5 other "Macon's") it made me somewhat unique in the North. I learned to appreciate it in a large office full of engineers when the telephone rang. The secretary would call out " Telephone Joe," and at least three guys wondered if it was for them. But when my name was called, no one was confused because I was the only "Macon" in the large department, probably in the whole company of 20,000.

Some of the fellows had fun with my name. Some would say, "What are you making, Macon?" Others would carry it a bit further by saying, "He's Making Epps," and the straight man would say, "What's Epps?" Some even said, "Watch out for Macon—he <u>may con</u> you!

When on a double date, the other guy would sometimes say, with a twinkle in his voice, "Are you Macon out?" I never answered the question orally, because the twinkle in my eye was sufficient. (Making out in those days was just hugging and kissing)

Some newcomers at work were surprised that I was male. They thought I was a girl named May Conepps!

But the worst errors concerning my name were when some heard it as "Malcolm X", and some junk mail people misspelled it as "Moron Epps." I hope the last one doesn't stick!

On a recent trip to Europe I ordered a compact disc from two musicians I heard. I printed my name and address carefully on the order form, but when it arrived it was addressed to: Mr. Mceon Eggs, 7 Cledoweter Dr., Dover, Nitt. 03820. Since I live at 7 Clearwater Dr. in N.H., hats off to the Postal Service for deciphering the many errors and delivering the package to me on time!

Our world is full of both praising and insulting nicknames, so I will conclude this piece with some that stick in my memory:

o "Lucky Lindy", for famous aviator and scientist <u>Charles Lindbergh</u>, the first man to fly over the Atlantic Ocean.

o "Wrong-way" Corrigan, for <u>Douglas Corrigan</u> who filed a flight plan from New York to California, and then flew across the Atlantic Ocean to Europe. He had more than his "fifteen minutes" of fame, but not a whole lot more.

o "<u>Tricky Dick" Nixon</u>, who turned out to be worse than tricky because he seriously abused his high office.

o "<u>Slick Willie" Clinton</u>, who blatantly lied to the American Public, violated his oath of office, and demeaned his high position, yet was "slick" enough to be forgiven by a gullible public. And they used to call <u>Ronald Reagan</u> the "Teflon Man"!

o And who can forget <u>Archie Bunker's</u> favorite nicknames for his wife and son-in-law: "<u>Dingbat</u>" and "<u>Meathead</u>"!

WOMEN AND THE SIX "L's"

As a man, it is risky for me to write about women and their needs and desires; but what the heck, I'm a risk taker, so here goes.

I believe that most women seek the first five "L's" all through their lives, starting when they are very young girls. I will explain the six "L's" as I discuss each one.

The first "L" stands for "Lovely". What girl or woman wouldn't like to have that appellation? To me, it is a better word than "pretty", "beautiful", or even "gorgeous". "Lovely" is a combination of outer attractiveness with inner charm and grace. Outer attractiveness can be a pleasant face, a reasonable figure, and perhaps one or two physical features that make a woman memorable.

Not all women score high in the outer attractiveness department. In fact, it is somewhat rare to see a physically attractive woman in any given crowd. Check it out yourself the next time you are shopping, and see how long it takes to find one that is unusual. But inner charm and grace abound in the female population, especially when compared to the brusque, sometimes rough, and insensitive characteristics of men.

Furthermore, inner charm and grace can be developed further through the years. Best of all, unlike physical attractiveness, it doesn't fade with age. It can even grow stronger all the way to old age and beyond. Even without much outer attractiveness, a woman can be "Lovely". Fortunate is the woman who has both outer and inner loveliness!

The second "L" stands for "Loving". That is a trait that seems to be inborn in women. Watch a little girl play with her doll, or a young mother with a new baby, or even an older woman with her teenaged son or daughter. Admittedly, teen-agers can strain the loving nature of a mother, but deep down their love remains through thick and thin times. And it is rare to see a grandmother who doesn't glow with love when her grandchildren enter the house.

Women are not only the principal givers of life, but seem to be the care givers of mankind by nature, or at least in their allotted role in most societies throughout the world. Therefore, it is unusual to find a woman who isn't a loving person, especially with those who are the closest in her life.

Those who aren't "loving" probably have been blown off course by the vicissitudes of life, and should be eased back into the loving channel whenever possible.

The third "L" stands for "Loveable". Show me a woman who is "Lovely" and "Loving", and odds are great that she is also "Loveable". Oh, there may be a few other traits that can embellish her "Lovability", but the first two are usually sufficient. Embellishments are such things as cute, witty, sensitive, unselfish, etc, but usually they are part of the total package under "Lovely" and "Loving".

The fourth "L" is "Loved". It almost follows, like dawn follows darkness, that those having the first three "L's" will be "Loved" by someone; and the stronger the first three "L's" the more people will love her. More important, the special people in her life should make her feel superbly loved!

The fifth "L" is "Lady". While it is true that all ladies are women, not all women are ladies. I'm not sure all women want to be called "ladies,"* but I believe that women who qualify for the above "L's", desire and deserve the term. I know that most of the men I'm acquainted with use the term with both respect and admiration, especially when they are in the presence of a true lady. While the term is used broadly when there's a group of women, both men and women realize that there may be some in the group that don't really qualify. Fortunately, we live in an age and in a country where a woman doesn't have to be of high social or economic rank to deserve the term. In my view, a woman who earns the term ranks higher than the highest-ranked noble "lady", who deep down may not be a true lady.

But what about men? Well, I hesitate to describe any man as "Lovely", but "Loving", "Loveable", and "Loved can apply in full force to men, and the term "gentleman" is the male equivalent of "lady". So once again the women have outdone the men by having five "L's" instead of three. It means that we men should try harder to cultivate our three "L's" and earn the term "gentleman". I'll bet that most women will applaud that goal.

Most of the great religions have placed "Love" as our principal goal in life, and have said that our creator not only loves us, but also expects us to love each other. So the bottom line is this: If we work hard to accomplish "Love" as our principal goal, it could transform our worrisome world into a semi-paradise.

The sixth "L" is "Life", for which women are the principal progenitors. Life could be transformed from a thing of worry and travail, into a thing of beauty and joy for all mankind if everyone followed as many of the "L's" as possible!

©2009 L. Macon Epps All rights reserved (2/ 8/06)

* During the Women's Liberation Movement I was chided for referring to a small group of women as "ladies". Fortunately, that sensitivity has died out, at least among the women I know. L.M.E.

WORD PLAY

I'm tired of tires-- they're tiresome.

Are you glad when you see gladiolas?

People from Bad, Switzerland, say that Badminton is bad.

If Boris Goudenoff is good enough for the Russians,
is he good enough for you?

Victor had a great victory when he conquered Victorla.

If they made flour out of flowers, maybe we could all bloom and flower!

She drank a cup of tea on the 9th tee, wearing a T-shirt to tease the golfers.

Of course the waiter served the main course on the golf course,
but his language was course.

I appreciate my antiques, especially when they appreclate in value.

The chairman sat In an easy chair near a table, but he wasn't charitable.

The politicians were standing in the stands,
but they didn't stand for anything important.

The Hungarian army squad was bottled up in a box canyon.
All they had for nourishment was two cases of bottled water.
After two weeks of being bottled up, they died from hunger!

The entertainer wasn't very entertaining, so the Board
entertained a motion to dismiss him.

We had eight guest for dinner at eight, but none ate very much.

When Herr Schiklegruber returned home, his wife had gone through
A bad "Hair" day, because a large hare entered the beauty shop.
It was a harrowing experience!

Just as I was about to open my Lite beer, the light went out.
But I was light-hearted about it and went up in a lighter-than air balloon.

When the gambler won by a "nose", no one knows why his nose started running faster than the horse that won the race by a nose.

When President Bush went into the bushes, he was bushwhacked. Once he was rescued, he felt "bushed."

She brushed her teeth, then gave me the brush-off and disappeared into the underbrush.

You can speak your mind when you're in a Speakeasy, but when you're speaking to the Speaker of the House of Representatives, speak carefully!

The Western steaks were so tasty that the vampire investor staked his fortune on them. When it turned out to be a big mistake, his fellow investors drove a stake in his heart.

Everyone thought he was a cool guy, but when the police put him in the cooler to cool-off, he got a cool reception from his friends, who now called him a "coolie.".

You fooled us once, they said, so don't fool around with us anymore. We're not fools, you know!

Why don't we ditch those plans to dig a big ditch?

As the head-hunter was searching for a headmaster, some headlights shone so brightly that he fell headlong into a bush. He then went to the head, but there wasn't enough headroom, so he headed home.

People that buy a four poster bed with a canopy on top should know that a can a pee belongs under the bed.

WRONG TIME, WRONG PLACE STORIES

ITSY-BITSY SPIDER

Remember the kid's rhyme of the itsy-bitsy spider that climbed into the waterspout? Well, this one is true, but with an unhappy ending for the spider. It happened as I turned on the hot water for my morning shower. I quickly noticed a little spider, fighting furiously to keep from being swept away by the rushing water. Before I could decide whether or not to save him, he was flushed down the drain. By then the water was so hot I had to turn it down a bit to make my shower livable before I entered. 'Poor little spider', I thought. 'If it didn't drown it was probably scalded to death.'

If it had been in the spout of the kid's rhyme, it could climb out again, but with hot shower water and a drain trap catching it, there was no way for a happy ending.

Wrong Time, Wrong Place!

A MOUSE'S MISTAKE

As I entered the kitchen of my rented house in Huntington, N.Y. in 1947 a little gray mouse ran behind the open back door to hide. It didn't know the door had hinges and could easily be moved, but I did. I quickly got a broom, closed the door, and smacked the little mouse until it stopped moving. I was still in my pajamas, so I re-opened the door, opened the screen door, and swept it into the back yard.

I never learned its fate, because after I got dressed and went outside to dispose it, it was gone. I like to think that it was only stunned and crept away, but a more probable fate was that a neighborhood cat ate it for breakfast.

Wrong Time, Wrong Place, for a mouse who was too ignorant to understand that a hinged door makes a bad-hiding place!

BATHING BEAUTY

I had gone to Jones Beach on Long Island, N.Y. with some fellow bachelors, and was the last one to stay in the exciting surf. I was still riding the waves and about to get out, when I spotted a very pretty girl in a strapless bathing suit coming into the water.

My thought process went something like this: 'Hmm- when the waves hit her, the water's buoyancy will lift her breast, and its downward motion will push the strapless bathing suit down, so there may be a big exposure. I'd better get into a good position in case it happens.'

Much to her embarrassment and my delight, my analysis was correct. Her two beauties were fully exposed and stayed exposed as she frantically tried to place them back into her suit. By the time she did, I had gotten an eyeful. I was even tempted to go closer and offer to help her put them back in, but decided she wouldn't appreciate my "kindness".

Wrong Time, Wrong Place for her, but Right Time, Right Place for me!

A CLIENT'S CATASTROPHE

This story involved the client of a Real Estate agent I knew, and not me. (Thank God) She was showing a male client the yard of a prospective house, when the cesspool over which the man was walking collapsed and he disappeared into the abyss. The agent called the fire department, and they rescued the unfortunate victim. He was barely injured because he fell in soft, smelly stuff, but what an awful experience. Needless to say, he didn't buy that house.

Wrong Time, Very Wrong Place!

GOLF CAN BE DANGEROUS

This story made the news many years ago, and it got embedded in my memory. Four men were playing golf and a sudden thunderstorm arose before they could get to shelter. A lightning bolt instantly killed one of them. When the friend nearest to him recovered from the shock, he went back to see if he could help his fallen friend. Just as he put his arms around to lift him, another bolt struck him and he fell to the ground.

Whoever said, "Lightning never strikes twice in the same place," was wrong, <u>dead wrong</u>. Fortunately for the helpful friend, Thor took pity and reduced the power of the second bolt, and he recovered.

Wrong Time, Wrong Place, especially for the first golfer!

GOLF CAN BE JUST

Another golf story I heard, but I'm not sure it's a true one. A deaf mute was playing golf alone, and overtook a foursome. He wrote on his pad, "May I play through?" The foursome leader was a selfish guy, so he wrote, "Hell no, wait your turn!"

Three holes later, after the foursome had starting moving away from their second shots, the deaf mute hit an unusually long drive that conked the foursome leader in the head. Did he apologize when he approached the selfish leader, who was still sitting and rubbing the bump on his head? Hell no, he handed him a piece of paper with this message: "FORE!"

Wrong Time, Wrong Place, but poetic justice for the selfish golfer!

MAD DOGS AND ENGLISHMEN?

<u>NO</u>. This story is about a mad dog and a little girl. It happened in the nineteen thirties to my sister, <u>Ruth</u>, who was in her early teens. She was walking home from school when the dog attacked her without provocation. She screamed and protected herself as well as she could, and the owner came out of the house and rescued her. I'm not sure of the sequence of events, but I think someone took Ruth to a doctor and my <u>Dad </u>got his shotgun and killed the dog.

The owner seemed more upset by the shooting than by the attack, but later apologized when the medical examiner verified that the dog was rabid and needed to be killed. Poor Ruth had to go through a number of painful shots so that the rabies wouldn't harm her. What an awful thing to happen to an innocent, sweet little girl, who was in the Wrong place at the Wrong time. When Dad shot the dog, it was The Right Time and the Right Place!

IRS AUDIT

A retired pediatrician friend of mine told me this story. While still in practice, he was notified by the IRS that his tax return had been audited and that there were serious questions about his charitable deductions. He was asked to come to the auditor's office and bring proof of his claims. He had given generously to his Synagogue, but figured that one of the reasons the IRS was disturbed was because of a Jewish custom-- making contributions of $18 or multiples thereof, which was believed to bring luck and blessings to the contributor

When he got to the IRS office, he waited his turn. As one of the men being audited left the interview, he spoke to my friend thusly: "Watch out for that auditor; she's very tough and a real bitch. I think she's also a racist!"

" But you're a white guy", my friend replied.

" Yeah, but she's a black woman" he responded. "I'm a lawyer and she knows more about tax law than I do, so be damn careful."

When my friend's turn came, he entered with some trepidation, expecting a tough session. Much to his surprise, the auditor said, "What are you doing here, Dr Treitman? You should be at the hospital saving lives, like you did when you saved my grandson!"

That remark helped him remember the woman and the circumstances to which she referred. She was at the hospital holding her grandson in her arms, when he realized that the kid had a serious breathing problem that needed immediate action. Any delay meant that his breathing would cease completely in a few minutes. He grabbed the kid and rushed him to the operating room for a tracheotomy, which saved the kid's life.

The tough auditor then said, "We must have made a mistake calling you here, so why don't you get back to the hospital and save some more lives?"

He thanked her, they shook hands and he left.

An IRS audit is the Wrong Time and Wrong Place for most of us, but not the good doctor; he had been in the Right Place at the Right Time when he saved her grandson, and she never forgot it!

A WARM, YELLOW FLUID

When I was around twelve years old, I had a paper route. Every afternoon after school and during summer vacation, I would deliver the Hickory Daily Record to my twenty customers. I made a dollar a week, except sometimes a stingy customer would cheat me out of a nickel or so.

One hot summer day, I spotted two of my friends, Earl Robinson and his brother, sitting on their front steps drinking water. Earl called out, "Hi, Macon! Come over here and set a spell and I'll get 'cha some cold water."

"Thanks," I replied, as I ambled over, sat on a step and relieved myself of my bulging paper bag. He fetched the cold water and I noticed that his five-year-old brother, Horace, was sitting in a chair on the porch behind me. We were talking amicably when I felt a warm, smelly fluid hitting my head. I immediately rose to see what was happening, and there stood little Horace peeing on me. Before I could do anything, Horace ran into the house and my two "friends" started laughing merrily and pointing at my wet, disheveled hair and wet clothes. Fortunately, my paper bag was spared.

Naturally, I wanted to do something to Horace, but the steps I was sitting on belonged to the Chief of Police in our little town, Newton, N.C., so I decided I had better take Horace's trick good naturedly. Besides, Earl was bigger, stronger and older than I, and would have protected his kid brother. To this day, I don't know whether Horace had done the dousing on his own, or if his older brothers had taught him to do it to make the hot summer days more exciting.

Wrong Time, Wrong Place, and the Wrong Type of Shower for me!

HONORARY FRATERNITY

When I was in college at North Carolina State, I played a baritone horn in three bands: Military, Concert, and a marching one for football games. The Music Department had an Honorary Fraternity called Mu Beta Psi, and you usually had to be a junior or senior before you were elected to it. They had some nice social events, which its members enjoyed.

Before you could be elected to Mu Beta Psi, you had to be inducted into a student organization called "The Yellow Dogs." Unlike Mu Beta Psi, it had an initiation ceremony. When my turn came, the regular members blindfolded me and sent me through an obstacle course. During my passage thru the course, I was paddled, yelled at, blown on with some bellows, and intimidated by other harmless, but somewhat frightening tricks.

The final ceremony involved being sworn in by the president of the group. I was still blindfolded, and somewhat surprised and apprehensive when they ordered me to lower my pants and underwear, thus exposing you know what. The president then read a number of things we had to do as loyal members, with my repeating each one after him. I remember the ending quite well, because he said, and I repeated: "...and I will not tell other inductees ...the secret of the little yellow dog... that peed on me!" This was followed by a stream of warm liquid squirted on my "you know what". There was laughter from the president and other officers, my blindfold was removed, and everyone shook my hand and congratulated me.

Wrong Time, Wrong Place for the warm liquid, but, unlike my Horace episode, it was just warm tap water and the resulting fellowship was worth it!

NURSERY BABIES

One of my N.C. State College friends also got a job with my employer, Grumman Aircraft Engineering Corporation. He married several years before I did, and as nature took its course, Jim and Helen Huntly had a baby boy. Naturally, I went to the local hospital to congratulate both my friends.

After spending time with them in Helen's hospital room, Jim said, "Macon, why don't you go down the hall and get the nurses to show you our new baby? Just tap on the glass and hold this name sign up, and they will bring little <u>Richard</u> to the window. Be sure and come back and tell us what you think of our little guy."

I followed his directions, and when the nurse brought the new baby to the window, I gazed at him admiringly. The nurse then said in a loud voice, "He looks just like you!"

When I returned to Helen's room, I praised the little guy, and then told them what the nurse had said. Helen giggled with laughter, but Jim had a serious look on his face as he said, "I thought you were my friend. What have you been doing behind my back?" Before I could respond, he roared with laughter.

For a few seconds I thought, Wrong Time, Wrong Place! Fortunately I was mistaken that time.

DRINKING AND WATER DON'T MIX

I was around seven years old when this adventure happened. It was summer time and some of the other kids and I had walked down to the old city dam near the edge of our small town. As usual, all we wore were short pants with an elastic waistband, and maybe some smelly tennis shoes. Some of us were barefooted.

Naturally, we picked up some stones and tossed them in the water to see the splash, and a few flat stones actually skipped along the water several times. As we were about to leave, a nearby man signaled for me to come to him, saying, "Come here and I'll give you a nickel."

The other kids left as I ambled over to him. I recognized him as <u>Slim Smith</u>, a guy I frequently saw hanging around town doing nothing. Once I got there, he said, "What's your name, kid?"

I told him, and then he said, "Can you swim?"

"No sir," I replied. I noticed that his breath smelled of whisky and he looked quite drunk, even to my young eyes.

"Well I'm gonna teach you. You know the best way to learn to swim?"

"No sir."

"Well, the best way is to be thrown into water that's over your head. That way you've got' a sink or swim! Here, I'll show ya." He then grabbed me and started taking me toward the deep water.

Somehow, I struggled free and started running away. He then yelled, "Come back, I was only kidding and you didn't get your nickel yet."

Call it instinct or common sense, but I knew that his drinking and that deep water didn't mix in case I started sinking, so I kept running. He staggered toward me to try to catch me, but I was sober and he wasn't, so I easily outran him.

Wrong Time, Wrong Place, but his booze and my instinct/common sense saved me.

HIGH SCHOOL BULLY BECOMES RICH

When I first entered High School, in Newton, NC, I encountered a senior-class boy named <u>Rome Jones</u>. He was a tall, good-looking guy, with light blond hair, and was much larger than I. He approached me just as the bell rang for us to go to our classes, saying, "You're Macon Epps, aren't cha?" Of course I replied affirmatively.

"Come with me, I wanta show you something." He then grabbed my arm and took me to a little-used lower entrance, which gave him the privacy he wanted.

He then said, "When your daddy was superintendent he gave me a beating for misbehavior. I can't do anything to him, so I'm gonna get even by beating you."

"But I didn't have anything to do with it," I replied. "It's not fair!"

"Maybe so," he responded, "but I'm gonna do it anyway, and if you tell anyone, I'll beat you even harder the next time." He then took off his belt, made me bend over, and strapped my little bottom about ten times in spite of my protests and cries of pain.

He then said, "There, I feel better. Remember, if you tell anyone the next beating will be even worse!" Naturally, I kept mum, but it was the Wrong Time, Wrong Place, and from my viewpoint, the Wrong Person he beat!

About thirty years later, I discovered that he had become wealthy by starting a small furniture manufacturing business in his garage, which grew into a much larger one. In fact, he was so successful that he was building a new mansion on a large piece of property with a man-made lake, near the edge of town. Once I heard about it, I toured it when it was nearly completed. I found it very impressive, but the road it was located on was surprising. It was named "Rome Jones Road'!

Rome died many, many years ago, while I am now 86. The injustice of his beating me was a small incident, and probably had nothing to do with his early demise and my longevity. But if he beat a 12-year-old kid, maybe he did other things that tipped the justice scales against him, but that's pure speculation. Anyway, I never forgot that beating, which occurred in 1932.

A MARBLE LESSON FROM THE CHAMP

<u>Zeb Yount</u> was a good-looking kid, and the best marble shooter in primary school. I had just received a pack of new marbles for my seventh birthday, and when Zeb learned about them he invited me to play with him. At first, I declined, saying, "You're too good, and I'm just learning to play. But I'll play just for fun, if you wanna."

Zeb was a savvy kid, so he replied, "Tell ya what I'll do. We'll play a few rounds and I'll give ya lessons and I'll always let cha go first. But we'll have to play for keeps so you'll try harder and learn faster."

I figured it would be worth a few of my marbles to learn from Zeb, so I agreed to play a few rounds. We each put about five marbles in a ring he drew with his finger, and he even gave me some preliminary lessons on the proper way to hold and shoot with the "steelie". My first shot missed, so

Zeb proceed to clear the ring with his accurate shots. He was kind enough to instruct me about his technique on each shot.

During a subsequent round, I even won one or two marbles, and Zeb told me, "Hey, you're catching on. You're gonna be a good marble shooter!"

About that time the bell rang to go to class, but Zeb convinced me to stay longer since I might not get the chance to learn again. I was caught up in the game, and agreed, but wondered if maybe I should stop. I still had a lot of marbles, so I stayed.

Our teacher missed us when she called the roll, and someone told her we were playing marbles, so she sent a little girl to tell us to come to class immediately or be punished. Again, I was ready to go in, but Zeb convinced me to stay by using his previous persuasion, adding, "Miss Thornton will just scold us a little as her punishment."

That was a bad decision, because Zeb won all of my marbles, and Miss Thornton sent us to the principal, who gave us both a beating for gross disobedience.

Wrong Time, Wrong Place, and a damn bad decision for a seven-year-old kid who lost all his marbles!

About twenty years later I noticed a WWII monument in my hometown. It had the names of native sons who had died in that massive conflict. I was very saddened when I saw Zeb's name engraved thereon, and wondered if he'd been in the Wrong Place at the Wrong Time during the war.

DRACULA STRIKES AGAIN

It was 1939, and I was in summer school at N.C. State College. All engineering students were required to take surveying after the junior year, and those who had some make-up work could stay three weeks longer so they would be on track for their senior year. I was one of the latter, but my roommate wasn't, so I spent those three weeks alone in my dormitory room. It was near the deserted end of the building, and there weren't even any students near me, so I felt a bit uneasy.

One Saturday night I stopped by the library and picked up a book to read. It was Dracula, by Bram Stoker. I had seen the movie, and felt it would be cool to read the original story. As I left the library, I stopped to talk with a friend and classmate, Tommy Haynes. He was all decked out for a date with a Raleigh belle, but was curious as to what I was reading. When he saw the title, he said, "That's a very scary story. Aren't you afraid to read it since you're living alone in the end of your dorm?"

"Nah", I responded. "It's only a book."

"Well I wouldn't have the nerve to read it, so I hope you'll be O.K."

He then left for his date and I for my lonely room. I sat at my desk reading it for several hours, and then decided to climb into my upper bunk bed to continue. Since it was a hot summer, and we didn't have air-conditioning in those days, I pulled the bunk bed over to the window so it would be cooler.

Earlier, I had locked my dorm room and was enjoying the book with some sense of security. While in my bunk bed, I reached the part where Dracula had murdered the entire crew of the ship that brought him to England, and had changed himself into a ferocious dog to leave the ship. Suddenly, I heard a loud growl at my window, only a few feet from my ears. I reacted by dropping the book and bouncing up in my bunk, half-frightened out of my wits.

I then heard peals of laughter, and Tommy saying, "I warned you not to read that book, didn't I?" I scolded him a bit, and he took it good-naturedly as he left for his dorm. When I tried to go to sleep, visions of Dracula striking at me ran through my head. I even pulled the bunk bed back to a safer place than the window, but that didn't help much. Eventually, I went to sleep, but my dreams weren't very reassuring. I finished the book the next day and returned it to the library and kept my bunk bed away from the window the remaining weeks. What an experience one little book caused.

Wrong Time, Wrong Place, Wrong Book, but Tommy took advantage of my situation to play his fiendish trick on me!

MAJOR DECISIONS

Dr. George Smith, head of the Engineering Mechanics Department at N.C. State, was one of my favorite professors. He was tough and demanding, but fair and considerate. I think he liked to be extra tough with his "Strength of Materials" students the first quarter of our senior year, so he could weed out the weaker students and have a smaller class with the stronger ones.

Fortunately, I was in the latter group and was pleased with his change in attitude with the smaller class. He was an excellent teacher, and gave us special attention and encouragement. I not only learned a lot from him, but also felt he liked and appreciated me. This was borne out when he asked me to come into his office one day.

After a few pleasantries, he offered me a job after graduation as a teaching fellow. He explained that I would teach the basics to juniors and would get to live in a dorm as a monitor, eat in the cafeteria, and have medical care in the infirmary, all free. More importantly, I could work on my master's degree, and perhaps my doctorate, free of tuition charges. Although there would be no cash income, it was 1940 and the Great Depression was still with us, so I realized it was a fine opportunity. Besides, I would have summers off and could earn spending money, as I had done previous summers in my dad's Printing Shop.

I think I would have jumped at the opportunity, except for a few other considerations. First was Hitler's war in Europe and the Japanese invasion of China. The world situation looked precarious, even to my youthful eyes. Second was an offer I had from an east-coast aircraft manufacturer. Third was the possibility of joining the U.S. Air Corp. I had taken its physical exam during a recruiting visit at the college, and had passed except for a small problem that could be fixed with minor surgery. I was a First Lieutenant in the college R.O.T.C, was about to get a degree in Mechanical Engineering, Aeronautical Option, and a private pilot's license through President Roosevelt's Civilian Pilot Training Association, so the Air Corp was my first choice. Unfortunately, I had no money for an operation and the Air Corp wouldn't do it for me, so I had to abort that possibility.

My situation was a major decision point in my life, and obviously required a lot of thinking. Working for an aircraft manufacturer was my ultimate career goal, but getting an advanced degree, or serving in the Air Corps, would certainly enhance it. Besides, Dr. Smith's offer might lead to a career as a college professor, which was appealing to me. I knew that it involved more than teaching and could include interesting research, profitable consulting, writing books, and considerable prestige.

I also thought that the Air Corp could be a long-term career, and perhaps some day I could rise to a lofty rank there, while having the thrilling and exciting life of a pilot of highly advanced aircraft. (Several of my college friends did just that, and one, who happened to be from my hometown, even became a Major General.)

I finally decided to take the aircraft manufacturer's offer, mostly because of the worsening world situation and the need for military aircraft. I believe it was a good decision for a 20-year-old youth, since I spent 37 years with my new employer, the Grumman Aircraft Engineering Corporation. Several of my early positions relied heavily on the knowledge I had learned from Dr. Smith, and my career involved many important projects that helped us win WWII, subsequent wars, and land men on the moon. Best of all, I found my life-long mate and mother of our two girls there. She was an engineering aide with a major in mathematics from Vassar College.

God only knows what would have happened if I had accepted Dr. Smith's offer. I might have lasted a year before I was called to military service via my pending reserve officer's commission, because Pearl Harbor happened on December 7th, 1941. I might have been killed or severely injured during the war, or perhaps found a long- term military career. I could even have returned to N.C. State after the war and lived the interesting and useful life of a faculty member. One thing seems certain. I doubt if I would have found the same life-long mate, and since we have now enjoyed 61 years of a happy and fulfilling marriage, that 20-year-old kid made a damn good decision.

So I guess that Dr. Smith's offer, although much appreciated, was at the Wrong Time, but not necessarily the Wrong Place. Under different world conditions, it could have been the Right Time and the Right Place!

DROWSY DRIVING DISASTER

My wife, Elizabeth, and I were driving on the parkway to Poughkeepsie,

NY one Saturday night after attending the Metropolitan Opera. I drove for about two hours with little traffic, but lots of fog, so the going was unusually slow. Once the fog cleared, Elizabeth insisted she drive so I could get some rest. She also told me to go to sleep, saying, "I'm wide-awake, so it'll be safe." Against my better judgment, I went to sleep.

I was rudely awakened when the car was going down a steep embankment headed for a large tree. Fortunately, some saplings had slowed us down, so when we hit the tree all it did was damage the left front fender and headlight. Once we ascertained that neither of us was hurt, I turned off the ignition to prevent potential fire. We exited from the car, I picked up our luggage, and we climbed the embankment to the parkway.

By then, it was after two a.m., so no other cars where in sight. Finally, we spotted one, so I stepped out and flagged it down by waving my hands. The driver and his wife stopped, I explained our situation, and the kind man offered to take us to Poughkeepsie, which happened to be his destination. I asked him to check his odometer so I could tell a tow truck how far we were from the Poughkeepsie exit. He was impressed that I could be so clear-headed after our frightening experience. He even drove us to Elizabeth's parent's home and declined my offer of money. What a nice couple, I thought.

After our car was repaired we again went to Poughkeepsie, but this time during daylight hours. I spotted the embankment we plunged down, and noticed several things. It was the fill part of a road cut-and-fill, and there was a guardrail to protect cars from going down the steep grade.

Unfortunately, Elizabeth had gone off the parkway just after the cut and just before the guardrail. A few seconds earlier, we would have hit the slope of the cut, awakened, and bounced back on the parkway automatically. A few seconds later and we would have hit the guardrail, awakened, and not gone down the steep embankment of the fill. About six or eight minutes later we would have been on level ground and just run into a flat, grassy area with no damage and very little fright.

Very Wrong Time, Very Wrong Place, but a happy ending.

METROPOLITAN OPERA PROBLEMS

In October, 1967, my wife, <u>Betty</u>, was picking me up after work to go to the Met, when a series of problems happened. First, I was meeting with <u>General Rip Bollander</u>, a NASA manager, to review recent design changes on the Lunar Module, for which I was Grumman Aerospace's assistant program manager. I knew my wife was waiting in our car, but Rip was such a thorough man that our review took longer than I had planned. Although it was about an hour after quitting time, I finally, got the courage to tell him I was going to the Met and must leave.

Although rush hour traffic slowed our drive to the city, Betty had packed some supper that let us reach the Met parking lot in time, but we had to wait in line. Just as we got near the entrance, they put up a sign:" Lot Full!"

Damn, I thought, now I've got to find another spot. I drove to a nearby lot, but there was a long line there too. Suddenly, I spotted an empty space across the street, and eased our car into it. When I got out, I looked for any "No Parking" signs; seeing none, I locked the car and we hurried to the Met on foot.

By then the opera had started, so we were ushered to a room for latecomers, where we saw and heard part of the first act on closed-circuit television. Once we took our seats, we enjoyed the remaining acts thinking, "All's well that ends well!"

We walked leisurely to our car, but much to our surprise it wasn't there. Were we in the wrong place? Was our car stolen? Did the police tow it away? Those were the questions we asked as we tried to solve the mystery. We finally decided that we were at the right place, so that left the other two choices. I spotted a sign at the corner, about 100 feet away, and much to my surprise it said, "No Parking. Reserved for Diplomats." We conclude that it had been towed away, but what to do now? I found a pay phone and called the Police Department, and was told, "Yeah, it was towed; you can get it at our lot on 10th and 29th streets once you pay the fine."

We took a cab, and the officer on duty said the fine would be $50. We didn't have that much with us, so we asked if he would take a check. He asked for identification, and since we lived in NY State, he accepted it. (Out of staters would be in trouble) Incidentally, it was Halloween night, so as I left with our car, I told the officer, "I didn't mind your towing away trick, but did you have to demand such an expensive treat?

There were several Wrong Time, Wrong Place events that Halloween night.